ISBN 978-0-484-59377-9
PIBN 10048183

THE

HARVEST OF THE SEA

A CONTRIBUTION TO
THE NATURAL AND ECONOMIC HISTORY OF
THE BRITISH FOOD FISHES

WITH SKETCHES OF FISHERIES & FISHER FOLK

By JAMES G. BERTRAM

POLONIUS.—Do you know me, my lord?
HAMLET.—Excellent well; you are a fishmonger.
Shakespeare.

SECOND EDITION WITH ILLUSTRATIONS

LONDON
JOHN MURRAY, ALBEMARLE STREET
1869

Printed by R. CLARK, *Edinburgh*.

PREFATORY NOTE TO THE
SECOND EDITION.

In bringing before the public a second Edition of the "Harvest of the Sea," I think it right to say that even if no new issue had been requisite I would have still considered that the book had fulfilled its purpose, as much greater attention has been paid to all questions of fishery economy, since its publication, than was before devoted to the subject, either by the general public or public journalists, and to the latter I owe grateful thanks for their cordial reception of the work. Some important corrections have been made in this new edition, and—so far as I know—the "Harvest of the Sea" is the only work in which an attempt has been made to bring before the public, in one view, the present position and future prospects of the food fisheries of Great Britain and Ireland, which are yearly becoming of greater importance as contributories to the national commissariat.

It is not my intention, however, to inflict upon the reader a formal preface, but it is proper that I should acknowledge the aid and information kindly afforded by the Emperor of the French, and various members of the French Government ;

also by Professor Coste of the French Institute ; M. Coumes of Strasbourg ; the authorities at Huningue ; the Intendant of the Jardin d'Acclimatisation of Paris ; the late Mr. Buist of Perth ; John Cleghorn, Esq. of Wick ; Jonathan Couch, Esq. ; Mr. H. Dempster ; Thomas Ashworth, Esq. ; Robert Cowie, Esq. ; Mr. R. P. Scott ; Edward Cooke, Esq., R.A., to whose kindness I am indebted for the characteristic sketches of " The Angler Fish," and " Jack in his Element." The various Fish Groups have been arranged and drawn by Mr. Stewart ; while the sketches of Lochfyne and elsewhere are from the pencil of Mr. J. R. Prentice of Edinburgh.

10TH OCTOBER 1868.

CONTENTS.

CHAPTER I.

FISH LIFE AND GROWTH.

CHAPTER II.

FISH COMMERCE.

CHAPTER III.

FISH CULTURE.

CHAPTER IV.

ANGLERS' FISHES.

CHAPTER V.

THE NATURAL AND ECONOMIC HISTORY
OF THE SALMON.

The Salmon our best-known Fish—Controversies and Anomalies
—Food of Salmon—The Parr Controversy—Experiments by
Shaw, Young, and Hogg—Grilse : its Rate of Growth—Do

CHAPTER VI.

THE NATURAL AND ECONOMIC HISTORY OF THE HERRING.

CHAPTER VII.

THE WHITE-FISH FISHERIES.

CHAPTER VIII.

THE NATURAL AND ECONOMIC HISTORY OF THE OYSTER.

CHAPTER IX.

OUR SHELL-FISH FISHERIES.

CHAPTER X.

THE FISHER-FOLK.

CHAPTER XI.

CONCLUDING REMARKS.

APPENDIX.

LIST OF ILLUSTRATIONS.

CHAPTER I.

FISH LIFE AND GROWTH.

Classification of Fish—Their Form and Colour—Mode and Means of Life—Curiously-shaped Fish—Senses of Smell and Hearing in Fish—Fish nearly Insensible to Pain—The Fecundity of Fish—Sexual Instinct of Fish—External Impregnation of the Ova—Ripening of a Salmon Egg—Birth of a Herring—Proposal for a Marine Observatory in order to note the Growth of our Sea Fish—Curious Stories about the Growth of the Eel—All that is known about the Mackerel—Whitebait : is it a Distinct Species?—Mysterious Fish : the Vendace and the Powan—Where are the Haddocks?—The Food of Fish—Fish as a rule not Migratory—The Growth of Fish Shoals—When Fish are good for Food—The Balancing Power of Nature.

FISH form the fourth class of vertebrate animals, and, as a general rule, they live in the water ; although in Ceylon and India there are found species that live in the earth, or, at any rate, that are able to exist in mud, not to speak of some that are said to occupy the trees of those countries ! The classification of fishes as given by Cuvier is usually adopted. That eminent naturalist has divided these animals into those with true bones, and those having a cartilaginous structure ; and the former again are divided into acanthopterous and malcopterous fish. Other naturalists have adopted more elaborate classifications ; but Cuvier's being the simplest has in my opinion a strong claim to be considered the best ; at least it is the one generally used.

A fish breathes by means of its gills, and progresses chiefly by means of its tail. This animal is admirably adapted for pro-

gressing through the water, as may be seen from its form, which
has been imitated more or less closely by the builders of ships,
the makers of weavers' shuttles, and others.   Fish are exceedingly beautiful as regards both form and colour.   There
are comparatively few persons, however, who have an opportunity of seeing them at the moment of their greatest brilliancy,
namely, just when they are brought out of the water.   I allude
more particularly to some of our sea fish—as the herring,
mackerel, etc.   The power of a fish to take on the colour of its
hiding-place may be mentioned.   I found, a few weeks ago, some
young fish of various kinds in the Tweed at Stobo, which
were, when in the water, quite undistinguishable from the vegetable matter among which they were taking shelter.   It is not
an easy matter to paint a fish so as accurately to transmit to
canvas its exquisite shape and glowing colours.   The moment
it is taken from its own element its form alters and its delicate hues fade; and in different localities fish have, like the
chameleon, different colours, so that the artist must have a
quick eye and a responding hand to catch the rapidly-fleeting
tints of the animal.   Nothing, for instance, can reveal more
beautiful masses of colour than the hauling into the boat of a
drift of herring-nets.   As breadth after breadth emerges from
the water the magnificent ensemble of the fish flashes with
ever-changing hues upon the eye—a wondrous pantomimic
mixture of glancing blue and gold, and silver and purple,
blended into one great burning glow of harmonious colour,
lighted into brilliant life by the soft rays of the newly-risen
sun.   But, alas for the painter! unless he can instantaneously
fix the burnished mass on his canvas, the light of its colour
will be extinguished, and its beauty be dimmed, long before
the boat has reached the harbour.   The brightly-coloured
fish of the tropics are indeed gorgeous, as is the plumage of
tropical birds; but as regards excellence of flavour, beautifully-
blended colours, and especially as a food power, they cannot

for a moment be compared with that plentiful poor man's fish —the beautiful common herring of our British waters.

If the breathing apparatus of a fish were to become dry the animal would at once be suffocated. A fish when in the water has very little weight to support, as its specific gravity is about the same as that of the water in which it lives, and the bodies of these animals are so flexible as to aid them in all their movements, while the various fins assist either in balancing the body or in helping it to progress. The motion of a fish is excessively rapid ; it can dash along in the water with lightning-like velocity. Many of our sea fish are curiously shaped, such as the hammer-headed shark, the globe-fish, the monk-fish, the angel-fish, etc. ; then we have the curious forms of the rays, the Pluronectidæ, and of some others that I may call " fancy fish ;" but fish of all kinds are admirably adapted to their mode of life and the place where they live—as for instance, in a cave where light has never penetrated there have been found fish without eyes. Fresh-water fish do not, however, vary much in shape, most of them being very elegant. Fish are nearly insensible to pain, and are cold-blooded, their blood being only two degrees warmer than the element in which they swim. It is worthy of being noted also that fish have small brains in comparison to the size of their bodies—considerably smaller in proportion than in the case of the birds or mammalia, but the nerves communicating with the brain are as large in fish, proportionately, as in either the birds or mammalia. So far as personal knowledge goes, I believe the senses of sight and hearing are well developed in most fish, as also those of smell and taste, particularly the sense of smell, which chiefly guides them to their food. We may take for granted, I think, that fish have a very keen sense of smell—more so than most other animals ; and thus it is that strong-smelling baits are so successful in fishing. The French people, for instance, when fishing for sprats and sardines, bait the ground with prepared cod-roe, which, by the way, adds very largely to the expense of that branch of fishing in the Bay of Biscay. I may also remind my readers, as an evidence of fish having a strong sense of smell, that salmon-roe used to be a deadly trout-bait, but fishing with salmon-roe is now illegal. It has been said by some naturalists that fish do not hear well, but that assertion is contrary to my own experience ; for on making repeated trials as to the sense of hearing in fish, I found them as quick in that faculty as they are sharp in seeing ; and have we not all read of pet fish being summoned by means of a bell, and of trouts that have been whistled to their food like dogs? Water is an excellent conductor of sound: it conveys a noise of any kind to a greater distance, and at nearly as great a speed as air. Benjamin Franklin used to experiment on water as a conductor, and soon arrived at the conclusion that its powers in this way were wonderful. By striking two stones together, the experimenter will find that the sound is conveyed to a great distance, and also that it is very loud. Most kinds of fish are voracious feeders, and prey upon each other without the slightest ceremony ; and the greatest difficulties of the angler are experienced after the fish have had a good feed, when even the most practised artist, with his most seductive bait, will not induce them to nibble, far less to bite. Many of our fish have a digestion so rapid as only to be comparable to the action of fire, and in good feeding-grounds the growth of a fish usually corresponds to its power of eating. In the sea there exists an admirable field for observing the cannibal propensities of the fish world, where shoals of one species have apparently no other object in life than to chase another kind with a view to eat them ; and what goes on in the sea on a wholesale scale is imitated on a smaller scale in the loch and the river. To compensate for the waste of life incidental to their place of birth and their ratio of growth, nature has en-

dowed this class of animals with an enormous power of reproduction. Fish yield their eggs by tens of thousands or millions, according to the danger that has to be incurred in the
progress of their growth.

All fish are enormously fecund ; indeed there is nothing
in the animal world that can in this respect be compared to
them, except perhaps a queen bee, which has fifty or sixty
thousand young each season; or the white ant, which produces
eggs at the rate of fifty per minute, and goes on laying for a
period of unknown duration ; not to speak of that terrible
domestic *bug*bear which no one likes more particularly to
name, but which is popularly supposed to become a great-grand-
father in twenty-four hours. The little aphides of the garden
may also be noted for their vast fecundity, as may likewise the
common house-fly. During a year one green aphis may produce one hundred thousand millions of young; and the house-
fly produces twenty millions of eggs in a season !

When I state that the cod-fish yields its eggs in millions,
and that a herring of six or seven ounces in weight is provided
with about thirty thousand ova, it will at once be seen that
the multiplying power of all kinds of fish is enormous ; but
then the drain on fish life, consequent on the *habitat* of these
animals, is immense, or at least of corresponding magnitude.
Although there may be thirty thousand eggs in a herring, the
reader must bear in mind that if these be not vivified by the
milt of the male fish, they just rot away in the sea, and never
become of any value, except perhaps as food to some minor
monster of the deep. Millions upon millions of the eggs that
are emitted by the cod or the herring never come to life at all
—many of them from the want of the fructifying power, and
others from being devoured by enemies. Then, again, of those
eggs that are so fortunate as to be ripened, it is pretty certain,
I think, from minute and careful inquiry, that fully ninety
per cent of the young fish perish before they are six months

old. Were only half of the eggs to come to life, and but one moiety of the young fish to live, the sea would so abound with animal life that it would soon be impossible for a boat to move in its waters. But we can never hope to realise such a sight ; and when it is considered that a single shoal of herrings consists of millions and millions of individual fish, and takes up a space in the sea far more than that occupied by the parks of London, and yet gives no impediment to navigation, my readers will see the magnitude of our fish supplies ; but, from the destruction of fish life by natural causes, the breeding supply is kept down to an amount that cannot, in my opinion, be very far from the point of extermination; and hence I am prepared to argue the urgent necessity of regulation, continued statistical inquiry, and the adoption of fish-culture as an adjunct to the natural supplies.

The figures of fish fecundity are quite reliable, and are not dependent on mere guessing or imagination, because different persons have taken the trouble, the writer amongst others, to count the separate eggs in the roes of some of our fish, in order to ascertain exactly their amount of breeding power. It is well known that the female salmon yields her eggs at the rate of about one thousand for each pound of her weight, and some fresh-water fish are still more prolific ; the sea fish, again, far excelling them in reproductive power. The sturgeon, for instance, is wonderfully fecund, as much as two hundred pounds weight of roe having been taken from one of these fish, yielding a total of 7,000,000 of eggs. I have in my possession the results of several investigations into the question of fish fecundity, which were conducted with careful attention to the details, and without any desire to exaggerate : these give the following results :—Cod-fish, 3,400,000 ; flounder, 1,250,000 ; sole, 1,000,000 ; mackerel, 500,000 ; herring, 35,000 ; smelt, 36,000. Mr. Frank Buckland, who some time ago investigated this part of the fish question, quite corroborates such numbers as being correct, having found equally great quantities in fish dissected by himself.

Any of my readers who wish to manipulate these figures may try by way of experiment a few calculations with the herring. The produce of a single herring is, let us say, thirty-six thousand eggs, but we may—and the deduction is a most reasonable one—allow that half of these never come to life, which reduces the quantity born to eighteen thousand. Allowing that the young fish will be able to repeat the story of their birth in three years, we may safely calculate that the breeding stock by various accidents will by that time be reduced to nine thousand individuals ; and granting half of these to be females, or let us say, for the sake of rounding the figures, that four thousand of them yield roe, we shall find by multiplying that quantity by thirty-six thousand (the number of eggs in a female herring) that we obtain a total of one hundred and forty-four millions as the produce in three years of a single pair of herrings ; and although half of these might be taken as the food of man as soon as they were large enough, there would still be left an immense breeding stock even after all deductions for casualties had been given effect to ; so that the devastations committed by man on the shoals while capturing for food uses must be enormous if they affect, as I suppose, the reproductiveness of these useful animals. Of course this is but guess-work, and is merely given as a basis for a more minute statement; but I have conversed with practical people who do not think that, taking all times and seasons into account, even five per cent of the roe of a herring comes to life, far less that such a percentage reaches maturity as table fish.

It is now well enough known, even to the merest *tyros* in the study of natural history, and to anglers and others interested as well, that the impregnation of fish-eggs is a purely external act ; but at one time this was not believed, and even so lately as six years ago a portion of the experiments at the Stor-

montfield salmon-breeding ponds was dedicated, by Mr. Robert
Buist, to a solution of this question, with what result may
be easily guessed. The old theory, so stoutly maintained
by Mr. Tod Stoddart and others, that it is contrary both to
fact and reason that fish can differ from land animals in
the matter of the fructification of their eggs, was signally
defeated, and the question conclusively settled at the ponds
in a very simple way—namely, by placing in the breeding-
boxes a quantity of salmon eggs which had not been brought
into contact with the milt, and which rotted away ; proving
emphatically that the sexes do not come into alliance at
the time of spawning, and that there is no way of rendering the eggs fruitful unless they are brought into immediate
contact with the milt. Curious ideas used to prevail on
this branch of natural history. Herodotus observes of the
fish of the Nile, that at the season of spawning they move
in vast multitudes towards the sea ; the males lead the
way, and emit the engendering principle in their passage ;
this the females absorb as they follow, and in consequence
conceive, and when their ova are deposited they are consequently matured into fry. Linnæus backed up this idea, and
asserted that there could be no impregnation of the eggs of any
animal out of the body, and as fish have no organs of generation, there was in the mind of the great naturalist no more
feasible explanation of their mode of reproduction than that
given in Beloe's *Herodotus*. It is this wonderfully exceptional
principle in the life of fish that has given rise to the art of
pisciculture—*i.e.* the artificial impregnation of the eggs of fish
forcibly exuded from these animals, which, as will be fully
explained in another portion of this work, are brought into contact with the milt, independent altogether of the animal.

The principle of fish life which brings the male and female
together at the period of spawning is unknown. It is supposed
by some naturalists that fish do not gather into shoals till they

are about to perform the grandest action of their nature, and that till that period each animal lives a separate and individual life. If we set down the sense of smell as the power which attracts the fish sexes, we shall be very nearly correct: such cold-blooded animals cannot very well have any more powerful instinct. A very clever Spanish writer on pisciculture hints that the fish have no amatory feeling for each other at that period, thus forming a curious exception to most other animals, and that it is the smell of the roe in the female that attracts the male. As the writer well expresses it—"The curious phenomenon of the fecundation of the eggs or spawn of the female fish away from the bowels of the mothers, and independent of their co-operation in every way, constitutes an interesting exception to the almost universal law of instinct and sympathy in the sexes—a law simple in its essence, as are all nature's laws, but most prolific in its results; for we see it pass through all the phases of an immense series, from the phenomena of organic attraction shown by the first-named living beings up to the great passions of love and maternity in the human species, forming the affectionate and solid bases of families and the imperishable foundation of society."

This idea—viz. as to the shoaling of the fish at the period of spawning only—has been prominently thrown out in regard to the herring by parties who do not admit even of a partial migration from the deep to the shallow water, which, however, is an idea that is stoutly held by some writers on the herring question. It is rather interesting, however, in connection with this phase of fish life, to note that particular shoals of herrings deposit their spawn at particular places, that the eggs come simultaneously to life, and that it is quite certain that the young fish remain together for a considerable period—a few months at least—after they are hatched. This is well known from the fact of large bodies of young herrings having been caught during the sprat season; these could not, of course, have been assembled to spawn—they were too young and had no development of milt or roe. This, if these fish separate, gives rise to the question—At what period do the herrings begin their individual wanderings? Sprats, of course—if sprats be sprats and not the young of the herring—may have come together at the period when they are so largely captured for the purpose of perpetuating their kind; but if so, they must live long together before they acquire milt or roe. And how is it that we so often find young herrings in the sprat shoals? Then, again, how comes it that the fishermen do not frequently fall in with the separate herrings during the white-fishing seasons? How is it that fishermen find particular kinds of fish always on particular ground? How is it that eels migrate in immense bodies? My opinion is, that particular kinds of fish do hold always together, or at all events gather at particular seasons into greater or lesser bodies. No doubt, life among the inhabitants of the sea, if we could know it, is quite as diversified as life on land, where we observe that many kinds of animals colonise—ants, bees, etc. Are the old stories about each kind of fish having a king so absolutely incredible after all? That there are schools of fish is certain; how the great bodies may be divided can only be guessed.

Whatever may be the attracting cause, and however powerful the sexual instinct may be among fish, it can scarcely be discussed fully in a work which makes no pretension to being scientific or even technological. It is noteworthy, however, that fish-eggs afford us an admirable opportunity of studying a peculiarly interesting stage of animal life—viz. the embryo stage—which naturally enough is rather obscure in all animals. Having had opportunities of observing the eggs of the salmon in all their stages of progress, from the period of their first contact with the milt till the bursting of the egg and the coming forth of the tiny fish, I will venture briefly to describe what I have seen, because salmon eggs are of a convenient size

for continued examination.   The roe of this fine fish is, I daresay, pretty familiar to most of my readers.   The microscope
reveals the eggs of the salmon as being more oval than round,
although they appear quite round to the naked eye.   A
yolk seems to float in the dim-looking mass, and the skin
or shell appears full of minute holes, while there is an appearance of a kind of canal or funnel, which opens from the
outside and is apparently closed at the inner end.   The milt
is found to swarm with a species of very small creatures
with big heads and long tails, apparently of very low
organisation.   On the contact of this fluid with the egg,
into which it enters by the canal I have described, an immediate change takes place—the ovum, so to speak, becomes
illuminated as if by some curious internal power, and the
aspect of the egg then appears a great deal brighter and clearer
than before ; and it is surely wonderful that on the mere
touching of the egg with this wonder-working sperm so great
a change should take place—a change which indicates that
the grand process of reproduction characteristic of all living
nature has begun in the ovum, and will go on with increasing
strength to maturity.

Beds containing salmon-spawn are so accessible, comparatively speaking, as to render it easy to trace the development
of the egg from the embryo to the complete animal.   I have
personally watched the egg from the date of its contact with
the milt till the little salmon has burst out of its fragile prison
and waddled away to the shady side of a friendly pebble, evidently anxious to hide its nakedness.   I was enabled, in fact,
to hatch a few salmon eggs, brought from Stormontfield last
Christmas-day, by means of a very simple apparatus in a
printing-office, and had therefore an opportunity of daily
observation.   As may be supposed, however, the transmutation
of a salmon egg into a fish is a tedious process, which takes
above a hundred days to accomplish.   The eggs of the female

under the natural system of spawning are laid in the secluded and shallow tributary of some choice stream, in a trough of gravel ploughed up by the fish with great labour, and are there left to be wooed into life by the eternal murmuring of the water. From November till March, through the storms and floods of winter, the ova lie hid among the gravel, slowly but surely quickening into life, and few persons would guess from a mere casual glance at the tributary of a great salmon stream that it held among its bubbling waters such a countless trea sure of future fish. A practised person will find out a burrow of salmon eggs with great precision, and a little bit of water may contain perhaps a million of eggs waiting to be summoned into life by the mysterious workings of nature. During the first three weeks from the milting of the egg scarcely any change is discernible in its condition, except that about the end of that period it contains a brilliant spot, which gradually increases in its brilliancy, when certain threads of blood begin faintly to prefigure the anatomy of the young fish. After another day or two, the bright spot seems to assume a ring-like form, having a clear space in the centre, and the blood-threads then become more and more apparent. These blood-like tracings are ultimately seen to take an animal shape; but it would be difficult at first to say what the animal may turn out to be—whether a tadpole or a salmon. After this stage of the development is reached, two bright black specks are then seen—the eyes of the fish. We can now, from day to day, note the form as it gradually assumes a more perfect shape ; we can see it change palpably almost from hour to hour. After the egg has been laved by the water for a hundred days, we can observe that the young fish is then thoroughly alive and, to use a common expression, kicking. We can see it moving and can study its anatomy, which, although as yet very rudimentary, contains all the elements of the perfect fish. Heat expedites the birth of the fish. The eggs of a minnow have been sensibly advanced towards maturity by being held on the palm of the hand. The spawn of the lobster has the advantage of being nursed on the tail of the animal till it is just on the point of ripening into life. Salmon eggs deposited early in the season, when the temperature is high, come sooner to life than those spawned in mid-winter : indeed there is a difference of as much as fifty days between those deposited in September and those spawned in December, the one requiring ninety days, the other one hundred and forty days to ripen into life. Salmon have been brought to life in sixty days at Huningue ; but the quickest hatching ever accomplished at the Stormontfield breeding-ponds was when the fish came to life in one hundred and twenty days.

I have endeavoured to illustrate these early stages of fish life by a drawing, which shows the eggs at about their natural size, as also the advance of the fish in size and shape.

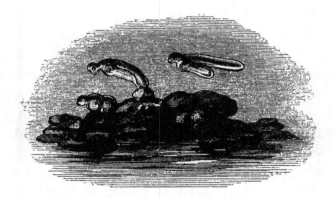

EGGS OF THE SALMON KIND JUST HATCHING.

At the salmon-ponds of Stormontfield the eggs laid down the first season were hatched in one hundred and twenty-eight days, but the eggs of other fish have been known to come to life a great deal sooner. The usual time for the hatching of salmon eggs in our northern rivers is one hundred and thirty days, or between four and five months, according to the openness or severity of the season. When at last the infant animal bursts from the shell, it is a clumsy, unbalanced, tiny thing, having attached to it the remains of the parental egg, which hamper its movements ; but after all, the remains of its little prison are exceedingly useful, as for a space of about thirty days the young salmon cannot obtain other nourishment than what is afforded by this umbilical bag.

SALMON A DAY OR TWO OLD.

We cannot, unfortunately, obtain a sight of the ripening eggs of any of our sea fish at a time when they would prove useful to us. No one, so far as I know, has seen the young herring burst from its shell under such advantageous circumstances as we can view the salmon ova ; but I have seen the bottled-up spawn of that fish just after it had ripened into life, the infant animal being remarkably like a fragment of cotton thread that had fallen into the water : it moved about with great agility, but required the aid of a microscope to make out that it was a thing endowed with life. Who could suppose, while examining those wavy floating threads, that in a few months afterwards they would be grown into beautiful fish, with a mechanism of bones to bind their flesh together, scales to protect their body, and fins to guide them in the water ? But young herring cannot be long bottled up for observation, or be kept in an artificial atmosphere ; for in that condition they die almost before there is time to see them live ; and when in the sea there are no means of tracing them, because they are speedily lost in an immensity of water.

There are points of contrast between the salmon and the herring which I cannot pass without notice. They form the St. Giles' and St. James' of the fish world, the one being a portion of the rich man's food, and the other filling the poor man's dish. The salmon is hedged round by protecting Acts of Parliament, but the herring gets leave to grow just as it swims, parliamentary statutes being thought unnecessary for its protection. The salmon is born in its fine nursery, and is wakened into life by the music of beautiful streams : it has nurses and night-watchers, who hover over its cradle and guide its infant ways ; but the herring, like the brat of some wandering pauper, is dropped in the great ocean workhouse, and cradled amid the hoarse roar of the ravening waters ; and whether it lives or dies is a matter of no moment, and no one's business. Herring mortality in its infantile stages is appalling, and even in its old age, at a time when the rich man's fish is protected from the greed of its enemies, the herring is doomed to suffer the most. And then, to finish up with the same appropriateness as they have lived, the venison of the waters is daintily laid out on a slab of marble, while the vulgar but beautiful herring is handled by a dirty costermonger, who hurls it about in a filthy cart drawn by a wretched donkey. At the hour of reproduction the salmon is guarded with jealous care from the hand of man, whilst at the same season the herring is offered up a wholesale sacrifice to the destroyer. It is only at its period of spawning that the herring is fished. How comes it to pass that what is a highly punishable crime in the one instance is a government-rewarded merit in the other ? To kill a gravid salmon is as nearly as possible felony ; but to kill a herring as it rests on the spawning-bed is an act at once meritorious and profitable !

Having given my readers a general idea of the fecundity of fish, and the method of fructifying the eggs, and of the development of these into fish—for, of course, the process will

be nearly the same with all kinds of fish eggs, the only difference perhaps being that the eggs of some varieties will
take a longer time to hatch than the eggs of others—I will
now pass on to consider the question of fish growth.

All fish are not oviparous. There is a well-known
blenny which is viviparous, the young of which at the time
of their birth are so perfect as to be able to swim about
with great ease ; and this fish is also very productive. Our
skate fishes (Raiæ) are all viviparous. "The young are enclosed in a horny capsule of an oblong square shape, with a
filament at each corner. It is nourished by means of an umbilical bag till the due period of exclusion arrives, when it
enters upon an independent existence." I could name a few
other fish which are viviparous. In the fish-room of the
British Museum may be seen one of these. It is known as
Ditrema argentea, and is plentifully found in the seas of
South America. But our information on this portion of the
natural history of fish is very obscure at present.

There are many facts of fish biography that have yet to
be ascertained, and which, if we knew them, would probably
conduce to a stricter economy of fish life and the better regulation of the fisheries. Beyond a knowledge of mere gene-
ralities, the animal kingdom of the sea is a sealed book. No
person can tell, for example, how long a time elapses from
the birth of any particular sea fish till the period when it is
brought to table. Sea fish grow up unheeded—quite, in a
sense, out of the bounds of observation. Naturalists can
only guess at what rate a cod-fish grows. Even the life of a
herring, in its most important phase, is still a mystery ; and
at what age the mackerel or any other fish becomes reproductive, who can say ? The salmon is the one particular fish
that has as yet been compelled to render up to those inquiring the secret of its birth and the ratio of its growth. (See
Natural and Economic History of the Salmon.) We have

imprisoned this valuable fish in artificial ponds, and by robbing it of its eggs have noted when the young ones were born
and how they grew. It would be equally easy to devise a
means of observing sea fish. Why should we not erect a
great marine observatory, where we could, as in the case of
the Stormontfield-bred salmon, watch the young fish burst
from its shell, and for a year or two observe and study the
progress of the animal, and ascertain its rate of growth, and
especially the period at which it becomes reproductive? The
government might act upon this suggestion, and vote a few
thousand pounds annually for the support of a series of marine
fish-ponds ; for something more is required than the resources
of an amateur naturalist to determine how fish live and grow.

What naturalists chiefly and greatly need in respect
of our sea fish is, precise information as to their rate
of growth. We have a personal knowledge of the fact of
the sea fish selecting our shores as a spawning-ground, but
we do not precisely know in some instances the exact time
of spawning, how long the spawn takes to quicken into life,
or at what rate the fish increase in growth.

The eel may be taken as an example of our ignorance of
fish life. Do our professed naturalists know anything about
it beyond its migratory habits?—habits which, from sheer
ignorance, have at one period or another been guessed as
pertaining to all kinds of fish. The tendency to the romantic,
specially exhibited in the amount of travelling power bestowed
by the elder naturalists on this class of animals, would
seem to be very difficult to put down.

About two years ago an old story about the eel was gravely
revived by having the larger portion of a little book devoted
to its elucidation—an old story seriously informing us that the
silver eel is the product of a black beetle. But no one need
wonder at a new story about the eel, far less at the revival of
this old one ; for the eel is a fish that has at all times experi-

enced the greatest difficulty in obtaining recognition as being anything at all in the·animal world, or as having respectable parentage of even the humblest kind. In fact, the study of the natural history of the eel has been hampered by old-world romances and quaint fancies about its birth, or, in its case, may I not say invention? "The eel is born of the mud," said one old author. "It grows out of hairs," said another. "It is the creation of the dews of evening," exclaimed a third. "Nonsense," emphatically uttered a fourth controversialist, "it is produced by means of electricity." "You are all wrong," asserted a fifth, "the eel is generated from turf;" and a sixth theorist, determined to outdo all the others and come nearer the mark than any of his predecessors, assures the public that the young fish are grown from particles scraped off the old ones! The beetle theorist tells us that the silver eel is a neuter, having neither milt nor roe, and is therefore quite incapable of perpetuating its kind; and, in short, that it is a romance of nature, being *one* of the productions of some wondrous lepidopterous animals seen by Mr. Cairncross (the author of the work alluded to) about the place where he lived in Forfarshire, its other production being of its own kind, a black beetle! The story of the rapid growth and transformation of the salmon is—as will by and by be seen—wonderful enough in its way, but it is certainly far surpassed by the extraordinary silver eel, which is at one and the same time a fish and an insect.

There can be no doubt that the eel is a curious enough animal even without the extra attributes bestowed upon it by this very original naturalist, for that fish is in many respects the opposite of the salmon: it is spawned in the sea, and almost immediately after coming to life proceeds to live in brackish or entirely fresh water. It is another of the curious features of fish life that about the period when eels are on their way to the sea, where they find a suitable spawning-ground, salmon are on their way from the sea up to the river-heads to fulfil the grand instinct of their nature—namely, reproduction. The periodical migrations of the eel, on which instinct has been founded the great fishing industry of Comacchio, on the Adriatic, described in another portion of this volume, can be observed in all parts of the globe, and they take place, according to the climate, at different periods from February to May ; the fish frequenting such canals or rivers as have communication with the sea. The myriads of young eels which ascend are almost beyond belief ; they are in numbers sufficient for the population of all the waters of the globe—that is, if there were protective laws to shield them from destruction, or reservoirs in which they might be preserved to be used for food as required. The eel, indeed, is quite as prolific as the generality of sea fish. As a corroboration of the prolificness of the animal, it may be stated that eels have been noted—but that was some years ago—to pass up the river Thames from the sea at the extraordinary rate of eighteen hundred per minute ! This *montee* was called eel-fair.

It is clear from certain facts in the history of this peculiar animal that, like all other fish, it can suit its life and growth to whatever circumstances it may be placed in, and seems to be quite able to multiply and replenish its species in rivers and lakes as well as in the sea. In Scotland eels are very seldom eaten, a strong prejudice existing in that country against the fish on account of its serpentine shape ; but for all that the eel is a nutritious and palatable fish, and is highly susceptible of the arts of the cook. At one time the eel was thought to be viviparous, but naturalists now know better, having found out that eels produce their young in the same way as most other fish do.

It would be interesting, and profitable as well, to know as much of any one of our sea fish as we now know of the salmon, but so little progress is being made in observing the natural history of fish that we cannot expect for some time to know much more than we do at present; everything in the fish world seems so much to be taken for granted that we are still inclined rather to revive the old traditions than to study or search out new facts. Naturalists are so ignorant of how the work of growth is carried on in the fish world—in fact, it is so difficult to investigate points of natural history in the depths of the sea—that we cannot wonder at less being known about marine animals than about any other class of living beings.

It is the want of precise information about the growth of the fish that has of late been telling heavily against our fisheries, for in the meantime all is fish that comes to the fisherman's net, no matter of what size the animals may be, or whether or not they have been allowed time to perpetuate their kind. No person, either naturalist or fisherman, knows how long a period elapses from the date of its birth before a turbot or cod-fish becomes reproductive. It is now well known, in consequence of the repeated experiments made with that fish, that the salmon grows with immense rapidity, a consequence in some degree of its quick digestive power. The cod-fish, again—and I reason from the analogy of its greatly slower power of digesting its food and from other corroborative circumstances—must be correspondingly slow in its growth; but people must not, in consequence of this slow power of digestion, believe all they hear about the miscellaneous articles often said to be found in the stomach of a cod-fish, as a large number of the curiosities found in the intestinal regions of his codship are often placed there by fishermen, either by way of joke or in order to increase the weight and so enhance the price of the animal.

As regards the natural history of one of our best-known food fishes, I have taken the pains to compile a brief *precis* of its life from the best account of it that is known, keeping in the background at present any knowledge or speculation of my own regarding it.   I allude to the mackerel; and the following facts are from an evidently well-studied chapter of Mr. Jonathan Couch's *Fishes of the British Islands,* by which it will be at once seen that our knowledge of the growing power of this well-known fish is very defective.

1. Mackerel, geographically speaking, are distributed over a wide expanse of water, embracing the whole of the European coasts, as well as the coasts of North America, and this fish may be caught as far southward as the Canary Islands. 2. The mackerel is a wandering unsteady fish, supposed to be migratory, but individuals are always found in the British seas.   This fish appears off the British coasts in quantity early in the year; that is, in January and February.   4. The male kind are supposed to be more numerous than the female.   5. The early appearance of this fish is not dependent on the weather.   6. The mackerel, like the herring, was at one time supposed to be a native of foreign seas.   7. This fish is laden with spawn in May, and it has been known to deposit its eggs upon our shores in the following month.

Such is a brief *resumé* of Mr. Couch's chapter on the mackerel.

Now, we have no account here of how long it is ere the spawn of the mackerel quickens into life, or at what age that fish becomes reproductive, although in these two points is unquestionably obtained the key-note to the natural history of all fishes, whether they be salmon or sprats.   In fact—and it is no particular demerit of Mr. Couch more than of every other naturalist—we have no precise information whatever on this point of growth power.   We have at best only a few guesses and general deductions, and we would like to know as regards all fish—1*st*, When they spawn : 2*d*, How long it is ere the spawn quickens into life ; and 3*d*, At what period the young

fish will be able to repeat the story of their birth. These points
once known—and they are most essential to the proper understanding of the economy of our fisheries—the chief remaining
questions connected with fishing industry would be of comparatively easy solution, and admit of our regulating the power
of capture to the natural conditions of supply.

As another example of our ignorance of fish life, I may
instance that diminutive member of the Clupea family—the

WHITEBAIT GROUND NEAR QUEENSFERRY.

whitebait. This fish, which is so much better known gastro-
nomically than it is scientifically, was thought at one time to
be found only in the Thames, but it is much more generally
diffused than is supposed.   It is found for certain, and in
great plenty, in three rivers—viz., the Thames, the Forth, and
the Hamble.   I have also seen it taken out of the Humber,
not far from Hull, and have heard of its being caught near the
mouth of the Deveron, on the Moray Firth ; and likewise of

its being found in plentiful quantities off the Isle of Wight. Mr. Stewart, the natural history draughtsman, tells me also that he has seen that fish taken in bushels on many parts of the Clyde, and that at certain seasons, while engaged in taking coal-fish, he has found them so stuffed with whitebait, that by holding the large fish by the tail the little silvery whitebait have fallen out in handfuls. The whitebait has become celebrated from the mode in which it is cooked, and the excuse it affords to Londoners for an afternoon's excursion, as also from its forming a famous dish at the annual fish-dinner of Her Majesty's ministers ; but truth compels me to state that there is nothing in whitebait beyond its susceptibility of taking on a flavour from the skill of the cook. It is poor feeding when compared to a dish of sprats, or (an illegal) fry of young salmon ; it has been said in joke that an expert cook can make up capital whitebait by means of flour and oil! But to eat whitebait is a fashion of the season, and the well-served tables of the Greenwich and Blackwall taverns, with their pleasant outlook to the river, and their inducements of chablis and other choice wines and comestibles, are undoubtedly very attractive, whether the persons partaking of these dainties be ministers of state or merchants' clerks.

The whitebait, however, if I cannot honestly praise it as a table fish, is particularly interesting as an object of natural history, there having been from time to time, as in the case of most other fish, some very learned disputes as to where it comes from, how it grows, and whether or not it be a distinct member of the herring family or the young of some other fish. The whitebait is a tiny animal, varying in length, when taken for cooking purposes, from two to four inches, and has never been seen of a greater length than five inches. In appearance it is pale and silvery, with a greenish back, and ought to be cooked immediately after being caught ; indeed if, like Lord Lovat's salmon, whitebait could leap out of the water into the frying-pan, it would be a decided advantage to those dining upon it, for if kept even for a few hours these fish become greatly deteriorated, and as a consequence, require all the more cooking to bring the flavour up to the proper pitch of gastronomic excellence.   Perhaps, as all fish are chameleon-like in reflecting not only the colour of their abode, but what they feed on as well, the supposed fine flavour of whitebait, so far as it is not conferred upon that fish by the cook, may arise from matter held in solution in the Thames water, and so the result from the corrupt source of the supply may be a quicker than ordinary decay.   The waters of the Forth at the whitebait ground—a little way above Inchgarvie, where the sprat-fishing is usually carried on, of which I have given a slight sketch—are clean and clear, and the whitebait taken there are in consequence slightly different in colour, and greatly so in taste, from those obtained in the Thames ; in fact, all kinds of fish, including salmon, are able to live and thrive in the Firth of Forth.   It is long since the refined salmon forsook the Thames, but then salmon are very delicate in their feeding, and at once take on the surrounding flavour, whatever that may be.   Creditable attempts are now being made to re-stock the Thames, especially the upper waters, with more valuable fish than are at present contained in that river, but whether these attempts will be successful yet remains to be seen.   I have been watching with great interest what is being done by Mr. Frank Buckland and others ; but salmon I fear cannot at present live in the Thames.   To thrive successfully, that fish must have access to the sea, and how a salmon can ever penetrate to the salt water with the river in its present state is a problem that must be left for future solution ; however, as Mr. Frank Buckland very truthfully remarks, if the salmon are not first sent down the Thames they cannot be expected ever to come up that noble river.

Returning, however, to our whitebait, it may be stated

that that fish was once thought to be the young of the shad, which is itself an interesting fish, coming, as we have been told by some naturalists, from the sea to deposit its spawn in the fresh waters. The shad was at one time thought to be the patriarch of the herring tribe ; and it was said, in the days when the old theory about the migration of the herring was believed in, that the great shoals which came to this country from the icy seas of the high latitudes were led on their wonderful tour by a few thousands of this gigantic fish. Pennant conjectured that whitebait was an independent species ; but so difficult is it to investigate such facts in the water, that it was not till many years had elapsed that the question was set at rest so far as to determine at anyrate that whitebait were not the young of either the Alice or the Twaite shad, which, by the by, are coarse and insipid fish.

As yet I have never at any season of the year found an example of whitebait containing either milt or roe, although it is said that examples may be taken full of both during the early winter months. This, of course, is not conclusive evidence of its being the young of some other fish, although its never being found with milt or roe would go some length in proving it a distinct species. What was only hinted at in the first edition of this work, namely, that whitebait were young herrings, may at length be asserted as truth. Dr. Gunther has determined this fact pretty conclusively. Not wishing to be dogmatic, I refrained from giving my own opinion on the question of the whitebait mystery, and it may sound quite a second-hand opinion *now* to say that I thoroughly agree in the conclusion arrived at by Dr. Gunther, and published in the 7th volume of the *Catalogue of Fishes* in the British Museum. My argument as to the whitebait was contained in the very simple question, " Where are the parent fish? " I never yet saw a whitebait that was more than half the size of a sprat. But the whitebait of a

London Tavern, it must be kept in mind, are generally a mixture of the fry of many different fishes, and the fish known
as whitebait at Blackwall, may not be the fish known as
whitebait at Queensferry ! so much for this tavern celebrity.
I may mention that this fish cannot be taken so far up
the river Thames as formerly.   Whitebait are now usually
caught between Gravesend and Woolwich, and are in their
best season between April and September.   It is not unusual for sea fish to ascend our rivers : the eel, as I have
already narrated, spawns in the sea, and the young of that
fish ascend to the fresh water, in which they live till they are
seized with the migratory instinct.

Besides whitebait there are other mysterious fish—especially in Scotland—which are well worthy of being alluded to.
The salmon itself—as will be by and by shown—is one of
these, and certainly not the least interesting among them.
An idea prevails in Scotland that the vendace of Lochmaben
and the powan of Lochlomond are really herrings forced into
fresh water, and slightly altered by the circumstances of a new
dwelling-place, change of food, and other causes.   One learned
person lately ascribed the presence of sea fish in fresh water
to the great wave which had at one time passed over the
country.   But no doubt the real cause is that these peculiar
fish were brought to those lakes ages ago by monks or other
persons who were adepts in the piscicultural art.

A brief summary of the chief points in the habits of these
mysterious fish may interest the reader.   The "vendiss," as
it is locally called, occurs nowhere but in the waters at Lochmaben, in Dumfriesshire ; and it is thought by the general
run of the country people to be, like the powan of Lochlomond,
a fresh-water herring.   The history of this fish is quite
unknown, but it is thought to have been introduced into the
Castle Loch of Lochmaben in the early monkish times, when
it was essential, for the proper observance of church fasts, to

have an ample supply of fish for fast-day fare.   It is curious
as regards the vendace that they float about in shoals, that they
make the same kind of poppling noise as the herring, and that
they cannot be easily taken by any kind of bait.   At certain
seasons of the year the people assemble for the purpose of
holding a vendace feast, at which times large quantities of the
fish are caught by means of a sweep net.   The fish is said to

LOCHMABEN.
The home of the Vendace.

have been found in other waters besides those of Lochmaben,
but I have never been able to see a specimen anywhere else.
There are a great number of traditions afloat about the vendace,
and a story of its having been introduced to the lake by Mary
Queen of Scots.   The country people are very proud of their
fish, and take a pride in showing it to strangers.   The principal
information I can give about the vendace, without becoming
technical, is, that it is a beautiful and very symmetrical fish,
about seven or eight inches long, not at all unlike a herring,
only not so brilliant in the colour ; and that the females of

the vendace seem to be about a third more numerous than the males—a characteristic which is also observed in the salmon family. The vendace spawn about the beginning of winter, and for this purpose gather, like the herring, into shoals. They are very productive, and do not take long to grow to maturity.

The peculiarities of the Lochleven trout may be chiefly ascribed to a peculiar feeding-ground. Having lived at one time on the banks of this far-famed loch, I had ample time and many opportunities of studying the habits and anatomy, as well as the fine flavour, of this beautiful fish, which, in my humble opinion, has no equal in any other waters. Feeding I believe to be everything, whether the subjects operated upon be cattle, capons, or carps. The land-locked bays of Scotland afford richer flavoured fish than the wider expanses of water, where the finny tribe, it may be, are much more numerous, but have not the same quantity or variety of food, and, as a consequence, the fish obtained in such places are comparatively poor both in size and flavour. Nothing can be more certain than that a given expanse of water will feed only a certain number of fish ; if there be more than the feeding-ground will support they will be small in size, and if the fish again be very large it may be taken for granted that the water could easily support a few more. It is well known, for instance, that the superiority of the herrings caught in the inland sea-lochs of Scotland is owing to the fish finding there a better feeding-ground than in the large and exposed open bays. Look, for instance, at Lochfyne : the land runs down to the water's edge, and the surface water or drainage carries with it rich food to fatten the loch, and put flesh on the herring; and what fish is finer, I would ask, than a Lochfyne herring? Again, in the bay of Wick, which is the scene of the largest herring fishery in the world, the fish have no land food, being shut out from such a luxury by a vast sea wall of everlasting rock ; and the consequence is, that the Wick herrings are not nearly so rich in flavour as those taken in the sea-lochs of the west of Scotland. In the same way I account for the rich flavour and beautiful colour of the trout of Lochleven. This fish has been acclimatised with more or less success in other waters, but when transplanted it deteriorates in flavour, and gradually loses its beautiful colour—another proof that much depends on the feeding-ground ; indeed, the fact of the trout having deteriorated in quality as a consequence of the abridgment of their feeding-range, is on this point quite conclusive. I feel certain, however, that there must be more than one kind of these Lochleven trouts ; there is, at any rate, one curious fact in their life worth noting, and that is, that they are often in prime condition for table use when other trouts are spawning.

The powan, another of the mysterious fish of Scotland, is also considered to be a fresh-water herring, and thought to be confined exclusively to Lochlomond, where they are taken in great quantities. It is supposed by persons versed in the subject that it is possible to acclimatise sea fish in fresh water, and that the vendace and powan, changed by the circumstances in which they have been placed, are, or were, undoubtedly herrings. The fish in Lochlomond also gather into shoals, and on looking at a few of them one is irresistibly forced to the conclusion, that in size and shape they are remarkably like the common herring. The powan of Lochlomond and the pollan of Lough Neagh are not the same fish, but both belong to the Coregoni : the powan is long and slender, while the pollan is an altogether stouter fish, although well shaped and beautifully proportioned.

I could analyse the natural history of many other fish, but the result in all cases is nearly the same, and ends in a repeated expression that what we require as regards all fish is the date of their period of reproduction ; all other information without this great fact is comparatively unimportant. It is difficult, however, to obtain any reliable information on the natural history of fish either by way of inquiry or by means of experiments. Naturalists cannot live in the water, and those who live on it, and have opportunities for observation, have not the necessary ability to record, or at any rate to gene-ralise what they see. No two fishermen, for instance, will agree on any one point regarding the animals of the deep. I have examined every intelligent fisherman I have met within the last ten years, numbering above one hundred, and few of them have any real knowledge regarding the habits of the fish which it is their business to capture. As an instance of fishermen's knowledge, one of that body recently repeated to me the old story of the migration of the herring, holding that the herring comes from Iceland to spawn, and that the sprat goes to the same icy region in order that it may fulfil the same instinct.

"Where are the haddocks ?" I once asked a Newhaven fisherman. "They are about all eaten up, sir," was his very innocent reply ; and I believe this to be true. The shore races of that fish have long disappeared, and our fishermen have now to seek this most palatable inhabitant of the sea afar off in the deep waters. Vast numbers of the haddock used to be taken in the Firth of Forth, but during late years they have become very scarce, and the boats now require to go a night's voyage to seek for them. If we knew the minu-tiæ of the life of this fish, we should be better able to regulate the season for its capture, and the percentage that we might with safety take from the water without deteriorating the breeding power of the animal. There are some touches of romance even about the haddock, but I need not further allude to these in this division of my book, as I shall have to refer to it again under the head of the "White Fish Fisheries." It is, like all fish, wonderfully prolific, and is looked upon by the fishermen as being also a migratory fish, as are also the turbot and many other sea animals.

The family to which the haddock belongs embraces many of our best food fish, as whiting, cod, ling, etc.; but of the growth and habits of the members of this family we are as ignorant as we are of the natural history of the whitebait or sprat. I have the authority of a rather learned Buckie fisherman (recently drowned, poor fellow! in the great storm on the Moray Frith) for stating that cod-fish do not grow at a greater rate than from eight to twelve ounces per annum. This fisherman had seen a cod that had got enclosed by some accident in a large rock pool, and so had obtained for a few weeks the advantage of studying its powers of digestion, which he found to be particularly slow, although there was abundant food. The haddock, which is a far more active fish, my informant considered to grow at a more rapid rate. On asking this man about the food of fishes, he said he was of opinion that they preyed extensively upon each other, but that, so far as his opportunities of observation went, they did not as a matter of course live upon each other's spawn ; in other words, he did not think that the enormous quantities of roe and milt given to fish were provided, as has been supposed by one or two writers on the subject, for any other purpose than the keeping up of the species. The spawn of all kinds of fish is extensively wasted by other means ; and these animals have no doubt a thousand ways of obtaining food that are yet unknown to man ; indeed, the very element in which they live is in a sense a great mass of living matter, and it doubtless affords by means of minute animals a wonderful source of supply. Fish, too, are less dainty in their food than is generally supposed, and some kinds eat garbage of the most revolting description with great avidity.

I take this opportunity of correcting the very common error that all fish are migratory. Some fishermen, and naturalists

as well, picture the haddock and the herring as being afflicted
with perpetual motion—as being wanderers from sea to sea
and shore to shore.   The migratory instinct in fish is, in my
opinion, very limited.   They do move about a little, without
doubt, but not further than from their feeding-ground to their
spawning-ground—from deep to shallow water.   Some plan
of taking fish other than the present must speedily be devised;
for now we only capture them—and I take the herring as an
example—over their spawning-ground, when, according to all
good authority, they must be in their worst possible condition,
their whole flesh-forming or fattening power having been bestowed on the formation of the milt and roe.   I repudiate
altogether this iteration of the periodical wandering instincts
of the finny tribes.   There are great fish colonies in the sea,
in the same way as there are great seats of population on
land, and these fish colonies are stationary, having, comparatively speaking, but a limited range of water in which to
live and die.   Adventurous individuals of the fish world
occasionally roam far away from home, and speedily find
themselves in a warmer or colder climate, as the case may
be ; but, speaking generally, as the salmon returns to its own
waters, so do sea fish keep to their own colony.

Our larger shoals of fish, which form money-yielding industries, are of wonderful extent, and must have been gathering and increasing for ages, having a population multiplied
almost beyond belief.   Century after century must have
passed away as these colonies grew in size, and were subjected
to all kinds of influences, evil or good : at times decimated
by enemies, or perhaps attacked by mysterious diseases, that
killed the fish in tens of thousands.   At Rockall, for instance, there was lately discovered a cod depôt, about which
a kind of sensation was made—perhaps by interested parties
—in the public prints, but the supply obtained at that place
was only of brief duration.   This fish colony, which had evi-

dently fixed upon a good food-giving centre, was too infantile to be able to stand the heavy draughts that were all at once made upon it. Schools or shoals of fish, when they are of such an extent as will admit of constant fishing, must have been forming during long periods of time ; for we know that, despite the wonderful fecundity of all kinds of sea fish, the expenditure of both seed and life is something tremendous. We may rest assured that, if a female cod-fish yields its roe by millions, a balancing-power exists in the water that prevents the bulk of them from coming to life, or at any rate from reaching maturity. If it were not so, how came it, in the days when there was no fish commerce, and when man only killed the denizens of the sea for the supply of his individual wants, that our waters were not, so to speak, impassable from a superfluity of fish? Buffon has said that if a pair of herrings were left to breed and multiply undisturbed for a period of twenty years, they would yield a fish bulk equal to the whole of the globe in which we live !

The subject of fish growth—particularly as regards the changes undergone by the salmon family—will be found further elucidated under the head of " Fish Culture," and incidentally in some other divisions of this work.

CHAPTER II.

———◆———

FISH COMMERCE.

Early Fish Commerce—Sale of Fresh-water Fish—Cured Fish—Influence of Rapid Transit on the Fisheries—Fish-ponds—The Logan Pond—Ancient Fishing Industries—The Dutch Herring Fishing—Comacchio—the Art of Breeding Eels—Progress of Fishing in Scotland—A Scottish Buss—Newfoundland Fisheries—The Greenland Whale Fishing—Speciality of different Fishing Towns—The General Sea Fisheries of France—French Fish Commerce—Statistics of the British Fisheries.

THERE was a time when man only killed the denizens of the deep in order to supply his own immediate wants, and it is very much to be regretted, in the face of the extensive fish commerce now carried on, that no reliable documents exist from which to write a consecutive history of the rise and progress of fishing.

In the absence of precise information, it may be allowed us to guess that even during the far back ages fish was esteemed as an article of diet, and formed an important contribution to the food resources of such peoples as had access to the sea, or who could obtain the finny inhabitants of the deep by purchase or barter. In the Old and New Testaments, and in various ancient profane histories, fish and fishing are mentioned very frequently ; and in what may be called modern times a few scattered dates, indicating the progress of the sea fisheries, may, by the exercise of great industry and research, be collected ; but these are not in any sense conse-

cutive, or indeed very reliable, so that we are, as it were, compelled to imagine the progress of fish commerce, and to picture
in our mind's eye its transition from the period when the mere
satisfaction of individual wants was all that was cared for, to
a time when fish began to be bartered for land goods—such as
farm, dairy, and garden produce—and to trace, as we best can,
that commerce through these obscure periods to the present
time, when the fisheries form a prominent outlet for capital,
are a large source of national revenue, and are attracting, because of these qualities, an amount of attention never before
bestowed upon them.

Fish commerce being an industry naturally arising out of
the immediate wants of mankind, has unfortunately, as regards the article dealt in, been invested with an amount of
exaggeration that has no parallel in other branches of industry.
Blunders perpetrated long ago in Encyclopædias and other
works, when the life and habits of all kinds of fish, from the
want of investigation, were but little understood, have been,
with those additions which under such circumstances always
accumulate, handed down to the present day, so that even
now we are carrying on some of our fisheries on altogether
false assumptions, and in many cases evidently killing the
goose for the sake of the golden egg : in other words, never
dreaming that there will be a fishing to-morrow, which must
be as important, or even more important, than the fishing of
to-day, beyond which the fisher class as a rule never look.

It is curious to note that there was in most countries a
commerce in fresh-water fish long before the food treasures of
the sea were broken upon. This is particularly noticeable in
our own country, and is vouched for by many authorities both
at home and abroad. We can all imagine also, that in the
pre-historic or very early ages, when the land was untilled and
virgin, and the earth was undrained, there were sources for
the supply of fresh-water fish that do not now exist in conse-

quence of the enhanced value of land. At the period to which I have been alluding there was a much greater water surface than there is now—rivers were broader and deeper, and so also were our lakes and marshes. In those early days, although not so early as the remote uncultivated age of which I have spoken, there were great inland stews populous with fish, especially in connection with monasteries and other religious houses, many examples of which, in their remains, are still to be seen in England or on the Continent. In fact, fish commerce, in despite of many curious industries connected with the productiveness of the fisheries, was not really developed till a few years ago, when the railway system of carriage began. Even up to the time of George Stephenson commerce in fish was generally speaking a purely local business, except in so far as the fishwives could extend the trade by carrying the contents of their husbands' boats away inland, in order, as in the still more primitive times, to barter the fish for other produce. The fishermen of Comacchio, for instance, still cure their eels, because they have not the means of sending them so rapidly into the interior of Italy as would admit of their being eaten fresh. Scotch salmon in the beginning of the present century was nearly all kippered or cured as soon as caught, because the demand for the fresh fish was only local, and therefore limited. With the discovery that salmon by being packed in ice could be kept a long time fresh, the trade began to extend and the price to rise. This discovery, which exercised a very important influence on the value of our salmon-fisheries, was made by a country gentleman of Scotland, Mr. Dempster of Dunnichen, in the year 1780. Steamboat and railway transit, when they became general, at once converted salmon into a valuable commodity; and such is now the demand, from facility of transport, that this particular fish, from its great individual value, has been lately in some danger of being exterminated through the greed of the fishery tenants; indeed, it cannot be said that it is yet safe; for every tenant thinks it legitimate to kill all the fish he can see.

The network of railways which now encircles the land has conferred upon our inland towns, so far as fish is concerned, all the advantages of the coast. For instance, the fishermen of Prestonpans send more of their fish to Manchester than to Edinburgh, which is only nine miles distant : indeed our most landward cities are comparatively well supplied with fresh fish and crustacea, while at the seaside these delicacies are not at all plentiful. The Newhaven fishwife is a common visitant in many of our larger Scottish inland towns, being able by means of the railway to take a profitable journey ; indeed, one consequence of the extension of our railways has undoubtedly been to add enormously to the demand for sea produce, and to excite the ingenuity of our seafaring population to still greater cunning and industry in the capture of all kinds of fish. In former years, when a large haul of fish was taken there was no means of despatching them to a distance, neither was there a resident population to consume what was caught. Railways not being then in existence, the conveyance inland was too slow for a perishable commodity like fish, and visitors to the seaside were also rarer than at present. The want of a population to eat the fish no doubt aided the comfortable delusion of our supplies being inexhaustible. But it is now an undoubted fact, that with railways branching out to every pier and quay, our densely-populated inland towns are better supplied with fish than the villages where they are caught—a result of that keen competition which has at length become so noticeable where fish, oysters, or other sea delicacies are concerned. The high prices now obtained form an inducement to the fishermen to take from the water all they can get, whether the fish be ripe for food or not. A practical fisherman, whom I have often consulted on these topics, says that forty years ago the slow system of carriage was a sure pre-

ventive of over-fishing, as fish, to be valuable for table purposes, require to be fresh. "It's the railways that has done all
the mischief, sir, depend on that ; and as for the fishing, sir,
it's going on at such a rate that there will very soon be a
complete famine. I've seen more fish caught in a day, sir,
with a score of hooks on a line than can now be got with
eight thousand ! "

As to fish-ponds: at the time indicated it was quite usual
for noblemen and other country gentlemen to have fish-ponds ;
in fact, a fish-pond was as necessary an adjunct of a large
country house as its vegetable or fruit garden. These ponds,
as the foregoing sketch will show, were of the most simple
kind, and were often enough constructed by merely stopping a
little stream at some suitable place, and so forming a couple of
artificial lakes, in which were placed a few large stones, or two

or three bits of artificial rock-work, so constructed as to afford shelter to the fish. There being in those days no railways or other speedy conveyance, there arose a necessity for fish-ponds to persons who were in the habit of entertaining guests or giving great dinner-parties ; hence also the multiplicity of recipes in our older cookery-books for the dressing of all kinds of fresh-water fishes ; besides, in the very ancient times, that is before the Reformation, when Roman Catholicism required a rigorous observance of the various church fasts, a fish-pond near every cathedral city, and in the precincts of every monastery, was a *sine qua non.* The varieties of fish bred in these ponds were necessarily very limited, being usually carp, some of which, however, grew to a very large size. There are traces also of some of our curious and valuable fishes having been introduced into this country during those old monastic times. Thus it is thought, as has been already stated, that the celebrated trout of Lochleven may have been introduced from foreign parts by some of the ancient monks who had a taste for gastronomy. The celebrated vendace of Lochmaben is likewise supposed to have been introduced in the same way from some continental fishery.

As I have already shown, most of the fish-ponds of these remote times were quite primitive in their construction—very similar, in fact, to the beautiful trout-pond that may any day be seen at Wolfsbrunnen, near Heidelberg. There were no doubt ponds of large extent and of elaborate construction, but these were comparatively rare; and even on the very sea-coast we used to have ponds or storing-places for sea fish. One of these is still in existence: I allude to Logan Pond in Galloway. This is only used as a place for keeping fish so as to have them attainable for table uses without the family having to depend on the state of the weather. This particular pond is not an artificially-constructed one, but has been improved out of the natural surrounding of the place. It is a basin, formed in the solid rock, ten yards in depth, and having a circumference of one hundred and sixty feet. It is used chiefly as a preserve to ensure a constant supply of fish, which are taken in the neighbouring bay when the weather is fine, and transferred to the pond, which communicates with the sea by a narrow passage. It is generally well stocked with cod, haddock, and flat fish, which in the course of time become very tame ; and I regret to say, from want of proper shelter, most of the animals become blind. The fish have of course to be fed, and they partake greedily, even from the hand of their keeper, of the mass of boiled mussels, limpets, whelks, etc., with which they are fed, and their flavour is really unexceptionable.

Coming back, however, to the subject of fresh-water fish-ponds, it may be stated that at one time some very large but simply-constructed fish-ponds, or stews as they were then called, existed in various parts of England, but that, as the commerce in sea fish gradually extended, these were given up, except as adjuncts to the amenities of gentlemen's pleasure-grounds. Ornamental canals and fish-ponds are not at all uncommon in the parks of our country gentlemen, although they are not required for fish-breeding purposes, as the fast London or provincial trains carry baskets of fish to a distance of one hundred miles in a very few hours, so that a turbot or whiting is in excellent condition for a late dinner.

All the ancient fishing industries, whether those that still exist or those that are extinct, except in their remains, bear traces of the times in which they originated. Pisciculture (which I shall describe at some length by and by) arose at a very ancient period, and was chiefly resorted to in connection with fresh-water fishes—the ova of such being the most readily obtainable ; or with the mollusca, as these could bear a long transport, having a reservoir of water in their shell. The sea fishers of the olden time dealt with the fish for the purpose of their being cured with salt or otherwise, simply, as has already been stated, because of the scarcity of rapid land carriage and a comparatively scanty local population.

The particular fishing industry which has bulked largest in literature, and which was pursued after a systematic fashion, is, or rather was, that of the Dutch, for Holland does not at present make her mark so largely on the waters as she was

PACKING· HERRINGS.

wont to do, being at present far surpassed in fishing enterprise by Scotland and other countries. The particular fish coveted by the Dutch people was the herring, and I have recently had the pleasure of examining a set of engravings procured in Amsterdam, that convey a graphic idea of the great import-ance that was attached by the Dutch themselves to their herring-fishery. This series of sixteen peculiarly Dutch plates begins at the beginning of the fishery, as is indeed proper it should, by showing us a party busy at a sea-side cottage knit-

ting the gerring nets; one or two busses are seen in the distance
busy at work.   We are then shown, on the banks of one of
the numerous Dutch canals, a lot of quaint-looking coopers
engaged in preparing the barrels, while next in order comes a
representation of the preparing and victualing of the buss,
which is surrounded by small boats, and crowded with an
active population all engaged in getting the vessel ready for
sea—barrels of provisions, breadths of netting, and various
necessaries, are being got on board.   Then follow plates, of
which the foregoing is a specimen, showing us the equipment
of various other kinds of boats, which again are succeeded by
a view of the busses among the shoals of herring, the big mast
struck, most of the sails furled, and the men busy hauling in
the nets, which are of course, as is fitting in a picture, laden
with fish.   Various other boats are also shown at work, as the
great hoy, a one-masted vessel, that is apparently furnished
with a seine-net, and the great double shore or sea-boar, which
is an open boat.   Then we have the herring-buss coming gal-
lantly into the harbour, with its sails all set and its flags all
flying—its hull deep in the water, which seems to frolic
lovingly round its prow as if glad at its safe return.   Next, of
course, there is a scene on the shore, where the pompous-look-
ing curer and his servants are seen congratulating each other
amid the bustle of surrounding commerce and labour ; dealers,
too, are figured in these engravings, with their wheelbarrows
drawn by dogs of unmistakable Dutch build, and there are also
to be seen in the picture many other elements of that industry
peculiar to all fishing towns, whether ancient or modern.

The next scene of this fishing panorama is the herring
banquet or feast, where the king, or mayhap the rich owner of
a fleet of busses, sits grandly at table, with his wife and daughter, attended by a butler and a black footman, partaking of
the first fruits of the fishery.   After this follows a view of the
fishmarket, with portraits of the fishwives, and altogether

thoroughly indicative of their peculiar way of doing business, which is always the same, whether the scene be laid in ancient Holland or in modern Billingsgate. Next comes a picture of the various buyers of the commodity on their way home, of course by the side of a canal, with their purchases of deep-sea, shore, state, and red herrings. The next scene of the series is a smoking-house, partially obscured by wreaths of smoke, where the herrings are being red-ed ; and the series is appropriately wound up with a tableau representing the important process of repairing the damaged nets—the whole conveying a really graphic, although not very artistic, delineation of this highly characteristic Dutch industry. A few plates illustrative of the whale-fisheries of Holland are appended to the series I have been describing—for whale-fishing in the seas of Greenland was also in those days one of the industries of the hardworking Dutch.

The old saying that Amsterdam was built on herring bones frequently used to symbolise the fishing power of Holland. It is thought that the industry of the Dutch people was first drawn to the value of the sea fisheries by the settlement of some Scottish fishermen in their country. I cannot vouch for the truth of this statement as to the Scottish emigration, but I believe it was a Fleming who first discovered the virtues of pickled herrings, and it is also known that the capture of the herring was a chief industry on the sea-board of all the Low Countries, and it is likewise instructive to learn that at a time when our own fisheries were very much undeveloped the Dutch people found our seas to be a mine of gold, so productive were they in fish, and so famous did the Dutch cure of herrings become. We are not called on, however, to credit all the stories of miraculous draughts taken, and store of wealth garnered up, by the plodding Hollanders. We must bear in mind that when the Dutch began to fish the seas as a field of industry were nearly virgin, and that that people had at one time this great source of wealth all to themselves. At that particular period, likewise, there was no limit to the supply, the fishermen having but to dip their nets in the water in order to have them filled.   No wonder, therefore, that the fisheries of Holland grew into a prominent industry, and became at one time the one absorbing hobby of the nation. Busses in large fleets were fitted out and manned, till in time the Dutch came to be reputed as the greatest fishers in the world.   But great as was the fishing industry of those days in Holland, and industrious as the Dutch undoubtedly were, it is evident that there has been a considerable amount of exaggeration as to the results, more especially in regard to the enormous quantities of fish that are said to have been captured and cured.   But whatever this total might be was not of great consequence.   The mere quantity of fish caught is perhaps, although a considerable one, the smallest of the many benefits conferred on a nation by an energetic pursuit of its fisheries.   The fishermen must have boats, and these must be fitted with sails, rigging, etc.; and, moreover, the boats must be manned by an efficient crew; then the curing and sale of the fish give employment to a large number of people as well; whilst the articles of cure—as salt, barrels, etc.—must of necessity be largely provided, and are all of them the result of some kind of trained industry : and all these varied circumstances of demand combine to feed the particular industrial pursuit I am describing.   And the fisheries provide, besides, a grand nursery for seamen, which is, perhaps, in a country like ours, having a powerful navy, the greatest of all the benefits conferred.

I have taken the pains to collate as many of the figures of the Dutch fishery as I could collect during an industrious search, and I find that, in the zenith of its prosperity, after the proclamation of the independence of the States of Holland, three thousand boats were employed in her own bays, while sixteen hundred herring busses fished industriously in British waters, while eight hundred larger vessels prosecuted the cod and whale fisheries at remote distances. In the year 1603 we are informed that the Dutch sold herrings to the amount of £4,759,000, besides what they themselves consumed. We are also told that in 1618 they had twelve thousand vessels engaged in this branch of the fishery, and that these ships employed about two hundred thousand men. It must have been a splendid sight, on every 24th of June, to witness the departure of the great fleet from the Texel; and as most of the Dutch people were more or less interested in the prosperity of the fishery, either as labourers or employers of labour, there would be no lack of spectators on these occasions. The Wick herring drave of twelve hundred boats is, as I will by and by endeavour to show, an industrial sight of no common kind, but it must give way before the picturesque fleet of Holland, as it sailed away from the Texel about three hundred years ago.

Long before the organisation of the Dutch fisheries there existed a quaint colony of Italian fisher people on the borders of a more poetic water than the Zuyder Zee. I allude to the eel-breeders of Comacchio on the Adriatic. This particular fishing industry is of very considerable antiquity, as we have well-authenticated statistics of its produce, extending back over three centuries. The lagoons of Comacchio afford a curious example of what may be done by design and labour. This place was at one time a great unproductive swamp, about one hundred and forty miles in circumference, accessible to the waves of the sea, where eels, leeches, and the other inhabitants of such watery regions, sported about unmolested by the hand of man; and its inhabitants—the descendants of those who first populated its various islands—isolated from the surrounding civilisation, and devoid of ambition, have long been contented with their obscure lot, and have even

remained to this day without establishing any direct communication with surrounding countries.

The precise date at which the great lagoon of Comacchio
was formed into a fish-pond is not known, but so early as the
year 1229 the inhabitants of the place—a community of
fishers as quaint, superstitious, and peculiar as those of Buckie
on the Moray Firth, or any other ancient Scottish fishing port
—proclaimed Prince Azzo d'Este Lord of Comacchio; and
from the time of this appointment the place grew in prosperity, and the fisheries from that date began to assume an
organisation and design which had not before that time been
their characteristic. The waters of the lagoon were dyked out
from those of the Adriatic, and a series of canals and pools
were formed suitable for the requirements of the peculiar
fishery carried on at the place, all of which operations were
greatly facilitated by the Reno and Volano mouths of the Po
forming the side boundaries of the great swamp; and, as a
chief feature of the place, the marvellous fish labyrinth celebrated by Tasso still exists. Without being technical, we may
state that the principal entrances to the various divisions of the
great pond—and it is divided into a great many stations—are
from the two rivers. A number of these entrances have been
constructed in the natural embankments which dyke out
the waters of the lagoon. Bridges have also been built over
all these trenches by the munificence of various Popes, and
very strong flood-gates, worked by a crank and screw, are
attached to each, so as to regulate the migration of the fish
and the entrance and exit of the waters. A very minute account of all the varied hydraulic apparatus of Comacchio would
only weary the reader; but I may state generally, and I speak
on the authority of M. Coste, that these flood-gates place at
the service of the fish-cultivators about twenty currents, which
allow the salt waters of the lagoon to mingle with the fresh
waters of the river. Then, again, the waters of the Adriatic

are admitted to the lagoon by means of the Grand Palotta Canal, which extends from the port of Magnavacca right through the great body of the waters, with branches stretching to the chief fishing stations which dot the surface of this inland sea, so that there are about a hundred mouths always ready to vomit into the lagoon the salt water of the Adriatic.

The entire industry of this unique place is founded on a knowledge of the natural history of the particular fish which is so largely cultivated there—viz. the eel. Being a migatory fish, the eel is admirably adapted for cultivation, and being also very prolific and of tolerably rapid growth it can be speedily turned into a source of great profit. About the end of the sixteenth century we know that the annual income derived from eel-breeding in the lagoons was close upon £12,000—a very large sum of money at that period. No recent statistics have been made public as to the money derived from the eels of Comacchio, but I have reason to know that the sum has not in any sense diminished during late years.

The inhabitants of Comacchio seem to have a very correct idea of the natural history of this rather mysterious fish. They know exactly the time when the animal breeds, which, as well as the question how it breeds, has in Britain been long a source of controversy, as I have already shown ; and these shrewd people know very well when the fry may be expected to leave the sea and perform their *montee*. They can measure the numbers, or rather estimate the quantity, of young fish as they ascend into the lagoon, and consequently are in a position to know what the produce will eventually be, as also the amount of food necessary to be provided, for the fish-farmers of Comacchio do not expect to fatten their animals out of nothing. However, they go about this in a very economic way, for the same water that grows the fish also grows the food on which they are fed. This is chiefly the aquadelle, a tiny little fish which is contained in the lakes in great numbers,

and which, in its turn, finds food in the insect and vegetable
world of the lagoons. ˙ Other fish are bred as well as the eel—
viz. mullet, plaice, etc.   On the 2d day of February the year
of Comacchio may be said to begin, for at that time the *montec*
commences, when may be seen ascending up the Reno and
Volano mouths of the Po from the Adriatic a great series of
wisps, apparently composed of threads, but in reality young

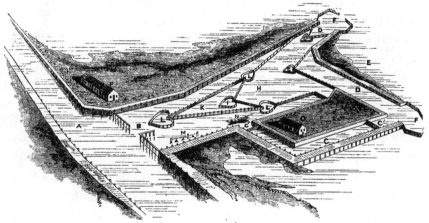

A DIVISION OF COMACCHIO.

A. Canal Palotta.	H. Second compartment.
B. Entrance from the canal.	I. Chamber of second compartment.
C. Canal for the passage of boats.	K. Third compartment.
C′. Sluices for closing canal.	L L L. Chambers of third compartment.
D. First compartment of the labyrinth.	M. Wickerwork baskets for keeping fish alive.
E. Outer basin.	N. Boat with instruments of fishing.
F. Antechamber of the first compartment.	O. Dwelling-house.
G. Chamber of the first compartment.	P. Storehouse.

eels; and as soon as one lot enters, the rest, with a sheeplike
instinct, follow their leader, and hundreds of thousands pass
annually from the sea to the waters of the lagoon, which can
be so regulated as in places to be either salt or fresh as required.   Various operations connected with the working of the
fisheries keep the people in employment from the time the
entrance-sluices are closed, at the end of April, till the commencement of the great harvest of eel-culture, which lasts from
the beginning of August till December.   The manner of life of

the people of Comacchio will be found detailed under the title of " The Fisher Folks" in another part of this volume. The engraving represents one of the fishing-places of the lagoon.

No country has, taking into account size and population, been more industrious on the seas than Scotland—the most productive fishery of that country having been the herring. There is no consecutive historical account of the progress of the herring-fishery. The first really authentic notice we have of a trade in herrings is nine hundred years old, when it is recorded that the Scots sold herrings to the people of the Netherlands, and we have some indications that even at that early period a considerable fishery for herrings existed in Scotland ; and even prior to this time Boethius alludes to Inverlochy as an important seat of commerce, and persons of intelligence consider that town to have been a resort of the French and Spaniards for the purchase of herring and other fishes. The pickling and drying of herrings for commerce were first carried on by the Flemings. This mode of curing fish is said to have been discovered by William Benkelen of Biervlet, near Sluys, who died in 1397, and whose memory was held in such veneration for that service that the Emperor Charles V. and the Queen of Hungary made a pilgrimage to his tomb. We have also incidental notices of the herring-fishery in the records of the monastery of Evesham, so far back as the year 709, and the tax levied on the capture of herrings is noticed in the annals of the monastery of Barking as herring-silver. The great fishery for herrings at Yarmouth dates from the earliest Anglo-Saxon times, and at so early a period as the reign of Henry I. it paid a tax of 10,000 fish to the king. We are told that the most ancient records of the French herring-fishery are not earlier than the year 1020, and we know that in 1088 the Duke of Normandy allowed a fair to be held at Fecamp during the time of this fishery, the right of holding it being granted to the Abbey of the Holy Trinity.

E

The Yarmouth fishery, even in these early times, was a great success—as success was then understood. Edward III. did all he could to encourage the fishery at that place. In 1357 he got his Parliament to lay down a body of laws for the better regulation of the fisheries, and the following year sixty lasts of herring were shipped at Portsmouth for the use of his army and fleet in France. In 1635 a patent was granted to Mr. Davis for gauging red-herrings, for which Yarmouth was famed thus early, at a certain price per last ; his duty was, in fact, to denote the quality of the fish by affixing a certain seal ; this, so far as we know, is the first indication of the brand system. His Majesty Charles II., being interested in the fisheries, visited Yarmouth in company with the Duke of York and others of the nobility, when he was handsomely entertained, and presented with four golden herrings and a chain of considerable value.

Several of the kings of Scotland were zealous in aiding the fisheries, but the death of James V. and the subsequent religious and civil commotions put a stop for a time to the progress of this particular branch of trade, as well as to every other industrial project of his time. In 1602 his successor on the throne, James VI., resumed the plans which had been chalked out by his grandfather. Practical experiments were made in the art of fishing, fishing-towns were built in the different parts of the Highlands, and persons well versed in the practice were brought to teach the ignorant natives ; but as the Highlanders were jealous of these "interlopers," very slow progress was made ; and, again, the course of improvement was interrupted by the king's accession to the throne of England and the union of the two Crowns. During the remainder of James's reign little progress was made in the art of fishing, and we have to pass over the reign of Charles I. and wait through the troublous times of the Protectorate till we have Charles II. seated on the throne, before much further encouragement is decreed to the fisheries. Charles II. aided the advancement of this industrial pursuit by appointing a Royal Council of Fishery, in order to the establishment of proper laws and regulations for the encouragement of those engaged in this branch of our commerce.

After this period the British trade in fish and the knowledge of the arts of capture expanded rapidly. It is said, as I have already stated, that during our early pursuit of the fishery the Dutch learned much from us, and that, in fact, while we were away founding the Greenland whale-fishery, the people of Holland came upon our seas and robbed us of our fish, and so obtained a supremacy in the art that lasted for many years. At any rate, whatever the Dutch accomplished, we were particularly industrious in fishing. Our seas were covered with busses of considerable tonnage—the average being vessels of fifty tons, with a complement of fourteen men and a master. The mode of fishing then was to sail with the ship into the deep sea, and then, leaving the vessel as a rendezvous, take to the small boats, and fish with them, returning to the large vessel to carry on the cure. The same mode of fishing, with slight modifications, is still pursued at Yarmouth and some other places in England.

The following note of the cost of building and sailing one of the old Scottish herring-busses will illustrate the fishery of the last century :—

Expenses of a Vessel of 60 *Tons Burden fitted out for the Herring-Fishery.*

To shipbuilder's account for hull - -	£345	0	0
To joiners' account - - -	21	10	0
To blockmaker's account (paint, etc.) -	18	0	0
To rope-work account (sails, etc.) - -	160	0	0
To smith's account (anchors, etc.) -	22	10	0
To spars, 3 fishing-boats, compasses, etc. -	56	0	0
Cost of Vessel (forward)	£623	0	0

Brought forward   -   £623   0   0

Outfit.

To 462 bushels of salt -	-	-	45	0	0
To 32 lasts herring barrels	-	-	80	0	0
To 15,000 square yards netting	-	-	78	5	0
To buoys, etc. -	-	-	-	8	4	0
To provisions for 14 men for 3 months	-	42	10	0
To spirits for men when at work	-	5	0	0
To wages, 13 men at 27s. per month	-	52	13	0
To shipmaster's wages -	-	-	10	0	0
To custom-house clearing	-	-	0	15	0

Cost of Outfit   -   -   £945   7   0

Supposing the above vessel to make one-half of her cargo of herrings yearly, which has not been the case for seven years back on an average, the state of account will stand as under :—

Voyage to Herring Fishers and Owners.   Dr.

To one-half of salt carried out	-	-	£22	10	0
To one-half of barrels used	-	-	48	0	0
To tear and wear on nets (one-third worn)	26	1	3
To provisions and spirits -	-	-	47	10	0
To wages, including skipper	-	-	62	13	0
To tear and wear of rigging and vessel, 5 per cent per month	-	-	-	-	30	11	2
To insurance on £957 for 3 months at 2½ per cent	-	-	-	-	27	16	0
To interest on £957 for 3 months	-	11	18	0
To waste on salt, etc., at 10 per cent	-	3	10	0
To freight of herrings to Cork, at 2s. per barrel, 192 barrels -	-	-	-	19	4	0
To duty on herrings in Ireland, at 1s. per barrel	9	12	0

£305   5   5

Brought forward   -   £305   5   5

Contra.   *Cr.*

By 192 barrels herrings at 20s.   £192   0   0
By debenture on herrings at 2s. 8d.   25 12   0
By bounty on 60 tons   -   -   90   0   0
                                               ——————   307 12   0

Gain on home fishery   £2   6   7

Extra Expenses on such Busses as go to the Irish
   Fishery—
To duty of 17¾ tons salt in Ireland £10 19 11
To duty on barrels   -   -   4 16   0
To fees on 3 boats at 42s.   -   6   6   0
                                               ——————   22   1 11

Loss if upon Irish fishery   £19 15   4

Much has also been written from time to time about the great cod-fishery of Newfoundland : it has been the subject of innumerable treatises, Acts of Parliament, and other negotiations, and various travellers have illustrated the natural products and industrial capabilities of these North American seas.   The cod-fishery of Newfoundland is undoubtedly one of the greatest fishing industries the world has ever seen, and has been more or less worked for three hundred and sixty years.   Occasionally there is a whisper of the cod grounds of Newfoundland being exhausted, and it would be no wonder if they were, considering the enormous capture of that fish that has constantly been going on during the period indicated, not only by means of various shore fisheries, but by the active American and French crews that are always on the grounds capturing and curing.   Since the time when the Red Indian lay over the rocks and transfixed the codfish with his spear, till now, when thousands of ships are spreading their sails in the bays and surrounding seas, taking the fish with ingenious instruments of capture, myriads upon myriads of valuable cod have been taken from the waters, although to the ordinary

eye the supply seems as abundant as it was a century ago.
When my readers learn that the great bank from whence is
obtained the chief supply of codfish is nearly six hundred
miles long and over two hundred miles in breadth, it will
afford a slight index to the vast total of our sea wealth and to
the enormous numbers of the finny population of this part of
our seas, and the population of which, before it was discovered,
must have been growing and gathering for centuries ; but
when it is further stated—and this by way of index to the
extent of this great food-wealth—that Catholic countries alone
give something like half a million sterling every year for the
produce of these North American seas, the enormous money
value of a well-regulated fishery must become apparent even
to the most superficial observer of facts and figures.

It is much to be regretted that we are not in possession
of reliable annual statistics of the fisheries of Newfoundland,
but there are so many conflicting interests connected with
these fisheries as to render it difficult to obtain accurate
statistics. Mr. Hind, in his recent work on Labrador, gives
us a few figures about the fisheries of Nova Scotia and Canada,
for which we are thankful. From this work we learn that the
fish exported from Nova Scotia in 1860 reached the large sum
of $2,956,788, and that 3258 vessels were engaged in the
fishery ; and Mr. Hind thinks that if we include the fish and
fish-oil consumed by the inhabitants, the present annual
value of the fisheries to British America must be above
$15,000,000, and this estimate even does not include much
of the fish that goes directly to Britain. The value of the
Labrador fisheries alone has been estimated at one million
sterling per annum, and the total value of the fisheries of the
Gulf of St. Lawrence and the coast of Labrador may be set
down as four millions sterling per annum, and the Canadian
fisheries, Mr. Hind informs us, are yet in their infancy !

Another fishing industry which has bulked large in the

annals of the sea is the whale-fishery. At one time a goodly
number of British vessels were fitted out in order to follow
this dangerous pursuit in the Arctic Seas, and many a thrilling
narrative has been founded on the adventures of enterprising
whalers. This fishery has fallen off very much of late years,
both as regards the pursuit of the right or the Greenland
whale, and also in the case of the sperm whale, the capture of
which used to be an "enterprise of great pith and moment"
in America, the head-quarters of the fishery being situated at
New Bedford. It is a good thing that the invention of gas
has superseded in a great measure our dependence on the
whale; and the discovery of other lubricants, vegetable and
mineral, suitable for machinery, has rendered us altogether
independent of the Leviathan of the deep. Although this
particular fishing industry may almost be said to be extinct, it
was at one time of considerable importance, at least to Scottish
commerce.

To come down to the present time, it is pleasant to think
that the seas of Britain are crowded with many thousand boats,
all gleaning wealth from the bosom of the waters. As one
particular branch of sea industry becomes exhausted for the
season another one begins. In spring we have our white
fisheries ; in summer we have our mackerel ; in autumn we
have the great herring-fishery ; then in winter we deal in
pilchards and sprats and oysters ; and all the year round we
trawl for flat fish or set pots for lobsters, or do some other work
of the fishing—in fact, we are continually day by day despoil-
ing the waters of their food treasures. When we exhaust the
inshore fisheries we proceed straightway to the deep waters.
Hale and strong fishermen sail hundreds of miles to the white-
fishing grounds, whilst old men potter about the shore, setting
nets with which to catch crabs, or ploughing the sand for
prawns. At different places we can note the specialities of the
British fisheries. In Caithness-shire we can follow the greatest

herring-fleet in the world ; at Cornwall, again, we can view
the pilchard-fishery ; at Barking we can see the cod-fleet ;
at Hull there is a wealth of trawlers ; at Whitstable we can
make acquaintance with the oyster-dredgers ; and at the
quaint fishing-ports on the Moray Firth, to be afterwards described, we can witness the manufacture of "Finnan haddies,"
as at Yarmouth we can take part in the making of bloaters ;
and all round our coasts we can see women and children
industriously gathering shell-fish for bait, or performing other
functions connected with the industry of the sea—repairing
nets, baiting the lines, or hawking the fish, for the fisherwomen
are true helpmates to their husbands. At certain seasons
everything that can float in the water is called into requisition
—little cobbles, gigantic yawls, trig schooners, are all required
to aid in the gathering of the sea harvest. Thousands of people
are employed in this great industry ; betokening that a vast
population have chosen to seek bread on the bosom of the
great deep.

Crossing the Channel we can see that the general sea
fisheries of France are also being prosecuted with great vigour,
and at those places which have railways to bear away the
produce with considerable profit. I am in possession of notes
and statistics pertaining to a large portion of the French seabord, giving plentiful details of the modern fishing industry
of that country ; and the fisheries of France are greatly noticed
just now, in the hope of their forming a splendid nursery for
seamen, the improvement of the navy being at present one of
the dominant objects of the Emperor of the French. The
Marine Department, having this object in view, have sagaci-
ously broken through all the old protective laws incidental to
the fisheries, and now allow the fishermen to carry on their
trade very much as they please ; trawling has therefore become pretty general at all those ports which maintain railway
communication with the interior : thus at Dunkerque there

are 60 trawlers; at Boulogne, 100; at Tourville, 109; at Treport, 53; at Calais, 84; with lesser numbers at smaller ports, most of them being engaged in supplying the wants of Paris with deep-sea fish; and as the coasts are provided with excellent harbours of refuge, the trawlers follow their avocations with regularity and success.

The modes of sea-fishing are so much alike in every country that it is unnecessary for us to do more than just mention that the French method of trawling is very similar to our own, about which I will by and by have something to say. But there are details of fishing industry connected with that pursuit on the French coasts that we are not familiar with in Britain. The neighbouring peasantry, for instance, come to the seaside and fish with nets which are called *bas parc;* and these are spread out before the tide is full in order to retain all the fish which are brought within their meshes. The children of these land-fishers also work, although with smaller nets, at these foreshore fisheries, while the wives poke about the sand for shrimps and the smaller crustacea. These people thus not only ensure a supply of food for themselves during winter, but also contrive during summer to take as much fish as brings them in a little store of money.

The perpetual industry carried on by the coast people on the French foreshores is quite a sight, although it is a fish commerce of a humble and primitive kind. Even the little children contrive to make money by building fish-ponds, or erecting trenches, in which to gather salt, or in some other little industry incidental to sea-shore life. One occasionally encounters some abject creature groping about the rocks to obtain the wherewithal to sustain life. To these people all is fish that comes to hand; no creature, however slimy, that creeps about is allowed to escape, so long as it can be disguised by cookery into any kind of food for human beings. Some of the people have old rickety boats patched up with still older pieces of wood or leather, sails mended here and there, till it is difficult to distinguish the original portion from those that have been added to it ; nets torn and darned till they are scarce able to hold a fish ; and yet that boat and that crippled machinery are the stock in trade of perhaps two or three generations of a family, and the concern may have been founded half a century ago by the grandfather, who now sees around him a legion of hungry gamins that it would take a fleet of boats to keep in food and raiment. The moment the tide flows back, the foreshore is at once overrun with an army of hungry people, who are eager to clutch whatever fishy *debris* the receding water may have left ; the little pools are eagerly, nay hungrily, explored, and their contents grabbed with an anxiety that pertains only to poverty. At some places of the coast, however, a happier life is dawning on the people —the discovery of pisciculture has led to a traffic in oysters that, as I will by and by show, is surprising ; indeed a new life has in consequence dawned on some districts, and where at one time there was poverty and its attendant squalor, there is now wealth and its handmaid prosperity.

On some parts of the French coasts, and it is proper to mention this, the fishery is not of importance, although the fish are plentiful enough. At Cancale, for instance, the fishermen have imposed on themselves the restriction of only fishing twice a week. In Brittany, at some of the fishing places, the people seem very poor and miserable, and their boats look to be almost valueless, reminding one of the state of matters at Fittie in the outskirts of Aberdeen. At the isle of Groix, however, there is to be found a tolerably well-off maritime and fishing community ; at this place, where the men take to the sea at an early age, there are about one hundred and thirty fishing boats of from twenty to thirty tons each, of which the people—*i.e.* the practical fishermen—are themselves the owners. At the Sands of Olonne there is a most extensive sardine-fishery—the capture of sprats, young herrings, and young pilchards, for curing as sardines, yielding a considerable share of wealth, as a large number of boats follow this branch of the business all the year round.   There are not less than 13,000 boats on the coast of Brittany devoted to the sardine trade, and when it is considered that, according to Mitchell, a sum of £80,000 is annually expended on cod and mackerel roe for bait in this fishery, my readers will see that the total value of the French fisheries must be very considerable.   Experiments in artificial breeding are now being made both with the white fish and the crustaceans, and sanguine hopes are entertained of having in a short time a plentiful supply of all kinds of shell and white fish, and as regards those parts of the French coast which are at present destitute of the power of conveyance, the apparition of a few locomotives will no doubt work wonders in instigating a hearty fishing enterprise.

In fact the industry of the French as regards the fisheries has become of late years quite wonderful, and there is evidently more in their eager pursuit of sea wealth than all at once meets the eye.   No finer naval men need be wished for any country than those that are to be found in the French fishing luggers, and there can be no doubt but that they are being trained with a view to the more perfect manning of the French navy.   At any rate the French people (? government) have discovered the art of growing sailors, and doubtless they will make the most of it, being able apparently to grow them at a greatly cheaper rate than we can do.   As regards the French fisheries in the North Sea, I may mention that the flotilla engaged in 1863, in that particular mine of industry, consisted of 285 ships, measuring 22,000 tons, and manned by nearly 4000 seamen—the whole, both ships and men, being an increase over those of the preceding year.   This fleet left the shores of France between the 20th of March and the 12th of April, and shortly after these dates arrived at

Iceland.   A very large number of codfish were taken, and the
report to the Minister of Marine says that the ships of war
on the station afforded help to eighty-three of the vessels, and
that the health of the crews was remarkably good during the
whole season, eighteen vessels only requiring the aid of the
surgeon, and these vessels had only two invalids each.   This
is instructive as showing the care that is taken in the selection
of healthy crews, and of the pains of their Government to keep
them healthy, and it must be admitted that, so far as physique
is concerned, the French seamen are fine-looking fellows.

The commercial system established in France for bringing
the produce of the sea into the market is of a highly-elaborate
and intricate character.   The direct consequence of this
system is, that the price of fish goes on increasing from its
first removal from the shore until it reaches the market.   This
fact cannot be better illustrated than by tracing the fish
from the moment they are landed on the quay by the fishermen through various intermediate transactions until they
reach the hands of the fishmonger of Paris.   The first agent
into whose hands they come is the *ecoreur*.   The *ecoreur* is
usually a qualified man appointed by the owners of the
vessels, the municipality, or by an association termed the
Société d'Ecorage.   He performs the functions of a wholesale
agent between the fisherman and the public.   He is ready to
take the fish out of the fisherman's hands as soon as they are
landed.   He buys the fish from the fisherman, and pays him
at once, deducting a percentage for his own services.   This
percentage is sometimes 5, 4, or even as low as $3\frac{1}{2}$ per
cent.   He undertakes the whole risk of selling the fish, and
suffers any loss that may be incurred by bad debts or bad
sale, for which he can make no claim whatever upon the
owner of the boat.   The system of *ecorage* is universally
adopted, as the fisherman prefers ready money with a
deduction of 5 per cent rather than trouble himself with any

repayment or run the risk of bad debts.   Passing from the *ecoreur* we come to the *mareyeur*—that is, the merchant who buys the fish from the wholesale agent.   He provides baskets to hold the fish, packs them, and despatches them by railway. He pays the carriage, the town-dues or duties, and the fees to the market-crier.   Should the fish not keep, and arrive in Paris in bad condition, and be complained of by the police, he sustains the loss.   As regards the transport arrangements, the fish are usually forwarded by the fast trains, and the rates are invariable, whatever may be the quality of the fish. Thus, turbot and salmon are carried at the same rate as monkfish, oysters, and crabs.   On the northern lines the rate is 37 cents per ton per kilometre ; upon the Dieppe and Nantes lines, 25 or 26 cents ; which gives 85 or 96 francs as the carriage of a ton of fish despatched from the principal ports of the north—such as St. Valery-sur-Somme, Boulogne, Calais, and Dunkerque—and 130 francs per ton on fish despatched from Nantes.

The fish, on their arrival in Paris, are subjected to a duty. For the collection of this duty the fish are divided into two classes—viz., fine fresh fish and ordinary fresh fish.   The fine fish—which class includes salmon, trout, turbot, sturgeon, tunny, brill, shad, mullet, roach, sole, lobster, shrimp, and oyster—pay a duty of 10 per cent of the market value.   The duty upon the common fresh fish is 5 per cent.   This duty is paid after the sale, and is then of course duly entered in the official register.

All the fish sent to Paris is sold through the agency of auctioneers (*facteurs à la criée*) appointed by the town, who receive a commission of 2 or 3 per cent.   The auctioneer either sells to the fishmonger or to the consumer.

It will be seen from the above statement that between the landing of the fish by the fisherman and the purchase of it by the salesman at Paris there is added to the price paid to the fisherman 5 per cent for the *ecorage ;* 90, 100, or 130 francs per ton for carriage ; 10 or 5 per cent, with a double tithe of war, for town-dues ; and 3 per cent taken by the auctioneer—or, altogether, 18 or 13 per cent, besides the war-tithe and the cost of transport. This is an estimate of the indispensable expenses only, and does not include a number of items—such as the profit which the *mareyeur* ought to make, the cost of the baskets, carriage from the market to the railway, and from the custom-house to the market in Paris ; and, besides, presumes that the merchant who buys in the market is the consumer, which is seldom the case.

Many other considerations must be taken into account, as, for instance, the quantity of fish not sold, or sold at a low price, the fish which arrive in Paris in bad condition, and that quantity which never leaves the fishing town.

Besides all this, if we bear in mind that the fish-despatcher tries to repay himself for losses incurred, it need not astonish us that he must put a high price upon the fish he sends to the market.

From these considerations it is evident, I think, that the high price of fish is not owing to any scarcity in the supply, or that an increase in the quantity brought to land will effectually reduce the price. Were the fisherman to give his labour for nothing, and the merchant, or rather commission-agent, who buys from him to seek no profit, there is still enough in carriage, toll, and duties, to put a price on the fish which would place it beyond the power of small purses to reach. To reduce the price we must lessen these intermediate expenses, and put the fisherman in direct communication with the Parisian salesman. This might be possible by the establishment of fishermen's societies, directed by skilful business men.

I question very much, however, if the fishermen would agree to such a plan, as they always prefer ready money and no risk. Another suggestion is to unite the offices of *ecoreur* and *mareyeur* in one person, or even, as is already done in some quarters, to combine these two functions with the owner's own special duties. Undoubtedly, a much more effectual plan than either of these is a reduction in the expenses of carriage and duties. The system of transport is manifestly defective, inasmuch as the rate is a uniform one for fine and ordinary fresh fish. The expenses of the carriage compel the fisherman in many cases to retain the ordinary or inferior qualities of fish and endeavour to make use of them otherwise than for sale by employing them for the food of their own households, feeding poultry, or manuring barren land. They in some instances cut off the superfluous parts of the monkfish—the tail, fins, etc.—to reduce the carriage weight ; and although the fish thus mutilated fetch a less price than they would otherwise bring, the depreciation of the selling-price is more than counterbalanced by the reduction in the freight.

It would be difficult to suggest a system which would at once meet the wishes of the owners of boats, the fish-merchants, and the railway directors. On the southern and western railway lines in Ireland the fish are divided into classes. Turbot, sole, plaice, whiting, eels, and shrimps, are charged two-thirds of the rate for salmon ; oysters, crabs, and lobsters, one-half ; and herring' and the common fish one-third. In France, as I have already said, the rate is uniform. The cost of transport depends upon the distance alone. The Commercial Treaty has brought foreign fish more abundantly into the market ; but those coming from England, being gutted to make them keep, have no longer the red gills by which the buyer distinguishes fresh fish ; and between a gutted fish and one with the gills intact the purchaser never hesitates to choose the latter, without the slightest regard to the place at which it has been caught.

The fish-carrier, again, tries, by cramming as many fish as possible into the large baskets, to diminish the number of packages, and thus destroys a number of his fish.

If there is little hope of a reduction of the railway tariffs, there is still less chance, we think, of any reduction of the town-duties. They are far too profitable to the city funds. The revenue derived by the city of Paris from the sale of fish amounted, in 1858, to 894,214 francs ; in 1859, to 928,925 ; and in 1860 it increased to 1,027,920 francs. This sum, however, only includes the dues levied upon fish carried to the market. There is a separate and distinct duty upon fish which arrive directly by railway to the consumer. In this case fine fresh fish are subjected to a duty of 60 francs the 100 kilogrammes ; common fish, 15 francs ; ordinary oysters, 5 francs ; and Ostend oysters, 15 francs per 100 kilogrammes. The exact revenue accruing to the city from this source embraces these two duties; and in estimating the full amount that the merchant must pay for bringing fish into the town and selling it in the market, we must add to these dues the expense of cartage, railway fare, the double tithe of war, and the fees to the crier.

From the official records of the market sales, we find that for six years there has been little difference in the price of fish. The tables of 1852 and 1862 show that mussels, shrimps, mullets, and salmon, are at the same price ; lobsters, sprats, turbot, and shad, are a little less ; and mackerel, whiting, monkfish, sardines, sole, tunny, trout, barbel, and flounder, are slightly raised. The prices vary so little that any increase in the revenue must arise from an increased quantity being brought into the market. Oysters, however, have increased greatly in price, although the quantity has diminished.

But allowing the French people to cultivate to the very utmost—as they especially do as regards the oyster—it is

impossible they can ever exceed, either in productive power
or money value, the fisheries of our own coasts. If, without
the trouble of taking a long journey, we desire to witness the
results of the British fisheries, we have only to repair to
Billingsgate to find this particular industry brought to a focus.

BILLINGSGATE.

At that piscatorial bourse we can see in the early morning the
produce of our most distant seas brought to our greatest seat
of population, sure of finding a ready and a profitable market.
The aldermanic turbot, the tempting sole, the gigantic codfish,
the valuable salmon, the cheap sprat, and the universal herring,
are all to be found during their different seasons in great
plenty at Billingsgate ; and in the lower depths of the market
buildings countless quantities of shell-fish of all kinds, stored
in immense tubs, may be seen ; while away in the adjacent
lanes there are to be found gigantic boilers erected for the pur-

F

pose of crab and lobster boiling. Some of the shops in the neighbourhood have always on hand large stocks of all kinds of dried fish, which are carried away in great waggons to the railway stations for country distribution. About four o'clock on a summer morning this grand piscatorial mart may be seen in its full excitement—the auctioneers bawling, the porters rushing madly about, the hawkers also rushing madly about seeking persons to join them in buying a lot, and so to divide their speculations ; and all over is sprinkled the dripping sea-water, and all around we feel that "ancient and fish-like smell" which is the concomitant of such a place.

No statistics of a reliable kind are published as to the total annual value of the British fisheries. An annual account of the Scottish herring-fishery is taken by commissioners and officers appointed for that purpose; which, along with a yearly report of the Irish fisheries, is the only reliable annual document on the subject that we possess, and the latest official report of the commissioners will be found analysed in another part of this volume. For any statistics of our white-fish fisheries we are compelled to resort to second-hand sources of information ; and, as is likely enough in the circumstances, we do not, after all, get our curiosity properly gratified on these important topics—the progress and produce of the British fisheries. As a proof of the difficulty of obtaining reliable statistics of our sea-harvest, I am compelled to have recourse to the quantities of all kinds of fish carried by the various railways as an indication of what we are doing on the waters. Large quantities of sea produce are still, however, carried by water. The supplies brought inland by the various railways are as follow :—

London and Brighton	-	-	5,174 tons.
Great Western	-	-	2,885 „
North British	-	-	8,303 „
Carry forward			16,362 tons.

Brought forward 16,362 tons.

Great Northern	-	-	-	11,930 „
North Eastern	-	-	-	27,896 „
South Eastern	-	-	-	3,218 „
Great Eastern	-	-	-	29,086 „

Making a total of - - 88,492 tons.

For Ireland the statistics of carriage for the same year are as follow :—

Great Southern and Western	-		1145 tons.
Midland and Great Western	-		785 „
Waterford and Limerick	-	-	374 „
Dublin and Drogheda	-	-	1004 „

Making a total of - - 3308 tons.

The best index, however, of the quantities of fish taken out of the British seas is the supply of that comestible required for London alone. Two attempts have been made to obtain a correct account of the quantities of each kind used for the commissariat of London. Fourteen years ago Mr. Mayhew gave a summation of the quantities of fish sold at Billingsgate, and the number of each kind as detailed is really astonishing ; as 203,000 salmon, nearly four millions of fresh herrings, and others in proportion. The second attempt to guage the fish-supply of the great metropolis was made by a Member of Parliament. In moving for a commission to inquire into the state of the British fisheries, he gave the following statistics :—

Codfish	-	-	-	-	500,000
Mackerel	-	-	-	-	25,000,000
Soles	-	-	-	-	100,000,000
Plaice	-	-	-	-	35,000,000
Haddocks	-	-	-	-	200,000,000
Oysters	-	-	-	-	500,000,000
Periwinkles	-	-	-	-	300,000,000
Cockles	-	-	-	-	70,000,000
Mussels	-	-	-	-	50,000,000
Lobsters, daily	-	-	-		10,000

There is likewise a very extensive demand for cured or pickled fish. Mayhew quoted 1,600,000 dried cod and 50,000,000 of red herrings as being a portion of the London fish-supply. Eels are also a very large item, being set down as nearly 10,000,000 per annum ; and as for crabs, prawns, shrimps, sprats, etc., they are required by the ton weight, and are hawked about London in millions !

CHAPTER III.

———✦———

FISH CULTURE.

Antiquity of Pisciculture—Italian Fish-Culture—Sergius Orata—Re-discovery
of the Art—Gehin and Remy—Jacobi—Shaw of Drumlanrig—The Ettrick
Shepherd—Scientific and Commercial Pisciculture—A Trip to Huningue—
Tourist Talk about Fish—Bale—Huningue described—The Water Supply—
Modus Operandi at Huningue—Packing Fish Eggs—An Important Ques-
tion—Artificial Spawning—Danube Salmon—Statistics of Huningue—
Plan of a Suite of Ponds—M. De Galbert's Establishment—Practical
Nature of Pisciculture—Turtle-Culture—Best Kinds of Fish to Rear—
Pisciculture in Germany—Stormontfield Salmon-Breeding Ponds—Design
for a Suite of Salmon-Ponds—Statistics of Stormontfield—Acclimatisation
of Fish—The Australian Experiment—Introduction of the *Silurus glanis*.

PISCICULTURE may be briefly described as the art of
fecundating and hatching fish-eggs, and of nursing young
fish under protection till they are of an age to take care of
themselves.

The art of pisciculture is almost as old as civilisation
itself. We read of its having been practised in the empire
of China for many centuries, and we also know that it was
much thought of in the palmy days of ancient Italy, when
expensively-fed fish of all kinds were a necessity of the
wonderful banquets given by wealthy Romans and Neapolitans.
There is still in China a large trade in fish-eggs, and boats
may be seen containing men who gather the spawn in various
rivers, and then carry it into the interior of the country for
sale, where the young fish are reared in great flocks or shoals

in the rice-fields.   One Chinese mode of collecting fish-spawn
is to map out a river into compartments by means of mats
and hurdles, leaving only a passage for the boats.   The mats
and hurdles intercept the spawn, which is skimmed off the
water, preserved for sale in large jars, and is bought by persons
who have ponds or other pieces of water which they may wish
to stock with gold or other fish.   One Chinese plan is to
hatch fish-eggs in paddy-fields, and in these places the spawn
speedily comes to life, and the flocks of little fishes are herded
from one field to another as the food becomes exhausted.
The trade in ova is so well managed, even in the present day,
that fish are plentiful and cheap—so cheap as to form a large
portion of the food of the people ; and nothing so much sur-
prises the Chinese who come here as the high price that is
paid for the fish of this country.   A Chinese fisherman was
much astonished, three years ago, at the price he was charged
for a fish-breakfast at Toulon.   This person had arrived in
France with four or five thousand young fish of the best
kinds produced in his country, for the purpose of their being
placed in the great marine aquarium in the Bois de Boulogne.
Being annoyed at the comparative scarcity of fish in France, the
young Chinaman wrote a brief memoir, showing that, with the
command of a small pond, any quantity of fish might be raised
at a trifling expense.   All that is necessary, he stated in the
memoir alluded to, is to watch the period of spawning, and
throw yolks of eggs into the water from time to time, by which
means an incredible quantity of the young fry are saved from
destruction.   For, according to the information conveyed by
this very intelligent youth, thousands of young fish annually
die from starvation—they are unable to seek their own food
at so tender an age.   We cannot believe all the stories we
hear about the Chinese mode of breeding fish, they are so
evidently exaggerated ; but I must notice one particularly
ingenious method of artificial hatching which has been resorted

to by the people of China and which is worth noting as a piscicultural novelty. These ingenious Celestials carry on a business in selling and hatching fish-spawn, collecting the impregnated eggs from various rivers and lakes, in order to sell to the proprietors of canals and private ponds. When the proper season for hatching arrives, they empty a hen's egg, by means of a small aperture, sucking out the natural contents, and then, after substituting fish-spawn, close up the opening. The egg thus manipulated is placed for a few days under a hen! By and by the shell is broken, and the contents are placed in a vessel of water, warmed by the heat of the sun only ; the eggs speedily burst, and in a short time the young fish are able to be transported to a lake or river of ordinary temperature, where they are of course left to grow to maturity without being further noticed than to have a little food thrown to them.

The luxurious Romans achieved great wonders in the art of fish-breeding, and were able to perform curious experiments with the piscine inhabitants of their aquariums; they were also well versed in the arts of acclimatisation. A classic friend, who is well versed in ancient fish lore, tells me that the great Roman epicures could run their fish from ice-cold water into boiling cauldrons without handling them! They spared neither labour nor money in order to gratify their palates. The Italians sent to the shores of Britain for their oysters, and then flavoured them in large quantities on artificial beds. The value of a Roman gentleman's fish in the palmy days of Italian banqueting was represented by an enormous sum of money. The stock kept up by Lucullus was never valued at a less sum than £35,000! These classic lovers of good things had pet breeds of fish in the same sense as gentlemen in the present day have pet breeds of sheep or horned cattle. Lucullus, for instance, to have such a valuable stock, must have been in possession of unique varieties derived from curious crosses, etc. Red mullet or fat carp, which sold for large prices, were not at all unusual. Sixty pounds we can ascertain as being given for a single mullet, and more than three times that sum for a dish of that fish; and enormous sums of money were lavished in the buying, rearing, and taming of the mullet; so much so, that some of those who devoted their time and money to this purpose were satirised as mullet-millionaires. One noble Roman went to a fabulous expense in boring a tunnel through a mountain, in order that he might obtain a plentiful supply of salt water for his fish-ponds. Sergius Orata invented artificial oyster-beds. He caused, as will be afterwards described when I come to speak of oyster-farming, to be constructed at Baiæ, on the Lucrine Sea, great reservoirs, where he grew the dainty mollusc in thousands; and in order that he and his friends might have this renowned shell-fish in its very highest perfection, he built a palace on the coast, in order to be near his oyster-ponds; and thither he resorted when he wanted to have a fish-dinner free from the care and turmoil of business. Many of the more luxurious Italians, imitating Sergius Orata, expended fabulous sums of money on their fish-ponds, and were so enabled, by means of their extravagance, to achieve all kinds of *outré* results in the fattening and flavouring of their fish. A curious story, illustrative of these times and of the value set on fish of a particular flavour, is related, in regard to the bass (*labrax lupus*) which were caught in the river Tiber. The Roman epicures were very fond of this fish, especially of those caught in a particular portion of the river, which they could tell by means of their taste and fine colour. An exquisite, while dining, was horrified at being served with bass of the wrong flavour, and loudly complained of the badness of the fish; the fact being that the real bass (the high-coloured kind) were flavoured by the disgusting food which they obtained at the mouth of a common sewer.

The modern phase of pisciculture is entirely a commercial

one, which as yet does not lie in imparting fanciful flavours to the fish—although, if such were wanted, it might easily enough be accomplished—but has developed itself both at home and abroad in the replenishing of exhausted streams with salmon, trout, or other kinds of fish. The present idea of pisciculture, as a branch of commerce, is due to the shrewdness of a simple French peasant, who gained his livelihood as a *pêcheur* in the tributaries of the Moselle, and the other streams of his native district, *La Bresse* in the *Vosges*. He was a thinking man, although a poor one, and it had long puzzled him to understand how animals yielding such an abundant supply of eggs should, by any amount of fishing, ever become scarce. He knew very well that all female fish were provided with tens of thousands of eggs, and he could not well see how, in the face of this fact, the rivers of La Bresse should be so scantily peopled with the finny tribes. Nor was the scarcity of fish confined to his own district : the rivers of France generally had become impoverished; and as in all Catholic countries fish is a prime necessary of life, the want of course was greatly felt. Joseph Remy was the man who first found out what was wrong with the French streams, and especially with the fish supplies of his native rivers— and better than that, he discovered a remedy. He ascertained that the scarcity of fish was chiefly caused by the immense number of eggs that never came to life, the enormous quantity of young fish that were destroyed by enemies of one kind or another, and the fishing-up of all that was left, in many instances, before they had an opportunity to reproduce themselves ; at any rate, without any care being taken to leave a sufficient breeding stock in the rivers, so that the result he discovered had become inevitable.

The guiding fact of pisciculture has been more than once accidentally re-discovered—that is, allowing that the ancient Romans knew it exactly as now practised ; but nothing came

of such discoveries, and till a discovery be turned to some
practical use, it is, in a sense, no discovery at all. After
being lost for many hundred years, the art of artificially
spawning fish was re-discovered in Germany by one Jacobi,
and practised on some trout more than a century ago. This
gentleman not only practised pisciculture himself, but wrote
essays on the subject as well. His elaborate treatise on
the art of fish-culture was written in the German language,
but also translated into Latin, and inserted by Duhamel du
Monceau, in his *General Treatise on Fishes*. Jacobi, who
practised the art for thirty years, was not satisfied with a
mere discovery, but at once turned what he had discovered to
practical account, and, in the time of Jacobi, great attention
was devoted to pisciculture by various gentlemen of scientific
eminence. Count Goldstein, a savan of the period, likewise
wrote on the subject. The Journal of Hanover also had
papers on this art, and an account of Jacobi's proceedings was
enrolled in the Memoirs of the Royal Academy of Berlin.
This discovery of Jacobi was the simple result of keen
observation of the natural action of the breeding salmon.
Observing that the process of impregnation was entirely an
external act, he saw at once that this could be easily imitated
by careful manipulation ; so that, by conducting artificial
hatching on a large scale, a constant and unfailing supply of
fish might readily be obtained. The results arrived at by
Jacobi were of vast importance, and obtained not only the
recognition of his government, but also the more solid reward
of a pension. I need not detail the experiments of Jacobi, as
they are very similar to those of others that I intend to describe at full length in this portion of my narrative.

Some persons dispute the claims of France to the honour
of this discovery, asserting that the peasant Remy had borrowed his idea from the experiments of Shaw of Drumlanrig,
who had by the artificial system undertaken to prove that parrs

were the young of the salmon.   As I shall again have occasion to allude to Mr. Shaw's experiments, I do not require to
say more at present on this part of my subject than that they
were brought to a successful conclusion long before the re-discovery of the art of pisciculture by Remy.   In my opinion the
honours may be thus divided, whether Remy knew of Shaw's
experiments or not : I would give to Scotland the honour of
having re-discovered pisciculture as an adjunct of science, and
to France the useful part of having turned the art to commercial uses.   In regard to what has been already stated here as
to the accidental discovery of artificial fish-breeding, I may
mention that James Hogg, the Ettrick Shepherd, was one of
the discoverers.   Hogg had an observant eye for rural scenes
and incidents, and anxiously studied and experimented on fish-
life.   He took an active share in the parr controversy.   Having
seen with his own eyes the branded parr assuming the scales
of the smolt, he never doubted after that the fact that the parr
was the young of the salmon.   In Norway, too, an accidental
discovery of this fish-breeding power was made ; and certainly if salmon-fishing in that country goes on at its present
rate cultivation will be largely required.   The artificial plan
of breeding oysters has been more than once accidentally discovered.   There is at least one well-authenticated instance of
this, which occurred about a century ago, when a saltmaker of
Marennes, who added to his income by fattening oysters, lost a
batch of six thousand in consequence of an intense frost, the
shells not being sufficiently covered with water ; but while engaged in mourning over his loss and kicking about the dead
molluscs, he found them, greatly to his surprise, covered with
young oysters already pretty well developed, and these, fortunately, although tender, all in good health, so that ultimately
he repeopled his salt-bed without either trouble or expense—
having of course to wait the growth of the natives before he
could recommence his commerce.

To return to Remy, however, his experiments were so instanteously crowned with success as even to be a surprise to himself; and in order to encourage him and Gehin, a coadjutor he had chosen, the Emulation Society of the Vosges voted them a considerable sum of money and a handsome bronze medal.   It was not, however, till 1849 that the proceedings of the two attracted that degree of notice which their importance demanded both in a scientific and economic sense.   Dr. Haxo of Epinal then communicated to the Academy of Sciences at Paris an elaborate paper on the subject, which at once fixed attention on the labours of the two fishermen—in fact, it excited a sensation both in the Academy and among the people. The government of the time at once gave attention to the matter, and finding, upon inquiry, everything that was said about the utility of the plan to be true, resolved to have it extended to all the rivers in France, especially to those of the poorer districts of the country.   The artificial system of fish-breeding was by this mode of action rapidly extended over the chief rivers of France, and added much to the comfort of the people, and in some cases little fortunes were realised by intelligent farmers who appreciated the system and had a pond or stream on which they could conduct their experiments in safety.

The piscicultural system has culminated in France, chiefly under the direction of Professor Coste, in the erection of a great establishment at Huningue, near Bale, for the collection and distribution of fish-eggs.   In order to see this place with my own eyes, and so be enabled to describe exactly how the piscicultural business of France is administered, I paid a visit to the great laboratory along with some friends in the autumn of 1863, having gone by way of Paris in order to see that city in its holiday trim during the *fêtes* of the Emperor.   The weather was so hot, and pleasure-seeking so fatiguing, that my little party made but a brief stay in the gay capital.   It was a pleasant relief indeed when we had obtained our tickets for

Mulhausen, done the penance of the *salle d'attente*, and then, attaining our seats, had left the sultry city behind us. The air became at once cool and moist, and the torturing Paris thirst left us—that fierce thirst which no quantity of well-mixed *vin ordinaire* and water, no amount of brandy and *eau de seltz*, could assuage. After reaching the outskirts of the city, and passing those manufactories, wood-yards, tile-depôts, brickfields, and stone-yards, which are common to the environs of all large towns, we could see well about us, and enjoy the sights and sounds of French agriculture—all but the perfume of the rotting flax in process of manipulation in the watery pits ; we certainly did not enjoy that potent compound of all that is awful in the way of smell. It was pleasant to note the industry of the small farmers, all busy with their wives and families on their little allotments, or rather estates, for numbers of them are owners or perpetual holders of the land on which they work ; and it looks curious to eyes accustomed to the large fields of England to see the little patches which compose the majority of French farms. We saw no particularly choice landscape scenery on the line of rail by which we travelled— *via* Troyes and Chalindrey—but there was no lack of pictur-esque villages and immense barns, giving cheerful token of a rude plenty, and there was no end of tall pollard trees, and numerous vineyards ; besides, here and there, upon a bit of stubble, we were agreeably surprised by the whitter of an occasional covey of partridges.

Bent on a piscatorial tour, I noted with care—to the occa-sional wonderment of my friends—the spots of water that pretty often fringed the line of rails, and wondered if they were populated by any of the finny tribe ; if so, by what kind of fish, and whether they had been replenished by the aid of pisciculture ? There was evidently fishing in the districts we passed through, because at many of the stations we encoun-tered the vision of an occasional angler, and a frequent " flop" in many of the pools which we passed convinced me that fair sport might be had ; and the entry of an occasional Waltonian into some of the stations with twenty pounds weight of trout quite excited everybody, and made some of us long to whip the waters of the district of Champagne, through which we were passing. And a close inspection of the national *etablissement de pisciculture* at Huningue has convinced me that if any river in France be still fishless, it is not through the fault of a paternal government.   •

Travelling is pleasant in France, for although the trains are slow, they are safe and punctual. The distance from Paris to Mulhausen is fifteen hours by the ordinary train, but we did not feel the journey at all tedious. In my compartment were a priest, who spoke a very " leetle" English, but who could evidently read a great deal of Latin ; a shrewd Edinburgh news-agent—who, like most Scotchmen, took nothing for granted, but saw and judged for himself ; and his daughter, a young lady on her way to " do" the Rhine, but who took no interest in pisciculture. Then there was a lively English gentleman, who seemed to have an intimate acquaintance with every fish in the Thames ; he had netted whitebait (and eaten them) off Blackwall, he had taken perch out of the East India Dock, killed a monster pike near Teddington, and had caught no end of gudgeon at various picturesque spots on the great river.

" Bah," said my Scotch friend, joining in the conversation, " did you ever kill a salmon, man ? I hate gudgeon and such small fry ; give me the river Isla, about the ' Brig o' Riven,' a good stout rod with no end of tackle, and an angry seventeen-pound fish sulking behind a big stone—then you may have sport ; or favour me with good trolling-tackle and a boat on deep Loch Awe, with the castle of Kilchurn glooming its great shadow over us, and the eternal hills rising tall around, and I will take out trout that will outweigh a hundred gudgeon ; or give me a trout-rod and a pleasant ramble along the picturesque Shochy, and I will manage to fill my basket with fish worth taking home ; but away with your Thames gudgeon, they can only satisfy a Cockney linendraper."

Verily my shrewd Scottish friend, with his reminiscences of monster fish and his fervid manner, waxed eloquent ; he even startled the priest ; and as for the Englishman he looked quite chapfallen. I had to come to the rescue, and defended as well as I could Thames angling, and reminded the enthusiastic Caledonian that they once had very fine salmon in the Thames, and would some day, if all goes well, have them again ; and that gudgeon-fishing in the midst of such fine scenery was at least a healthy and happy way of having a pleasant day's " out," even if the sport was not quite so fierce as hunting for salmon in the river Isla at the " Brig o' Riven."

The salmon of the Tay, it was also hinted to the news-agent, were not so famous as those of the Severn. " But we have twenty for your one," was the quick reply, " and at the Stormontfield breeding-ponds we are raising them by the hundred thousand. The rental of the Tay, sir, is equal to what the whole revenue of the French fisheries was a year or two ago." " Very likely, sir," I replied ; " but then the Tay is what you may call a Highland stream—good for fish, no doubt ; and the Thames is a splendid river in its own way, but no one pretends that it is a fish river ; it is the highway of the greatest commerce in the world, and ———" " Pooh, man," said the Scotchman, " the Tay is as celebrated for commerce as for fish. Have you ever been to Dundee?" And then, chuckling to himself at his rather rich idea of comparing Dundee to London, my friend sank back in his corner of the carriage and looked as if he could have slain a thousand London gudgeon-fishers, and the twinkle in his eye waxed brighter and brighter as he continued his chuckle.

As even the longest journey will come to an end, the train arrived in due time at Mulhouse, or Mulhausen, as it is called

in the German, and it being late and dark, and our whole
party being somewhat fatigued, we allowed ourselves to be
carried to the nearest hotel, a large, uncomfortable, dirty-look-
ing place, where apparently they seldom see British gold, and
make an immense charge for *bougies*. Had we had the necessary time to spare, my little party would have been interested
in seeing Mulhouse, which is a manufacturing town of considerable size, where many of the operatives are the owners
of their own houses ; but being within scent of Switzerland,
having the feeling that we were in the shadow of its mountains, and almost within hearing of the noise made by its many
waters, we hurried on by the first train to Bale. The distance
is short, and the conveyance quick. Almost before we had
time to view the passing landscape, which is exceedingly
beautiful, being rich in vineyards and orchards, and rapidly
turning Swiss in its scenery, we were stopped at St. Louis by
the custom-house authorities, who, it is but proper to say, are
exceedingly polite to all honest travellers. I would advise any
one in search of the *etablissement de pisciculture* at Huningue
to leave the train at this station. Not knowing its proximity
at the time of my visit, I went right on to Bale.

Poets might go into raptures about Bale—Bale the beautiful—with the flowing Rhine cutting it into two halves, its
waters green as the icefields which had given them birth, its
houses quaint, its streets so clean, its fountains so antique ;
but we had no time to go into raptures—our business was to
get to Huningue, and curiously enough we had wandered into
the fishmarket before we knew where we were. Like various
other fishmarkets which we have visited, it contained no
fish that we could see, but it is so picturesque that I determined to place a view of it in this work. Hailing a
voiture, our party had no end of difficulty to get the coachman
to understand where we wanted to be driven. I said, "To
Huningue ;" he then suggested that it must be "Euiniguen,"

and my Scotch young lady friend, who was all in a glow about
the " beautiful Rhine," as, of course, a young lady ought to be,
suggested that the pronunciation might be " Hiningue," which
proved a shrewd guess, as immediately on hearing it we were
addressed in tolerable but very broken English by a quiet-
looking coachman, who said, " Come with me ; I have study
the English grammaire ; I know where you want to go, and

THE FISHMARKET AT BALE.

will take you." Although I could not help wondering that a
celebrated place, as we all thought Huningue ought to be, was
not better known, I felt pretty sure our coachman knew it ;
and having persuaded my Scotch friend and his young lady to
take a drive, we at once started for the *etablissement de pisciculture*, where we were all of us most hospitably received
by the superintendent, who at once conducted us over the
whole place with great civility and attention.

The series of buildings which have been erected at
Huningue are admirably adapted to the purpose for which
they have been designed. The group forms a square, the
entrance portion of which—two lodges—is devoted to the

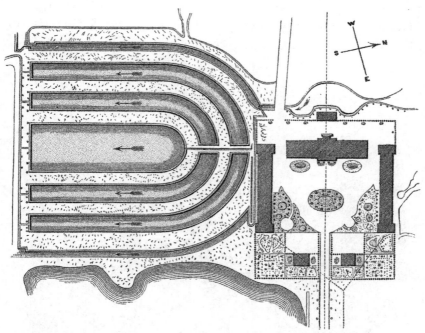

GROUND-PLAN OF THE PISCICULTURAL ESTABLISHMENT AT HUNINGUE.

Showing the disposition of the buildings and the situation of the experimental watercourses.

corps de garde, and the centre has been laid out as a kind of
shrubbery, and is relieved with two little ponds containing
fish. The whole establishment, ponds and buildings, occupies
a space of eighty acres. The suite of buildings comprise at
the side two great hatching-galleries, 60 metres in length and
9 metres broad, containing a plentiful supply of tanks and
egg-boxes ; and in the back part of the square are the offices,
library, laboratory, and residences of the officers. Having
minutely inspected the whole apparatus, I particularly
admired the aptitude by which the means to a certain end

had been carried out. The egg-boxes are raised in pyramids, the water flowing from the one on the top into those immediately below. The eggs are placed in rows on glass frames which fit into the boxes, as will be seen by examining

VIEW OF HUNINGUE.

the drawings. The grand agent in the hatching of fish-eggs being water, I was naturally enough rather particular in making inquiry into the water supplies of Huningue, and these I found were very ample : they are derived from three sources—the springs on the private grounds of the establishment, the Rhine, and the Augraben stream. The water of the higher springs is directed towards the buildings through an underground conduit, whilst those rising at a lower level are used only in small basins and trenches for the experiments in rearing fish outside. Being uncovered, however, they are easily frozen, and are besides frequently muddy and troubled. As a general rule, fish are not bred at Hun-

ingue, the chief business accomplished there being the collection and distribution of their eggs; but there is a large supply
of tanks or troughs for the purpose of experimenting with
such fish as may be kept in the place.   The waters of the

HALL OF INCUBATION.

Rhine, being at a higher level than the springs, can be at once
employed in the *appareils* and basins.   The waters of the
Augraben stream, which cross the grounds, are of very little
use.   Nearly dry in summer, rapid and muddy after rain,
they have only hitherto served to supply some small exterior
basins.   Of course, different qualities of water are quite
necessary for the success of the experiments in acclimatisation
carried on so zealously at this establishment.   Some fish
delight in a clear running stream, while others prefer to pass
their life in sluggish and fat waters.   The engineering of the
different water-supplies, all of them at different levels, has

been effectually accomplished by M. Coumes, the engineer of this department of the Rhine, who, in conjunction with Professor Coste, planned the buildings at Huningue ; indeed the machinery of all kinds is as nearly as possible perfect.

BASINS FOR THE YOUNG FISH.

The course of business at Huningue is as follows :—The eggs are brought chiefly from Switzerland and Germany, and embrace those of the various kinds of trout, the Danube and Rhine salmon, and the tender ombre chevalier. People are appointed to capture gravid fish of these various kinds, and having done so to communicate with the authorities at Huningue, who at once send an expert to deprive the fishes of their spawn and bring it to the breeding or store boxes, where it is carefully tended and daily watched till it is ready to be despatched to some district in want of it. The mode of artificial spawning is as follows, and I will suppose the

subject operated upon to be a salmon :—Well, first catch
your fish ; and here I may state that male salmon are a great
deal scarcer than female ones, but fortunately one of the
former will milt two or even three of the latter, so that the

GUTTERS FOR HATCHING PURPOSES.

scarcity is not so much felt as it might otherwise be. The
fish, then, having been caught, it should be seen, before
operating, that the spawn is perfectly matured, and that being
the case, the salmon should be held in a large tub, well buried
in the water it contains, while the hand is gently passed
along its abdomen, when, if the ova be ripe, the eggs will
flow out like so many peas. The eggs must be carefully
roused or washed, and the water should then be poured off.
The male salmon may be then handled in a similar way, the
contact of the milt immediately changing the eggs into a
brilliant pink colour. After being again washed, the eggs

may be ladled out into the breeding-boxes, and safely left to come to maturity in due season. Very great care is necessary in handling the ova. The eggs distributed from Huningue are all carefully examined on their arrival, when the bad ones are thrown out, and those that are good are counted and entered upon the records of the establishment, which are carefully kept. The usual way of ascertaining the quantity is by means of a little stamped measure, which varies according to the particular fish-eggs to be counted. The ova are watched with great care so long as they remain in the boxes at Huningue, and any dust is removed by means

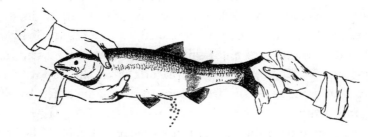

ARTIFICIAL MODE OF SPAWNING.

of a fine camel-hair brush, and from day to day all the eggs that become addled are removed. The applications to the authorities at Huningue for eggs, both from individuals and associations, are always a great deal more numerous than can be supplied; and before second applications from the same people can be entertained, it is necessary for them to give a detailed account of how their former efforts succeeded. The eggs, when sent away, are nicely packed in boxes among wet moss, and they suffer very little injury if there be no delay in the transit.

"How about the streams from which the eggs are brought?" I asked. "Does this robbery of the spawn not injure them?"

"Oh, no; we find that it makes no difference whatever. The fish are so enormously fecund that the eggs can be got in any quantity, and no difference be felt in the parent waters;

what we obtain here are a mere percentage of the grand totals deposited by the fish."

Of course, as the operations are pursued over a large district of two countries, no immediate difference will be felt ; but how if these Huningue *explorateurs* go on for years taking away tens of thousands of eggs ? Will that not ultimately prove a case of robbing Peter to pay Paul ? I know full well that all kinds of fish are enormously prolific, and the reader would see from the figures given in a former section that it is so ; but suppose a river, with the breeding power of the Tay, was annually robbed of a few million eggs, the result must some day be a slight difference in the productive power of the water. I would like to know with exactitude if, while the waters of France are being replenished, the rivers in Switzerland and Germany are not beginning to be in their turn impoverished ? It surely stands to reason that if the impoverishment of streams resulting from natural causes be aided by the carrying away of the eggs by zealous *explorateurs,* they must become in a short time almost totally barren of fish. The best plan, in my opinion, is for each river to have its own breeding-ponds on the plan of those of Stormontfield on the river Tay which I will by and by describe.*

---

* On this part of the piscicultural question I had the following conversation with a *pêcheur* who has a little place in the suburbs of Strasbourg, on the road to the Bridge of Boats —

" By your system you collect the eggs of fish in the rivers of Switzerland and Germany, either from the spawning-beds, or direct from the parents, which are then barbarously killed and sold, as we were told at Huningue, and the eggs may be sent off to enrich some private speculator in the north of France. Now, will not the rivers from whence the spawn is taken be impoverished in their turn ?"

" Oh, no ; it is considered by the piscicultural system that we only obtain that portion of the spawn that would otherwise be lost."

" What do you think is the proportion of young salmon that arrives at marketable size under the ordinary conditions of growth ?"

It would scarcely pay to breed the commoner fishes of the lakes and rivers, as pike, carp, and perch ; the commonest fish bred at Huningue is the *fera*, whilst the most expensive is the beautiful ombre chevalier, the eggs of which cost about a penny each before they are in the water as 'fish. The general calculation, however, appertaining to the operations carried on at Huningue gives twelve living fish for a penny. The *fera* is very prolific, yielding its eggs in thousands ; it is called the herring of the lakes ; and the young, when first born, are so small as scarcely to be perceptible. The superintendent at Huningue told me that several of them had escaped by means of the canal into the Rhine, where they had never before been found. I inquired particularly as to the Danube salmon, but found that it was very difficult to hatch, especially at first, great numbers of the eggs, as many sometimes as 60 or 70 per cent, being destroyed ; but now the manipulators are getting better acquainted with the *modus operandi,* and it is

"It is very small. An eighteen-pound fish will yield eighteen thousand eggs. Well, one-third of these will in all probability escape the fecundating principle of the milt, another third most likely will never come to life—the eggs will either be destroyed from natural causes or be eaten up by other fish ; so that you see only six thousand, or one-third of the whole eggs, will ever come to life."

"Well, that is so far good ; but you do not protect the infant fish at all, you only insure the transmission of the eggs from Huningue."

"Yes ; but the eggs are more than half the battle. Out of eighteen thousand salmon-ova you will, by giving protection, hatch at least fifteen thousand fish ; and then these won't be sent into the water till they are well able to take care of themselves, and fight the battle of life."

"Supposing it to be as you say, and that you can rear the fish in remunerative quantities, will not an extension of the piscicultural system ultimately injure the breed ?"

"I don't think it will. We have been carrying out the system in France now on a lesser or greater scale for more than twenty years, and I can hear of no damage being done to the fish."

expected that by and by the assistants at Huningue will be as successful with this fish as they are with all others. Even allowing for a very considerable loss in the artificially-manipulated ova—and it is thought that two-thirds at least of the eggs of this fish are in some way lost—it is certain that the artificial system of protection is immensely more productive in fish than the natural one, for it has been said, in reference especially to the salmon of the river Tay, that hardly one in a thousand of the eggs ever reaches to maturity as a proper table-fish, such is the enormous destruction of eggs and young fry ; and the percentage of destruction in Catholic countries is greatly larger, because during the fast-days enjoined by the church fish *must* be obtained.

Up to the season of 1863-64 the total number of fresh-water fish-eggs distributed from Huningue was far above 110,000,000, and nearly the half of these were of the finer kinds of fish, there being no less than 41,000,000 of eggs of salmon and trout.

I have complied a tabular statement, which I insert at this place, of the number of fish-eggs collected and distributed at Huningue for the two years previous to my visit :—

1860-61.

Species.	Time of Operations.	Ova provided.	Loss.	Quantity despatched from the Establishment.	Retained for Experiments at Huningue.
Common trout Salmon trout Great lake trout Rhine salmon Ombre chevalier	1860-61. Oct. 20 to Mar. 17, 149 days.	5,729,100	1,943,100 34 per cent.	3,153,500	632,500
Fera . . .	Nov. 14 to Dec. 30, 46 days.	8,997,000	22,000	5,573,000	3,402,000
Total . .	. . . .	14,726,100	1,965,100	8,726,500	4,034,500

Destination of the Ova despatched from the Establishment.

278 demands for establishments in 70 departments of France, and 29 demands from establishments in Belgium, Switzerland, Bavaria, and Wurtemberg.

1861-62.

Species.	Time of Operations.	Ova provided.	Loss.	Quantity despatched from the Establishment.	Retained for Experiments at Huningue.
Common trout ⎫ Salmon trout ⎪ Great lake trout ⎬ Rhine salmon ⎪ Ombre chevalier ⎭	1861-62. ⎧ Oct. 24 ⎫ ⎨ to Mar. 7, ⎬ ⎩ 135 days. ⎭	6,382,900	2,602,400	3,360,000	420,500
Fera . . .	⎧ Nov. 16 ⎫ ⎨ to Dec. 25, ⎬ ⎩ 39 days. ⎭	11,995,000	12,000	9,519,000	2,464,000
Total . .	. . . .	18,377,900	2,614,400	12,879,000	2,884,500

296 demands for establishments in 76 departments of France, and 39 demands from other parts of Europe.

So far as I could ascertain, the right of fishing in France is claimed by the Government in all navigable rivers and canals, but private persons can purchase the power to fish ; and the rent payable by those using nets varies from £1 to £4 per annum. In common streams that are not navigable, and in lakes, the fishery belongs to the proprietors of the surrounding land, and no person can fish in these without permission. As to the larger river fisheries, they are so mapped out as to prevent all possibility of dispute, no fisherman being permitted to work his nets on a portion of water which does not belong to him. Fishing of some kind goes on all the year round.

The following figures will indicate the money rental and the value of the produce of the whole of the French fisheries :—

4719 miles navigable rivers - -	£23,025
3105 miles of canals -	5,845
310 miles of estuaries of rivers - -	46,140
930 miles of rivers and canals belonging to individual proprietors - - -	2,700

114,889 miles of rivers and streams not navigable.
493,750 acres of lakes and ponds.

The money value of the fish caught in these waters may be stated as follows :—

From State Returns for rivers and canals	£28,880
The estuaries yield £46,140, of which the fresh waters supply one-half, giving -	23,080
Rivers and canals belonging to private individuals	2,680
114,889 miles of watercourses - -	148,000
493,750 acres of lakes and ponds -	400,000
Total - - -	£602,640

If the profits of the cultivators and expenses of the fishery be added to the produce, we have—

Canals and watercourses - -	£400,000
Lakes and ponds - - -	400,000
Total production of profits and produce	£800,000

The piscicultural establishment of M. de Galbert, one of the most important of the kind which exists in France, is worthy of notice. It is situated at Buisse in the canton of Voiron in Isere, a department on the south-east frontier of France. The works, of which the accompanying engraving is a plan, comprise four ponds for the reception of the fish in various stages of growth. The first (1 in the plan) is about 100 metres long by 3 m. 50 in breadth, with a mean depth of 1 metre. It is almost divided into two parts, a sheet of water and a stream, by a peninsula, and the division is completed by a grating which prevents the mixing of the fish contained in each part, and also arrests the ascent or descent of the fry. The sheet of water is supplied from sources of an elevated temperature which diverge into the stream, and thence into pond No. 2 at N. This basin (2) is 150 metres long, with a mean breadth of 8 metres, and a depth varying from 1 to 2 metres. Besides the waters from the first pond, this basin is supplied from the springs, and from the mill-stream which rises from a rock situated at a distance of 200

metres. This pond contains fish of the second year. A sluice
or water-gate (J), placed in the deepest part of the pond,

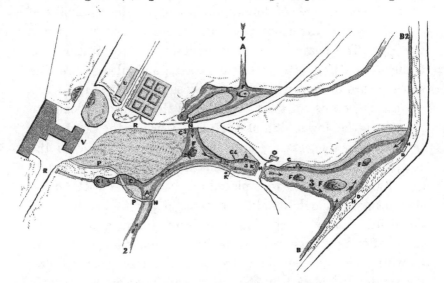

PISCICULTURAL ESTABLISHMENT AT BUISSE.

affords the means of turning the water and the fish contained therein into the pond No. 3. Courses of rough stones
and weeds line the banks of the pond, and form places of
shelter for the fish, besides encouraging the growth of such
shell-fish as shrimps, lobsters, etc. The third pond (3) has a
surface of about 5000 yards, with a depth equal to that of the
second pond. An underground canal (G) runs along the eastern
side, and at distances of 2 metres trenches lined with stones
loosely thrown together join the canal to the basin, and allow
the fish to circulate through these subterranean passages, where
every stone becomes a means of shelter and concealment.
The adult trout can conceal themselves in the submerged holes
and crevices of the islands (F) of which there are three in the
pond. The narrowest part of the basin is crossed by a viaduct
of 8 metres (N), to the arch of which is fitted an iron grating
with rods in grooves to receive either a sluice or a snare. The

sluice, formed of fine wire, keeps out the fish that would destroy the spawn at the time of fecundation. The spawn is
covered with a layer of fine round gravel, to the thickness of
0 m. 30, which the trout can easily raise as fast as it bursts
the egg. The snare or netting encloses the fish destined for
artificial breeding without hurting them, and also secures the
fish that are to be consumed, and those which it is necessary
to destroy because of their voracity, as the pike. A floodgate
placed at the lower end of the pond permits the pond to be
emptied when necessary, and an iron grating prevents the
escape of the fish. All the ponds are protected by a double
line of galvanised iron wire placed on posts armed with hooks,
and yet low enough to allow a boat to pass. The water of
the ponds finally passes into the Isere, where a permanent
snare allows strange fish to penetrate into the ponds. At
spawning time a great many trout deposit their spawn there.
The small pond (4) fed by the mill-stream is a sort of reservoir
for large fish destined for sale or domestic use. Throughout
the year the fish caught in the nets of the third pond are
placed in this basin, so when the spawning season arrives it
is a vast nursery for the purpose of reproduction. In the
house (O) built near the bridge (N) of the third pond lodge the
guard and the hatching-apparatus. The *appareils* are similar
to those employed at the Collége de France and are supplied
from a spring. One particular appareil, placed in a source of
which the temperature never varies, is slightly different from
the other models : it is simply zinc boxes pierced with very
fine holes. This apparatus, which has been in use for three
years, has given great satisfaction. It may be added that the
establishment at Buisse can supply 40,000 or 50,000 young
trout in the year at five centimes each, a result which is
mainly due to the care and solicitude with which M. de Galbert has conducted his operations.

What strikes us most in connection with the history of

French fish-culture is the essentially practical nature of all the experiments which have been entered upon. There has been no toying in France with this revived art of fish-breeding. The moment it was ascertained that Remy's discoveries in artificial spawning were capable of being carried out on the largest possible scale, that scale was at once resolved upon, and the government of the country became responsible for its success, which was immediate and substantial. The discoverer of the art was handsomely rewarded ; and the great building at Huningue, used as a place for the reception and distribution of fish-eggs, testifies to the anxiety of France to make pisciculture one of the most practical industries of the present day. Unceasing efforts are still being made by the government to extend the art, so that every acre of water in that country may be as industriously turned to profit as the acres of land are. Why should not an acre of water become as productive as an acre of land? We have an immensity of water space that is comparatively useless. The area occupied by the water of our lakes and rivers may be estimated from the Thames, which occupies a space of five thousand square miles. The French people are now beginning thoroughly to appreciate the value of their lakes and rivers. Think of the fish-ponds of Doombes being of the extent of thirty thousand acres ! No wonder that in France pisciculture has become a government question, and been taken under the protecting wing of the state.

The different kinds of water in France are carefully considered, and only fish suitable for them placed therein. In marshy places eels alone are deposited, whilst in bright and rapid waters trout and other suitable fish are now to be found in great plenty. Attention is at present being turned to sea-fish, and the latest "idea" that has been promulgated in connection with the cultivation of sea-animals is turtle-culture. The artificial multiplication of turtle, on the plan of securing the eggs and protecting the young till they are able to be left to their own guidance, is advocated by M. Salles, who is connected with the French navy, and who seems to have a considerable knowledge of the nature and habits of the turtle. To some extent turtle-culture is already carried on in the island of Ascension—so far at least as the protection of the eggs and watching over the young is concerned. M. Salles proposes, however, to do more than is yet done at Ascension ; he thinks that, to arrive quickly at a useful result, it would be best to obtain a certain number of these animals from places where they are still abundant, and transport them to such parks or receptacles as might be established on the coasts of France and Corsica, where, at one time, turtles were plentiful. Animals about to lay would be the best to secure for the proposed experiments ; and these might be captured when seeking the sandy shores for the purpose of depositing their eggs. Male turtles might at the same time be taken about the islets which they frequent. A vessel of sufficient dimensions should be in readiness to bring away the precious freight ; and the captured animals, on arriving at their destination, should be deposited in a park chosen under the following considerations :—The formation of the sides to be an inclosure by means of an artificial barrier of moderate height, formed of stones, and perpendicular within, so as to prevent the escape of the animals, but so constructed as to admit the sea, and, at the same time, allow of a large sandy background for the deposition of the eggs, which are about the size of those laid by geese. As the turtles are herbivorous, the bottom of the park should be covered with sea-weeds and marine plants of all kinds, similar to those the animal is accustomed to at home. A fine southern exposure ought to be chosen for the site of the park, in order to obtain as much of the sunshine as possible, heat being the one grand element in the hatching of the eggs. Turtles are very fond of sunshine, and float lazily about in the tropical water, seldom coming to the shore except to lay.

This they do in the night-time : crawling cautiously ashore, and scraping a large hole in a part of the sand which is never reached by the tide, they deposit their eggs, and carefully cover them with the sand, leaving the sun to effect the work of quickening them into life.

It may be as well to state here that the French people eat all kinds of fish, whether they be from the sea, the river, the lake, or the canal. In Scotland and Ireland the salmon only is bred artificially as yet, and chiefly because it is a valuable and money-yielding animal, and no other fresh-water fish is regarded there as being of value except for sport. In France large quantities of eels are bred and eaten ; but in Scotland, and in some parts of England, the people have such a horror of that fish that they will not touch it. This of course is due to prejudice, as the eel is good for food in a very high degree. In all Roman Catholic countries there are so many fast-days that fish-food becomes to the people an essential article of diet ; in France this is so, and the consequence is that a good many private amateurs in pisciculture are to be found throughout the empire ; but the mission of the French Government in connection with fish-culture is apparently to meddle only with the rearing and acclimatising of the more valuable fishes. It would be a waste of energy for the authorities at Huningue to commence the culture of the carp or perch. In our Protestant country there is no demand for the commoner river or lake fishes except for the purposes of sport ; and with one or two exceptions, such as the Lochleven trout, the charr, etc., there is no commerce carried on in these fishes. One has but to visit the fishmarket at Paris to observe that all kinds of fresh-water fish and river crustacea are there ranked as saleable, and largely purchased. The mode of keeping these animals fresh is worthy of being followed here. They are kept alive till wanted in large basins and troughs, where they may at all times be seen swimming about in a very lively state.

As soon as the piscicultural system became known, it was rapidly extended over the whole continent of Europe, and the rivers of Germany were among the first to participate in the advantages of the artificial system. In particular may be noticed the efforts made to increase the supplies of the Danube salmon, a beautiful and excellent food-fish, with a body similar to the trout, but still more shapely and graceful, and which, if allowed time, is said to grow to an enormous size. The young salmon of the Danube are always of a darker colour than those a little older, but they become lighter in colour as they progress in years. The mouth of this fish is furnished with very strong teeth ; its back is of a reddish grey, its sides and belly perfectly white; the fins are bluish white ; the back and the upper part of both sides are slightly and irregularly speckled with black and roundish red spots. This fish is also very prolific. Professor Wimmer of Landshut, the authorities at Huningue mentioned, had frequently obtained as many as 40,000 eggs from a female specimen which weighed only eighteen pounds. Our own *Salmo salar* is not so fecund, it being well understood that a thousand eggs per pound weight is about the average spawning power of the British salmon. The ova of the Danube salmon are hatched in half the time that our salmon eggs require for incubation—viz. in fifty-six days—while the young fry attain the weight of one pound in the first year ; and by the third year, if well supplied with the requisite quantity of food, they will have attained a weight of four pounds. The divisions of growth, as compared with *Salmo salar*, are pretty nearly as follows :—That fish, curiously enough, may at the end of two years be eight pounds in weight, or it may not be half that number of ounces. One batch of a salmon hatching go to the sea at the end of the first year, and rapidly return as grilse, handsome four-pound fish, whilst the other moiety remain in the fresh water till the expiry of the second year from the time of birth, so that *they* require about thirty months to become four-pound fish, by which time the first moiety are salmon of eight or ten pounds! These are ascertained facts. This is rapid work as compared with the Danube fish, which, after the first year, grows only at about the rate of eighteen ounces per annum. But even at that rate, fish-cultivation must pay well. Suppose that by the protected or piscicultural system a full third (*i.e.* 13,500) of the 40,000 eggs arrive in twelve months at the stage of pound fish, and are sold at the rate of threepence per pound weight, a revenue of £162 would thus result in one year's time from a single pair of breeding salmon! Two pairs would, of course, double the amount, and so on.

A series of well-conducted operations in fish-culture has been carried on for about twelve years on the river Tay about five miles from Perth ; and as these have attracted a great amount of attention, they merit a somewhat lengthened description. The breeding-ponds at Stormontfield are beautifully situated on a sloping haugh on the banks of the Tay, and are sheltered at the back by a plantation of trees. The ground has been laid out to the best advantage, and the whole of the ponds, water-runs, etc., have been planned and constructed by Mr. Peter Burn, C.E., and they have answered the purpose for which they were designed admirably. The supply of water is obtained from a rapid mill-stream, which runs in a line with the river Tay, as is shown by a small plan on the next page. The necessary quantity of water is first run from this stream into a reservoir, from which it is filtered through pipes into a little watercourse at the head of the range of boxes from whence it is laid on. These boxes are fixed on a gentle declivity, half-way between the mill-race and the Tay, and by means of the slope the water falls beautifully from one to another of the three hundred " procreant cradles" in a gradual but constant stream, and collects at the bottom of the range of boxes in a kind of dam, and thence runs into a small lake or depôt where the young fish are kept. Until lately only one such pond was to be

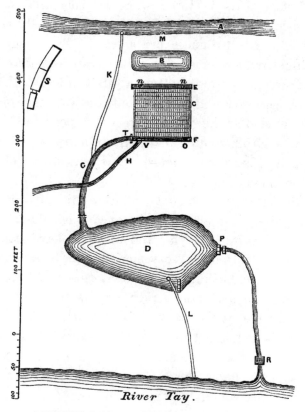

ORIGINAL BREEDING-POND AT STORMONTFIELD.

A. Mill-race.
B. Filtering-pond.
C. Hatching-boxes.
D. Rearing-pond.
E. Upper canal.
F. Lower canal.
G. Connecting stream of C and D.
H. By-run to river.
K. Pipe from mill-race to pond.

L. Pipe to empty pond.
M. Pipe from mill-race to filtering-pond.
n n. Discharge-pipes from do.
O. Do. do. to lower canal.
P. Sluices from pond.
R. Marking-box.
S. Keeper's house.
T V. Sluices from lower canal.

found at Stormontfield, but another pond for the smolts has now been added in order to complete the suite. A sluice made of fine wire-grating admits of the superfluous water being run off into the Tay, so that an equable supply is invariably kept up. It also serves for an outlet to the fish when it is deemed expedient to send them out to try their fortune in the greater deep near at hand, and for which their pond experience has been a mode of preparation. The planning of the boxes, ponds, sluices, etc., has been accomplished with great ingenuity ; and one can only regret that the whole apparatus is not three times the size, so that the Tay proprietors might breed annually a million of salmon, which would add largely to the productiveness of that river, and of course aid in increasing the rental.

For the purpose of showing the level of the pond at Stormontfield I beg to introduce what the French people call " a profile."

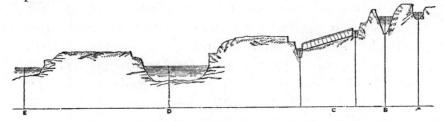

PROFILE OF STORMONTFIELD SALMON-BREEDING PONDS.

A. Source of water-supply.	C. Egg-boxes.
B. Pond from which to filter water on boxes.	D. Pond for young fish.
	E. River Tay.

The salmon-breeding operations at Stormontfield originated at a meeting of the proprietors of the river Tay held in July 1852, when a communication by Dr. Eisdale was read on the subject of artificial propagation ; and Mr. Thomas Ashworth of Poynton detailed the experiments which had been conducted at his Irish fisheries. This gentleman, who takes a great and practical interest in all matters relating to fisheries and the breeding of fish—and to whom I am greatly indebted for practical information—said that he had long entertained the opinion that it would be quite as easy to propagate salmon artificially in our rivers as it is to raise silkworms on mulberry leaves, though the former were under water and the latter in the open air ; "indeed it has become an established fact," said Mr. Ashworth, "that salmon and other fish may be propagated artificially in ponds in numbers amounting to millions, at a small cost, and thus be protected from their natural enemies for the first year or two of their existence, after which they will be much more able, comparatively speaking, to take care of themselves, than can be the case in the earlier stages of their existence." Mr. Ashworth estimates the expense of artificial propagation as about one pound for each thousand fish, or one farthing per salmon. On the suggestion of Mr. Ashworth, a practical pisciculturist was engaged to inaugurate the breeding operations at Stormontfield, and to teach a local fisherman the art of artificial spawning. The operation of preparing the spawn for the boxes was commenced on the 23d of November 1853, and in the course of a month 300,000 ova were deposited in the 300 boxes, which had been carefully filled with prepared gravel, and made all ready for their reception. Mr. Ramsbottom, who conducted the manipulation, says the river Tay is one of the finest breeding streams in the world, and thinks that it would be presumptuous to limit the numbers of salmon that might be bred in it were the river cultivated to the full extent of its capabilities.

The date when the first of the eggs deposited was observed to be hatched was on the 31st of March, a period of more than four months after the stocking of the boxes ; and during April and May most of the eggs had started into life, and the fry were observed waddling about the breeding-boxes, and were in June promoted to a place in the reception-pond, being then tiny fish a little more than an inch long. Sir William Jardine, who has taken a warm interest in the Stormontfield operations, thought that the first year's experiments were remarkably successful in showing the practicability of hatching, rearing, and maintaining in health, a very large number of young fish, at a comparatively trifling cost. The artificial breeding of salmon is still carried on at these ponds, and with very great success, when their limited extent is taken into account. They have sensibly increased the stock of fish in the Tay, and also, as I will by and by relate, under the sepa-

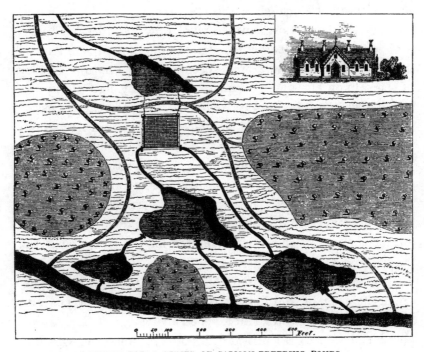

DESIGN FOR A SERIES OF SALMON-BREEDING PONDS.

Source of supply at top.	Adult salmon pond to the left.
Breeding-boxes next.	River at foot of plan.
Parr-pond after.	Ornamental walks.
Smolt-pond to the right.	Clumps of trees, etc., according to taste.

rate head of "The Salmon," contributed greatly to the solution of the various mysteries connected with the growth of that fish. The fish, it is remarkable, suffer no deterioration of any kind by being bred in the ponds, and can compare in every respect with those bred in the river.

The plan of the ponds at Stormontfield, as originally constructed, will be a better guide to persons desiring information than any written description. The engraving, with the double pond, shows a design of my own, founded on the Stormontfield suite ; it contains a separate pond for the detention, for a time, of such large fish as may be taken with their spawn not fully matured. Cottages for the superintendent of the ponds and his assistants are also shown in the plan.

The ponds at Stormontfield were originally designed with a view to breed 300,000 fish per annum, but after a trial of two years it was found, from a speciality in the natural history of the salmon elsewhere alluded to, that only half that number of fish could be bred in each year. Hence the necessity for the recently-constructed smolt-pond, which will now admit of a hatching at Stormontfield of at least 350,000 eggs every year. An additional reason for the construction of the new pond was the fact of the old one being too small in proportion to the breeding-boxes. Its dimensions were 223 feet by 112 feet at its longest and broadest parts. The new pond is nearly an acre in extent, and is well adapted for the reception of the young fish.

The egg-boxes at Stormontfield, unlike those at Huningue, are in the open air, and in consequence the eggs are exposed to the natural temperature, and take, on an average of the seasons, about 120 days to ripen into fish. For instance, the eggs laid down in November 1863 had not come to life at the time of my visit to the ponds in the second week of March 1864. The young fish, as soon as they are able to eat—which is not for a good few days, as the umbilical bag supplies all the food that is required for a time by the newly-hatched animal—are fed with particles of boiled liver. On the occasion of my last visit (December 22, 1864), Mr. Marshall threw a few crumbs into the pond, which caused an immediate rising of the fry at that spot in great numbers. It would, of course, have been a simple plan to turn each year's fish out of the ponds into the river as they were hatched, but it was thought advisable rather to detain them till they were seized with the migratory instinct and assumed the scales of smolthood, which occurs, as already stated in other parts of this work, at the age of one and two years respectively. Indeed, the experiments conducted at the Stormontfield ponds have conclusively settled the long-fought battle of the parr, and proved indisputably that the parr is the young of the salmon, that it becomes transformed to a smolt, grows into a grilse, and ultimately attains the honour of full-grown salmonhood.

The anomaly in the growth of the parr was also attempted to be solved at Stormontfield, but without success. In November and December 1857 provision was made for hatching in separate compartments the artificially-impregnated ova of—1, parr and salmon ; 2, grilse and salmon ; 3, grilse pure ; 4, salmon pure. It was found, when the young of these different matches came to be examined early in April 1859, that the sizes of each kind varied a little, Mr. Buist, the superintendent of fisheries, informing us that—"1st, the produce of the salmon with salmon are 4 in. in length ; 2d, grilse with salmon, 3½ in. ; 3d, grilse with grilse, 3½ in. ; 4th, parr with grilse, 3 in. ; 5th, smolt from large pond, 5 in." These results of a varied manipulation never got a fair chance of being of use as a proof in the disputation; for, owing to the limited extent of the ponds at the time, the experiments had to be matured in such small boxes or ponds as evidently tended to stunt the growth of the fish. Up to the present time the riddle which has so long puzzled our naturalists in connection with the growth of the salmon has not been solved. A visitor whom I met at the ponds was of opinion that a sufficient quantity of milt was not used in the fructification of the eggs, as the male fish were scarcer than the female ones, and that those eggs which first came into contact with the milt produced the stronger fish.

"Peter of the Pools " (Mr. Buist) says that what strikes a stranger who visits the 'ponds most is the great disparity in the size of fish of the same age, the difference of which can only be that of a few weeks, as all were hatched by the month of May. That there are strong and weak fry from the moment that they burst the covering admits not of a doubt, and that the early fish may very speedily be singled out from among the late ones is also quite certain. In the course of a few weeks the smolts that are to leave at the end of the first year can be noted. The keeper's opinion is that at feeding-time the weak are kept back by the strong, and therefore are not likely to thrive so fast as those that get a larger portion of the food ; he lays great stress on feeding, and his opinion on that subject is entitled to consideration.

At the time of the visit alluded to one of the ponds (the original one) was swarming with young salmon hatched out in March and April 1864, the eggs having been placed in the boxes in November and December 1863. Half of these would depart from the ponds as smolts during May 1865 ; the other half, I suppose, would be transferred to the new pond, as there is direct communication with both of the ponds from the canal at the foot of the suite of breeding-boxes, which have been lately renewed and improved. The requirements of spawning only once in two seasons have not been strictly observed of late years, so that eggs were laid down in both the years 1862 and 1863. In the former of those years the ova laid down were 250,000, and in 1863 about 80,000 ; indeed, no more could be obtained, in consequence of the river being in an un-favourable state for capturing the gravid fish.

The guiding of the smolts from the ponds to the river is easily managed through the provision made at Stormontfield for that purpose, and which consists of a runlet lined with wood, protected at the pond by a perforated zinc sluice, and terminating near the river in a kind of reception-chamber, about four feet square, which is likewise provided with a zinc sluice (also perforated), to keep the fish from getting away till the arranged time, thus affording proper facilities for the marking and examination of departing broods. [See plan.] The sluice being lifted, the current of water is sufficiently strong to carry the fish down a gentle slope to the Tay, into which they proceed in considerable quantities, day by day, till all have departed ; the parrs, strange to say, evincing no desire to remove, although, of course, being in the same breeding-ponds, they have a good opportunity of reaching the river.

It was a great drawback in former years at Stormontfield, during the hatching seasons, that many fish were caught with their eggs not sufficiently matured, and which could not be used in consequence. To remedy this, a plan has been adopted of keeping all the salmon that are caught, if they be so nearly ripe for spawning as to warrant their detention. These are confined in the mill-race till they become thoroughly ready for the manipulator, and are kept within bounds by strong iron gratings, placed about 100 yards from each other. These gravid fish are taken out as they are required, or rather as they ripen, by means of a small sweep-net, and it is noteworthy that the animals, after being once or twice fished for, become very cunning, and hide themselves in such bottom holes as they can discover, in order that the net may pass over them. I have no doubt that the Stormontfield mill-race forms an excellent temporary feeding-place for these fish, as its banks are well overhung with vegetation, and its waters are clear as crystal, and of good flavour. It is a decided convenience to be able thus to store the egg-and-milt-producing fish till they are wanted, and will render the annual filling of the breeding-boxes a certainty, which, even under the old two-year system, was not so, in consequence of floods on the river Tay, and from many other causes besides.

The latest has been the best spawning season experienced since the commencement of the Stormontfield artificial spawning operations. On the 22d of December (1865) I found that Peter Marshall, the resident pisciculturist, had up to that date deposited in the breeding-boxes more than 300,000 salmon eggs, and that he still had three adult fish to spawn, from which he calculated upon obtaining something like 50,000 additional eggs, and he told me that that number would complete the total quantity required that season—viz. 350,000 ; indeed, the boxes cannot conveniently hold many more, although another row has been constructed.

Upwards of a million of pond-bred fish have now been thrown into the river Tay, and the result has been a satisfactory rise in the salmon-rental of that magnificent stream.

I have compiled the following summary of what has been achieved in salmon-breeding at the Stormontfield ponds :—

On the 23d November 1853 the stocking of the boxes commenced, and before a month had expired 300,000 ova were deposited, being at the rate of 1000 to each box, of which at that time there were 300. These ova were hatched in April 1854, and the fry were kept in the ponds till May 1855, when the sluice was opened, and one moiety of the fish departed for the river and the sea. About 1300 of these were marked by cutting off the dead or second dorsal fin. The smolts marked were about one in every hundred, so that about 130,000 must have departed, leaving more than that number in the pond. The second spawning, in 1854, was a failure, only a few thousand fish being produced. This result arose from the imperfect manipulation of the fish by those intrusted with the spawning. The third spawning took place between the 22d November and the 16th December 1855, and during that time 183,000 ova were deposited in the boxes. These ova came to life in April 1856. The second migration of the fry spawned in 1853 took place between the 20th April and 24th May 1856. Of the smolts that then left the ponds, 300 were marked with rings, and 800 with cuts in the tail. Many grilses having the mark on the tail were re-taken, but none of those marked with the ring. The smolts from the hatching of 1856 left the pond in April 1857. About 270 were marked with silver rings inserted into the fleshy part of the tail ; about 1700 with a small hole in the gill-cover ; and about 600 with the dead fin cut off in addition to the mark in the gill-cover. Several grilses with the mark on the gill and tail were caught and reported, but no fish marked with the ring. The fourth spawning took place between the 12th November and the 2d December 1857, when 150,000 ova were deposited in the boxes. These came to life in March 1858. Of the smolts produced from the previous hatching, which left the pond in 1858, 25 were marked with a silver ring behind the dead fin, and 50 with gilt copper wire. Very few of this exodus were reported as being caught. The smolts produced from the hatching of 1858 left the pond in April 1859, and 506 of them were marked. The fifth spawning, from 15th November to 13th December 1859, produced 250,000 ova, which were hatched in April 1860. Of the smolts that left in 1860, 670 were marked, and a good many of them were reported as having been caught on their return from the sea. The smolts of the hatching of 1860 left the pond in May 1861, but none of them were marked.* The number of eggs deposited in the

---

* As I assisted personally at the exodus of 1861, I subjoin a brief report of what took place from the *Perth Courier :—*

" On Saturday last, Mr. Buist, accompanied by Mr. Bertram of Edinburgh and other gentlemen, visited the ponds of Stormontfield, for the purpose of ascertaining the state of the fish and giving instructions as to the liberation of the smolts. For eight days past the keeper had observed strong indications of a desire for freedom on the part of a considerable proportion of his finny wards, and numbers had gone into the runlet which leads to the reservoir by the side of the river where the

breeding-boxes in the spawning season of 1862 (November
and December) was about 250,000 ; and in 1863 not more

fish were formerly caught and marked. When the party arrived they
found a good many of the fish in the reservoir, being those which had
sought egress during the night. The smolts were large and in fine
condition ; and one fish, which has been detained for three years for
the purpose of discovering whether the species will grow in fresh water
without being permitted to visit the sea, was found to be fully twice
the size of the largest smolt. A number of parrs, too, of the same
age as the smolts, and spawned of the same parents, were found about
the size of minnows, and bearing the parr-mark distinctly defined. On
seeing the state of matters, Mr. Buist gave instructions for removing
the sluices, and allowing those bent on migration to have their liberty
without being marked this season. A considerable number at once
sought the river, and no impediment will now be placed in the way of
a free migration. The ova of which the present fry is the produce were
placed in the boxes at various times during the period from 15th
November to 13th December 1859 ; and the departure of the smolts
commenced on the 18th instant. The whole fry—amounting, it is
estimated, to somewhat approaching 200,000 fish—is the produce of 19
male and 31 female salmon. The anomaly of one-half of the fry
reaching the condition of smolts, and leaving the ponds when only
a year old, and the other half remaining, has been hitherto supposed to
be accounted for upon the supposition of the earlier fish being the
produce of salmon, while the later were that of grilse. The experiment
of this year sets that question at rest by negativing the supposition.
Mr. Buist gave orders in November 1859 that none but salmon should
be taken for the purposes of the ponds. The result is the same anomaly.
Although all the fry this year in the ponds are the produce of salmon,
as is usual only a moiety of them have yet attained to the condition of
smolts, while the remainder have all the appearance of continuing
parrs as before. This is perhaps the most important feature in the
operations of the year. In the early part of the year 1860, from the
unfavourable nature of the season for hatching, the whole brood seemed
particularly stunted and ill-grown, and it was hardly expected that
any of them would become smolts this year at all. About a month
ago, however, early fears were dispelled ; a goodly portion of the fry
began to approach the smolt state, and since the beginning of May
have been putting on their silvery livery, and now are fully as far
advanced as those in the open river."

than 80,000 ova could be obtained, in consequence of the unfavourable state of the river for capturing gravid salmon. Peter Marshall has proved a most able pisciculturist. The loss of eggs under his management forms an almost infinitesimal proportion of the total quantities hatched at Stormontfield.

Mr. Buist has favoured me with the following notes, which were compiled from his day-books at an early stage of the Stormontfield experiments :—

" 1. Of the marked fish which were liberated from the pond at Stormontfield, four out of every hundred were re-captured, either as grilse or salmon.

" 2. We find that more than 300,000 fish were reared in the pond, and allowed to go into the Tay. Thus forty fish out of every thousand were re-captured ; and as 300,000 were in all liberated, it follows that 12,000 of the salmon taken in the Tay were pond-bred fish. But as the fish did not all go away in one year, this 12,000 must be distributed over two years.

" 3. We find the average number of salmon and grilse ·taken in each year is 70,000. It follows, then, if there be any truth in figures, that nearly one-tenth of the fish taken in the Tay for the last two years were artificially bred. This is equivalent to a rise of 10 per cent in the rental of the fishings ; and such we find is the result.

" It may be urged that if the salmon from which the ova were taken had been left at liberty, the result would have been the same ; but this we know could not have been the case, for, according to a careful calculation made by Mr. Thomas Tod Stoddart and others, each pair of salmon, although they produce upon an average 30,000 eggs, do not rear above five fish. Three female fish, if every egg they deposit was to produce a salmon, would produce all the fish in the Tay. When left in their natural state, 30,000 ova produce four or five fish fit for the table ; whereas the same number of ova, when carefully protected in the breeding-ponds, produce about 800. This is supposing that one-third of the ova deposited in the boxes perishes—does not hatch, and comes to nothing. Therefore the increase in the number of salmon taken within the last year is accounted for. Had there been any increase in the number of fish in the other rivers of Scotland, doubts might arise; but there has been no such increase, last year being a bad one for every river in Scotland with the exception of the Tay."

In addition to the group of salmon-breeding ponds at Stormontfield, a very successful suite of breeding-boxes has been laid down on the river Dee, in the Stewartry of Kirkcudbright, by Messrs. Martin and Gillone, the lessees of the river Dee salmon-fisheries. Mr. Gillone, who is an adept in the art of fish-culture, was one of the earliest to experiment on the salmon, and so long ago as 1830 had arrived at the conclusion that parr were young salmon, and that that tiny animal changed at a given period into a smolt, and in time became a valuable table-fish. These early experiments of Mr. Gillone's were not in any sense commercial; they were conducted solely with a view to solve what was then a curious problem in salmon-growth. In later years Mr. Gillone and his partner have entered upon salmon-breeding as an adjunct of their fisheries on the river Dee, for which, as tacksmen, they pay a rental of upwards of £1200 per annum. The breeding-boxes of Messrs. Martin and Gillone have been fitted up on a very picturesque part of the river at Tongueland, and the number of eggs last brought to maturity is considerably over 100,000. The present series of hatchings for commercial purposes was begun in 1862-63 with 25,000 eggs, followed in the succeeding year by a laying down of nearly double that number. The hatchings of these seasons were very unsuccessful, the loss from many causes being very great, for the manipulation of fish eggs during the time of their artificial extraction and impregnation requires great care—a little maladroitness being sufficient to spoil thousands.

The last hatching (spring 1865) has been most successfully dealt with. Messrs. Martin and Gillone's breeding-boxes are all under cover, being placed in a large lumber-store connected with a biscuit manufactory. This chamber is seventy feet long, and there is a double row of boxes extending the whole length of the place. These receptacles for the eggs are made of wood; they are three feet long, one foot wide, and four inches deep, and into the whole series a range of frames has been fitted containing glass troughs on which to lay the eggs. The edges of the glass are ground off, and they are fitted angularly *across the current* in the shape of a V. The eggs are laid down on, or rather sown into, these troughs, from a store bottle, on to which is fitted a tapering funnel. The flow of water, which is derived from the river, and is filtered to prevent the admission of any impurity, is very gentle, being at the rate of about fifteen feet per minute, and is kept perfectly regular. The boxes are all fitted with lids, in order to prevent the eggs from being devoured, as is often done, by rats and other vermin, and also to assimilate the conditions of artificial hatching as much as possible to those of the natural breeding-beds—where, of course, the eggs are covered up with gravel and are hatched in comparative darkness.

It may be of some use, particularly to those who are interested in pisciculture, to note a few details connected with the capturing of the gravid fish and the plan of exuding the ova practised at Tongueland. The river Dee is tolerably well stocked with fish, as may be surmised from the rent I have named as being paid for the right of fishing. Mr. Gillone adopts the plan, now also in use at Stormontfield, of capturing his fish in good time—in fact, as a general rule, before the eggs are ripe—and of confining them in his mill-race till they are thoroughly ready for manipulation. Last season—*i.e.* in November and December 1864, and January 1865—as many as thirty-six female fish were taken for their roe, the number of milters being twenty-five, the total weight of the lot being 454 lbs., or, on the average, six and a half pounds each fish. According to rule, the weight of the female fish taken having been 283 lbs., these ought to have yielded 283,000 eggs, but as several of the fish were about ripe at the time they were caught, they spawned naturally in the mill-race, where the eggs in due time came to life. The plan of spawning pursued at Tongueland is as follows :—Whenever the fish are supposed to be ripe for that process, the water is shut out of the dam, and the animal is first placed in a box filled with water in order to its examination ; if ready to be operated upon, it is then transferred to a trough filled with water about three feet and a half long, seven inches in breadth, and of corresponding depth, and the roe or milt is pressed out of the fish just in the position in which it swims. As soon as the eggs are secured, a portion of the water is poured out of the wooden vessel, and the male fish is then similarly treated. The milt and roe are mixed by hand stirring, and the eggs then being washed are distributed into the boxes.

Mr. Gillone carries on all his operations with the greatest possible precision. He has a large clear glass bottle marked off in divisions, each of which contains 800 eggs, and he numbers the divisions allotted to each particular fish, which are sown into a similarly numbered division in his box, so that by referring to his index-book he can trace out any peculiarity in the eggs, etc.

Although pisciculture has been shown by means of what has been achieved on the Continent and at Stormontfield to be eminently practical, yet nothing beyond a few toy experiments, so to speak, have been made in England ; indeed, we have had a great deal of " toying" with the subject ; but all honour to Messrs. Buckland and Francis—they are evidently doing their best to create public opinion on the subject. Lectures have been delivered on fish-culture, and letters have been thickly sent to the daily papers, advocating the extension of the art; but no great movement has been made beyond stocking the upper waters of the Thames with a few thousand trout and some fancy fish. Salmon also have been hatched ; but can they reach the sea in the present state of the river ?

PISCICULTURAL APPARATUS.

In order that gentlemen who have a bit of running water on their property may try the experiment of artificial hatching, I give a drawing of an apparatus invented by M. Coste suitable for hatching out a few thousand eggs—it could be set up in a garden or be placed in any convenient outhouse. I may state that I am able to hatch salmon eggs in the saucer of a flower-pot ; it is placed on a shelf over a fixed wash-hand basin, and a small flow of water regulated by a stopcock falls into it. The vessel is filled with small stones and bits of broken china, and answers admirably. Out of a batch of about two hundred eggs brought from Stormontfield, only fifteen were found to have turned opaque in the first five weeks. Eggs hatched in this homely way are very serviceable, as one can examine them day by day and note how they progress, and in due time observe the development of the fish for a few days. The young animals can only be kept in the saucer about ten or twelve days, and should then be placed in a larger vessel or be thrown into a river.

As regards England, I should like to see one of the great rivers of that country turned into a gigantic salmon "manufactory." Ponds might be readily constructed on one or two places of the Severn, or on some of the other suitable salmon streams of England or Wales, capable of turning out a million fish per annum, and at a comparatively trifling cost. The formation of the ponds would be the chief expense ; a couple of men could watch and feed the fry with the greatest ease. The size adopted might be three times that of the ponds on the river Tay, and the original cost of these was less than £500. I would humbly submit that the ponds should be constructed after the manner of the plan I have elsewhere given. Except by the protecting of the spawn and the young fish from their numerous enemies, there is no way of meeting the present great demand for salmon, which, when in season, is in the aggregate of greater value than the best butchers' meat. The salmon is an excellent fish to work with in a piscicultural sense, because it is large enough to bear a good deal of handling, and it is very accessible to the operations of mankind, because of the instinct which leads it to spawn in the fresh water instead of the sea. It is only such a fish as this monarch of the brook that would individually pay for artificial breeding, for, having a high money value as an animal, it is clear that salmon-culture would in time become as good a way of making money as cattle-feeding or sheep-rearing.

There are waste places in England—the Essex marshes, for instance, or the fens of Norfolk—where it would be profitable to cultivate eels or other fish after the manner of the inhabitants of Comacchio. I observed lately some details of a plan to rescue a quantity of land in Essex from the water ; it would perhaps pay as well to convert the broad acres in question, from their being near the great London market, into a fish-farm.   The English people are fond of eels, and would be able to consume any quantity that might be offered for sale, and the place being in such close proximity to the Thames, other fish might be cultivated as well.   All the best portions of the hydraulic apparatus of Comacchio might be imitated, and to suit the locality, such other portions as might be required could be invented.   The art of pisciculture is but in its infancy, and we may all live in the hope of seeing great water farms—but, to be profitable, they must be gigantic— for the cultivation of fish, in the same sense as we have extensive grazing or feeding farms for the breeding and rearing of cattle.

In Ireland, Mr. Thomas Ashworth, of the Galway fisheries, finds it as profitable and as easy to breed salmon as it is to rear sheep.   His fisheries are a decided success ; and, if we except the cost of some extensive engineering operations in forming fish-passes to admit of a communication with the sea, the cost of his experiments has been trifling and the returns exceptionally large.   Mr. Ashworth put into his fisheries no less than a million and a half of salmon eggs in the course of two seasons—viz., 659,000 eggs in 1861, and 770,000 in 1862.* I am anxious to obtain a consecutive and detailed account of the operations carried out by the Messrs. Ashworth, but have not been able to get correct particulars.   Mr. Ashworth

---

* " In order that the public may understand what a vast number of fish 770,000 would be, I would mention that it has been calculated by ' the chronicler,' Mr. James Lowe, that the number of human beings assembled to welcome the arrival of the Princess of Wales was 700,000 : imagine a salmon for each human being, and you will have an idea of the number of fish Mr. Ashworth has hatched out as a stock for his fisheries."—Lecture by Mr. Buckland.

has lately visited the oyster-farms of the Isle of Re, and has a high opinion of the efforts made for the multiplication of that favourite mollusc.   He has very obligingly communicated to me a number of interesting statistics as to French oyster-culture, which I have incorporated into my account of the shell-fish fisheries.

Two recent achievements in the art of fish-culture, or at any rate in the art of acclimatisation, deserve to be chronicled in this division of the "Harvest of the Sea."   I allude to the successful introduction into Australia of the British salmon, and the equally successful bringing to this country of a foreign fish—the *Silurus glanis*.

Grave doubts at one time prevailed among persons interested in acclimatisation and pisciculture as to whether or not it were possible to introduce the British salmon into the waters of Australia ; and an interesting controversy was about three years ago carried on in various journals as to the best way of taking out the fish to that country. Those very wise people who never do anything, but are largely endowed with the gift of prophecy, at once proclaimed that it could not be done ; that it was impossible to take the salmon out to Australia, etc. etc.   But happily for the cause of progress in natural science, and the success of this particular experiment, there were men who had resolved to carry it out and who would not be put down. Mr. Francis Francis, Mr. Frank Buckland, and Mr. J. A. Youl, took a leading part in the achievement ; but before they fell upon their successful plan of taking out the ova in ice, hot discussions had ensued as to how the salmon could be introduced into the rivers of the Australian Continent. Many plans were suggested: some for carrying out the young fish in tanks, and others for taking out the fructified ova, so that the process of hatching might be carried on during the voyage.   One ingenious person promulgated a plan of taking the parr in a fresh-water tank a month or two before it changed into a smolt, saying that after the change it would be easy to keep the smolts supplied with *fresh* salt water direct from the sea as the ship proceeded on her voyage.

The mode ultimately adopted was to pack up the ova in a bed of ice, experiments having first been made with a view to test the plan. For that purpose a large number of ova were deposited in an ice-house in order to ascertain how long the ripening of the egg could be deferred—a condition of the experiment of course being that the egg should remain quite healthy. The Wenham Lake Ice Company were so obliging as to allow boxes containing salmon and trout ova, packed in moss, to be placed in their ice vaults, and to afford every facility for the occasional examination of the eggs. Satisfactory results being obtained—in other words, it having been proved that the eggs of the salmon could with perfect safety be kept in ice for a period exceeding the average time of a voyage to Australia—it was therefore resolved that a quantity of eggs, properly packed in ice, should be sent out. The result of this experiment is now well known, most of the daily papers having chronicled the successful exportation of the ova, and announced that the fish had come to life and were thriving in their foreign home.

I do not wish to weary my readers, but must crave their indulgence while I give a few of the more interesting details connected with this important experiment.

The number of ova sent out to Australia was 100,000 salmon and 3000 trout. The vessel selected for the conveyance of the eggs was the *Norfolk*, which on one or two occasions had made very rapid voyages. The ova were procured from the Tweed, the Severn, the Ribble, and the Dovey rivers ; thus England, Scotland, and Wales contributed to this precious freight. One hundred and sixty-four boxes, containing about 90,000 ova, were placed at the bottom of the ice-house, with a solid mass of ice nine feet thick on the top, so that every particle of this mass must melt before the ova would suffer. Sixteen boxes, containing above 13,000 ova, were placed in other parts of the ice-house, with ice below and above, as well as all round the boxes. The ova were taken between the 13th and 15th January, placed on board the ship on the 18th, and the *Norfolk* left the docks on the morning of the 21st, and Plymouth on the 28th January. Thirty tons of Wenham Lake ice were used in the experiment.

The ship arrived at Hobson's Bay, Melbourne, on the 15th of April, having been seventy-seven days on the voyage. A few of the boxes containing the eggs were at once opened and placed in a suitable hatching apparatus, but the larger portion were sent off to Tasmania and reached Hobart Town on the 20th of April, where they were at once deposited in the pond which had been carefully prepared for them on the river Plenty. The following extract from a letter, written by the Hon. Dr. Officer, Speaker of the House of Assembly, will show what was done on the arrival of the eggs :—" Soon after the arrival of the first half of the boxes, the process of opening them and depositing the ova in their watery beds commenced, and you may be sure an anxious process it was. In the first two boxes that were opened by far the greater number of the ova had perished, but as we proceeded much more fortunate results were obtained, and in many of the packages the living predominated over the dead. I could not attempt to state to you, even approximately, at the present moment, the actual number of healthy ova that were found in the moss and placed in the hatching-boxes, beyond saying that they amount to many thousands, and are amply sufficient, if they should all continue to thrive and should become living fish, to insure the complete success of our experiment. All the boxes have now been opened except fifteen, and the ova first taken out have been about twenty-four hours in the water. Among these some of them can be observed with the eyes quite prominent, and visibly indicating the near approach of hatching, so that not many days will elapse until the ultimate result of the experiment is known.   The remnant of the ice, amounting to about eight tons, obtained from the *Norfolk*, was brought up here with very little loss, and has of course been used in cooling the water in the hatching-boxes.   Mr. Ramsbottom thinks it will last as long as he will require its aid, although it melts very quickly.   The water of the Plenty, which had fallen below 50 degrees, had been again raised by a week of warm sunny weather to 54 degrees, which was its temperature yesterday, but it was reduced to 45 degrees by the introduction of ice.   To-day the weather has been more suitable, and the natural temperature is not much over 50 degrees, and will in all probability soon decline several degrees lower.   One or two of the ova which were deposited in the water in apparently sound health have been observed to become opaque and die, while some others have been seen to retain all their clearness. These observations have necessarily been of very limited extent.   In one of the two boxes of trout ova, nearly all were dead ; in the other nearly all alive, and of a remarkably clear and brilliant appearance.   These have been placed in a compartment separated from the salmon-boxes."

The commissioners appointed to receive the ova sent to Tasmania made a formal report to the Government of the colony.   One of the local papers supplies a summary of what was reported, which is as follows :—"They state that upon examination of the cases on arrival, it was found that a close and almost unvarying relation existed between the fate of the ova and the condition of the moss in which they were enveloped.   Where the moss retained its natural green hue and elasticity, there a large proportion of the ova retained a healthy vitality ; where, on the contrary, the moss was of a brown colour, and in a collapsed or compressed form, few of the ova were found alive, and all were more or less entangled in a network of fungus. The smallest amount of mortality was invariably found to have taken place in those boxes in which the moss had been most loosely packed and the ova subjected to the least amount of pressure. On the 4th of May the first trout made its appearance, followed on the succeeding day by the first salmon that had ever been seen in Australia, or south of the equator. The further hatching of the trout and salmon proceeded very slowly for some days, but then became more rapid—especially among the trout. Among these the process was completed about the 25th May, producing upwards of two hundred healthy fish. The hatching of the salmon is more protracted, and was not concluded until the 8th June, on which day the last little fish was observed making its escape from the shell. As they continued to make their appearance from day to day, their numbers were counted by Mr. Ramsbottom with tolerable accuracy up to about 1000, after which it was no longer possible to keep any reckoning. The great undertaking of introducing the salmon and trout into Tasmania has now, the commissioners believe, been successfully accomplished. Few countries of the same extent possess more rivers suited to the nature and habits of this noble fish than Tasmania. A stranger acquainted with the salmon rivers of Europe could scarcely behold the ample stream and sparkling waters of the Derwent without fancying that they were already the home of the king of fish. And the Derwent is but one of many other large and ever-flowing rivers almost equally suited to become the abode of the salmon. When these rivers have been stocked, they cannot fail to become a source of considerable public revenue, and of profit and pleasure to the people."

Mr. Ramsbottom, a son of the well-known English practical pisciculturist, went out in charge of the eggs, and aided in their accouchement, watching over the progress of the experiment with much zeal.   Véry great anxiety was evinced by those interested for the proper hatching out of the eggs, and the mortality which was soon visible among the ova—it was at one time at the rate of one hundred each day—was viewed with great alarm.   The first eggs were hatched in the ponds of Tasmania.   Of the Victoria consignment, the first egg was hatched at an ice company's establishment on the 7th of May, twenty-two days after the arrival of the ship.   In a letter, dated 11th May 1864, Dr. Officer communicates many interesting details of the experiment, as the following extract will show :—" By our last out-going mail I reported the hatching of the first trout and the first salmon on May 4 and 5.   We have now forty trout and nine salmon, but of the latter two are deformed, and, therefore, not likely to survive long.   The first-born salmon is now nine days old, and is quite healthy and visibly grown.   The mortality among the ova, which had been about one hundred per diem for some days, has very much decreased again, and for the last two days has been quite trifling. The weather and temperature of the water have continued favourable.   The temperature of the Plenty and ponds has not exceeded 49 degrees, nor descended below 46 degrees.   This equality is of course highly conducive to the health and progress of our charge.   We expected to have seen more salmon by this time, but our impatience has outrun probability and the teachings of experience.   The authorities tell us that a few always precede the great body of fish by a good many days, and are not usually so vigorous as those that are hatched at a later period.   As to the trout we may, I think, regard them as safe.   Only one out of the whole number hatched has died.   As I looked at their box this afternoon, I observed several in the act of escaping from the shell.   Mr. Ramsbottom's attentions are indefatigable, and, I believe, nothing has been neglected that could insure success."

The process of hatching was much more protracted than

was anticipated ; it was not till the 8th of June that the last
of the eggs gave forth its little tenant.   An account of the
daily hatching was kept up till the time that 1000 of the
eggs had arrived at maturity, but after that the hatching
went on with such rapidity as to render it impossible to keep
a correct record.   Up to the 16th of June the trout had not
been artificially fed, but for all that they looked healthy and
grew fat.   Mr. Ramsbottom computed that he had at least
3000 healthy salmon, rather a small percentage certainly to
obtain out of the 30,000 eggs, but quite sufficient to solve the
grand problem of whether or not it were possible to introduce
the British salmon into Australian waters.   The latest accounts
tell us that the young parr are doing well, though they are
not growing so fast as the trout.*   The further progress of the
experiment will be watched with great anxiety both at home
and abroad.   The Tasmanian Legislature have voted a further
sum of £800 for the purpose of introducing another batch of
ova ; this sum will be augmented by £400 voted by the
Victorian Acclimatisation Society ; so that no means will be
left untried to bring to a successful conclusion this great
experiment—the ultimate result of which, I have no doubt,
will be, that the salmon will become as valuable a fish in the
waters of the great Australian Continent as it is in the waters
of our own islands.

The naturalisation of fish, to which a brief reference has
already been made, is a subject that is not very well under-

---

* Since the above was written intelligence has been received in
England of the loss, by escape into the river (which would be no loss),
or the death, or more truly "mysterious disappearance" of a large number
of the fry—only five hundred being left in the pond.   These have been
allowed to make their escape into the river, and we may yet hope to
hear of their safety and welfare.   I hope those interested will lose
no time, now that they know the way to success, in sending out another
batch of eggs, so as to ensure the sending into the river of a few thousand
young fish.

stood ; but so far as practical experience goes, I have seen
nothing to prevent our breeding in England some of the most
productive foreign kinds. Among the fishes of China, for
instance, in addition to the golden carp—now quite common
here, and bred in thousands in nearly every factory pond, and
which is looked upon as simply an ornamental fish—there is
the lo-in, or king of fish, which frequently measures seven feet
in length, and weighs from fifty to two hundred pounds, the
flesh being excellent ; the lien-in-wang and the kan-in, almost
as good, and even larger than the other. Then there is the
li-in, the usual weight of which is about fifteen pounds, and
is said to be of a much finer flavour than our European carp.
There are many other choice fishes of exquisite flavour, which
it is unnecessary to enumerate ; but I have no doubt that,
besides these natives of Chinese seas, there are numerous
other fine fish that might be acclimatised in our rivers and
firths. The seir fish of Ceylon may be named : it is a kind of
scomberoid, and in shape and size is similar to the British
salmon. We must not, however, build ourselves much on
the acclimatisation of foreign fish, especially tropical fish, as
—although fish can bear great extremes of temperature—it
would be no easy matter to habituate them to our climate.
Indeed some writers think it will be found impossible to
habituate tropical fish, however valuable, to our cold waters,
but the experiment is, I believe, being tried in France. The
bass of Lake Wennern may also be mentioned as a suitable fish
for British waters, as well as the ombre chevalier of the Lake
of Geneva, a few of which latter are now, I believe, along with
some other varieties, being tried in the river Thames. So great
is the increasing interest of pisciculture becoming, that new
ideas are being daily thrown out regarding it. A few months
ago a writer in the *Times* suggested the introduction of a
white fish from the Canadian lakes to our fresh waters :—
" This fish (*Coregonus albus*), of the salmon family, is from

three to four pounds weight, as delicious as a Dublin Bay haddock when fresh, and when barrelled considered a luxury in the Central and Southern States of America and the West Indies, bringing 50 per cent over the price of barrelled trout. Different from our fresh-water fish, it is a vegetarian, living on weeds and moss. It is a great article of food in the North-Western States of America and Canada, the exports of it being $464,479 in 1861 from the states on the lakes; but I have no return from Canada, which may be about one-half more, making a total of over $700,000, or £140,000 a year."

The latest achievement in pisciculture has been the introduction to this part of Europe of "the Wels" (*Silurus glanis*), an interesting account of which lately appeared in the *Field* newspaper. Great expectations have been formed that this gigantic fish may be successfully reared in England. It is, I believe, the largest European fresh-water fish, commonly attaining a weight of from fifty to eighty pounds, and individuals have been found of the extraordinary size of four cwts. ! Dr. Gunther, the eminent ichthyologist, remarks that this is the only foreign fish which it would be worth while to introduce into this country; and thinks that, in several of our lakes, particularly those in peat soil, it might be usefully placed.

The following particulars regarding this new food fish have been printed by the Acclimatisation Society, to whom the greatest praise is due for its introduction :—Its appearance is not pleasant, the large flattened head having a capacious mouth, which is capable of seizing the largest kind of prey ; so that if this fish be successfully propagated in our streams and lakes, the pike, the water-wolf of the British waters, will meet with more than its match. The habits of the *Silurus glanis* are said to be most ferocious, and its growth, provided there be a sufficient supply of food, very rapid. The body is less elongated than the eel, and there are,

stretching from the head, long tapering barbels ; the eyes are
frog-like, and there are many other points of resemblance to
the frog. The new fish is like the eel in its habits, being
a wallowing fish, fond of burrowing in the mud, and
hiding amongst the rotten roots of trees. There are dark
charges made against some of the largest specimens of the

SILURUS GLANIS.

Silurus glanis, in the stomachs of which it is reported that
portions of human bodies have been found. However, this is
probably an exaggeration. There can, however, be no doubt
of the extraordinary appetite and fierceness of this fish. In
the floods of the Danube the silurus finds plentiful prey in
· the multitude of frogs which pass into the river ; but at
other times, fish, small animals, worms, indeed anything
which comes near, afford a supply of food ; and there may be
fear that, notwithstanding the valuable qualities of the silurus

as a means of supply to our tables, it may more than balance
its value in this way by the immense destruction of fish which
is needed for its support.   It is said that the silurus, when the
prey is plentiful, will attain over fifty-six pounds in four years;
and Englishmen who have tasted it report that in flavour it
is superior to the salmon.   Specimens of the wels have been
brought alive from a distance of nearly two thousand miles
to the station of the society at Twickenham by the exertions
of Sir Stephen Lakeman and Mr. Lowe, a gentleman who
takes a great interest in all questions of natural science.   In all,
fourteen of these young fish were brought from Kapochien,
in Wallachia, where Sir Stephen Lakeman has an estate.
The Argich river, which flows past there, abounds in these
and other valuable fish, which are found more or less throughout central Europe and in Scandinavia.   In the Danube and
many of its tributaries the number is abundant; and in those
wide waters the *Silurus glanis* is said to reach the enormous
weight of three hundred pounds.

CHAPTER IV.

—◆—

ANGLERS' FISHES.

Fresh-Water Fish not of much Value—The Angler and his Equipment—
Pleasures of the Country in May—Anglers' Fishes—Trout, Pike, Perch,
and Carp—Gipsy Anglers—Angling Localities—Gold Fish—The River
Scenery of England—The Thames—Thames Anglers—Sea Angling—
Various Kinds of Sea-Fish—Proper kinds of Bait—The Tackle Neces-
sary—The Island of Arran—Corry—Goatfell, etc.

ALTHOUGH it may be deemed necessary in a work like
the present to devote some space to the subject, I do
not set much store by the common anglers' fishes, so far,
at least, as their food value is concerned; for although we
were to cultivate them to their highest pitch, and by means of
artificial spawning multiply them exceedingly, they would
never (the salmon, of course, excepted) form an article of any
great commercial value in this beef-eating country. In France,
where the Church enjoins so many fasts and has such strict
sumptuary laws, the people are differently situated, and require, especially in the inland districts, to have recourse to the
meanest produce of the rivers in order to carry out the injunctions of their priests. The fresh waters are therefore assiduously cultivated in nearly all continental countries; but the
fresh-water fishes of the British Islands have at present but a
very slight commercial value, as they are not captured, either
individually or in the aggregate, for the purposes of commerce;
but to persons fond of angling they afford sport and healthful

K

recreation, whether they are pursued in the large English or Scottish lakes, or caught in the small rivulets that feed our great salmon streams.

Although Britain is possessed of a seabord of 4000 miles, and a large number of fine rivers and lakes, the total number of British fishes is comparatively small (about 250 only), and the varieties which live in the fresh water are therefore very limited; those that afford sport may be numbered with ease on our ten fingers. Fishers who live in the vicinity of large cities are obliged in consequence to content themselves with the realisation of that old proverb which tells them that small fish are better than no fish at all; hence there is a race of anglers who are contented to sit all day in a punt on the Thames, happy when evening arrives to find their patience rewarded with a fisher's dozen of stupid gudgeons. But in the north, on the lakes of Cumberland or on the Highland lochs of Scotland, such tame sport would be laughed at. Are there not charr in the Derwent and splendid trout in Loch Awe? and these require to be pursued with a zeal, and involve an amount of labour not understood by anglers who punt for gudgeon or who haunt the East India Docks for perch, or the angler who only knows the usual run of Thames fish— barbel, roach, dace, and gudgeon. To kill a sixteen-pound salmon on a Welsh or Highland stream is to be named a knight among anglers; indeed, there are men who never lift a rod except to kill a salmon; such, however, like the Duke of Roxburghe, are the giants of the profession. For sport there is no fish like the monarch of the brook, and great anglers will not waste time on any fish less noble. An angler, with a moderate-sized fish of the salmon kind at the end of his line, is not in the enjoyment of a sinecure, although he would not for any kind of reward allow his work to be done by deputy. I have seen a gentleman play a fish for four hours rather than yield his rod to the attendant gillie, who could have landed the fish in half-an-hour's time. It is a thrilling moment to find that, for the first time, one has hooked a salmon, and the event produces a nervousness that certainly does not tend to the speedy landing of the fish. The first idea, naturally enough, is to haul our scaly friend out of the water by sheer force ; but this plan has speedily to be abandoned, for the fish, making an astonished dash, rushes away up stream in fine style, taking out with it no end of " rope ;" then when once it obtains a bite of its bridle away it goes sulking into some rocky hiding-place. In a brief time it comes out again with renewed vigour, determined as it would seem to try your mettle ; and so it dashes about till you become so fatigued as not to care whether you land it or not. It is impossible to say how long an angler may have to "play" a salmon or a large grilse ; but if it sinks itself to the bottom of a deep pool, it may be a business of hours to get it safe into the landing-net, if the fish be not altogether lost, as in its exertions to escape it may so chafe the line as to cause it to snap and thus regain its liberty ; and during the progress of the battle the angler has certainly to wade, aye and be pulled once or twice through the stream, so that he comes in for a thorough drenching, and may, as many have to do, go home after a hard day's work without being rewarded by the capture of a single fish.

There is abundance of good salmon-angling to be had in the season in the north of Scotland, where there are always a great variety of fishings to be let at prices suitable for all pockets ; and there is nothing better either for health or recreation than a day on a salmon stream. There are one or two places on Tweed frequented by anglers who take a fishing as a sort of joint-stock company, and who, when they are not angling, talk politics, make poetry, bandy about their polite chaff, and generally "go in" as they say for any amount of amusement. These societies are of course very select, and

not generally accessible to strangers, being of the nature of a
club. The plan which every angler ought to adopt on going
to a strange water is to place himself under the guidance of
some shrewd native of the place, who will show him all the
best pools and aid him with his advice as to what flies he
ought to use, and give him many useful hints on other points
as well. Anglers, however, must divide their attention, for it
is quite as interesting (not to speak of convenience) for some
men to spend a day on the Thames killing barbel or roach as
it is to others to kill a ten-pound salmon on the Tweed or
the Spey. It is good sport also to troll for pike in the
Lodden or to capture grayling in beautiful Dovedale. And
so pleasant has of late years become the sport that it is no
uncommon sight to see a gentle-born lady handling a salmon-
rod with as much vigour as grace on some one of our
picturesque Highland streams. In fact, angling is a recreation
that can be made to suit all classes, from the child with his
stick and crooked pin to the gentleman with his well-mounted
rod and elaborate tackle, who hies away in his yacht to the
fiords of Norway in search of salmon that weigh from twenty to
forty pounds and require a day to capture. For those, however,
who desire to stay at home there is abundant angling all the
year round. From New-Year's Day to Christmas there needs
be no stoppage of the sport; even the weather should never
stop an enthusiastic angler; but on very bad days, when it is
not possible to go out of doors, there is the study of the fish,
and their natural and economic history, which ought to be
interesting to all who use the angle, and to the majority of
mankind besides; and there is spread out around the angler
the interesting book of nature inviting him to perusal. He
can see the white seal of winter opened, and observe the balmy
spring put forth its vernal power; note the turbid streams of
winter as they are slackening their volume of water; see the
swelling buds and the bursting leaves; admire the cowslip and

the primrose grow into blossom almost as he looks at them ; hear the sweet notes of the cuckoo, and the unceasing carol of noisier birds; watch the sportive lamb or the timid hare; and chronicle the ever-changing seasons as they roll away on their everlasting journey of progress.

Without pretending to rival the hundred and one guides to angling that now flood the market, I shall take a glance at a few of the more popular of the anglers' fishes ; not, however, in any scientific or other order of precedence, but beginning with the trout, seeing that the salmon is discussed in a separate division of this work.

Of all our fresh-water fishes, the one that is most plentiful, and the one that is most worthy of notice by anglers, is the trout. It can be fished for with the simplest possible kind of rod in the most tiny stream, or be captured by elaborate apparatus on the great lochs of Scotland. There are so many varieties of it as to suit all tastes ; there are well-flavoured burn trout, not so large as a small herring, and there are lake giants that, when placed in the scales, will pull down a twenty pound weight with the greatest ease. The usual run of river trout are about six or eight ounces in weight ; a pound trout is an excellent reward for the patient angler. Where a trouting stream flows through a rich and fertile district of country, with abundant drainage, the trout are usually well-conditioned and large, and of good flavour ; but when the country through which the stream flows is poor and rocky, with no drains carrying in food to enrich the stream, the fish will, as a matter of course, be lanky and flavourless ; they may be numerous, but they will be of small size. It is curious, too, to note the difference of the fish of the same stream: some of the trout taken in Tweed, and in other rivers as well, are sharp in their colour, have fine fat plump thick shoulders, great depth of belly, and beautiful pink flesh of excellent flavour; others again are lean and flavourless. The colour of trout is of course dependent on the quality and abundance of its food; those are best which exist on ground-feeding, living upon worms and such fresh-water crustaceans as are within reach. Fly-taking fish—those that indulge in the feed of ephemeræ that takes place a few times every day—are comparatively poor in flesh and weak in flavour. As to where fishers should resort, must be left to themselves. I was once beguiled out to the Dipple, but it was a hungry sort of river, where the trout were on the average about three ounces and scarce enough; although I must say that for a few minutes, when "the feed" was on the water, there was an enormous display of fish, but they preferred to remain in their native stream, a tributary of the Clyde I think. The mountain streams and lochs of Scotland, or the placid and picturesque lakes of Cumberland and Westmorland, are the paradise of anglers.

For trout-fishing we would name Scotland as being before all other countries. "What," it has been asked, "is a Scottish stream without its trout?" Doubtless, if a river has no trout it is without one of its greatest charms, and it is pleasant to record that, except in the neighbourhood of very large seats of population, trout are still plentiful in Scotland. It is true the railway, and other modes of conveyance, have carried of late years a perfect army of anglers into its most picturesque nooks and corners, and therefore fish are not quite so plentiful as they were thirty years ago, in the old coaching days, when it was possible to fill a washing-tub in the space of half an hour with lovely half-pound trout from a few pools on a burn near Moffat. But there are still plenty of trout; indeed there is a noted fisher who can fill his basket even in streams that, being near the large cities, have been too often fished; but then it is given to him to be a man of great skill in his vocation, and moreover capable of instructing others, for he has written a work that in some degree has revolutionised the art of angling.

The place to try an angler is a fine Border stream or a grand Highland loch; but I shall not presume to lay down minute directions as to *how* to angle, for an angler, like a poet, must be born, he can scarcely be bred, and no amount of book lore will confer upon a man the magic power of luring the wary trout from its crystalline home. The best anglers, and I may add fish-poachers, are the gipsies. A gipsy will raise fish when no other human being can move them. If encamped near a stream, a gipsy band are sure to have fish as a portion of their daily food; and how beautifully they can broil a trout or boil a grilse those only who have had the fortune to dine with them can say. Your gipsy is a rare good fisher, and with half a rod can rob the river of a few dozens of trout in a very brief space of time, and he can do so while men with elaborate "fishing machines," fitted up with costly tackle, continue to flog the water without obtaining more than a questionable nibble, just as if the fish knew that they were greenhorns, and took a pleasure in chaffing them. Mr. Cheek, who wrote a capital book for the guidance of what I may call Thames anglers, says that the best way to learn is to see other anglers at work—which is better than all the written instructions that can be given, one hour's practical information going farther than a folio volume of written advice. It is all in vain for men to fancy that a suit of new Tweeds, a fair acquaintance with Stoddart or Stewart, and a large amount of angling "slang," will make them fishers. There is more than that required. Besides the natural taste, there is wanted a large measure of patience and skill; and the proper place to acquire these best virtues of the angler is among the brawling hill streams of Scotland, or on the expansive bosom of some of the great Cumberland lakes, while trying for a few delicious charr. A congregation of fish brought together by means of a scatter of food and an angler's taking advantage of the piscine convention over its diet of worms, is no more angling than a battue is sport.　An American that I have heard of has a fish-manufactory in Connecticut, where he can shovel the animals out by the hundred ; but then he does not go in for sport, his idea—a thoroughly American one—is money !　But despite this exceedingly commercial idea, there are a few anglers in America, and as there are much water and many game fishes, there is plenty of sport.　In North America there are to be found in large quantities both the true salmon and the brook trout; and as a great number of the American fishes visit the fresh and salt water alternately, they, by reason of their strength and size, afford excellent employment either to the river or sea angler.　One of the best of the American fishes is called the Mackinaw salmon.

To come back, in the meantime, to Scotland and the trout, and where to find them, I may mention that that particular fish is the stock in trade of the streams and lochs of Scotland,—Scotland, the "land of the mountain and the flood,"—and there is an ever-abiding abundance of water, for the lochs and streams of that country are numberless.　One county alone (Sutherland, to wit) contains a thousand lochs, and one parish in that county has in it two hundred sheets of water, and all of these abounding with fine trout, affording rich sport to the angler—rewarding all who persevere with full baskets.　As I have already hinted, the fisher must study his locality and glean advice from well-informed residents.　The gipsies of a district can usually give capital advice as to the kind of bait that will please best.　Many a time have anglers been seen flogging away at a stream or lake that was troutless, or at their wit's end as to which of their flies would please the dainty palate of my lord the resident trout.　But I shall not further dogmatise on such matters ; most people who are given to angling are quite as wise as the writer of these remarks ; and there are as fine trout in England, I daresay, as there are in Scotland ; indeed there are a thousand streams in this Great

Britain, Ireland, and Wales of ours, where we càn find fish—
there are splendid trout even in the Thames. Then there are
the Dove and the Severn, as well as rivers that are much
farther away, so that on his second day from London an active
angler may be whipping the Spey for salmon, or trolling on
Loch Awe for the large trout that inhabit that sheet of water.

ANGLERS' FISHES.

1. Great lake trout (*Salmo ferox*).　　　2. *Salmo fario*.　　　3. Trout.

The change of scene is of itself a delight, no matter what river
the visitor may choose. At the same time the physical exertion undergone by the angler flushes his cheek with the hue
of health, and imparts to his frame a strength and elasticity
known only to such as are familiar with country scenes and
pure air. May and the Mayfly are held to inaugurate the
angler's year; for although a few of the keenest sportsmen
keep on angling all the year round, most of them lay down
their rod about the end of October, and do not think of again

resuming it till they can smell the sweet fragrance of the advancing summer. Although few of our busy men of law or commerce are able to forestall the regular holiday period of August and September, yet a few do manage a run to the country at the charming time of May, when the days are not too hot for enjoyment nor too short for country industry. In August and September the landscape is preparing for the sleep of winter, whilst in May it is being robed by nature for the fêtes of summer, and, despite the sneers of some poets and naturalists, is new and charming in the highest degree. Town living people should visit the country in May, and see and feel its industry, pastoral and simple as it is, and at the same time view the charms of its scenery in all its vivid freshness and fragrance.

Some anglers delight in pike-catching, others try for perch; but give me the trout, of which there is a large variety, and all worth catching. In Loch Awe, for instance, there is the great lake trout, which, combined with the beauty of the scenery, has sufficed to draw to that neighbourhood some of our best anglers. The trout of Loch Awe, as is well known, are very ferocious, hence their scientific name of *Salmo ferox*. This trout attains to great dimensions; individuals weighing twenty pounds have been often captured; but its flavour is indifferent and the flesh is coarse, and not of a prepossessing colour. This kind of trout is found in nearly all the large and deep lochs of Scotland. It was discovered scientifically about the end of last century by a Glasgow merchant, who was fond of sending samples of it to his friends as a proof of his prowess as an angler. The usual way of taking the great lake trout is to engage a boat to fish from, which must be rowed gently through the water. The best bait is a small trout, with at least half-a-dozen strong hooks projecting from it, and the tackle requires to be prodigiously strong, as the fish is a most powerful one, although not quite so active as some others of the trout kind, but it roves about in these deep waters enacting the parts of the bully and the cannibal to all lesser creatures, and driving before it even the hungry pike. Persons residing near the great lochs capture these large trout by setting night lines for them. As has been already mentioned, they are exceedingly voracious, and have been known to be dragged for long distances, and even after losing hold of the bait to seize it again with great eagerness, and so have been finally captured. These great lake trout are also to be found in other countries.

In Lochleven, at Kinross, in the county of Fife, twenty-two miles from Edinburgh, there will be found localised that beautiful trout which is peculiar to this one loch, and which I have already referred to as one of the mysterious fishes of Scotland. This fish—although its quality is said to have been degenerated by the drainage of the lake in 1830, at which period it was reduced by draining to a third of its former dimensions—is of considerable commercial value; it cannot be bought in Edinburgh under two shillings a pound weight; and if it was properly cultivated might yield a large revenue. I have not been able to obtain recent statistics of " the take" of Lochleven trout, but in former years during the seven months of the fishing season it used to range from fifteen thousand to twenty thousand pounds weight, and at the time referred to all trout under three-quarters of a pound in weight were thrown back into the water by order of the lessee. Eighty-five dozen of these fine trout have been known to be taken at a single haul, while from twenty to thirty dozen used to be a very common take. As to perch, they used to be caught in thousands. Little has or can be said about Lochleven trout, except that they are a speciality. Some learned people (but I take leave to differ from them) consider the Lochleven fish to be identical with *Salmo fario*, but never in any of my piscatorial wanderings have I found its equal in colour, flavour, or shape.

It has been compared with the *Fario Lemanus* of the Lake of Geneva, and having handled both fishes I must allow that there is very little difference between them; but still there are differ-. ences. Boats can be hired at Kinross for an hour or two's fishing on Lochleven. Mr. Barnet, the editor of the local paper, himself a keen fisher, will, I have no doubt, put gentlemen in the way of enjoying a day's pike or trout fishing on the loch.

I need not go over all the varieties of fresh-water trout *seriatim*, for their name is legion, and every book on angling contains lists of those that are peculiar to the districts treated upon. If anglers' fishes ever become valuable as food, it will be by the cultivation of our great lochs. With such a vast expanse of water as is contained in some of these lakes, and having ample river accommodation at hand for spawning purposes, there could be no doubt that artificial breeding, if properly gone about, would be successful. The Lochleven trout in particular might be made a subject of piscicultural experiment ; it is already of great money value commercially, and could be cultivated so as to become a considerable source of revenue to the proprietor of the lake and amusement to the angler.

There are some pretty big pike in Lochleven ; I lately examined a very large one, weighing sixteen pounds, that had been feeding very industriously on the dainty trout of the loch. As every angler knows, the pike affords capital sport, and may be taken in many different ways. Pike spawn in March and April, when the fish leaves its hiding-place in the deep water and retires for procreative purposes into shallow creeks or ditches. The pike yields a very large quantity of roe on the average, and the young fish are not long in being hatched. Endowed with great feeding power, pike grow rapidly from the first, attaining a length of twenty-two inches. Before that period a young pike is called a jack, and its increase of weight is at the rate of about four pounds a year when well supplied with food. The appetite of this fish is very great, and, from its being so fierce, it has been called the pirate of the rivers. It is not easily satisfied with food, and numerous extraordinary stories of the pike's powers of eating and digesting have been from time to time related. I remember, when at school at Haddington (seventeen miles from Edin-

JACK IN HIS ELEMENT.

burgh), of seeing a pike that inhabited a hole in the "Lang Cram" (a part of the river Tyne), which was nearly triangular in shape, supposed to be the exact pattern of its hiding-place, and which devoured every kind of fish or animal that came in its way. It was caught several times, but always managed to escape, and must have weighed at least twenty-five pounds. Upon one occasion it was hooked by a little boy, who fished for it with a mouse, when it rewarded him for his cleverness

by dragging him into the water; and had help not been at
hand the boy would· assuredly have been drowned, as the
water at that particular spot was deep.   As to the voracity of
this fish many particulars have been given.   Mr. Jesse, in
one of his works, says that a pike of the weight of five pounds
has been known to eat a hundred gudgeon in three weeks;
and I have myself seen them killed in the neighbourhood
of a shoal of parr, and, notwithstanding their rapidity of digestion, I have seen four or five fish taken out of the stomach of
each.   Mr. Stoddart, one of our chief angling authorities, has
calculated the pike to be amongst the most deadly enemies
of the infant salmon.   He tells us that the pike of the Teviot,
a tributary of the Tweed, are very fond of eating young smolts,
and says that, in a stretch of water ten miles long, where there
is good feeding, there will be at least a thousand pike, and
that these during a period of sixty days will consume about a
quarter of a million of young salmon!

One would almost suppose that some of the stories about
the voracity of pike had been invented; if only half of them
be true, this fish has certainly well earned its title of shark of
the fresh water.   There is, for instance, the well-known tale of
the poor mule, which a pike was seen to take by the nose and
pull into the water; but it is more likely I think that the
mule pulled out the pike.   Pennant, however, relates a story of
a pike that is known to be true.   On the Duke of Sutherland's
Canal at Trentham, a pike seized the head of a swan that was
feeding under water, and gorged as much of it as killed both.
A servant, perceiving the swan with its head below the surface for a longer time than usual, went to see what was wrong,
and found both swan and pike dead.   A large pike, if it has the
chance, will think nothing of biting its captor; there are several authentic instances of this having been done.   The pike is
a long-lived fish, grows to a large size, and attains a prodigious
weight.   There is a narrative extant about one that was said

to be two centuries and a half old, which weighed three hundred and fifty pounds, and was seventeen feet long. There is abundant evidence of the size of pike : individuals have been captured in Scotland, so we are told in the Scots Magazine, that weighed seventy-nine pounds. In the London newspapers of 1765 an account is given of the draining of a pool, twenty-seven feet deep, at the Lilishall Limeworks, near Newport, which had not been fished for many years, and from which a gigantic pike was taken that weighed one hundred and seventy pounds, being heavier than a man of twelve stone ! I have seen scores of pike which weighed upwards of half a stone, and a good many double that weight, but, as in the case of the salmon, the weight is now on the descending ratio, the giants of the tribe having been apparently all captured. Formerly there used to be great hauls of this fish taken out of the water. Whether or not a pike be good for food depends greatly on where it has been fed, what it has eaten, and how it has been cooked. In fact, as I have already endeavoured to show, the animals of the water are in respect of food not unlike those of the land—their flavour is largely dependent on their feeding ; and pike that have been luxuriating on Lochleven trout, or feeding daintily for a few months on young salmon, cannot be very bad fare. As a general rule, however, pike are not highly esteemed as a dish even when cooked *à la Walton*, who recommended them to be roasted, and basted during the process with claret, anchovies, and butter. Old Isaac says a dish of pike so prepared is too good for any but anglers or very honest men. The pike is a comparatively ugly fish as regards its shape, but at certain seasons is very brilliant in colour. It is extensively distributed, and is found over the greater part of Europe, and also in America and Asia The mascalogne, *Esox estor*, is the name of the largest American pike ; it is found only in the great lakes and waters of the St. Lawrence basin, and grows to a very large size, thirty pounds being a common enough weight, but individuals have been captured ranging from sixty to eighty pounds. The mascalogne, like all its tribe, is a bold and voracious fish. There is also the northern pickerel, another American pike, which does not grow so large as the above, but is quite as fierce and bold as our own pike ; and as the fish is not good for food, although an excellent game fish, affording no end of sport, I need not recommend the acclimatisation of any of these American savages.

The carp family (Cyprinidæ) is very numerous, embracing among its members the barbel, the gudgeon, the carp-bream, the white-bream, the red-eye, the roach, the bleak, the dace, and the well-known minnow. There is one of the family which is of a beautiful colour, and with which all are familiar—I mean the golden carp, which may be seen floating in its crystal prison in nearly every home of taste, and which swarms in the ponds at Hampton Court and in the tropical waters of the Crystal Palace at Sydenham. The gold and silver fish are natives of China, whence they were introduced into this country by the Portuguese about the end of the seventeenth century, and have become, especially of late years, so common as to be hawked about the streets for sale. In China, as we can read, every person of fashion keeps gold-fish by way of having a little amusement. They are contained either in the small basins that decorate the courts of the Chinese houses, or in porcelain vases made on purpose ; and the most beautiful kinds are taken from a small mountain-lake in the province of Che-Kyang, where they grow to a comparatively large size, some attaining a length of eighteen inches and a comparative bulk, the general run of them being equal in size to our herrings. These lovely fish afford great delight to the Chinese ladies, who tend and cultivate them with great care. They keep them in very large basins, and a common earthen pan is generally placed at the bottom of these in a reversed position, and so perforated with holes as to afford shelter to the fish from the heat and glare of the sun. Green stuff of some kind is also thrown upon the water to keep it cool, and it (the water) must be changed at least every two days, and the fish, as a general rule, must never be touched by the hand. Great quantities of gold-fish are often bred in ponds adjacent to factories, where the waste steam being let in the water is kept at a warmish temperature. At the manufacturing town of Dundee they became at one time a complete nuisance in some of the factories, having penetrated into the steam and water pipes, and occasionally brought the works to a complete stand. In England the golden carp usually spawns between May and July, the particular time being greatly regulated by the warmth of the season. The time of spawning may be known by the change of habit which occurs in this fish. It sinks at once into deep water instead of basking on the top, as usual ; previous to which the fish are restive and quick in their movements, throwing themselves out of the water, etc. It may be stated here, to prevent disappointment, that golden carp never spawn in a transparent vessel. When the spawn is hatched the fish are very black in colour, some darker than others : these become of a golden hue, while those of a lighter shade become silver-coloured. As is the case with the salmon, it is some time before this change occurs, some colouring at the end of one year, and others not till two or three seasons have come and gone. These beautiful prisoners seldom live long in their crystal cells, although the prison is beautiful enough, one would fancy :—

> " I ask, what warrant fixed them (like a spell
>   Of witchcraft fixed them) in the crystal cell ;
>   To wheel with languid motion round and round,
>   Beautiful, yet in mournful durance bound ?

> Their peace, perhaps, our slightest footstep marr'd,
> Or their quick sense our sweetest music jarr'd ;
> And whither could they dart, if seized with fear ?
> No sheltering stone, no tangled root was near.
> When fire or taper ceased to cheer the room,
> They wore away the night in starless gloom ;
> And when the sun first dawned upon the streams,
> How faint their portion of his vital beams !
> Thus, and unable to complain, they fared,
> While not one joy of ours by them was shared."

Gold-fish ought not to be purchased except from some very respectable dealer. I have known repeated cases where the whole of the fish bought have died within an hour or two of being taken home. These golden carp, which are reared for sale, are usually spawned and bred in warmish water, and they ought in consequence to be acclimatised or "tempered" by the dealer before they are parted with. Parties buying ought to be particular as to this, and ascertain if the fish they have bought have been *tempered*.

Returning to the common carp, I may speak of it as being a most useful pond-fish. It is a sort of vegetarian, and it may be classed among the least carnivorous fishes ; it feeds chiefly upon vegetables or decaying organic matter, and very few of them prey upon their kind, while some, it is thought, pass the winter in a torpid state. There is a rhyme which tells us that

> Turkeys, carp, hops, pickerel, and beer,
> Came into England *all* in one year.

But this couplet must, I think, be wrong, as some of these items were in use long before the carp was known ; indeed, it is not at all certain when this fish was first introduced into England, or where it was brought from, but I think it extremely possible that it was originally brought here from Germany. In ancient times there used to be immense ponds filled with carp in Prussia, Saxony, Bohemia, Mecklenburg, and Holstein, and the fish was bred and brought to market with as much regularity as if it had been a fruit or a vegetable. The carp yields its spawn in great quantities, no fewer than 700,000 eggs having been found in a fish of moderate weight (ten pounds); and, being a hardy fish, it is easily cultivated, so that it would be profitable to breed in ponds for the fishmarkets of populous places, and the fish-salesmen assure us that there would be a large demand for good fresh carp. It is necessary, according to the best authorities, to have the ponds in suites of three—viz., a spawning-pond, a nursery, and a receptacle for the large fish—and to regulate the numbers of breeding fish according to the surface of water. It is not my intention to go minutely into the construction of carp-ponds; but I may be allowed to say that it is always best to select such a spot for their site as will give the engineer as little trouble as possible. Twelve acres of water divided into three parts would allow a splendid series of ponds—the first to be three acres in extent, the second an acre more, and the third to be five acres; and here it may be again observed that, with water as with land, a given space can only yield a given amount of produce, therefore the ponds must not be overstocked with brood. Two hundred carp, twenty tench, and twenty jack per acre is an ample stock to begin breeding with. A very profitable annual return would be obtained from these twelve acres of water; and, as many country gentlemen have even larger sheets than twelve acres, I recommend this plan of stocking them with carp to their attention. There is only the expense of construction to look to, as an under-keeper or gardener could do all that was necessary in looking after the fish. A gentleman having a large estate in Saxony, on which were situated no less than twenty ponds, some of them as large as twenty-seven acres, found that his stock of fish added greatly to his income. Some of the carp weighed fifty pounds each, and upon the

occasion of draining one of his ponds, a supply of fish weighing
five thousand pounds was taken out ; and for good carp it
would be no exaggeration to say that sixpence per pound
weight could easily be obtained, which, for a quantity like
that of this Saxon gentleman, would amount to a sum of
£125 sterling.   Now, I have the authority of an eminent fish-
salesman for stating that ten times the quantity here indicated
could be disposed of among the Jews and Catholics of London
in a week, and, could a regular supply be obtained, an unlimited
quantity might be sold.

I have been writing about Highland streams and northern
lochs ; but the river scenery of England is, in its way, equally
beautiful, and no river is more charming than the Thames.
It is a classic stream, and its praises have been sung by the
poets and celebrated by the historian.   After Mrs. S. C. Hall
and Thorne, it were vain to repeat its praises :—

> " Glide gently, thus for ever glide,
>   O Thames ! that anglers all may see
>   As lovely visions by thy side,
>   As now, fair river, come to me.
>   Oh, glide, fair stream, for ever so
>   Thy quiet soul on all bestowing,
>   Till all our minds for ever flow
>   As thy deep waters are now flowing."

The Thames takes its rise in Gloucestershire, about three
miles from the town of Cirencester ; and at that place, and for
some miles of its course, it is known as the Isis, and not till
the waters of the Thame join it in Oxfordshire is it known as
the *Thames*.   This celebrated river is small at first, and flows
through some beautiful scenery and highly-cultivated country ;
its banks are studded with castles and palaces, beautiful towns
and snug villages ; while well-stored gardens and cultivated
fields give smiling evidence of plenty all along its course.
When we consider that the Thames flows past Windsor,

Hampton Court, and Richmond ; that it laves the grassy lawns of Twickenham, waters the gardens of Kew, and that it bears upon its bosom the gigantic commerce of London—we can at once realise its importance, and can understand its being called the king of British rivers, although it is neither so long, nor does it contain so voluminous a body of water as some other of our British streams. The total length of the river Thames is 215 miles, and the area of the country it waters is 6160 square miles. It has as affluents a great many fine streams, including the river Lodden, as also the Wey and the Mole. I am not entitled to consider it here in its picturesque aspects —my business with it is piscatorial, and I am able to certify that it is rich in fish of a certain kind—

> " The bright-eyed perch with fins of Tyrian dye,
> The silver eel in shining volumes rolled,
> The yellow carp in scales bedropp'd with gold,
> Swift trout diversified with crimson stains,
> And pike, the tyrants of the watery plains."

Considering that all its best fishing points are accessible to an immense population, many of whom are afflicted with a mania for angling, it is quite wonderful that there is a single fish of any description left in it ; and yet but a year or two ago, the " pen of the war" bagged a seven-pound trout near Walton Bridge ! I may be allowed just to run over a few Thames localities, and note what fish may be taken from them. Above Teddington at different places an occasional trout may be pulled out, but, although the finest trout in the world may be got in the Thames, they are, unfortunately, so scarce in the meantime, that it is hardly worth while to lose one's time in the all but vain endeavour to lure them from their home. Pike fishing or trolling will reward the Thames angler better than trouting. There are famous pike to be taken every here and there—in the deep pools and at the weirs : and, as the pike is voracious, a moderately good angler, with proper bait,

is likely to have some sport with this fish.   But the speciality
of the Thames, so far at least as most anglers are concerned,
is the quantity of fish of the carp kind which it contains, as
also perch.   This latter fish may be taken with great certainty
about Maidenhead, Cookham, Pangbourne, Walton, Labham,
and Wallingford Road ; and a kindred fish, the pope, in great
plenty, may be sought for in the same localities.   Then the
bearded barbel is found in greater plenty in the Thames than
anywhere else, and, as it is a fish of some size and of much
courage, it affords great sport to the angler.   The best way to
take the barbel is with the "Ledger," and the best places for
this kind of fishing are the deeps at Kingston Bridge, Sunbury
Lock, Halliford, Chertsey Weir, and in the deeps at Bray,
where many a time and oft have good hauls of barbel
been taken.   The best times for the capture of this fish are
late in the afternoon or very early in the morning.   Chub are
also plentiful in the Thames ; and Mr. Arthur Smith, who
wrote a guide to Thames anglers, specially recommended the
island above Goring for chub, also Marlow and the large island
below Henley Bridge.   This fish can be taken with the fly,
and gives tolerable sport.   The roach is a fish that abounds in
all parts of the Thames, especially between Windsor and Richmond ; and in the proper season—September and October—it
will be found in Teddington Weir, Sunbury, Blackwater,
Walton Bridge, Shepperton Lock, the Stank Pitch at Chertsey,
and near Maidenhead, Marlow, and Henley Bridges.   At
Teddington I may state that the dace is abundant, and there
is plenty of little fish of various kinds that can be had as bait
at most of the places we have named.   In fact, in the Thames
there is a superabundance of sport of its kind, and plenty of
accommodation for anglers, with wise fishermen to teach them
the art ; and although the best sport that can be enjoyed on
this lovely stream is greatly different from the trout-fishing of
Wales or Scotland, it is good in its degree, and tends to health

and high spirits, and an anxiety to excel in his craft, as one can easily see who ventures by the side of the water about Kew and Richmond.

> " With hurried steps,
> The anxious angler paces on, nor looks aside,
> Lest some brother of the angle, ere he arrive,
> Possess his favourite swim."

THAMES ANGLERS.—FROM AN OLD PICTURE.

I come now to the perch, a well-known because common fish, about which a great deal has been written, and which is easily taken by the angler. There are a great number of species of this fish, from the common perch of our own canals and lochs to the "lates" of the Nile, or the beautiful golden-tailed mesoprion, which swims in the seas of Japan and India and flashes out brilliant rays of colour. The perch was assiduously cultivated in ancient Italy, in the days when pisciculture was an adjunct of gastronomy, and was thought to equal the mullet in flavour. In Britain, the fish, left to its natural growth and no care being taken to flavour it artificially, is surpassed for table purposes by the salmon and the trout ; but perch being abundant afford plenty of good fishing. The perch usually congregate in small shoals, and delight in streams, or water with a clear bottom and with overhanging foliage to shelter them from the overpowering heats of summer. These fish do not attain any considerable weight, the one recorded as being taken in the Serpentine, in Hyde Park, which weighed nine pounds, being still the largest on record. Perch of three and four pounds are by no means rare, and those of one pound or so are quite common. The perch is a stupid kind of fish, and easily captured. Many of the foreign varieties of perch attain an immense weight. Some of the ancient writers tell us that the " lates" of the Nile attained a weight of three hundred pounds ; and then there is the vacti of the Ganges, which is often caught five feet long. The perch, after it is three years old, spawns about May. It may be described as rather a hardy fish, as we know it will live a long time out of water, and can be kept alive among wet moss, so that it may be easily transferred from pond to pond. Its hardy nature accounts for its being found in so many northern lochs and rivers, as in the olden times of slow conveyances it must have taken a long time to send the fish to the great distances we know it must have been carried to. On the Continent, living perch are a feature of nearly all the fishmarkets. The fish, packed in moss and occasionally sprinkled with water, are carried from the country to the cities, and if not sold are taken home and replaced in the ponds. This particular fish, which is very prolific, might be " cultivated" to any extent. We do not see why a fish-pond should not be as much a portion of a country gentleman's commissariat as his kitchen-garden or his cow-paddock. Perch are useful in more ways than are generally known. The Laplanders make glue and also jelly out of their skins. Exquisite dishes for fastidious gourmets can be concocted from their milts, and choice ornaments can be formed out of their scales. The sea-perch, as it is called (the basse), may be mentioned here. Some varieties of it are very plentiful on the coast of America, where they grow to a large size, and are much esteemed for their flavour. Another variety of the perch is the common pike-perch, which might be acclimatised with advantage in our seas, where it is at present unknown. It is common in the Danube and the Elbe, as also in the Caspian and Black Seas. It is a fish that grows rapidly and attains a considerable weight, and its flesh is most agreeable. It is surprising that no pains are taken to acclimatise new varieties of fish in Britain, although it could be easily accomplished. There is, for instance, the black basse of the Huron, which might be advantageously introduced; and there are many other fishes, both of the salt and fresh water, which would flourish in this country and add to our commissariat. I have chronicled in another place the introduction of the *Silurus glanis*, and I would have been only too glad to have recorded the introduction of a dozen other fish.

As I have said so much about the Scottish lochs, it would be but fair to say a few words about those of England; but in good honest truth it would be superfluous to descant at the present day on the beauties of Windermere, or the general lake scenery of Cumberland and Westmorland: it has been described by hundreds of tourists, and its praises have been sung by its own poets—the lake poets. It is with its fish that we have business, and honesty compels us to give the charr a bad character. It is not by any means a game fish, so far as sport is concerned; nor is it great in size or rich in flavour. But potted charr is a rare breakfast delicacy. This fish, which is said by Agassiz to be identical with the ombre chevalier of Switzerland, is rarely found to weigh more than a pound; specimens are sometimes taken exceeding that weight,

but they are scarce. The charr is found to be pretty general
in its distribution, and is found in many of the Scottish lochs.
It spawns about the end of the year, some of the varieties
depositing their eggs in the shallow parts of the lake, while
others proceed a short way up some of the tributary streams.
In November great shoals of charr may be seen in the rivers
Rothay and Brathay, particularly the latter, with the view of
spawning. The charr, we are told by Yarrell, afford but scant
amusement to the angler, and are always to be found in the
deepest parts of the water in the lochs which they inhabit.
"The best way to capture them is to trail a very long line
after a boat, using a minnow for a bait, with a large bullet of
lead two or three feet above the bait to sink it deep in the
water; by this mode a few charr may be taken in the beginning of summer, at which period they are in the height of
perfection both in colour and flavour."

As I am on the subject of anglers' fishes, the reader will
perhaps allow me to suggest that "no end of sport" may be
obtained in the sea; that capital sea-angling may be enjoyed
all the year round, and all round the British coasts; and that
there are fighting fishes in the waters of the great deep that
will occasionally try both the cunning and the nerve of the
best anglers. The greatest charm of sea-angling, however, lies
in its simplicity, and the readiness with which it can be
engaged in, together with the comparatively homely and inex-
pensive nature of the instruments required. A party living at
the seaside can either fish off the rocks or hire a boat, and
purchase or obtain the loan (for a slight consideration) of such
simple tackle as is necessary; though it must not be too
simple, for even sea-fish will not stand the insult of supposing
they can be caught as a matter of course with anything; and
as the larger kinds of hooks are often scarce at mere fishing
villages, it is better to carry a few to the scene of action.

"Well then, what sport does the sea afford?" will most

likely be the first question put by those who are unacquainted with sea-angling. I answer, anything and everything in the shape of fish or sea-monster, from a sprat to a whale. This is literally true. It is not an unfrequent occurrence for tourists in Orkney, or other places in Scotland, to assist at a whale-battue; and some of my readers may remember a very graphic description of an Orcadian whale-hunt, given in *Blackwood's Magazine* a few years ago, by the late Professor Aytoun, who was Sheriff and Admiral of Orkney. The kind of sea-fish, however, that are most frequently taken by the angler, both on the coasts of England and Scotland, are the whiting, the common cod, the beautiful poor or power cod, and the mackerel; there is also the abundant coal-fish, or sea-salmon as I call it, from its handsome shape. This fish is taken in amazing quantities, and in all its stages of growth. It is known by various names, such as sillock, piltock, cudden, poddly, etc.; indeed most of our fishes have different names in different localities; but I shall keep to the proper name so as to avoid mistakes. The merest children are able, by means of the roughest machinery, to catch any quantity of young coal-fish; they can be taken in our harbours, and at the sea-end of our piers and landing-places. The whiting is also very plentiful, so far as angling is concerned, as indeed are most of the Gadidæ. It feeds voraciously, and will seize upon anything in the shape of bait; several full-grown pilchards have been more than once taken from the stomach of a four-pound fish. Whiting can be caught at all periods of the year, but it is of course most plentiful in the breeding season, when it approaches the shores for the purpose of depositing its spawn—that is in January and February. The common cod-fish is found on all parts of our coast, and the sea-anglers, if they hit on a good locality—and this can be rendered a certainty—are sure to make a very heavy basket.

The pollack, or, as it is called in Scotland lythe, also affords capital sport; and the mackerel-herring and conger-eel can also be taken in considerable quantities. I can strongly recommend the lythe-fishing to gentlemen who are *blasés* of salmon or pike, or who do not find excitement even among the birds of lone St. Kilda. Then, as will afterwards be described,

THE ANGLER FISH.

there is the extensive family of the flat fish, embracing brill, plaice, flounders, soles, and turbot. The latter is quite a classic fish, and has long been an object of worship among gastronomists; it has been known to attain an enormous size. Upon one occasion an individual, which measured six feet across, and weighed one hundred and ninety pounds, was caught near Whitby. The usual mode of capturing flat fish is by means of the trawl-net, but many varieties of them may be caught with a hand-line. A day's sea-angling will be chequered by many little adventures. There are various minor monsters of the deep that vary the monotony of the day by occasionally devouring the bait. A tadpole-fish, better known as the sea-devil or "the angler," may be hooked, or the fisher may have a visit from a hammer-headed shark or a pile-fish, which adds greatly to the excitement; and if "the dogs" should be at all plentiful, it is a chance if a single fish be got out of the sea in its integrity. So voracious are this species of the Squalidæ, that I have often enough pulled a mere skeleton into the boat, instead of a plump cod of ten or twelve pounds weight.

I shall now say a few words about the machinery of cap-ture. The tackle in use for handline sea-fishing is much the same everywhere, and that which I de-scribe will suit almost any locality. It 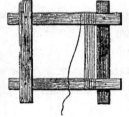 consists of a frame of four pieces of wood-work about a foot and a half in length, fastened together in the shape of such a machine as ladies use for certain worsted work. Round this is wound a thin cord, generally tanned, of from ten to twenty fathoms in length. To the extreme end of this line is attached a leaden sinker, the weight of which varies according as the current of the tide

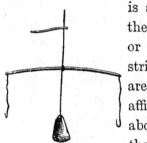 is slow or rapid. About two feet above the sinker is a cross piece of whalebone or iron, to the extremities of which the strings on which the hooks are dressed are attached. Sometimes a third hook is affixed to an outrigger, about two feet above the other hooks. The length of the cords to which the lower hooks are attached should be such as to allow them to hang about six inches higher than the bottom of the sinker. In some parts of the Western Highlands a rod consisting of thin fir is used, but from the length of line required it is rather a

clumsy instrument, as after the fish has been struck the rod
has to be laid down in the boat, and the line to be hauled in
by hand.

As to bait, it is quite impossible to lay down any strict
rule. The bait which is the favourite in one bay or bank
is scouted by the fish of other localities. At times almost
anything will do : numbers of mackerel have been taken with
a little bit of red cloth attached to the hook ; on certain
occasions the fish are so voracious that they will swallow
the naked iron ! On the English coasts, and among the
Western Islands of Scotland, the most deadly bait that is
used is boiled limpets, which require to be partially chewed by
the fisher before placing them on the hooks ; in other places
mussels are the favourites, and in others the worms procured
among the mud of the shore. The limpet has this one advantage, that it is easily fixed on the hook, and keeps its hold
tenaciously. A very excellent bait for the larger kinds of fish
is the soft parts of the body of small crabs, which are gathered
for that purpose at low tide under the stones ; a good place for
procuring them is a mussel-bed. The best time for fishing is
immediately before ebb or flow. The hooks being baited, the
line is run over the side of the boat until the lead touches the
bottom, when it is drawn up a little, so as to keep the baits
out of reach of the crabs, who gnaw and destroy both bait
and tackle. The line is held firmly and lightly outside the
boat, the other hand, inside the boat, also having a grip of
the line. The moment a fish is felt to strike, the line is
jerked down by the hand inside, thus bringing it sharply
across the gunwale and fixing the hook. A little experience
will soon enable the angler to determine the weight of the
fish, and according as it is light or heavy must he quickly or
slowly haul in his line. When the fish reaches the surface,
he should, if practicable, seize it with his hand, as it is apt,
on feeling itself out of water, to wriggle off. A landing-clip

or gaff, such as is used in salmon-fishing, is useful, as, in the event of hooking a conger or a ray, there is much difficulty, and even some danger.

In fishing for lythe—the most exciting of all sea-angling —a very strong cord is used, on which, in order to prevent the fouling of the line, one or two stout swivels are attached. The hooks also cannot be too strong; those used for cod or ling fishing are very suitable. The baits in general use are the body of a small eel, about half a foot in length, skinned and tied to the shaft; or a strip of red cloth, or a red or white feather similarly attached. A piece of lead is fixed on the line at a short distance above the hook.

The boat must be rowed or sailed at a moderate rate, and from five or ten fathoms of the line allowed to trail behind. The boat end of the line should be turned once or twice round the arm, and held tightly in the hand; if the line were fastened to the boat, there is every chance that a large lythe—and they are frequently caught upwards of thirty pounds weight— would snap the tackle. The fish, when hooked, gives considerable play, and rather strongly objects to being lifted into the boat. The clip or gaff is in this case always necessary. In fishing for lythe, mackerel and dogfish are not unfrequently caught. The best place for prosecuting this sport is in the neighbourhood of a rocky shore; and the best times of the day are the early morning and evening. This fish will also take readily during any period of a dull but not gloomy day.

The most amusing kind of sea-angling is fly-fishing for small lythe and saithe (coal-fish). The tackle is exceedingly simple : a rod consisting of a pliant branch about eight feet in length ; a line of light cord of the same length, and a small hook roughly busked with a small white, red, or black feather.

The fly is dragged on the surface as the boat is rowed along, and the moment the fish is struck it is swung into the boat. The fry of the lythe and saithe may also be fished for from rocks and pier-heads, using the same tackle. A very ingenious plan for securing a number of these little fish is carried on in the Firth of Clyde and elsewhere. A boat similar in shape to a salmon-coble, with a crew of two—one to row and one to fish—goes out along the shore in the evening, when the sea is perfectly calm or nearly so. The fisher has charge of half-a-dozen rods or more, similar to the one already mentioned. These rods project across the square stern of the boat, and their near ends are inserted into the interstices of a seat of wattled boughs, on which the fisher sits, not steadily, but bumping gently up and down, communicating a trembling motion to the flies. The course of the coble is always close in shore, and, if the fish are taking well, the same ground may be fished over many times during the course of the evening.

As to set-line-fishing, it can only be practised in places where the tide recedes to a considerable distance. The cord used is of no defined length, and at certain distances along its entire extent are affixed corks to prevent the hooks sinking in the sand or mud. The shore-end is generally anchored to a stone, and the further end fastened to the top of a stout staff firmly fixed in the beach, and generally attached also to a stone to prevent it drifting ashore in the event of being loosened from its socket. From the staff almost to the shore, hooks are tied along the line at distances of a yard. The hooks are baited at low tide, and on the return of next low tide the line is examined. This is neither a satisfactory nor sure method of fishing, as many of the fish wriggle themselves free, and clear the hook of the bait, and many, after being caught, fall a prey to dogfish, etc., so that the disappointed fisher, on examining his line, too often finds a row of baitless hooks, alternating with the half-devoured bodies of haddocks, fiounders, saithe, and other shore fish.

I may just name another mode of obtaining sport, which is by spearing flat fish, such as flounders, dab, plaice, etc.   No rule can be laid down on this method of fishing. It has been carried on successfully by means of a common pitchfork, but some gentlemen go the length of having fine spears made for the purpose, very long and with very sharp prongs; others, again, use  a three-pronged farm-yard "graip," which has been known to do as much real work as more elaborate utensils specially contrived for the purpose.   The simplest directions I can give to those who try this style of fishing are just to spear all the fish they can see, but the general plan is to stab in the dark with the kind of instrument delineated above.   At the mouths of most of the large English rivers there is usually abundance of all the minor kinds of flat fish.

Lobsters and crabs can be taken at certain rocky places of the coast ; mussels can be picked from the rocks, and cockles can be dug for in the sand.   Shrimps can also be taken, and various other wonders of the sea and its shores may be picked up.   After a storm a great number of curious fishes and shells 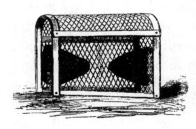 may be gathered, and some of these are very valuable as specimens of natural history.   The apparatus for capturing lobsters and crabs is like a cage, and is generally made of wicker work, with an aperture at the top or the side for the animal to enter by ; it can be baited with any sort of garbage that is at hand. Having been so baited, the lobster-pot is sunk into the water, and left for a season, till, tempted by the mess within, the game enters and is

M

caged. Those who would induce crabs to enter their pots must set them with fresh bait; lobsters, on the other hand, will look at nothing but garbage. Very frequently rock-cod, saithe, and other fish, are found to have entered the pots, intent both on foul and fresh food. Shell-fish for bait can be taken by means of a wooden box or old wicker basket sunk near a rocky place, and filled with garbage of some kind ; the whelks and small crabs are sure to patron-ise the mass extensively, and can thus be obtained at con-venience. It is impossible to tell in the limits of a brief chapter one-half of the fishing wonders that can be accomplished during a sojourn at the seaside. A visit to some quaint old fishing town, on the recurrence of "the year's vacation sabbath," as some of our poets now call the annual month's holiday, might be made greatly productive of real knowledge ; there are ten thousand wonders of the shore which can be studied besides those laid down in books.

As will be noted, I have avoided as much as possible the naming of localities, preferring to state the general practice. In all seaside towns and fishing villages there are usually three or four old fishermen who will be glad to do little favours for the curious in fish lore—to hire out boats, give the use of tackle, and point out good localities in which to fish. For such as have a few weeks at their disposal, I would sug-gest the western sea-lochs of Scotland as affording superb sport in all the varieties of sea-angling. Fish of all kinds, great and small, are to be found in tolerable quantity, and there is likewise the still greater inducement of fine scenery, cheap lodgings, and moderate living expenses. But the entire change of scene is the grand medicine ; nothing would do an exhausted London or Manchester man more good than a month on Lochfyne, where he could not only angle in the great water for amusement, but also watch the commercial fishers, and enjoy the finely-flavoured herring of that loch as a

portion of his daily food. If persons in search of sea-angling
wish to combine the enjoyment of picturesque scenery with
their pleasant labours on the water, they cannot do better
than select, as I did, the rural village of Corry, on the Island
of Arran, as a centre from which to conduct their operations.

May I be allowed to say a few words about this wonderful
island, just by way of a whet to the eye-appetite of those who
have never seen it? Our angler, having arrived at Glasgow,
can go down the Clyde by steamboat direct to Arran. There
is another and a quicker way—viz. by railway to Ardossan
and steamboat to Brodick, but most strangers prefer the
river; and let me say here, without fear of contradiction, there
is no pleasure river equal to the Clyde, especially as regards
accessibility. The steamers from Glasgow peer at stated intervals into every nook and cranny of the water, and, on
the Saturdays especially, deposit perfect armies of people at
various towns and villages below Greenock, who are thus enabled to pass the Sunday in the bright open air by the clear
waters of this great stream. Any kind of lodging is put up
with for the sake of being " down the water;" and all sorts of
people—merchants even of high degree and " Glasgow bodies"
of lower social standing—are contented, chiefly no doubt at
the instigation of their better halves, to sojourn in places that
when at home they would think quite unsuitable for even the
Matties of their households. The banks of the Clyde have
become wonderfully populous within the last twenty-five
years—villages have expanded into towns, hamlets have
grown into villages, and single cottages into hamlets. Now
the railway to Greenock is insufficient as a daily travelling aid
to persons whose half hours are of large commercial value; and
as a consequence, a new line of rails has been constructed to
come upon the water at Wemyss Bay, about twelve miles below Greenock. To your thorough business man time is money,
and if he is alternately able to leave his place of business and

his place of pleasure half an hour later each way, he is all the better pleased with both.   To speculators in want of an idea I would say : Rush to the Clyde, and buy up every inch of land that can be had within a mile of the water, build upon it, and from the half million of human beings who tenant Glasgow and the surrounding towns I will engage to find two competing occupants for every house that can be put up.   Building has progressed even in Arran, and this too in despite of the late Duke of Hamilton's dislike to strangers, so that there is now a population on the island of about 6000.   A friend of mine says that such an important entity as a duke has no right to do as he likes with his own, and consequently that Arran ought to be built upon, and the blackcocks and other game birds be left to take their chance.   Even with such limited accommodation as can be now obtained, Arran is a delightful summer residence ; were it to be generally built upon, it would realise from ground-rents alone an annual fortune to his Grace the Duke of Hamilton, who owns the greater part of it, and he might have capital shooting into the bargain.

Arran, I may state to all who are ignorant of the fact, is a very paradise for geologists ; and amateur globe-makers— persons who think they are better at constructing worlds than the Great Architect who preceded them all—are particularly fond of that island, being, as they suppose, quite able to find upon it *materiel* sufficient for the erection of the largest possible "theories."   Figures, it is said, can be made to prove either side of a cause ; so can stones.   Each geologist can build up his own pet world from the same set of rocks ; and so active geologists proceed to stucco over with their own compositions—" adumbrate " a friend calls the process— the sublime works of the greatest of all designers.   None of the sciences have given rise to so much controversy as the science of geology.   I make no pretensions to much geologic

knowledge, although I do know a little more than the man
who wondered if the granite boulders which he saw on a
brae-side were on their way up or down the hill, and argued
that it was a moot point. What I would like to see would
be a good work on geology, divested entirely of the learned
and scientific slang which usually make such books entirely
useless to ninety-nine out of every hundred persons who
attempt to read them. I would like, moreover, a work that
would not bully us with a ready-made theory.

Arran is a rugged island, and, as I have said, is full of
interesting and almost unique geologic features. There is a
mountain upon it which it is a kind of necessity for all
visitors to ascend. It is called Goatfell—its proper name
being Goath-Bhein, or hill of winds. At Corry I was told of
persons who had ascended Goatfell and come down again—
the mountain is 2865 feet high—in less than three hours ;
but I very soon found that I could not do the going up from
Corry in that period of time, not to speak of the coming down,
which to some people, especially if, like myself, they carry
about with them a solid weight of fourteen stones, is still more
fatiguing ; but then I had the disadvantage of a wet forenoon,
necessitating an occasional sojourn beneath a granite boulder
in order that *we*—that is, myself and a friend who essayed the
ascent with me—might keep ourselves tolerably dry. It was
toilsome, too, wading up to the knees in heather, even
although the heather was in its fullest bloom ; but by perseverance and the good guiding of an intelligent shepherd
whom we took with us as a guide, and who knew the best
paths, we did in time reach the top, and must confess that we
obtained upon our arrival an exceeding rich reward, the view
from the summit being very grand and extensive, embracing
what I may be allowed to call a sublimely-painted diorama of
portions of the three kingdoms.

It would be commonplace indeed to say of the view from

the top of Goatfell that it was either beautiful, picturesque, or sublime, for it is grand—I might say a mysterious combination of all these qualities; for it cannot be contemplated without a certain feeling of awe gradually becoming incidental to the situation. We obtain, first of all, in the distance, a faint and dreamlike view of mountains in Ireland, —away, however, over a far expanse of sea. Nearer at hand, looking another way, the giant crag of Ailsa rises perpendicular from the water, and we can almost hear the screaming of the myriads of wild fowl which float over it like a cloud. Then at our feet lie in rich profusion the green islands of the Clyde—Bute and the Cumbraes close at hand ; Argyle, with its lovely bays of glassy water, farther away ; and more distant still, the cragged peaks of Skye. Opening up from all parts of the river, which glitters brilliantly in the sun, there may be discovered glimpses of lovely scenery—hill-tops melting into clouds, and lofty mountains so abundantly clothed with wood that the very branches dip into the water. Here and there, distance no doubt lending enchantment to the view, we can see deep glens and gloomy ravines, with trickling brooks and a rare wealth of foliage, penetrated ever and anon by flashing sunbeams that light up the picture for a moment and then leave it darker and grander than before. Pastoral hill-sides too we can see covered with kine ; while every here and there steamboats dot the water and show their hazy trail of smoke. Lochfyne, covered with tiny skiffs, is in view, the waters yielding up their wealth of nourishment to the industrious fisherman. There too are the winding Kyles of Bute, as much worthy of being immortalised in verse as the well-sung Isles of Greece. The eye loves to linger on the soft-looking waters of the inland seas ; and again and again we gaze upon the Cobbler as he keeps watch over the waters of Loch Long, or scan the placid expanse of Lochfyne.

The late Miss Catharine Sinclair very happily said

that a portion of Lochfyne is fine only in name, and I can
well agree with her while looking at the rocky sides of
Cantyre ; but giving reins to the imagination, we can fill up
the scene and picture the savages of a few thousand years
ago fishing from the rocks with their bone-tipt spears, and
hauling the produce of their skill out of the waters with
rough branches of trees ; and, as time flies onward, we can
note in our mind's eye the rude canoes as they progress into
ships becoming instruments of commerce and tokens of civilisation.　At our very feet are the immense masses of granite
that form the mountain on which we stand ; and near at
hand, towering up alongside, are the cones of two other hills,
forming with Goatfell a silent council of three that seem to
be ever engaged in mysterious communing.　The silence on
the mountain-tops is wonderful, indeed oppressive : there is not
a sound to relieve the ear except perhaps a roar of water,
howling and hissing and boiling in endless torture in one of
the valleys ; and as the wind fitfully moans as it soughs adown
some weird vale, half hidden from us by the clouds that float
over it, the scene looks

> " So wondrous wild, the whole might seem
> The scenery of a fairy dream."

Looking around, one could feel that the island has a
history, if we could but ascertain it.　Books have been
written about Arran, and the stone period and the metal-
lurgic period, as illustrated by the antiquities of the place,
have been canvassed with a keen zest ; in fact, Arran is, if
that be possible, more interesting to the antiquary than the
geologist.　Its chambered cairns and cromlechs are silent
monuments of great events, as also are its standing-stones ;
and the place is rich in those grey monoliths that would speak
to us, if we could but interpret their silent eloquence, of deeds
achieved ages ago by the valiant warriors of a long past time.

There are vestiges of a prehistoric age in Arran that indicate a population as long before the Celtic period as that age preceded our own. There have doubtless been heroes on Mauchrie Moor worthy to have their praises sung in Ossianic strains; for scattered all over the island there are marks and tokens and scathed ruins that give rise to profound speculations as to the past history of this dark and mountainous island. And the irresistible conclusion of any amount of imagining is, that Arran is not alone the paradise of the geologist, but is the heaven of the botanist as well, while the antiquary may find in its moors and glens rich memorials indicating even in the present age the great and troubled life which the huge mass of rock and its gigantic and peaked protuberances have passed through as time with an invisible pencil was recording its history.

Having sufficiently studied the changing scenery, and rested and refreshed ourselves with some oat cakes and whisky, my friend proposed that we should do our speculation on the geology and history of the island at home over the dinner-table, or under the mild influence of the cup that not inebriates. This was a sensible proposal, especially as the rain was becoming more than a mere indication, and the shepherd, who knew the dangers of the hill-top in wet clothes, impatient; so I gave way, the more especially as beautiful views do not last for ever: the bright scene fades and the colours deaden—the sea looks gloomy, the mists gather, the rain falls, and the wind dashes the falling water rudely in our face, giving us warning to hurry away before worse befalls us.

When we again reached the plateau from which the rocky dome of Goatfell takes its rise, the fair sun once more shone out, and we had to note the botanical wealth of the island, and especially how rich in heaths and ferns are the slopes of the mountain. Indeed the same may be said of all the Clyde

islands. Cantyre is rich in ferns also. A botanical friend,
while I was lingering on a recent occasion in a bend of Lochfyne, waiting for that prince of river steamers the newest *Iona*,
picked up in a few minutes seven different varieties, and told
me that he had no doubt of finding double that number had
we had time to look for them. Our shepherd guide, while
descending with us from the mountain, seemed to hint that
the reason why Arran was not more generally allowed to be
built upon by the late duke was because of the game. I had
heard before that the duke thought of keeping the Island of
Arran as a gigantic game-preserve ; indeed it is admirably
suited for such a purpose, having an area of 165 square miles,
and being entirely isolated from any poaching population.
Our guide, on being asked, was quite of my opinion as to the
declining grouse supplies : we are overshooting our game birds
in the very same way as we have been overfishing our salmon.
Where are the grouse? can only be answered by the death-
dealing brigade of sportsmen, gamekeepers, and gillies, who
every "twelfth" assemble on the hills and moors to perform
their annual shooting task. The grand brag over all the
cohort of guns is who will have the biggest bag ; and now,
what with overshooting and the mysterious disease that ever
and anon attacks the birds, we are likely to run out of grouse.
What a calamity ! not only to real sportsmen, but to all others
who have extensive tracts of moor or mountain land, the only
wealth of which has hitherto been the stock of game. Once
upon a time the capercailzie abounded in the Island of Arran,
and in many places of Scotland besides ; but that bird has long
been very scarce, and renewed attempts to breed it have not
as yet resulted in any great success. The wild boar was at
one time also to be found on the island, and there are still a
few wild deer that rush with fleet steps about the mountain-
sides ; and on rare occasions, although not very lately, eagles
have been seen on the mountain-tops, where ptarmigan are

yet occasionally found.   Arran is lavishly populated with grouse and black game, while on the lowland parts partridges and pheasants have been bred by the duke.

We were exceedingly glad, after our hot and toilsome forenoon's work, to refresh our bodies with cold water, and then to sit down to our homely dinner of stewed mutton and well-boiled potatoes, which, it is needless to say, we ate with decided relish.   During this rest we became still better acquainted with our landlady.   She had passed nearly all her life on the island as a domestic servant, and now, when she had fallen into "the sere the yellow leaf," she had, by "good speaking," and the payment of a rent of one pound a year, obtained permission to reside in her present little cottage, which, when it was handed over to her, was ruined and roofless : she had, therefore, to put on a straw roof, and is bound to keep it in repair.   "How did she live ?" my friend asked.   "Well, sir, I don't live very well ; I'm not in good health and can't see to do much with my needle.   I have some sewing work at which I can earn a penny a day.   It is called 'veining,' and is used to trim ladies' underclothing.   Occasionally I let my bit place to Glasgow gentlemen, who come down by the Saturday steamboat.   The few shillings that I will get from you, if you stay out the week, will be money to me.   A gentlemen living in Edinburgh is kind enough to pay my rent, and when my beds are let, I sleep in the garret."   Such are the short and simple annals of the poor; and I could not help being impressed with this example of patient womanhood, who, rather than be a recipient of parish relief, would toil on from day to day, acting over again Hood's song of the shirt, in order to the earning of a "sair-won penny fee."

I have just indicated by the little story of this woman the one drawback of the island—the scarcity of house accommodation, and consequently of good lodgings.   To give my readers a practical idea of how matters stand, let me relate

the experience of my last visit, when, accompanied by the same
friend, I made a hurried run down to the island one Saturday
evening to make some inquiries anent the Western herring-
fishery.

We had been landed from the steamboat on a massive
grey boulder, on the sides of which, thick as was the atmosphere, we observed dozens of limpets and crowds of " buckies,"

CORRY HARBOUR.

and other sea-ware, giving us token of ample employment
when we could obtain leisure for a more minute survey of
the rocks and stray stones which sprinkle the sea-beach of
Corry.   In the meantime, that is just after landing, the great,
the momentous question on this and every other Saturday
night is—is *the* inn full ?   A hurried scramble over the jagged
stones, and a rush past the very picturesque residence of Mr.
Douglas' pigs, brought us to the inn, and at once decided the

question. Mrs. Jamison, the landlady, shook her lawn-
bedizened head—the inn, alas, *was* full, overflowing in fact,
for a gentleman had engaged the coach-house! It was feared,
too, that every house in the village was in a like predicament,
and further inquiry soon confirmed this to us rather awful
statement, and so I was left standing at the inn-door, with
a bitingly shrewd companion, to solve this problem—Given the
barest possible accommodation throughout all Corry for only
forty-eight strangers, how to shake fifty into the village, so
that each might have somewhere to lay his head? This is a
problem, I suspect, that few can answer. What was to be
done? The steamboat had gone! Were we then to tramp on
to Brodick, with more than a suspicion of a rainy night in the
moist atmosphere, or try a shake-down of clean straw in a
lime quarry? It might have come to that, and as both of us
had before then camped out for a night by the sheltered side
of a haystack, we might have arranged, fortified by the aid of
a dram, or perhaps two, to pass a tolerable night in the lime
cavern beside a very canny-looking horse-of-all-work that we
caught a glimpse of through the gloom of the place while
peeping into it.

But a Douglas to the rescue! And who is Douglas? it
will be asked. Well, the ever-active Douglas in his own person combines the offices of boatman, quarrier, postman,
butcher, grocer, and general merchant, and is, in fact, to use a
Scotch phrase, the "Johnny A'things" of the village—a dealer
in—

> "Meal, barley, butter, and cheese ;
> Soap, starch, blue, and peas ;
> Train-oil, tobacco, pipes, and teas ;
> And whisky and loch leeches."

It fortunately occurred that a modest maiden lady, a very
"civil-spoken" woman indeed, by name Grace Macalister, had
been disappointed of two Glasgow gentlemen, who had engaged

her whole house, and so the two benighted travellers from the east were accepted, at the instigation of the aforesaid Mr. Douglas, in lieu of them. Taking possession of our lodgings at once, we formed ourselves into a committee of supply, which resulted in a prompt expenditure of a sum of six shillings and threepence, the particulars of which, for the benefit of my readers, and to show how primitive we had all at once become, I beg to subjoin—namely, bread, 7d. ; mutton, 2s. 4d. ; butter, 6½d. ; tea, 6d. ; sugar, 3d. ; milk, ½d. ; herring, 2d. This sum, with eighteenpence added for whisky, threepence for potatoes, and one penny for a candle, represented the total commissariat expenses of two persons in Corry for five wholesome but homely meals. Our bed cost us one shilling each per night, and our attendance and washing were charged at the rate of a shilling a day, so long as we used the Hotel Macalister, but even this did not very much swell the grand total of the bill, which, at such rates, was by no means heavy at the end of our holiday ramble over Arran, especially when it is considered that the Arran season does not very greatly exceed one hundred days. Our quarters were certainly primitive enough—namely, half of a thatched cottage, or rather hut we may call it, consisting of one apartment containing two beds, four chairs, a small table, and a little cupboard. The beds were curtained by a series of blue striped cotton fragments of three different patterns of an old Scotch kind, and the walls were papered with five different kinds of paper ; but the low roof was the greatest treat of all—it was covered with old numbers of the *Witness* newspaper, at the time when it was edited by Hugh Miller, and these had, no doubt, been left in the cottage by previous travellers. The floor was covered with fragments of canvas laid down as a carpet. Many tourists would perhaps turn up their noses at this humble cottage, but to my friend and myself it was a delightful change.

I have not space in which to particularise all the beauties

of Arran, but I must say a word or two about Glen Sannox.
Near the golden beach of Sannox Bay is situated the solitary
churchyard of Corry, with its long grass waving rank over the
graves, and its borders of fuchsias laden with brilliant blos-
soms.   There was, we observed, on peeping over the wall, a
new-made grave, that of an orphan girl who had been drowned
while bathing.   Passing the churchyard—there was once a
church at the place, but all trace of it, save one stone built
into the wall of the churchyard, has long passed away—we
came upon a brawling stream, which led us up to the ruins of
what had been a barytes-mill.   The stones lay around in great
masses, as if they had been suddenly undermined by the passing stream, and had fallen cemented as they stood.   In a year
or two they will be grown over with weeds, and in a century
hence some persons may ingeniously speculate on the ruins,
and give a learned disquisition as to what building once stood
there, and its uses.   My friend and I wondered what it had
been, but an old man told us all about it; and, strange to say,
in the course of conversation, we found this old resident reciting
scraps of Ossian's poems.   He told us, too, that the bard had
died in the very parish in which we were standing.   He believed Ossian to have been a great priest and teacher of the
people, and this was an idea that was quite new to us.   We
had heard before, or rather read, that the poet was by some
esteemed a great warrior, and by others a necromancer—perhaps to esteem him a teacher is right enough ; his poems, at
any rate, were at one time as familiar in the mouths of the
West Highlanders as household words.

  The scenery of Arran would certainly inspire a poet.   As
we penetrated into Glen Sannox it became most interesting,
whether we noted the brawling and bubbling brook, or the
rich carpet of heath and wild flowers upon which we trod.
The luxuriance of its wild flowers is remarkable, and of its
rabbits equally so.   As we proceed up the glen, the lofty hills

with their granitic scars frown down upon us, and one with a
coroneted brow looks kingly among the others, as the mist
floats upon their shoulders, like a waving mantle, and with their
bold and rugged precipices they seem as if they had just been
suddenly shot out from the bosom of the earth.　Glen Sannox
is sublime indeed ; its magnitude is remarkable, and it is so
hemmed in with hills as to look at once, even without any
details, or the aid of history, a fitting hiding-place for the
gallant Bruce and his devoted followers.　About three miles
north from this glen we can view—and, we venture to say, not
without astonishment—the falling fragments of the broken
mountain ; a stream of large stones that lie crowded on the
declivity of the hill, till they in one long trail reach the ocean.
But to enumerate a tithe even of the scenic and antiquarian
beauties of the island would require—nay, it has obtained, and
more than once—a volume.　I could dwell upon the blue
rock near Corry, and picture the overhanging cliffs of the
neighbourhood mantled o'er with ivy.　The visitor might
enter some of the caves which have been scooped out by the
sea, or wander among the rock pools of the indented shore,
rich with treasures wherewith to feed the greedy eye of the
naturalist, and view the ladies, with kilted coats, doing their
daily lessons from Glaucus, collecting pretty shells, bottling
anemones, or gathering sea-weeds wherewith to ornament their
botanic albums.　At last, after a long day's work of wandering and climbing, we long for a quiet seat and a refreshing
cup of tea, and by and by, when the night shuts us out from
active labour, we hie us to our box bed, in order to stretch
our wearied limbs in Miss Macalister's well-lavendered
sheets ; and, as we are just attempting to coax the balmy god-
dess to close our eyes with her soft fingers, we hear the landlady in her garret reading her nightly chapter from her Gaelic
Bible, with that genuine droning sound incidental to the West
Highland voice.

I have more than once after nightfall passed a quiet half-hour at our cottage door inhaling the saline breath of the mighty sea. The look-out at midnight is very beautiful : the Cumbrae light looked like a monitor telling us that even at that dread hour we were watched over. On the opposite coast of Ayr a huge ironwork threw a lurid glare upon the bosom of the sea, and almost at my feet the restless waves were playing a mournful dirge on the boulder-crowded beach. I could see along the water to Holy Island, and could almost feel the silence that at that moment would render the cave of old Saint Molio a wondrous place for holding a feast of the imagination, the viands being brought forward from a far-back time, and the island again peopled with the quaint races that had passed a brief span of life upon its shores—who had been warmed by the same sun as had that day shone upon me, and whose nights had been illumined by the same moon that was now shimmering its soft radiance upon the liquid bosom of the sparkling waters.

CHAPTER V.

————◆————

THE NATURAL AND ECONOMIC HISTORY OF THE SALMON.

The Salmon our best-known Fish—Controversies and Anomalies—Food of Salmon—The Parr Controversy—Experiments by Shaw, Young, and Hogg—Grilse : its Rate of Growth—Do Salmon make Two Voyages to the Sea in each Year ?—The Best Way of marking Young Salmon—Enemies of the Fish—Avarice of the Lessees—The Rhine Salmon—Size of Fish—Killing of Grilse—Rivers Tay, Spey, Tweed, Severn, etc.—The Tay Fisheries—Report on English Fisheries—Upper and Lower Proprietors.

SO many books have been written during the last few years about this beautiful and valuable animal that I do not require to occupy a very large portion of this work with either its natural or economic history ; for of the two hundred and fifty kinds of fish which inhabit the rivers and seas of Britain, the salmon (*Salmo salar*) is the one about which we know more than any other, and chiefly for these reasons :—It is of greater value as property than any other fish ; its large size better admits of observation than smaller members of the fish tribe ; and, in consequence of its migratory instinct, we have access to it at those seasons of its life when to observe its habits is the certain road to information. And yet, with all these advantages, or rather in consequence of them, there has been a vast amount of controversy, oral and written, as to the birth, breeding,

N

and growth of the salmon.   There have been controversies as
to the impregnation of its eggs, as to the growth of the fish
from the parr to the smolt stage ; also as to the kind of food
it eats, how long it remains in the salt water, and whether it
makes one or two voyages to the sea per annum.   There has
likewise been a grilse controversy, as well as a rate-of-growth
quarrel.   These scientific and literary combats have been
fought at intervals, and, to speak generally, have exhibited
the temper and the learning of the combatants in about equal
proportions.   The dates of these controversies are not so
easily fixed as might be desired, seeing that they are either
scattered at intervals throughout the Transactions of learned
societies, buried in heavy encyclopædias, or altogether lost in
the columns of newspapers.   It is scarcely an exaggeration to
say that during the past quarter of a century there has been a
committee of inquiry either in the House of Lords or Commons,
a royal commission, a blue book, or an Act of Parliament, every
year on behalf of the salmon, besides numerous publications
by private individuals.

Although no person now believes the assertion of the
Billingsgate naturalist, that salmon-eggs come to maturity in
a period of forty-eight hours, or that other authority who
told the world that as soon as the fish burst from the ovum
—a smolt six inches long coming out of a pea !—it was conducted to the sea by its parents, there is much of the romantic
in the history of this monarch of the brook, and about the
manner in which the varied disputed points have been solved,
if indeed some of these points be yet completely settled.

I shall not again enter into the impregnation theory, having said as much as was necessary about that portion of my
subject in a previous division of this work ; but will proceed
at once to give a summary of the parr controversy, and a few
statements about the grilse and the full-grown fish as well.

According to the state of knowledge some five-and-thirty

years ago—and I need not go further back at present—the smolt was said to be the first stage of salmon-life, and the abounding parr was thought to be a distinct fish.   Now we know better, and are able to regulate our salmon-fisheries accordingly.   The spawn  deposited by the parent fish in October, November, and December, lies in the river till about April or May, when it quickens into life.   I have already described the changes apparent in the salmon-egg from the time of

 its fructification till the birth of the fish.   The infant fry are of course very helpless, and are seldom seen during the first week or two of their existence, when they carry about with them as a provision for food a portion of the egg from whence they emanated.   At that time the fish is about half an inch in size, and presents such a very singular appearance that no person seeing it would ever believe that it would grow into a fine grilse or salmon.   About fifty days is required for the animal to assume the shape of a perfect fish ; before that time it might

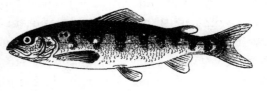

be taken for anything else than a young salmon.   The engravings on this and the succeeding pages, which are exactly half the size of life, show the progress of the salmon during the first two years of its existence, at the end of which time it is certain to have changed into a smolt.   After eating up its umbilical bag, which it takes a period of from twenty to forty days to accomplish, the young salmon may be seen about its birthplace, timid and weak, hiding about the stones, and always apparently of the some colour as the surroundings of its sheltering place.   The transverse bars of the parr very speedily become apparent, and the fish begins to grow with considerable rapidity, especially if it is to be a twelvemonth's smolt, and this is very speedily seen at such a good point of observation as the Stormontfield ponds. The smallest of the specimens given in the preceding page represents a parr at the age of two months; the next in size shows the same fish two months older; and the remaining fish is six months old. The young fish continue to grow for a little longer than two years before the whole number make the change from parr to smolt and seek the salt water. Half of the quantity of any one hatching, however, begin to change at a little over twelve months from the date of their coming to life; and thus there is the extraordinary anomaly, as I shall by and by show, of fish of the same hatching being at one and the same time parr of half an ounce in weight and grilse weighing four pounds. The smolts of the first year return from the sea whilst their brothers and sisters are timidly disporting in the breeding shallows of the upper streams, having no desire for change, and totally unable to endure the salt water, which would at once kill them. The sea-feeding must be favourable, and the condition of the fish well suited to the salt water, to ensure such rapid growth—a rapidity which every visit of the fish to the ocean serves but to confirm. Various fish, while in the grilse stage, have been marked to prove this; and at every migration they returned to their breeding stream with added weight and improved health. What the salmon feeds upon while in the salt water is not well known, as the digestion of that fish is so rapid as to prevent the discovery of food in their stomachs when they are captured and opened. Guesses have been made, and it is likely that these approximate to the truth; but the old story of the rapid voyage of the salmon to the North Pole and back again turns out, like the theory upon which was built up the herring-migration romance, to be a mere myth.

None of our naturalists have yet attempted to elucidate that mystery of salmon life which converts one-half of the fish into sea-going smolts while as yet the other moiety remain as parr. It has been investigated so far at the breeding-ponds at Stormontfield, but without resolving the question. There is another point of doubt as to salmon life which I shall also have a word to say about—namely, whether or not that fish makes two visits annually to the sea ; likewise whether it be probable that a smolt remains in the salt water for nearly a year before it becomes a grilse. As a salmon only stays, as is popularly supposed, a very short time in the salt water, and as it is one of the quickest swimming fishes we have, so that it is able to reach a distant river in a very short space of time, it is most desirable that we should know what it does with itself when it is not migrating from one water to the other ; because, according to the opinion of some natural-ists, it would speedily become so deteriorated in the river as to be unequal to the slightest exertion.

The mere facts in the biography of the salmon are not very numerous ; it is the fiction and mystery with which the life of this particular fish has been invested by those ignorant of its history that has made it a greater object of interest than it would otherwise have become. This will be obvious as I briefly trace the amount of controversy and state the arguments which have been expended on the three divisions of its life.

THE PARR CONTROVERSY.—None of the controversies con-cerning the growth of the salmon have been so hotly carried on or have proved so fertile in argument as the parr dispute. At certain seasons of the year, most notably in the months of spring and early summer, our salmon streams and their tri-butaries become crowded, as if by magic, with a pretty little fish, known in Scotland as the parr, and in England as the brandling, the peel, the samlet, etc. The parr was at one time so wonderfully plentiful, that farmers and cottars who

resided near a salmon river used not unfrequently, after filling
the family frying-pan; to feed their pigs with the dainty little
fish!   Countless thousands were annually killed by juvenile
anglers, and even so lately as twenty years ago it never occurred either to country gentlemen or their farmers that these
parr were young salmon.   Indeed, the young of the salmon, as
then recognised, was only known as a smolt or smout.   Parr
were thought, as I have already said, to be distinct fish of the
minor or dwarf kind.   Some large-headed anglers, however,
had their doubts about the little parr, and naturalists found

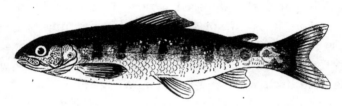

PARR ONE YEAR OLD.
Half the natural size.

it difficult to procure specimens of the fish with ova or milt
in them.   Dr. Knox, the anatomist, asserted that the parr
was a hybrid belonging to no particular species of fish, but a
mixture of many ; and it is curious enough that although
this fish was declared over and over again to be a separate
species, no one ever found a female parr containing roe.   The
universal exclamation of naturalists for many a long year
was always : It is a quite distinct species, and not the young
of any larger fish.   The above drawing represents a parr, the
engraving being exactly half the size of life.

This "distinct-species" dogma might have been still prevalent, had not the question been taken in hand and solved
by practical men.   Before mentioning the experiments of Shaw
and Young, it will be curious to note the varieties of opinion
which were evoked during the parr controversy, which has
existed in one shape or another for something like two hun-

dred years. As a proof of the difficulty of arriving at a correct conclusion amidst the conflict of evidence, I may cite the opinion of Yarrell, who held the parr to be a distinct fish. "That the parr," he says, "is not the young of the salmon, or, indeed, of any other of the large species of Salmonidæ, as still considered by some, is sufficiently obvious from the circumstance that parr by hundreds may be taken in the rivers all the summer, long after the fry of the year of the larger migratory species have gone down to the sea." Mr. Yarrell also says, "The smolt or young salmon is by the fishermen of some rivers called 'a laspring;'" and explains, "The laspring of some rivers is the young of the true salmon; but in others, as I know from having had specimens sent me, the laspring is really *only a parr*." Mr. Yarrell further states the prevalence of an opinion "that parrs were hybrids, and all of them males." Many gentlemen who would not admit that parr were salmon in their first stage have lived to change their opinion.

My friend Mr. Robert Buist, the intelligent and very obliging conservator of the Stormontfield breeding-ponds, is one of the gentlemen who now finds, from the results of most accurate experiments conducted under his own personal superintendence, that he was in error in holding the parr to be a distinct fish. A very eminent living naturalist, who has now seen all the stages of the question, said at one time that the parr had no connection whatever with the migratory salmon; and also that "males are found so far advanced as to have the milt flow on being handled; but at the same time, and indeed all the females which I have examined, had the roe in a backward state, and they have not been discovered spawning in any of the shallow streams or lesser rivulets, like the trout." Such extracts could be multiplied to almost any extent, but I can only give one more, and it is from the same writer. After minutely describing the anatomy of the fish, he thus sums up: "In this state, therefore, I have no hesitation in considering the parr not only distinct, but one of the best and most constantly marked species we have."

The first person who "took a thought about the matter"— *i.e.* as to whether the parr was or was not the young of the salmon—and arrived at any solid conclusion, was James Hogg, the Ettrick Shepherd, who, in his usual eccentric way, took some steps to verify his opinions. He had, while herding his sheep, many opportunities of watching the fishing-streams, and, like most of his class, he wielded his fishing-rod with considerable dexterity. While angling in the tributaries of some of the Border salmon-streams he had often caught the parr as it was changing into the smolt stage, and had, after close observation, come to the conclusion that the little parr was none other than the infant salmon. Mr. Hogg did not keep his discovery a secret, and the more his facts were controverted by the naturalists of the day the louder became his proclamations. He had suspected all his life that parr were salmon in their first stage. He would catch a parr with a few straggling scales upon it ; he would look at this fish and think it queer ; instantly he would catch another a little better covered with silver scales, but all loose, and not adhering to the body. Again he would catch a smolt, manifestly a smolt, all covered with the white silver scales, yet still rather loose upon its skin, and these would come off in his hand. On removing these he found the parr, with the blue finger-marks below the new scales ; and that these were young salmon then became as manifest to the shepherd as that a lamb, if suffered to live, would become a sheep. Wondering at this, he marked a great number of the lesser fish, and offered rewards (characteristically enough of whisky) to the peasantry to bring him any fish that had evidently undergone the change predicted by him. Whenever this conclusion was settled in his mind, the Shepherd at once proclaimed his new-gained knowledge. "What will the fishermen of Scotland think,"

said he, " when I assure them, on the faith of long experience
and observation, and on the word of one who can have no
interest in instilling an untruth into their minds, that. every
insignificant parr with which the Cockney fisher fills his
basket is a salmon lost?" These crude attempts of the im-
pulsive shepherd of Ettrick—and he was hotly opposed by Mr.
Buist, now of Stormontfield—were not without their fruits ;
indeed they were so successful as quite to convince him that
parr were young salmon in their first stage.

As I have had occasion to mention the opinions of James
Hogg on the salmon question, I may be allowed to state here
that the following amusing bit of dialogue on the habits of the
salmon once took place between the Ettrick Shepherd and a
friend :—

Shepherd—" I maintain that ilka saumon comes aye back
again frae the sea till spawn in its ain water."

Friend—" Toots, toots, Jamie ! hoo can it manage till do
that ; hoo, in the name o' wonder, can a fish, travelling up a
turbid water frae the sea, know when it reaches the entrance
to its birthplace, or that it has arrived at the tributary that
was its cradle ?"

Shepherd—" Man, the great wonder to me is no hoo the
fish get back, but hoo they find their way till the sea first ava,
seein' that they've never been there afore !"

The parr question, however, was determined in a rather more
formal mode than that adopted by the author of " Bonny Kil-
menny." Mr. Shaw, a forester in the employment of the Duke
of Buccleuch, took up the case of the parr in 1833, and suc-
ceeded in solving the problem. In order that he might watch
the progressive growth of the parr, Mr. Shaw began by capturing seven of these little fishes on the 11th of July 1833; these
he placed in a pond supplied by a stream of excellent water,
where they grew and flourished apace till early in April 1834,
between which date and the 17th of the following May they

became smolts ; and all who saw them on that day when they
were caught by Mr. Shaw were thoroughly convinced that they
were true salmon smolts.   In March 1835 Mr. Shaw repeated
his experiments with twelve parrs of a larger size, taken also
from the river.   On being transferred to the pond, these so
speedily acquired the scales of the smolt that Mr. Shaw
assumed a period of two years as being the time at which the
change took place from the parr to the smolt.   The late Mr.
Young of Invershin, a well-known authority on salmon life, was
experimenting at the same time as Mr. Shaw, and for the same
purpose—namely, to determine if parr were the young of the
salmon, and, if so, at what period they became smolts and proceeded to the sea.   Well, Mr. Shaw said two years, and Mr.
Young, who was at that time manager of the Duke of Sutherland's fisheries, said the change.took place in twelve months ;
others, again, who took an interest in the controversy, said
that three years elapsed before the change was made.   The
various parties interested held each their own opinion, and it
may even be said that the disputation still goes on ; for
although a numerous array of facts bearing on the migration
have been gathered, we are still in ignorance of any regulating
principle on which the migratory change is based, or to account for the impulse which impels a brood of fish to proceed
to sea divided into two moieties.   Mr. Shaw watched his young
fry with unceasing care, and described their growth with great
minuteness, for a period extending over two years, when his
parrs became smolts.   Mr. Young, in a letter from Invershin,
dated January 1853, says, pointedly enough—" The fry remain in the river one whole year, from the time they are
hatched to the time they assume their silvery coat and take
their first departure for the sea.   All the experiments we have
made on the ova and fry of the salmon have exactly corre-
sponded to the same effects, and none of them have taken
longer in arriving at the smolt than the first year."

Mr. Buist, in one of his letters on the progress of artificial breeding at the Stormontfield ponds, says : "There is at present a mystery as regards the progress of the young salmon. There can be no doubt that all in our ponds are really and truly the offspring of salmon ; no other fish, not even the seed of them, could by any possibility get into the ponds. Now we see that about one half have gone off as smolts, returning in their season as grilses ; the other half remain as parrs, and the milt in the males is as much developed, in proportion to the size of the fish, as their brethren of the same age seven to ten pounds weight, whilst these same parrs in the ponds do not exceed one ounce in weight. This is an anomaly in nature which I fear cannot be cleared up at present. I hope, however, by proper attention, some light may be thrown upon it from our experiments next spring. The female parrs in the pond have their ova so undeveloped that the granulations can scarcely be discovered by a lens of some power. It is strange that both Young's and Shaw's theories are likely to prove correct, though seemingly so contradictory, and the much-disputed point settled, that parrs (such as ours at least) are truly the young of the salmon."

It is quite certain that parr are young salmon, and that a parr becomes a smolt and goes to the sea, although there are still to be found, no doubt, a few wrong-headed people who will not be convinced on the point, but pridefully maintain all the old salmon theories and prejudices. With them the parr is still a distinct fish, the smolt is the true young of *Salmo salar* in its first stage, and a grilse is just a grilse and nothing more. However, these old-world people will in time pass away (there is no hope of convincing them), and then the modern views of salmon biography, founded as they are on laborious personal investigation, will ultimately prevail.

THE SMOLT AND GRILSE.—But the great parr mystery is still unsolved—that is to say, no one knows on what *principle*

the transformation is accomplished ; how it is that only half
of a brood ripen into smolts at the end of a year, the other
moiety taking double that period to arrive at the same stage
of progress. Some scientific visitors to the Stormontfield ponds
say that this anomaly is natural enough, and that similar
ratios of growth may be observed among all animals ; but it is
curious that just exactly the half of a brood—and the eggs be
it remembered all from adult salmon, and therefore similar in
ripeness and other conditions—should change into smolts at
the end of a year, leaving a moiety in the ponds as parr for
another twelvemonth.

The most remarkable phase in the life of the salmon is its
extraordinary instinct for change.   After the parr has become
a smolt, it is found that the desire to visit the sea is so intense,
especially in pond-bred fish, as to cause them to leap from
their place of confinement, in the hope of attaining at once
their salt-water goal ; and of course the instinct of river-bred
fish is equally strong on this point—they all rush to the sea at
their proper season.   There are various opinions as the cause
of the migratory instinct in the salmon.   Some people say it
finds in the sea those rich feeding-grounds which enable it to
add so rapidly to its weight.   It is quite certain that the fish
attains its primest condition while it is in the salt water ;
those caught in the estuaries by means of stake or bag nets
being richer in quality, and esteemed far before the river fish.
The moment the salmon enters the fresh water it begins to decrease in weight and fall from its high condition.   It is a curious fact, and a wise provision of nature, that the eel, which is
also a migratory fish, descends to spawn in the sea as the
salmon is ascending to the river-head for the same purpose ;
were the fact different, and both fish to spawn in the river, the
roe of the salmon would be completely eaten up.   In due
time then, we find the silver-coated host leaving the rippling
cradle of its birth, and adventuring on the more powerful

stream, by which it is borne to the sea-fed estuary, or the briny ocean itself. And this picturesque tour is repeated year after year, being apparently the grand essential of salmon life.

It is pleasant, rod in hand, on a breezy spring day, while trying to coax "the monarch of the brook" from his sheltering pool, to watch this annual migration, and to note the passage of the bright-mailed army adown the majestic river, that hurries on by busy corn-mill and sweeps with a murmuring sound past hoar and ruined towers, washing the pleasant lawns of country magnates or laving the cowslips on the

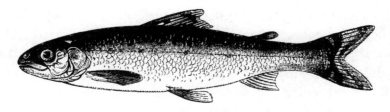

SMOLT TWO YEARS OLD.
Half the natural size.

village meadow, and as it rolls ceaselessly ocean-ward, giving a more picturesque aspect to the quaint agricultural villages and farm homesteads which it passes in its course. During the whole length of its pilgrimage the army of smolts pays a tribute to its enemies in gradual decimation : it is attacked at every point of vantage ; at one place the smolts are taken prisoners by the hundred in some well-contrived net, at another picked off singly by some juvenile angler. The smolt is greedily devoured by the trout, the pike, and various other enemies, which lie constantly in waiting for it, sure of a rich feast at this annually-recurring migration. But the giant and fierce battle which this infantile tribe has to fight is at the point where the salt water begins to mingle with the stream, where are assembled hosts of greedy monsters of the sea of all shapes and sizes, from the porpoise and seal down to the young coal-fish, who dart with inconceivable rapidity upon the defenceless shoal and play havoc with the numbers.

Many naturalists dispute most lustily the assertion that the smolt returns to the parental waters as a grilse the same year that it visits the sea ; and some writers have maintained that the young fish makes a grand tour to the North Pole before it makes up its mind to " hark back." It has been pretty well proved, however, that the grilse may have been the young smolt of the same year. A most remarkable fact in the history of grilse is, that we kill them in thousands before they have an opportunity of perpetuating their kind ; indeed on some rivers the annual slaughter of grilse is so enormous as palpably to affect the " takes" of the big fish. It has been asserted, likewise, that the grilse is a distinct fish, and not the young of the salmon in its early stage. There has been a controversy as to the rate at which the salmon increases in weight ; and there have been numerous disputes about what its instinct had taught it to " eat, drink, and avoid."

It has been authoritatively settled, however, that grilse become salmon ; and, notwithstanding a recent opening up of this old sore, I hold the experiments conducted by his Grace the Duke of Athole and the late Mr. Young of Invershin to be quite conclusive. The latter gentleman, in his little work on the salmon, after alluding to various points in the growth of the fish, says :—" My next attempt was to ascertain the rate of their growth during their short stay in salt water, and for this purpose we marked spawned grilses, as near as we could get to four pounds weight ; these we had no trouble in getting with a net in the pools below the spawning-beds, where they had congregated together to rest, after the fatigues of depositing their seed. All the fish above four pounds weight, as well as any under that size, were returned to the river unmarked, and the others marked by inserting copper wire rings into certain parts of their fins : this was done in a manner so as not to interrupt the fish in their swimming operations nor be troublesome to them in any way. After their journey to sea and back again, we found that the four pound grilses had grown into beautiful salmon, varying from nine to fourteen pounds weight. I repeated this experiment for several years, and on the whole found the results the same, and, as in the former marking, found the majority returning in about eight weeks; and we have never among our markings found a marked grilse go to sea and return a grilse, for they have invariably returned salmon."

The late Duke of Athole took a considerable interest in the grilse question, and kept a complete record of all the fish that he had caused to be marked; and in his Journal there is a striking instance of rapidity of growth. A fish marked by his Grace was caught at a place forty miles distant from the sea; it travelled to the salt water, fed, and returned in the short space of thirty-seven days. The following is his entry regarding this particular fish:—" On referring to my Journal, I find that I caught this fish as a kelt this year, on the 31st of March, with the rod, about two miles above Dunkeld Bridge, at which time it weighed exactly ten pounds; so that, in the short space of five weeks and two days, it had gained the almost incredible increase of eleven pounds and a quarter; for, when weighed here on its arrival, it was twenty-one pounds and a quarter." There could be no doubt, Mr. Young thinks, of the accuracy of this statement, for his Grace was most correct in his observations, having tickets made for the purpose, and numbered from one upwards, and the number and date appertaining to each fish was carefully registered for reference.

As the fish grew so rapidly during their visit to the salt water, people began to wonder what they fed on, and where they went. A hypothesis was started of their visiting the North Pole; but it was certain, from the short duration of their visit to the salt water that they could proceed to no great distance from the mouth of the river which admitted them to the sea.   Hundreds of fish were dissected in order to ascertain what they fed upon ; but· only on very rare occasions could any traces of food be found in their stomachs.   What, then, do the salmon live upon ? was asked.   It is quite clear that salmon obtain in the sea some kind of food for which they have a peculiar liking, and upon which they rapidly grow fat ; and it is very well known that after they return to the fresh water they begin to lose their flesh and fall off in condition. The rapid growth of the fish seems to imply that its digestion must be rapid, and may perhaps account for there never being food in its stomach when found ; although I am bound to mention that one gentleman who writes on this subject accounts for the emptiness of the stomach by asserting that the salmon vomits at the moment of being taken.   The codfish again is frequently found with its stomach crowded ; in fact, I have seen the stomach of a large cod which formed quite a small museum, having a large variety of articles " on board," as the fisherman said who caught it.   Salmon seldom now attain a weight of more than from fifteen to eighteen pounds. Long ago sixty-pound fish were by no means rare, and twelve years back salmon weighing thirty and forty pounds used frequently to be seen on our fishmongers' counters.   In the golden age of the fisheries salmon are said to have been very plentiful, and attainable for food by all classes of the community, the price being a mere trifle ; but railways now carry away our sea produce with such rapidity to far-off cities and populous towns, where there is an increasing demand that the price has risen to such a point as to make this fish a luxury for the rich, and so induce the capture of salmon of all weights.   On all these points there has been a great amount of disputation, chiefly carried on in the Transactions of learned societies, and not therefore accessible to the general reader.

It is supposed by some writers that the salmon makes two voyages in each year to the sea, and this is quite possible, as we may judge from the data already given on this point ; but sometimes the salmon, although it can swim with great rapidity, takes many weeks to accomplish its journey because of the state of the river. If there is not sufficient water to flood the course, the fish have to remain in the various pools they may reach till the state of the water admits of their proceeding on their journey either to or from the sea. The salmon, like all other fish, is faithful to its old haunts ; and it is known, in cases where more than one salmon-stream falls into the same firth, that the fish of one stream will not enter another, and where the stream has various tributaries suitable for breeding purposes, the fish breeding in a particular tributary invariably return to it.

But, in reference to the idea of a double visit to the salt water, may we not ask—particularly as we have the dates of the marked fish for our guidance—what a salmon that is known to be only five weeks away on its sea visit does with itself the rest of the year ? A salmon, for instance, spawning about " the den of Airlie," on the Isla, some way beyond Perth, has not to make a very long journey before it reaches the salt water, and travelling at a rapid rate would soon accomplish it ; but supposing the fish took forty days for its passage there and back, and allowing a period of six weeks for spawning and rest, there are still many months of its annual life unaccounted for. It cannot, according to the ideas of some writers, remain in the river forty-seven weeks, because it would become so low in condition from the want of a proper supply of nourishing food that it would die. It is this fact that has led to the supposition of a double journey to the sea. The Rev. Dugald Williamson, who wrote a pamphlet on this subject, entertains no doubt about the double journey. " Salmon migrate twice in the course of the year, and the instinct which

drives them from the sea in summer impels them to the sea
in spring. · Let the vernal direction of the propensity be
opposed, let a salmon be seized as it descends and confined in
a fresh-water pond or lake, and what is its fate? Before preparing to quit the river it had suffered severely in strength,
bulk, and general health, and, imprisoned in an atmosphere
which had become unwholesome, it soon begins to languish,
and in the course of the season expires : the experiment has
been tried, and the result is well known. This being an
ascertained and unquestionable fact, is it a violent or unfair
inference that a similar result obtains in the case of those
salmon that are forced back, from whatever cause, to the sea,
that the salt-water element is as fatal to the pregnant fish of
autumn as the fresh-water element is to the spent fish in
spring? . . . If there is any truth in these conjectures,
they suggest the most powerful reasons for *resisting* or *removing*
obstructions in the estuary of a river." The riddle of this double
migration of the salmon is likely still to puzzle us. It is said
that the impelling force of the migratory instinct is, that the
fish is preyed upon in the salt water by a species of crustaceous
insect, which forces it to seek the fresh waters of its native
river; again, that while the fresh water destroys these sea-lice
a new kind infests it in the river, thus necessitating a return
to the sea. My own experience leads me to believe that
salmon can exist perfectly well in the fresh water for months
at a time, suffering but little deterioration in weight, but
never, so far as I could ascertain, growing while in the fresh
streams, although it is certain they feed. It is a well-known
fact that the parr cannot live in salt water. I have both tried
the experiment myself and seen it tried by others ; the parr
invariably die when placed in contact with the sea-water.

Mr. William Brown, in his painstaking account of *The
Natural History of the Salmon*, also bears his testimony on
this part of the salmon question :—"Until the parr takes on

the smolt scales, it shows no inclination to leave the fresh water. It cannot live in salt water. This fact was put to the test at the ponds, by placing some parrs in salt water — the water being brought fresh from the sea at Carnoustie ; and immediately on being immersed in it the fish appeared distressed, the fins standing stiff out, the parr-marks becoming a brilliant ultramarine colour, and the belly and sides of a bright orange. The water was often renewed, but they all died, the last that died living nearly five hours. After being an hour in the salt water, they appeared very weak and unable to rise from the bottom of the vessel which contained them, the body of the fish swelling to a considerable extent. This change of colour in the fish could not be attributed to the colour of the vessel which held them, for on being taken out they still retained the same brilliant colours."

All controversies relating to the growth of salmon may now be held as settled. It has been proved that the parr is the young of the salmon ; the various changes which it undergoes during its growth have been ascertained, and the increase of bulk and weight which accrues in a given period is now well understood. But we still require much information as to the " habits " of fish of the salmon kind.

In a recent conversation with Mr. Marshall of Stormontfield, while comparing notes on some of the disputed points of salmon growth, we both came to the conclusion that the following dates, founded on the experiments conducted at Stormontfield, might be taken as marking the chief stages in the life of a salmon. An egg deposited in the breeding-boxes say in December 1852 yielded a fish in April 1853 ; that fish remained as a parr till a little later than the same period of 1854, when, being seized with its migratory instinct, and having upon it the protecting scales of the smolt, it departed from the pond into the river Tay on its way to the sea, having previously had conferred upon it a certain mark by which it could be

known if recaptured on its return.   It was recaptured as a
grilse within less than three months of its departure (July),
and weighed about four pounds.   Being marked once more, it
was again sent away to endure the dangers of the deep; and lo!
was once more taken, this time a salmon of the goodly weight
of ten pounds !   But there comes in here the question if it was
the same fish, for it is said that the smolt in some cases
remains a whole winter in the sea, and therefore that the fish
I have been alluding to was a smolt that had never come back
as a grilse.   I have a theory that half of the brood of smolts
sent to sea do remain over the winter and come back as salmon,
while the others come back almost immediately as grilse.   It
is possible, however, that any particular fish may lose its river
for a season, and be in some other water for a time as a grilse,
and then finding its birth-stream come once again to its
" procreant cradle."   The rapidity of salmon growth, however,
I consider to be undoubtedly proved.

A good deal has been said in various quarters about the
best way of marking a young salmon so that at some future
stage of its life it may be easily identified.   Cutting off the
dead fin is not thought a good plan of marking, because such
a mark may be accidentally imitated and so mislead those
interested, or it may be wilfully imitated by persons wishing
to mislead.   Of the smolts sent away from the Stormontfield ponds during May 1855, 1300 were marked in a rather
common way—viz. by cutting off the second dorsal fin—and
twenty-two of these marked fish were taken as grilse during
that same summer, the first being caught on the 7th of July,
when it weighed three pounds.   Mr. Buist, who took charge of
the experiments, was quite convinced that a much larger
number of the marked fish than twenty-two was caught, but
many of the fishermen, having an aversion to the system of
pond-breeding, took no pains to discover whether or not the
grilse they caught had the pond-mark, and so the chance of

still further verifying the rate of salmon growth was lost. A reward offered by Mr. Buist of 2s. per pound weight for each grilse that might be brought to his office, led to an imitation of the mark and the perpetration of several petty frauds in order to get the money. The mark was frequently imitated, and one or two fish were brought to Mr. Buist which almost deceived him into the belief of their being some of the real marked fish. As Mr. Buist says—"So cunningly had this deception been gone about, that a casual observer might have been deceived. When the fin was cut off the recent wound was far too palpable ; and to hide this the man cut a piece of skin from another fish and fixed it upon the wounded part. I examined this fish, which was lying alongside of an undoubted pond-marked fish, which had the skin and scales grown over the cut, and I am satisfied that it would be impossible to imitate the true mark by any process except by marking the fish while young."* Peter Marshall and also Mr. Buist agree with me in saying that the number of fish taken, each being minus the dead fin, was a sufficient proof that these fish were really the pond-bred ones returned as grilse. It is impossible that twenty or thirty grilse could have all been accidentally maimed within a few weeks, and

* In a very old number of the *Scots Magazine* I find the following: —" I was told by a gentleman who was present at a boat's fishing on Spey near Gordon Castle in the month of April, that in hauling, the weight of the net brought out a great number of smouts which the fishers were not willing to part with ; but that a gentleman, who knew the natural propensity of the salmon to return to their native river, persuaded them to slip them back again into the water, assuring them that in two months they would catch most of them full-grown grilses, which would be of much greater value. He at the same time laid a bet of five guineas with another gentleman present, who was somewhat dubious, that he should not fail in his prediction. The fishers agreed. He accordingly clipt off a part of the tail-fins from a number of them before he dropped them into the river ; and within the time limited the fishers actually caught upwards of a hundred grilses thus marked, and soon after many more."

each present the same—the very same appearance. Various other plans of marking were tried by the authorities at Stormontfield, some of which were partially successful, and added another link to the chain of evidence, which proves at any rate that many individual fish have grown from the smolt to the grilse state in the course of a very few weeks.

FISHES OF THE SALMON FAMILY.

1. Salmon.   2. Grilse.   3. Sea-trout.   4. Herling.

Leaving the salmon as an object of natural history, and looking at it as an article of commerce, I find that there exists a considerable dread of its speedy extinction, which, taking into account the state of the fisheries, is not at all to be wondered at. The English salmon-fisheries have utterly declined ; the Irish fisheries are decaying ; and the eagerness with which the Scotch people are rushing to Parliament for new laws indicates a fear of a similar fate overtaking the fisheries of the North. The "breeches-pocket" view of the question has recently become of considerable importance, in consequence of this fear of failing supplies ; for the commerce

carried on in this particular fish has been at the rate of over
£100,000 a year ; and although our salmon-fisheries are not
nearly equal in value to the herring and white fisheries, still
the individual salmon is our most tangible fish, and brings to
its owner a larger sum of money than any other member of
the fish family.   Indeed, of late years this "monarch of the
brook" has become emphatically the rich man's fish ; its price
for table purposes, at certain seasons of the year, being only
compatible with a large income ; and liberty to play one's rod
on a salmon river is a privilege paid for at a high figure per
annum.   Such facts at once elevate *Salmo salar* to the highest
regions of luxury : certainly, salmon can no longer find a
place on the tables of the poor ; for we shall never again hear
of its selling at twopence per pound, or of farm-servants bargaining not to be compelled to eat it oftener than twice a week.

At every stage of its career the salmon is surrounded by
enemies.   At the very moment of spawning, the female is
watched by a horde of devourers, who instinctively flock to
the breeding-grounds in order to feast on the ova.   The
hungry pike, the lethargic perch, the greedy trout, the very
salmon itself, are lying in wait, all agape for the palatable roe,
and greedily swallowing whatever quantity the current carries
down.   Then the water-fowl eagerly pounces on the precious
deposit the moment it has been forsaken by the fish ; and if
it escape being gobbled up by such cormorants, the spawn
may be washed away by a flood, or the position of the bed
may be altered, and the ova be destroyed perhaps for want of
water.   As an instance of the loss incidental to salmon-spawn-
ing in the natural way, I may just mention that a whitling of
about three-quarters of a pound weight has been taken in the
Tay with three hundred impregnated salmon ova in its
stomach !   If this fish had been allowed to dine and breakfast at this rate during the whole of the spawning season it
would have been difficult to estimate the loss our fisheries

sustained by his voracity. No sooner do the eggs ripen, and the young fish come to life, than they are exposed, in their defenceless state, to be preyed upon by all the enemies already enumerated ; while as parr they have been taken out of our streams in such quantities as to be made available for the purposes of pig-feeding and as manure ! Some economists estimate that only one egg out of every thousand ever becomes a full-grown salmon. Mr. Thomas Tod Stoddart calculated that one hundred and fifty millions of salmon ova are annually deposited in the river Tay ; of which only fifty millions, or one-third, come to life and attain the parr stage ; that twenty millions of these parrs in time become smolts, and that their number is ultimately diminished to 100,000 ; of which 70,000 are caught, the other 30,000 being left for breeding purposes. Sir Humphrey Davy calculates that if a salmon produce 17,000 roe, only 800 of these will arrive at maturity. It is well, therefore, that the female fish yields 1000 eggs for each pound of her weight ; for a lesser degree of fecundity, keeping in view the enormous waste of life indicated by these figures, would long since—especially taking into account the various very destructive modes of fishing that used a few years ago to be in use—have resulted in the utter extinction of this valuable fish.

The root of the evil as regards the scarcity of salmon is to be found in the avarice of the lessees of fisheries, who have overfished the rivers to an alarming extent. The increased value of all kinds of fish food during late years has engendered in these parties a greed of money that leads to the capture and sale of almost everything that bears the shape of fish. The tenant of a salmon-fishery has but one desire, and that is to clear his rent and get as much profit as he can. To achieve this end he takes all the fish that come to his net, no matter of what size they may be. It is not his interest to let a single one escape, because if he did so his neighbour above or below him on the water would in all probability capture it.　As a general rule, the tenant has no care for future years ; he has no personal interest in stocking the upper waters with breeding fish.　He is forced by the competition of his rivals to do all he can in the way of slaughter ; and were there not a legal pause of so many hours in the course of the week, and a close-time of so many days in the year, it is questionable if a score

SALMON-WATCHER'S TOWER ON THE RHINE.

of fish would make their way past the engines devoted to their capture.　A watcher can stand on the bridge of Perth, and at certain seasons can signal or count every fish that passes in the water below him, and every fish passing can be caught by those on the look-out ; and I have seen the same watch kept on the Rhine,* and on other salmon rivers.　The accompany-

* The Rhine is an excellent salmon stream and yields a large num-ber of fish.　The five fishing stations at Rotterdam are very productive,

ing sketch of a salmon-watcher's tower on the great German river may interest some of my readers who have never been on that beautiful water.

This unhealthy competition will always continue till some new system be adopted, such as converting each river into a joint-stock property, when the united interests of the proprietors, both upper and lower, would be considered. The trade in fresh salmon, which has culminated in some rivers by the total extermination of the fish, dates from the time of Mr. Dempster's discovery of packing in ice. Half-a-century ago, when we had no railways, and when even *fast* coaches were too slow for the transmission of sea-produce, the markets were exceedingly local. Then salmon was so very cheap as to be thought of no value as food, and was only looked upon by the population with an eye of good-humoured toleration—nobody ever expected to hear of it as a luxury at five shillings a pound weight. No Parisian market existed then for foul fish, and fifty years ago people only poached for amusement. But in the excessive poaching which now goes on during close-time we have a minor cause nearly as productive of evil as the primary and legal one ; for of course it is *legal* for the tacksman of the station to kill all the fish he can. Add to these causes the extraordinary quantities of infant fish which are annually killed, coupled with that phase of insanity which leads to the capture of grilse (salmon that have never spawned), and we obtain a rough idea of the progress of destruction as it goes on in our salmon rivers. Fifty or sixty years ago men caught a salmon or shot a pheasant for mere sport, or at most for the supply of an individual want. Now poaching is a trade or business entered into as a means of securing a weekly or annual income ; it has its complex

each of them yielding about 40,000 salmon per annum ; and it would not be extravagant to estimate the produce of these fisheries as of the value of £25,000 per annum.

machinery—its nets, guns, and other implements. There are men who earn large wages at this illicit work, who take to "the birds" in autumn and the fish in winter with the utmost regularity; and there are middlemen and others who encourage them and aid them in disposing of the stolen goods. A few men will band themselves together, and in the course of a night or two sweep fish from off the spawning-beds which are totally unfit for human food. There is a ready market always to be found even for spawning fish. Few of my readers can have any idea of the immense number of salmon which are destroyed by this cause, and at the very time when they are at their greatest value, intent on the propagation of their kind. Indeed, on the very spawning-bed itself, the " deadly leister" is hurled with unerring aim and mighty force ; and the slain fish, safely hidden in the poacher's bag, is carried off to be kippered and sold for the English market. A party will start at nightfall, and, dividing into two companies, sweep the Tweed with a net from shore to shore, and capture everything of the salmon kind that comes within reach. The takes upon such occasions average from ten to forty fish. The first night upon which my informant—a weaver—went out, the result was seventeen large fish, three of which weighed ninety pounds. Upon the second occasion the take was much larger, thirty-eight salmon of a smaller size being the reward of their iniquity, weighing in the aggregate four hundred and forty pounds, and producing in cash £8 sterling, divided among eleven people. These stolen fish pass through numerous hands. A person comes at a given time and takes away the spoil ; all that the actual poacher obtains as his share is a few pence per pound weight. They are bought from the thieves by middlemen, who again dispose of them to certain salesmen—each party, of course, obtaining a profit.

In former times, as at present, there were more ways of killing a salmon than by angling for it. Parties used to be made up for the purpose of "burning the water," a practice which prevailed largely on the Tweed, and which afforded good rough sport. The burning took place a little after sunset, when an old boat was commissioned for the purpose, and flaming torches of pinewood were lighted to lure the fish to their destruction. The leister, a sharp iron fork, was used on these occasions with deadly power ; rude mirth and song were usually the order of the night ; and the practice being illegal was not without a spice of danger, or at least a chance of a ducking. Burning the water, it must, however, be confessed, was more a picturesque way of poaching than a means of adding legitimately to the produce of the fisheries as a branch of commerce. It would have been well for the salmon-fisheries had the arts of poaching never extended beyond the rude practice here alluded to ; but now poaching, as I have endeavoured to show, has become a business, and countless thousands of the fish are swept off the breeding-beds and sold to dealers. There is on most rivers an organised system of taking and disposing of the fish ; France, till very lately, affording the chief outlet for this kind of food—an outlet, however, which a recent Act of Parliament has done much to close up. Legislation on the salmon question has of late been greatly extended, some powerful Acts of Parliament having been passed for the better regulation of the various British salmon-fisheries.*

It is recorded that at one time great hauls of salmon could be taken either in the rivers of Scotland or Ireland, and that in England salmon were also quite plentiful. One miraculous

---

* The French government took off the import-duty on salmon in 1856, when foul salmon began to be exported to that country during the British close-times at the rate of £7000 per annum. A late writer in *Fraser's Magazine* was informed by a leading fish-salesman, on the 16th November, that on that day *ten tons* of Tweed salmon, freshly caught, were in Billingsgate, two months after close-time, and despite of what was thought to be effective special legislation for that river !

draught is mentioned as having been taken out of the river Thurso, on which occasion the enormous number of two thousand five hundred fish were captured.   We shall never again see such a haul, unless we give the rivers a rest for a space of five years or so.   A jubilee would greatly help to restore the *status quo*.   The discovery of packing in ice by Mr. Dempster led, as was to be expected, to so large a trade in fresh salmon between Scotland and England, that it at once effected a great rise in the price of the fish.   High prices had their usual consequence with the producer.   Every device was put in requisition to catch fish for London and the Continent ; and if this was the case at the beginning, it will be readily understood how rapidly the fish-trade rose in importance as new modes of transit became common.   The demand and supply at once assumed such enormous proportions as to tell with fatal effect on the fisheries ; and the high prices led at the same time to such extensive and organised poaching as I have attempted to describe, and which, notwithstanding much police organisation, still exists.

At one time there were famous salmon in the Thames, and hopes are entertained of fish being successfully cultivated in that river.   It is certain that much deleterious matter has been allowed to get into that stream and also into that famous salmon river the Severn ; and in the rivers of Cornwall I believe the hope of ever breeding salmon has been entirely given up in consequence of the poisonous matters which flow from the mines.   Many rivers which were known to contain salmon in abundance in the golden age of the fisheries are now tenantless from matter by which they are polluted, such as the refuse of gasworks, paper-mills, etc.

Another fertile source of harm to the salmon-fisheries are the fixed engines of capture which so many people think it right to use, and which the Lord Advocate's Salmon Bill of 1862 left almost *in statu quo*, except that a little power on this part of the salmon question is given to the commissioners appointed to carry out the Act. Stake and bag nets in Scotland are known to have been very destructive, as have the putchers, butts, and trumpets of the English and Welsh rivers. It would be tedious to describe the different fixed engines invented for the capture of salmon ; what I desire to show is that they have injured the fisheries. A controversy has been raging in Scotland for some years back on this point of the salmon question, which, there can be no doubt, will ultimately result in their *entire* extinction. That they have been a most fruitful cause of injury to the fisheries has been proved by a long array of facts and figures. A striking example of the effect of bag-nets occurred with regard to the Tay. The system having been extended to that river, the productiveness of the upper portions of the stream was very speedily affected ; and again, shortly after their removal, the fisheries became greatly more productive, as will be seen by and by when it becomes necessary to deal with the figures denoting the rental of that river.

Although I have already referred to it, it is most important to note here much more particularly the fact that, with probably the solitary exception of the Tweed (and there the deterioration has only recently been arrested), the size and weight of salmon are annually diminishing, and, as some fishermen think, their condition and flavour also. There can be no doubt that in the golden age of the fisheries they attained much larger proportions than they do now. I need scarcely quote in support of this opinion the fish mentioned by Yarrell, which was exhibited by Mr. Groves, and weighed eighty-three pounds ; nor that alluded to by Pennant, which was only ten pounds lighter ; nor the fact that in all virgin salmon-rivers the fish average a greater weight than any now taken in the British streams. It is within the memory of anglers that fish of forty pounds were by no means rare in the

Scottish rivers ; that salmon of thirty pounds and thirty-five pounds weight were quite common ; and that the general run of fish were in the aggregate many pounds heavier than those of the present day.   Mr. Anderson, the lessee of some of the best salmon-fisheries on the Firth of Forth, a gentleman who is master of his business, is of opinion that the average weight of fish now is reduced to about sixteen pounds ; and by the Tweed Tables, the average weight of those killed by the net between July and September, though apparently on the increase, in no month rises to fifteen pounds.   How is it, then, that we have no giants of the river in these days?   The answer, I think, is simple and convincing.   Let us suppose, for example, that the fish grows at the rate of five pounds per annum : it would, therefore, take ten years to achieve a growth of fifty pounds.   Now it is needless to say that, in British waters at any rate, we never either see or hear of a fish of that weight.   The fact is, we do not give our salmon time to grow to that size.   The greater portion of the fish that we kill are two years old, or at the most three—fish running from eight pounds to sixteen pounds in weight.   It is clear that, if we go on for a year or two longer at the rate of slaughter we have been indulging of late years, there will speedily not be even a three-year-old fish to pull out of the water.   It is very suggestive of the state of the salmon-fisheries that we have now eaten down to our three-year-olds.

Another fertile source of destruction is the killing of grilse ; the grilse being a virgin fish, its slaughter is just analogous to the killing of lambs without due regulation as to quantity.   In this respect, " the conduct of salmon proprietors is as rational as high-farming with the help of tile-drains, liquid-manure, and steam-power, would be for the purpose of eating corn in the blade."   As many as 100,000 grilses have been taken from one river in a year—a notable example of killing the goose for the golden egg.   If we had an Act of Parliament to pre-

vent the capture of grilse, we should never want salmon.
The parr and smolt are protected. Why? Because they are
the young of the salmon. Well, so is grilse the young of the
salmon, and grilse also are sadly in want of protection.

Recent debates in the House of Commons on the English
and Scottish Salmon Fisheries Bills brought out very distinctly

STAKE-NETS ON THE RIVER SOLWAY.

the worst phase of the salmon question—viz. the prevalence of
stake and bag nets. These machines have exercised a bane-
ful influence on the fisheries, and have in numerous instances
intercepted about one-half of the salmon of particular rivers,
before they could reach their own waters. These nets are
erected in the tideways, not far from the shore, and as the fish
are coasting along towards their own particular spawning-
ground, they are intercepted either in the chambers of the
bag-net, or in the meshes of the stake-net. It is said, too,
that fish taken in the tidal estuaries are in far finer condi-

tion than those caught in the fresh-water division of the large salmon rivers ; hence they are in greater demand, and bring a slightly better price.   There is no consideration among tacksmen of river fishings, or proprietors of bag or stake nets, for the preservation of the fish ; it seems to be a rule with these gentlemen to kill all they can.   It is obvious that, if the upper proprietors of the waters were to act in the same spirit, and kill all the salmon that reached the breeding-grounds, that fine fish, not unaptly called the " venison of the waters," would very speedily become extinct.

As may be known to most of my readers, the chief British salmon streams, so far at least as productiveness is concerned, are the Tay, the Tweed, the Spey, and the Esk.   I have not space in which to sketch the whole of these rivers, but I desire, on behalf of English readers particularly, to say a few words about two of our Scottish salmon streams ; and I select the Tay and the Spey.

The Tay is equal to a basin of 2250 square miles, and it discharges, after a run of about 150 miles, a greater volume of water than any other Scottish river.   " As ascertained by Dr. Anderson, the quantity which is carried forward per second opposite the city of Perth averages no less than 3640 cubic feet."   The main river and its affluents, and *their* varied tributaries, afford splendid breeding-ground for the salmon.   As an instance we may take the Earn.   It flows from Loch Earn in the far west of Perthshire, and is, when it leaves the lake, a considerable river, and over the greater part of its course its current is very rapid.   A slight drawback to its capabilities as a fish-breeding river is the fact of its sometimes overflowing its banks ; but its tributaries afford plenty of excellent ground for salmon-breeding.   Indeed, on all the tributaries of the Tay there is ample accommodation for the fish.   I have in my mind's eye some excellent salmon-beds near Airlie Castle, on the Isla.   The banks of the river are overhung by foliage, and the salmon sport industriously in the deep pools, resorting to the gravel at the proper season in order to dig beds in which to deposit their eggs, and when in due time these are vivified and grow from the fry to the parr state, I have seen the youthful "natives" catching them in scores.

The Tay deserves special honour, for it must rank as the king of Scottish rivers, receiving as it does the tribute of so many streams, and running its course through such a variety of fine scenery. Loch Tay is generally accounted the source of this river, but if it be considered that the loch is chiefly fed by the river Dochart, the source of this latter river is actually the fountain-head of the Tay. The Dochart rises in the extreme west of Perthshire, and, after striking the base of the "mighty Ben More" and the Dochart Hills, falls into Loch Tay at the village of Killin, before reaching which place it assumes the dimensions of a considerable river. There is fine angling to be had in the vicinity of Killin ; indeed, the salmon rod-fisheries there are of some value, and trout can be taken in great plenty both in the Dochart and the Lochay. Loch Tay contains abundance of fish, and, as that sheet of water is of considerable size, there is ample room to ply the angle, either for salmon, trout, or charr. The loch is about sixteen miles in length, and is overshadowed on the north by Ben Lawers—one of the loftiest of our Scottish mountains. The river Tay issues from the loch within a mile of Taymouth Castle, one of the fine seats of the noble family of Breadalbane ; and, after flowing eastward for a few miles, its waters are augmented by those of the Lyon, whose source is about twenty-six miles distant from its junction with the Tay. Passing over several minor streams and proceeding eastwards, the next important tributary of the Tay is the Tummel, the junction taking place at the ancient and once famous burgh of Logierait. This river, which is the largest tributary of the Tay, is the outlet of Loch Rannoch, situated in the extreme

north-west of Perthshire.   The loch is well stocked with trout,
and large specimens of the *Salmo ferox* are frequently caught ;
but the true salmon (*Salmo salar*) is not found either in Loch
Rannoch or Loch Tummel, their ascent being checked by the
Falls of Tummel.   Below the falls, however, there are several
salmon-fisheries, but they are not very productive.   The Tay,
after receiving the waters of the Tummel and Garry at Logierait, flows onward through beautiful scenery till it reaches
Dunkeld, where it receives the tributary stream of the Braan,
which has for its source a small sheet of water named Loch
Freuchie, situated in Glen Quoich.   The scenery around the
junction of the Braan and Tay is hallowed by numberless
associations of bygone times.   Passing beneath the noble
arches of Dunkeld Bridge, the Tay flows eastward till it is
joined by the Isla, when it again takes a southerly direction
until it reaches Perth.   On its way thither it receives the
tribute of the Almond, the Shochie, and the Ordie.   The Isla
is a large and important stream, draining as it does a considerable extent of country, and lending its aid both to miller and
manufacturer.   The Almond is the next river in importance,
but a tradition connected with it is better known than the
river itself.   On Lynedoch Braes, which are near the foot of
the stream, dwelt the heroines of the poetic legend of Bessie
Bell and Mary Gray, in the house which they "biggit" with
their own hands, and "theekit ower wi' rashes."   The Shochie
and Ordie cannot claim the name of rivers, but they are celebrated as being named in a prophecy attributed to Thomas the
Rhymer :—

> " Says the Shochie to the Ordie
> Where shall we meet ?
> At the cross of Perth,
> When a' men are asleep."

The Isla, Almond, and the two rivers last named, in common
with all the tributaries of the Tay, afford excellent sport to

the angler.   The country bordering the banks of this portion
of the Tay is a mixture of pastoral and agricultural.   Rippling
past the Stormontfield breeding-ponds, now a feature of the
river, and the palace of Scone, the Tay speedily reaches the
links of Perth's fair city ; and after being joined by the Earn,

SALMON-FISHING STATION AT WOODHAVEN ON TAY.

also an excellent salmon stream, it widens into a broad estuary, and, speedily sweeping past the manufacturing town of
Dundee, is lost in the German Ocean.

   A few local inquiries as to angling on the Tay will elicit
more valuable information than I can give here.   At some
places on the lower portion of the water the aid of a boat (a
Tay boat) is necessary, as the best pools are otherwise inaccessible to the angler.   The cost of a boat and man ranges, I
think, from three to six shillings, and on the smooth parts
of the river one man is generally enough for attendance.

Some parts of the Tay are quite free to all comers, especially about Kinfauns ; and, if I mistake not, up all the way from Perth to the breeding-ponds at Stormontfield. Perth forms a capital centre for the angler : it is a good place in which to obtain information or tackle, and it is easy to get away from the "Fair City" to places and streams of note. And if the angler wants to " harl" the Tay itself, Perth is the very best place to obtain instructions in the art of "harling," which is very attractive. The commercial fishings may be seen in operation at and below Perth : they are carried on by means of the net and coble. A boat sails out with the net, and taking in a sweep of the water returns, in its progress enclosing any of the salmon kind that may be in that part of the river. The operation is usually repeated several times each day at every fishing station.

The Tay salmon-fisheries are owned by various noblemen, gentlemen, and corporations ; and they yield a gross annual rent of nearly £17,000. To give an idea of the individual value and the occasional fluctuations of even the best fisheries, we may cite some of the figures connected with the rental of the river Tay. Lord Gray, for instance, has drawn from his fisheries more than £100,000 during the last thirty-five years. The salmon and grilse obtained for this sum run from 10,000 to 28,000 a year. It has been frequently asserted that our salmon-fisheries are a lottery, and in confirmation of this it may be stated that in 1831, when 10,000 fish were taken, the rental of this fishery was £4000 ; and that in 1842, when the capture was 28,453 fish, the rental was £1000 less. Dividing the income for the two years, we have the following result :—Averaging the fish at 5s. each gives as a loss to the tenant on the 10,000 year of £1500, while on the other year there is the large profit of £4000 ! But the value of the Tay fisheries will be better estimated by mentioning that in some seasons the number of fish taken from the mouth of the

Isla down to the sea has ranged from 70,000 to upwards of 100,000. Ten of the fishing-stations between Perth and Newburgh used to produce an annual rental of about (on the average) £700 each.

As to the much-discussed stake-net question, the following figures may be quoted :—About the end of last century, *before* the existence of stake-nets, the average number of fish taken at the Kinfauns fishery was—salmon, 8720 ; grilse, 1714. In the first ten years of the present .century, the average annual catch of salmon fell to 4666, and the grilse numbered 1616. *After* the stake-nets were removed, and in the ten years from 1815 to 1824, the average number of salmon caught was 9010 per annum, and of grilse 8709. I have purposely avoided filling up my space with an accumulation of proof on this point, but were further proof required of the deadly influence of stake and bag nets on the salmon rivers, it could easily be had ; indeed, ample testimony has, from time to time, been recorded in Parliament, both against the stake-nets, and that " chamber of horrors" for the salmon, the deadly bag. A stream like the Tay ought to have a stock of breeding-fish sufficient to produce more than 100,000,000 of eggs, because the destruction of the spawn and the young fish is so enormous as to require provision for a large amount of waste ; hence the value of artificial cultivation. By the natural system of spawning it is supposed that only one egg in each thousand comes to the fisherman's net as a twenty-five pound fish.

The river Spey is an excellent salmon-producing stream ; in fact, size considered, it is the richest in Scotland, the fishings at Speymouth being worth £12,000 per annum. The Spey is about a hundred and twenty miles on its course before it falls into the sea, and some parts of the river are very picturesque.

" Dipple, Dundurcus, Dandaleith, and Dalvey
Are the bonniest haughs on the run of the Spey."

The stream is very rapid, having in its course a fall of twelve hundred feet ; it rushes on in one continuous gallop from its mountain well to the sea, giving rise to the local proverb of their being "no standing water in Spey," although there are pools thirty feet deep. Still, as a rule, the river is shallow, having generally a depth of about three feet ; and there are places which, when the water is a little low, may be crossed by a man on foot.

I have seen the rafts of wood coming down from the hills at the rate of ten miles an hour ; and the Spey is not only the most rapid, but also the wildest of all our large Scottish rivers. "The cause of this is easily explained. The river drains thirteen hundred miles of mountains, many of whose bases are more than a thousand feet above the level of the sea. The Dulnain, draining the southern part of the Monagh Lea Mountains, runs more than forty miles before entering Spey ; and the Avon, with a course as long, brings down the waters of Glenavon, which lies between the most majestic mountains in Britain. Besides these great tributaries, the Spey has the Truim, the Tromie, the Feshie, the Fiddoch, and other affluents, swelling her volume with the rapidly-descending waters of a mountainous country." The river Spey is an example of a well-managed stream, and in the late Duke of Richmond's time produced a very handsome revenue. It was well managed, because the duke fished it himself ; and, of course, it was his interest to have it well protected, and to keep a handsome stock of breeding fish. For instance, in the years 1858 and 1859 the duke drew on the Spey for upwards of 107,000 salmon and grilse, and the fish in that river are as plentiful as ever. On the Spey, however, there is no confusion of upper and lower proprietors to fight against and take umbrage at each other, the river belonging mostly to one proprietor. Other Scottish rivers also yield, or did at one time yield, large annual sums in the shape of rental ;

and on the larger salmon rivers of Scotland the income
derived by many of the " lairds" from the salmon forms a very
welcome addition to their land revenues.   Mr. Johnstone, the
lessee of the Esk fisheries at Montrose, stated at a public
meeting held some time ago in Edinburgh to protest against
the removal of stake-nets, that he estimated the Duke of Sutherland's fisheries at £6000 a year, and quoted his own rents as
£4000 per annum, giving him the privilege to fish on two
different rivers, on one of which he had eight miles of water,
on the other six.   The rents of the sea salmon-fisheries of
Scotland (stake and bag nets), which the recent bill of the
Lord Advocate proposed to abolish, range from £20 to £1000
per annum.   Princely rentals have been drawn from the
salmon rivers of that division of the United Kingdom.

The Tweed alone at one period gave to its proprietors an
annual income of £20,000 ; but although the price of fish has
greatly increased of late years, the rental fell at one time to
about a fifth part of that sum, and the take of fish sank from
40,000 to 4000.   Persons interested in the salmon have been
watching very keenly during late years the effects of the
legislation of 1857 and 1859 upon the Tweed fisheries, the
rent of that river being now little more than a third of what
it once was.   The principal changes introduced by the two
Tweed Acts of 1857 and 1859 may be shortly stated to be:—

1. The entire abolition of bag, stake, and other fixed nets
of every description in the river, and the restriction and regulation of stake-nets on the sea-coast, and no net except the
common sweep-net, rowed out and immediately drawn in again,
has been allowed on the Tweed since 1857.   2. The entire prohibition of leistering.   3. A slight increase of the weekly
close-time, and an increase of the annual close-time for nets by
four weeks.   4. The permission of rod-fishing for an extended
period, so as to interest proprietors to a greater degree in the
protection of the river.   And last, not least, the absolute pro-

hibition of killing unclean or unseasonable fish at any time of the year, and an enactment that all such fish caught during the fishing season should be returned to the water.

Much curiosity has existed as to the results achieved by the Tweed Acts, the first really stringent code enforced on any British river; and although statistics in such matters, unless taken over very extended periods, are not to be too implicitly relied on, and much allowance must be made for the variations caused by weather and unfavourable seasons during so short a period as has elapsed, yet it is well worth while to ascertain what can be learned concerning this experiment. With this view I have consulted the very valuable and interesting series of tables which have been compiled and printed for private circulation by Alexander Robertson, Esq., one of the Tweed Commissioners, and a director of the Berwick Shipping Company. A brief reference to the figures in these tables shows at once whether or not there has been an improvement in the fishing. The total capture of salmon, grilse, and trout, in Tweed for the six years preceding 1857 was 50,209 salmon, 153,515 grilse, and 294,418 trout; making a yearly average of 8368 salmon, 25,586 grilse, and 49,069 trout. In the six years succeeding the Act—viz. 1858 to 1863—the total capture was 60,726 salmon, 124,182 grilse, and 175,538 trout; being an average of 10,121 salmon, 20,697 grilse, and 29,256 trout. These are improving figures, taking into account that the fishing season had been curtailed by a period of four weeks. The total rent of the river in 1857 was about £5000; it is now above £7500, and is on the rise.

The English salmon-fisheries, generally speaking, have been allowed to fall into so low a state that I fear it will be impossible to recruit them in a moderate period of time without foreign aid. Some of the rivers, indeed, are as nearly as possible salmonless. It is difficult to select an English river that will in all respects compare with the Tay, but the Severn produces the finest salmon of any of the English salmon rivers ; and it is a noble stream, containing many kinds of fish, which afford great sport to the angler. If the river flowed in a direct course from its source to the sea, it would be eighty miles in length ; as it is, by various windings, it flows for two hundred miles. It has many fine affluents, and in its course passes through some beautiful scenery. It rises in Wales, high up the eastern side of Plinlimmon, at a place in the moors called Maes Hafren, which gave at one time its title to the river, Hafren being its ancient name. After flowing through several counties it falls into the sea at Bristol Channel. Had the fisheries of the Severn been as free from obstacles and as well preserved as those on the river Tay, they would still have been of immense value, as it possesses some very fine breeding-grounds. The Severn could be speedily restored to its primary condition as one of our finest salmon streams ; that is, if the various interests could be consolidated, and artificial breeding be extensively carried on for a few years. The Severn still possesses a tolerable stock of breeding-fish, which might be turned to good account in a way similar to those at Stormontfield on the Tay.

Mr. Tod Stoddart, who is an authority on the salmon question, and particularly on matters relating to angling, says that a river like the Tay or the Tweed requires 15,000 pairs of breeding-fish to keep it in stock, the average weight of the breeders to be ten pounds each. Proceeding on these data, and taking the period of growth of the fish as previously stated, it may be interesting if we inquire how soon a fine river like the Severn could be made a property. Allowing that there is at present a considerable stock of breeding fish in that river—say 10,000 pairs—and that for a period of two years these should be allowed a jubilee, the river during that time to be carefully watched; that plan alone would soon work a favourable change; but if supplemented by an extensive resort to artificial nurture and protection, in the course of three years the Severn would be, speaking roundly, a mine of fish wealth. A series of ponds capable of breeding 1,000,000 fish might, I think, be constructed for a sum of £2000 ; there ought of course to be two reception-ponds, so that a brood could be hatched annually. [See plan in "Fish Culture."] Thus, in a year's time, half a million of well-grown smolts would be thrown into the river from the ponds alone, a moiety of which in the course of ten weeks would be saleable grilse ! Next year these would be doubled, and added to the quantity naturally bred would soon stock even a larger river than the Severn. There can be no doubt of the practicability of such a scheme. What has been achieved in Ireland and at Stormontfield can surely be accomplished in England. An ample return would be obtained for the capital sunk, and in all probability a large profit besides.

A recent report of the Inspectors of the English Fisheries embraces a summary of the condition of ninety rivers ; and I can gather from it that considerable progress has already been made in arresting the decay of these valuable properties, and that there is every prospect of the best rivers being speedily re-peopled with salmon to an extent that will secure them, under proper regulations, from again falling into so low a condition. A careful perusal of this report shows that fixed nets have been nearly abolished ; that portions of rivers not hitherto accessible to fish have been made so, passes and gaps having been created by hundreds. Poachers have been caught and punished with great success ; and, according to a review of the report in the *Field*, a journal which is well versed in fishery matters, " salmon have been seen in large quantities in places where they have not been seen these forty years."

In reference to the Act for the regulation of the salmon-fisheries of England and Wales of 1861, and its supplement of 1865, a good deal can be said as to the increase of salmon, but it is perhaps best that Mr. Ffennell, one of the Commissioners, should be allowed to say it for himself. The increase in the productiveness of the English rivers then—and this is stated in the fourth annual report of the inspectors—"far exceeds the anticipations of those who were most sanguine in regard to the good results which might have been expected from the operation of the Act of 1861 ; and the zeal of many who from the first took an active part in administering the law has been greatly stimulated by the telling effects of their exertion ; while others, who may have hesitated in the commencement from doubts of success, have been led on by the force of good example, as well as by the more powerful incentive arising from the many proofs so soon forthcoming that salmon can be abundantly produced in the rivers of England."

As to the amendment or rider to the Act of 1861, which was passed in the present session (1865), its chief objects are to provide funds for the payment of the wages of water-bailiffs, and of other expenses connected with the due protection of the English salmon-fisheries, and for the appointment of a body of able and responsible persons to whom the duties of raising and expending such fund are to be entrusted. The first of these is attained by the annual licensing of rods, nets, and other engines used in the capture of salmon, at fixed sums, the proceeds of which licence-duties are to be expended (after the formation of a river or rivers into a fishery district by order of the Secretary of State) on the protection of the fisheries within that district only where such licence-duties are raised, and in that district only are the licences available for use ; and the second, where a fishery district lies wholly in one county, by the magistrates of that county in quarter-sessions at once appointing a board of conservators for the district ; but where a fishery district lies in several counties, such appointment will be made by committees of the various courts of quarter-sessions interested, under prescribed arrangements.

In either case after the appointment, the board of conservators will be a body corporate, and have the entire control of the salmon-fisheries within their district. The Act also provides for the issuing of a special commission to inquire into the titles and rights of all "fixed engines" used in the capture of salmon throughout England and Wales. These devices have since the late improvement in our fisheries very much increased in number; but now such only may hereafter be employed as are proved to the satisfaction of the Commissioners to have been lawfully used in either of the years 1857, 1858, 1859, 1860, or 1861. There are also other useful and necessary provisions in the Act, affording protection to trout in the months of November, December, and January, when they spawn, fixing a minimum penalty for a second offence; requiring all salmon intended to be exported between the 3d September and 2d February to be entered with the proper officer of customs; and in other minor but important particulars amending the Act of 1861, with which the Act of 1865 is to be understood as incorporated. The associations on the Severn, the Usk, and the Yorkshire rivers have already taken up the Act, and intend applying, through the court of quarter-sessions at their next October sessions, for the formation of fishery districts, and the appointment of boards of conservators. It is anticipated that in the lower part of the Severn £600, on the Wye £400, and on the Usk £300, will be then derived from licences, and from the first year's revenue of these respective boards; and it is to be hoped that all necessary preliminaries will be adjusted in time to permit the various boards of conservators to enter upon their duties with the commencement of the next open season.

As a guide to the productiveness in salmon of the different divisions of the three kingdoms, the following table may be taken. It was furnished by Messrs. Wm. Forbes Stuart and Co. of 104 Lower Thames Street, London, and shows the quantity of salmon (*i.e.* the number of boxes weighing one hundred and twelve pounds each) sent to London from 1850 to the end of the open fisheries of 1865 :—

	Scotch.	Irish.	Dutch.	Norwegian	Welsh.
1850	13,940	2,135	105	54	72
1851	11,593	4,141	203	214	40
1852	13,044	3,602	176	306	20
1853	19,485	5,052	401	1208	20
1854	23,194	6,333	345	None.	128
1855	18,197	4,101	227	None.	59
1856	15,438	6,568	68	5	200
1857	18,654	4,904	622	None.	220
1858	21,564	6,429	973	19	499
1859	15,630	4,855	922	None.	260
1860	15,870	3,803	849	40	438
1861	12,337	4,582	849	60	442
1862	22,796	7,841	568	87	454
1863	24,297	8,183	1,227	180	663
1864	22,603	8,344	1,204	837	752
1865	19,009	6,858	1,479	1069	868
	287,651	87,731	10,218	4079	5135

One of the least understood, although one of the most hotly-contested parts of the salmon question, is the relation between the upper and lower proprietors. A great salmon river may pass through the estates or mark the property boundaries of a large number of gentlemen ; and some portions of this river are sure to be much more valuable than others. As has been already stated, some of the proprietors on the river Tay derive a large revenue from their fisheries ; while others only obtain a little angling, although they very likely furnish the breeding-ground for a few thousands of the fish which aid in producing the large rentals lower down. This part of the salmon question has been so well argued by my friend Mr. Donald Bain, that I here reproduce a portion of one of his letters on the subject :—

" Considering that at present the only chance of having fish in the rivers depends upon the excellence and care of the breeding-grounds at the river-heads, while the river-head proprietors, by disturbing the shingle (which should be protected) at the period of depositing and hatching the roe, could destroy all chance, and yet be legally unchallengeable, these river-head proprietors are hardly recognised as proprietors at all, which therefore should be altered. . . . I propose that the river, from its highest breeding-ground to its mouth, and so far into the sea as private or public interests can extend, should be made a common property and a common care ; improved where improvable, at the general expense of the whole proprietors along its banks ; fished, not savagely, and as if extermination were a laudable object, but prudently, and with a view to permanent interests ; the fish allowed to go unmolested to the breeding-grounds, at least so far as to secure a full brood, and protected against destruction in returning when unfit for food ; and the expense and the profit to be divided *pro rata*, according to the mileage along the banks ; unless, in the judgment of intelligent and equitable men, a degree of preference should be given in the case of grounds of acknowledged excellence for breeding or feeding.

" It may be said it would be malicious in the proprietors of breeding-grounds to consider it necessary to repair their gravel-walks with shingle from the river at the very time when depositing or hatching the roe was going on ; but could it be prevented ?—and would it be more inequitable than anticipating every fish worth catching at the mouth of the river or along their course, and allowing the proprietors of the head-waters no share ?"

In the meantime, it is satisfactory to see that all classes of the community are thoroughly aroused to the danger which menaces our king of fishes. There must of course be a limit to the productiveness of even the most prolific salmon river; and if this be overpassed and the capital stock be broken upon, it is clear that a decrease will at once begin, and that the production must annually become weaker, till the fish are in course of time completely exterminated. Considering the constant enormous waste of fish life, there ought at least, I think, to be twice as many fish left in a river as are taken out of it. A care as to this would in time have a good effect.

An evident anxiety to improve the salmon-fisheries is now apparent, and the problem to be solved is how to restore the *status quo*, and obtain a supply of salmon equal to the demand. There are but two ways to a solution of the question. The experience of the Tweed, though still imperfect, shows that the decay of that river has been arrested, and that large salmon of some age—the best and surest breeders—now abound in its waters, and that this result is in the main to be attributed to improved legislation. The first thing therefore to be done is to extend our legislation for all our salmon rivers in the same direction that has been so successful on the Tweed; in other words, to eradicate, as soon as may be, those dams, engines, and fixed nets still really left untouched. The other, and as it seems to me the principal field for improvement, is the adoption of artificial culture wherever it can be carried out. Why should we not cultivate our water as we cultivate our land? Few measures could be more effectual than some check on the annual destruction of grilse; but, especially on the rivers in the hands of many proprietors, such as the Tweed, it is not easy to say how this can be practically effected; but might not artificial breeding supply the deficiency caused by this slaughter of the innocents? By means of pisciculture the French people have recreated their fisheries; why should not we try what they have done? Let us by all means clean our rivers by removing impurities of all kinds. Let us do our best to prevent poaching;

and, above all, let us take care not to encourage legal "over-fishing;" and, as gentlemen occasionally give their grouse a year of jubilee, let me prescribe an occasional similar indulgence to the salmon. Every little helps ; and as we have now a considerable knowledge of the natural history of the fish, we should avail ourselves of it not only in our legislation, but also in the practical management of the fisheries. If in our greed we still continue to overfish, after the numerous warnings we have had, we must take the consequences in the probable extermination of the salmon and its numerous congeners.

CHAPTER VI.

THE NATURAL AND ECONOMIC HISTORY OF THE HERRING.

Description of the Herring—The Old Theory of Migration—Geographical
Distribution of the Herring—Mr. John Cleghorn's Ideas on the Natural
History of the Herring—Mr. Mitchell on the National Importance of
that Fish—Commission of Inquiry into the Herring-Fishery—Growth
of the Herring—The Sprat—Should there be a Close-time ?—Caprice of
the Herring—The Fisheries—The Lochfyne Fishery—The Pilchard—
Herring Commerce—Mr. Methuen—The Brand—The Herring Harvest—
All Night at the Fishing—The Cure—The Curers—Herring Boats—
Increase of Netting—Are we Overfishing ?—Proposal for more Statistics.

THE common herring is one of our most beautiful and
abundant fishes, and is so well known as scarcely to
require description ; but it has one or two peculiarities of
structure that may be briefly alluded to. Its belly, for
instance, is keeled (as the Scotch fisher folk call carinated),
and is well protected by strong scales, giving us reason to
suppose that it is therefore a ground-feeder ; and having a very
large pectoral fin, and an air-bag of more than usual dimensions, it is thus endowed with a very rapid moving power. I
gather from personal observation of many herring stomachs —
and the stomach of the herring is unusually large—that this
fish is a devouring feeder, that it preys upon its own young or
upon the roe of its congeners when other food is scarce. Its
lobes of roe or milt are larger in proportion to its body than
those of any other fish. The herring has a fine instinct for

selecting a nursery for its young, contriving, when not obstructed, to deposit its ova on such bottoms as will ensure the adherence of its eggs and the favourable nourishment of the young fish.

The herring is taken throughout the year in vast quantities, thus affording a plentiful supply of cheap and wholesome food to the poorer classes, whilst its capture and cure afford remunerative employment to a large body of industrious people. It is greatly to be regretted, therefore, that recent fluctuations in the quantity caught have given occasion for well-grounded fears of an ultimate exhaustion of some of our largest shoals, or at all events of so great a diminution of their producing power as probably to render one or two of the best fisheries unproductive. This is nothing new, however, in the history of the herring-fishery : various places can be pointed out, which, although now barren of herrings, were formerly frequented by large shoals, that, from overfishing or other causes, have been dispersed.

This supposed overfishing of the herring has resulted chiefly from our ignorance of the natural history of that fish—ignorance which has long prevailed, and which we are only now beginning to overcome. Indeed, much as the subject has been discussed during the last ten years, and great as the light is that has been thrown on the natural and economic history of our fish, considering the elemental difficulty which stands in the way of perfect observation, there are yet persons who insist upon believing all the old theories and romances pertaining to the lives of sea animals. We occasionally hear of the great sea-serpent ; the impression of St. Peter's thumb is still to be seen on the haddock ; " Moby Dick," a Tom Sayers among fighting whales, still ranges through the *squid* fields of the Pacific Ocean; and I know an old fisherman who once borrowed a comb from a polite mermaid !

Not very long ago, for instance, the old theory of the

migration of the herring to and from the Arctic Regions was
gravely revived in an unexpected quarter, as if that romance of
fish-life was still believed by modern naturalists to be the chief
episode in the natural history of *Clupea harengus;* indeed in
the present edition of the *Encyclopædia Britannica* this migratory theory is still sustained (see article "Ichthyology"). The
original migration story—which was invented by Pennant, or
rather was constructed by him from the theories of fishermen
—old as it is, is worthy of being briefly recapitulated, as
affording a good point of view for a consideration of the
natural and economic history of the herring as now ascertained : it was to the effect that in the inaccessible seas of the
high northern latitudes herrings were found in overwhelming
abundance, securing within the icy Arctic Circle a bounteous
feeding-ground, and at the same time a quiet and safe
retreat from their numerous enemies. At the proper season,
inspired by some commanding impulse, vast bodies of this
fish gathered themselves together into one great army, and in
numbers far exceeding the power of imagination to picture
departed for the waters of Europe and America. The particular division of this great *heer*, which was destined annually
to repopulate the British seas, and afford a plenteous food-
store for the people, was said to arrive at Iceland about
March, and to be of such amazing extent as to occupy a
surface more than equal to the dimensions of Great Britain
and Ireland, but subdivided, by a happy instinct, into
battalions five or six miles in length and three or four in
breadth, each line or column being led, according to the ideas
of fishermen, by herrings (probably the *Alice* and *Twaite
shad*) of more than ordinary size and sagacity. These
heaven-directed strangers were next supposed to strike on the
Shetland Islands, where they divided of themselves, as we are
told; one division taking along the west side of Britain, whilst
the other took the east side, the result being an adequate and

well-divided supply of this fine fish in all our larger seas and rivers, as the herrings penetrated into every bay, and filled all our inland lochs from Wick to Yarmouth. Mr. Pennant was not contented with the development of this myth, but evidently felt constrained to give *éclat* to his invention by inditing a few moral remarks just by way of a *tag*. "Were we," he says, "inclined to consider this migration of the herring in a moral light, we might reflect with veneration and awe on the mighty power which originally impressed on this useful body of His creatures the instinct that directs and points out the course that blesses and enriches these islands, which causes them at certain and invariable times to quit the vast polar depths, and offer themselves to our expectant fleets. This impression was given them that they might remove for the sake of depositing their spawn in warmer seas, that would mature and vivify it more assuredly than those of the frigid zone. It is not from defect of food that they set themselves in motion, for they come to us full and fat, and on their return are almost universally observed to be lean and miserable."

Happily, the naturalists of the present day know a vast deal more of the natural history of the herring than Mr. Pennant ever knew, and, on the authority of the most able inquirers, it may be taken for granted that the herring is a local and not a migratory fish. It has been repeatedly demonstrated that the herring is a native of our immediate seas, and can be caught all the year round on the coasts of the three kingdoms. The fishing begins at the island of Lewis, in the Hebrides, in the month of May, and goes on as the year advances, till in July it is being prosecuted off the coast of Caithness; while in autumn and winter we find large supplies of herrings at Yarmouth; and there is a winter fishery in the Firth of Forth: moreover, this fish is found in the south long before it ought to be there, if we were to believe in Pennant's theory. It has been deduced, from a consideration of the figures of the annual takes of many years, that the herring exists in distinct races, which arrive at maturity month after month ; and it is well known that the herrings taken at Wick in July are quite different from those caught at Dunbar in August or September : indeed I would go further and say that even at Wick each month has its changing shoal, and that as one race ripens for capture another disappears, having fulfilled its mission of procreation. It is certain that the herrings of these different seasons vary considerably in size and appearance ; and it is very well known that the herrings of different localities are marked by distinctive features. Thus, the well-known Lochfyne herring is essentially different in its flavour from that of the Firth of Forth, and those taken in the Firth of Forth differ again in many particulars from those caught off Yarmouth.

In fact, the herring never ventures far from the shore where it is taken, and its condition, when it is caught, is just an index of the feeding it has enjoyed in its particular locality. The superiority in flavour of the herring taken in our great land-locked salt-water lochs is undoubted. Whether or not it results from the depth and body of water, from more plentiful marine vegetation, or from the greater variety of land food likely to be washed into these inland seas, has not yet been determined; but it is certain that the herrings of our western sea-lochs are infinitely superior to those captured in the more open sea. It is natural that the animals of one feeding locality should differ from those of another : land animals, it is well known, are easily affected by change of food and place ; and fish, I have no doubt, are governed by the same laws. But on this part of the herring question I need scarcely waste any argument, as there is but one writer who still persists in the old "theory" of migration. He is the same gentleman who has doubts about a grilse becoming a salmon !

Moreover, it is now known, from the inquiries of the late

Mr. Mitchell and other authorities on the geographical distribution of the herring, that that fish has never been noticed as being at all abundant in the Arctic Regions ; and the knowledge accumulated from recent investigations has dispelled many of what may be termed the minor illusions once so prevalent about the life of the herring and other fish.   People, however, have been very slow to believe that fish were subject to the same natural laws as other animals.   In short, seeing that the natural history of all kinds of fish has been largely mixed up with tradition or romance, it is no wonder that many have been slow to discard Pennant's pretty story about the migratory instinct of the herring, and the wonderful power of sustained and rapid travelling by which it reached and returned from our coasts.   Even Yarrell, as will by and by be shown, wrote in a weak uncertain tone about this fish ; indeed his account of it is not entitled to very much consideration, being a mere compilation, or rather a series of extracts, from other writers.

It was not till the year 1854 that anything like an authentic contradiction to Pennant's theory was obtained. Before that time one or two bold people asserted that they had doubts about the migration story, and thought that the herring must be a local animal, from the fact of its being found on the British coasts all the year round ; while one daring man said authoritatively, from personal knowledge, that there were no herrings in the Arctic seas.   During the year I have mentioned, a paper, which was communicated to the Liverpool Meeting of the British Association by Mr. Cleghorn of Wick, directed an amount of public attention to the herring-fishery, which still continues, and which, at the time, was thought sure ultimately to result in an authentic inquiry into the natural and economic history of that fish.   Such an investigation has now been made by persons qualified to undertake the task, and the result of their inquiries has been summed up in a most interesting report, which, along with the evidence taken

by the commissioners, I shall have occasion to refer to in
another part of the present chapter; the labours of Cleghorn,
Mitchell, and others, claiming priority of notice, as the ideas
promulgated by these gentlemen, although often hotly opposed
and combated, have gone a great way to guide public opinion
on the subject, and have evidently helped to influence recent
investigators.

In his paper communicated to the British Association at
Liverpool, Mr. Cleghorn stated that, living at Wick, the chief
seat of the fishery—" the Amsterdam of Scotland " in fact—his
attention had been directed to the herring-fishery by the
fluctuations in the annual take. That season (*i.e.* 1854) there
were 920 boats engaged in the fishing, and the produce was
95,680 barrels. On comparing the fishing of 1854 with
that of 1825, it was found to be 14,000 barrels short; and
as compared with 1830, 57,000 barrels less. It was found to
be the smallest fishing since 1840, and 61,000 barrels short of
the previous year. Various surmises were hazarded as to the
cause of the deficiency, but the generally-received opinion was,
that the falling off was attributable to the two rough nights
on which the boats did not put to sea, while great shoals
of herrings were on the coast. That this is an erroneous and
very partial view of the matter Mr. Cleghorn infers, because at all the stations between Noss Head and Cape Wrath
the fishing was a complete failure; and the same may be said
of Orkney and Shetland; while for the whole of Scotland the
shortcoming, perhaps, was one-third of the previous year.

Mr. Cleghorn—of whom it is proper to state that while in
business in Wick he suffered much local persecution for his
views of the herring question—says that he believes the fluctuations in the capture to be caused by " overfishing," as in the
case of the salmon, the haddock, and other fish. The points
brought forward by Mr. Cleghorn in order to prove his case were
as follow:—1. That the herring is a native of waters in which

it is found, and never migrates.   2. That distinct races of it
exist at different places.   3. That twenty-seven years ago the
extent of netting employed in the capture of the fish was much
less than what is now used, while the quantity of herrings
caught was, generally speaking, much greater.   4· There were
· fishing stations extant some years ago which are now exhausted;
a steady increase having taken place in their produce up to a
certain point, then violent fluctuations, and *then* final extinction.   5. The races of herrings nearest our large cities have
disappeared first; and in districts where the tides are rapid, as
among islands and in lochs, where the fishing grounds are
circumscribed, the fishings are precarious and brief; while on
the other hand, extensive seabords having slack tides, with
little accommodation for boats, are surer and of longer continuance as fishing stations.   6. From these premises it follows
that the extinction of districts, and the fluctuations in the
fisheries generally, are attributable to overfishing.   In the
commercial portion of this chapter I shall again have occasion
to refer to Mr. Cleghorn's investigations on the subject of the
netting employed, but it occurred to me to state Mr. Cleghorn's
theory at this place, as it has been the key-note to much of
the recent discussion on the subject of the natural history of
the herring.

    ·   Before the reading of Mr. Cleghorn's statistics, the natural
history of the herring was not well understood even by naturalists; so difficult is it to make observations in the labora-
tories of the sea.   Only a few persons, till recently, were
intimate with the history of this fish, and knew that, instead
of being a migratory animal, as had been asserted by Anderson and Pennant, the herring was as local to particular coasts
as the salmon to particular rivers.

    The late Mr. J. M. Mitchell, the Belgian Consul at Leith
(who published a work on the *National Importance of the
Herring*), in a paper which he read before the British Asso-

ciation at Oxford, three years ago, settled with much care and very effectually the geographical part of the herring question. His idea also is that the herring is a native of the coast on which it is found, and that immediately after spawning the full-sized herrings make at once for the deep waters of their own neighbourhood, where they feed till the spawning season again induces them to seek the shallow water. Mr. Mitchell gives his reasons, and states that the herrings resorting to the various localities have marked differences in size, shape, or quality ; those of each particular coast having a distinct and specific character which cannot be mistaken ; and so well determined are those particulars that practical men, on seeing the herrings, can at once pronounce the locality from whence they come ; as, indeed, is the case with salmon, turbot, and many other fishes and crustaceans.

On the southern coast of Greenland the herring is a rare fish ; and, according to Crantz, only a small variety is found on the northern shore, nor has it been observed in any number in the proper icy seas—as it would undoubtedly have been had it resorted thither in such innumerable quantities as was imagined by the naturalists of the last century. Another proof that the herring is local to the coasts of Britain lies in the fact of the different varieties brought to our own markets. As expert fishers know the salmon of particular rivers, so do some men know the different localities of our herring from merely glancing at the fish. A Lochfyne fish differs in appearance from a herring taken off the coast of Caithness, while the latter again differs from those taken by the Dunbar boats off the Isle of May. Experienced fishmongers know the different localities of the same kinds of fish as easily as a farmer will separate a Cheviot sheep from a Southdown. Thus they can at once distinguish a Severn salmon from one caught in the Tweed or the Spey, and they can tell at a glance a Lochfyne *matie* from a Firth of Forth one.

Turning now to the report of the commissioners appointed to inquire into the operation of the Acts relating to trawling for herring on the west coast of Scotland, we obtain some interesting information as to the spawning and growth of the herring.   Upon these branches of the subject the public have hitherto been very ill informed.   As has been already stated, Yarrell's account of this particular fish is a mere compilation from Dr. M'Culloch, W. H. Maxwell, Dr. Parnell, and others, and is thus very disappointing.   Again, the account in the *Naturalist's Library* is compressed into five small pages, referring chiefly to authorities on the subject, with quotations from Yarrell!   It is only by searching in Blue Books, by perusing much newspaper writing of a controversial kind, and by arduous personal inquiry, that I have been able to complete anything like an accurate *precis* of the natural and economic history of this very plentiful fish.

As to the periods at which herrings spawn, the commissioners appointed to conduct the latest inquiry that has been made inform us that they met with "singularly contradictory" statements, and after having collected a large amount of valuable evidence, *they* arrived at the conclusion that herrings spawn at two seasons of the year—viz. in the spring and autumn.   They have no evidence of a spawning during the solstitial months—viz. June and December ; but in nearly all the other months gravid herrings are found, and the commissioners assert that a spring spawning certainly occurs in the latter part of January, as also in the three following months, and the autumn spawning in the latter end of July, and likewise in the following months up to November : "Taking all parts of the British coast together, February and March are the great months for the spring spawning, and August and September for the autumn spawning."   The spawn, it may be stated in passing, is deposited on the surface of the stones, shingle, and gravel, and on old shells, at the various spawning places, and it adheres tenaciously to whatever it happens to fall upon. This, as will be seen, brings us exactly back to Mr. Cleghorn's ideas of the herring existing in races at different places and in separate bodies, and thereby rendering the fluctuations of the great series of shoals at Wick more and more intelligible, especially when we take into account the fact that winter shoals have recently been found at that place, giving rise to what may ultimately prove a considerable addition to the great autumn fishery yet carried on there. Indeed I consider this point proved, and having taken great pains in sifting the evidence (of different spawning seasons) given on the question, both oral and written, I feel entitled to say so much.

As to the question of how long herrings take to grow, from the period of the deposition of the egg, there are various opinions, for no naturalist or practical fisherman has been able definitely to fix the time. There is reason to believe, we are told in the report, that the eggs of herrings are hatched in, at most, from two to three weeks after deposition. This is very rapid work when we consider that the eggs of the salmon require to be left for a period of ninety or a hundred days, even in favourable seasons, before they quicken into life, and that the eggs of a considerable number of fish are known to take a much longer period than three weeks to ripen. The rate of growth of the herring, and the time at which it begins to reproduce itself, are not yet well understood; indeed, it seems particularly difficult to fix the period at which it reaches the reproductive stage.* I have had young her-

* As an example of the numerous absurd statements that have been circulated about fish, the reader may study the following paragraph :—" Old fishermen about Dunbar say the way herring spawn is —first, the female herrings deposit their roe at some convenient part on sand or shingly bottom ; second, the male fish then spread their milt all over the roe to protect it from enemies, and the influence of

rings of all sizes in my possession, from those of an inch long upwards. The following are the measurements of a few specimens which were procured about the end of February 1861, and not one of which had any appearance of either roe or milt, while some (the smaller fish) were strongly serrated in the abdominal line, and others, as they advanced in size, lost this distinguishing mark, and were only very slightly serrated. The largest of these fish—and they must all have been caught at one time—was eight inches long, nearly four inches in circumference at the thickest part of the body, and weighed a little over two ounces. The smallest of these herring-fry did not weigh a quarter of an ounce, and was not quite three inches in length. One of them, again, that was six inches long, only weighed three-quarters of an ounce ; whilst another of the same lot, four and a half inches long, weighed a quarter of an ounce exactly. I do not propose at present to enter at great length into the sprat controversy; but, if the sprat be the young of some one of the different species of herring, as I take leave to think it is, then the question of its growth and natural economy will become highly important. Some people say that the herring must have attained the age of seven years before it can yield milt or roe, whilst a period of three years has been also named as the ultimate time of this event; but there are persons who think that the herring attains its reproductive power in eighteen months, while others affirm that the fish grows to maturity in little more than half that time. If the average size of a herring may be stated as eleven and a half inches, individual fish of *Clupea harengus*

the tide and waves from moving it about. The fishermen also say that when the young herrings are hatched they can see and swim ; the milt covering bursts open, and they are free to roam about. Some naturalists think the roes and milts of herring are all mixed together promiscuously, and left on the sands to bud and flourish. The fishermen's idea seems to be the most likely of the two opinions."

have been found measuring seventeen inches, and full fish have been taken only ten inches in length, when should the example, noted above as being eight inches long, reach its full growth? and how old was it at the time of its capture? And, again, were the fish—all taken out of the same boat, be it observed, and caught in the same shoal—all of one particular year's hatching? Is this the story of the parr over again, or is it the case that the fishermen had found a shoal of mixed herrings—some being of one year's spawning, some of another? I confess to being puzzled, and may again remind the reader that my largest fish had never spawned, and had not the faintest trace of milt or roe within it. Then, again, as to the time when herrings spawn, I have over and over again asserted in various quarters that they spawn in nearly every month of the year—an assertion, as I have just shown, which has been proved by the recent inquiry.

As to the place of spawning, development of the ova, and other circumstances attendant on the increase of the herring, I promulgated the following opinions some years ago, and I see no reason to alter them :—The herring shoal keeps well together till the time of spawning, whatever the fish may do after that event. Some naturalists think that the shoal breaks up after it spawns, and that the herring then live an individual life, till again instinctively moved together for the grand purpose of procreating their kind. It is quite clear, I think, that the herring moves into the shallow water because of its increased temperature, and its being more fitted in consequence for the speedy vivifying of the spawn. The same shoal will always gather over the same spawning ground, and the fish will keep their position till they fulfil the grand object of their life. The herrings will rise buoyantly to the top water after they have spawned ; before that they swim deep and hug the ground. The herring, in my opinion, must have a rocky place to spawn upon, with a vegetable growth of some kind to

receive the roe ; shoals may of course accidentally spawn on
soft ground. It is not accurately known how long a period
elapses till the spawn ripens into life. I think, however,
that herring spawn requires a period of about six weeks to
ripen. It is known that young herrings have appeared on a
spawning ground in myriads within fifty days after the departure of a shoal, and fishermen say that no spawn can be found
on the ground after the lapse of a few weeks from the visit of
the gravid shoal—that the eggs in fact have come to life, and
that the fish are swimming about ; and some fishermen assert
that the little whitebait is the herring in its first stage.

It is generally known that the sprat (*Clupea sprattus*) is a
most abundant fish, so plentiful as to have been used at times
for manure. The fact of its great abundance has induced a
belief that it is not a distinct species of fish, but is, in reality,
the young of the herring. It is true that many distinguishing
marks are pointed out as belonging only to the sprat—such as
its serrated belly, the relative position of the fins, etc. But
there remains, on the other side, the very striking fact of the
sprat being rarely found with either milt or roe ; indeed, the
only case I *know* of this fish having been found in a condition
to perpetuate its species was detailed by the late Mr. Mitchell,
Belgian Consul at Leith, who exhibited before one of the
learned societies of Edinburgh a pair of sprats having the roe
and milt fully developed. Dr. Dod, an ancient anatomist,
says : " It is evident that sprats are young herrings. They appear immediately after the herrings are gone, and seem to be
the spawn just vivified, if I may use the expression. A more
undeniable proof of their being so is in their anatomy ; since,
on the closest search, no difference but size can be found between them." After the nonsense which was at one time
written about the parr, and considering the anomalies of
salmon growth, it would be unsafe to dogmatise on the sprat
question. As to the serrated belly, we might look upon it as

we do the tucks of a child's frock—viz. as a provision for growth. The fin-rays of this fish have also been cited in evidence as not being the same in number as those of the herring, but as I can testify, from actual counting, the fin-rays of the latter fish vary considerably, therefore the number of fin-rays is not evidence in the case. The slaughter of sprats which is annually carried on in our seas is, I suspect, as decided a killing of the goose for the sake of the golden eggs as the grilse-slaughter which is annually carried on in our salmon rivers.

The herring is found under four different conditions :—1st, Fry or sill ; 2d, *Maties* or fat herring ; 3d, Full herring ; 4th, Shotten or spent herring. All herrings under five or six inches in length come under the first denomination. The *matie* is the finest condition in which a herring can be used for food purposes ; and if the fishery could be so arranged, that is the time at which it should be caught for consumption. At that period it is very fat, its feeding-power being all developed on its body ; the spawn is small, the growth of the roe or milt not having yet demanded the whole of the nutriment taken by the fish. A full herring is one in which the milt or roe is fully developed. The *maties* develop into spawning herring with great rapidity—in the course of three months, it is said. The herrings at the spawning season come together in vast numbers, and proceed to their spawning places in the shallower and consequently warmer parts of the sea. As Gilbert White says, "the two great motives which regulate the brute creation are love and hunger ; the one incites them to perpetuate their kind, the latter induces them to preserve individuals." In obedience to these laws the herring congregate on our coast, for there only they find an abundant supply of food to mature with the necessary rapidity their milt and roe, as well as a sea-bottom fitted to receive their spawn ; and they are thus brought within the reach of man at what many persons consider the wrong time of their life.

As to this division of the question, it has been said that it matters not at what period you take a herring, whether it be old or young, without or with spawn; that fish cannot again be caught, and will never spawn again; and it is argued, therefore, that the taking of fish in "the family way" no more prevents it from reproducing than if it had been killed in the condition of a *matie*. The same argument was used in the case of the young salmon; and it was asked : If you kill all your grilse, where are you to find your salmon? but I shall have more to say on this part of my topic by and by.

The herring breeds, then, and is caught in greater or lesser quantities, during every month of the year. There is no general close-time for the herring in Scotland. On one or two parts of the west coast it has hitherto been illegal to capture this fish at certain seasons, although the restrictions are not general. How is it that the time selected by fishermen for the capture of this fish corresponds with the period when it is a crime to take a salmon? If a gravid salmon be unwholesome, is a gravid herring good for food? Do not the same physical laws affect both of these fish? There cannot be a doubt but that at the period of spawning, this fish, as well as all other fish, is in its worst condition so far as its food-yielding qualities are concerned, because at that time of its life its whole nutritive power is exerted on behalf of its seed, and its flesh is consequently lean and unpalatable. Yet it is a great fact that the time which the herring selects in order to fulfil the grandest instinct of its nature is the very time appointed by man for its capture ! In fact, that is the period when herrings are at a premium; they must be "full fish," or they cannot obtain the official brand; in other words, *shotten* herrings—*i.e.* fish that have spawned—are not of much more than half the value of the others. When it is taken into account that each pair of full fish (male and female) are killed just as they are about to give us the chance of

R

obtaining an increase of the stock to the extent say of thirty
thousand, the ultimate effect must be to disturb and cripple
the producing powers of the shoal to such a degree that it will
break up and find a new breeding-ground, safe for a time perhaps from the spoliation of the greedy fishermen.   The Lochfyne commissioners give as a reason for their non-recommen-
dation of a close-time the fact, that were there to be a cessation
from labour, the enemies of the herring would so increase,
that the jubilee given would be nugatory.   But surely there is
a great want of logic in this argument !   How is it that a close-
time operates so favourably in the case of the salmon—not
only a seasonal close-time, but a weekly one as well ?   Would
not the herring, with its almost miraculous breeding-power,
increase in the same ratio, or even in a greater ratio than its
enemies, especially if, as the commissioners tell us and we
believe, it is engaged in multiplying its kind during ten
months of the year ?   Are not the enemies of the herring at
work during the fishing season as well as at other periods ?
I could understand the logic of denying a close-time on the
ground that, as the herring never ceases breeding, it is impossible to fix a correct period.   But, according to the deliver-
ance made by the commissioners in the natural history
portion of their inquiry, a close-time is quite possible.   I have
ever been of opinion, notwithstanding the practical difficulties
that would have to be encountered in carrying it out, that the
want of a close-time, especially for the larger kinds of sea-
fish, is one of the causes which are so obviously affecting the
supplies.   It is certain also, from chemical and sanitary investigation, that all fish are unwholesome at the period of
spawning ; the salmon at that time of its life is looked upon
as being little better than carrion.   But, without dwelling on
this phase of the question, or considering the effect of unwholesome fish on the public health, I must point out most
strongly that the want of a well-defined close-time is one of

the greatest and severest of our fish-destroying agencies.   We
give our grouse a breathing space ; nay, we sometimes afford
to that bird a whole jubilee year ; we do not shoot our hares
during certain months of the year, nor do we select their
breeding season as the proper time to kill our oxen or our
sheep ; but we do not at dinner-time object to an *entrée* composed of cod-roe, and we evidently rather believe in the propriety of killing only our seed-laden herrings !   This lavish
destruction of fish-life has arisen in great part from the well-
known fecundity of all kinds of sea-fish, some of which yield
their eggs by the million, and this has given rise to the idea
that it is impossible to exhaust the shoals.   But when it is
considered that this wonderful fecundity is met by an unparal-
leled destruction of the seed and also of the young fish, we
need not be astonished at the ever-recurring complaint of
scarcity.   A recent, but no doubt exaggerated complaint, sets
forth that the beam-trawl is one of the most destructive
engines employed in the sea, five hundred tons of spawn being
said to be destroyed by the trawlers in twenty-four hours.
It is well known also that tons of broken fish and spawn are
sold in the south as manure for the land at threepence per
bushel !   There can be no doubt that there is annually an
enormous waste of fish-life, through the accidental destruction
of very large quantities of spawn, herring-spawn as well as all
other kinds.

As to the food of the herring, the report already alluded
to tells us that it " consists of crustacea, varying in size from
microscopic dimensions to those of a shrimp, and of small fish,
particularly sandeels.   While in the *matie* condition, they feed
voraciously, and not unfrequently their stomachs are found
immensely distended with crustacea and sandeels, in a more
or less digested condition."   I have personally examined the
stomachs of many herrings, and have found in them the remains of all kinds of food procurable in the place frequented

by the particular animal examined—including herring-roe,
young herrings, sprats, etc.; but the sandeel seems to be its
favourite food.

One of the wonders connected with the natural history of
the herring is the capricious nature of the fish. It is always
changing its *habitat*, and, according to vulgar belief, from the
most curious circumstances. I need not add to the necessary
length of this chapter by giving a great number of instances
of the capricious nature of the herring; but I must cite a
few, in order to make my recapitulation of herring history as
complete as possible, and at the same time it is proper to
mention that superstition is brought to bear on this point.
The fishermen of St. Monance, in Fife, used to remove their
church-bell during the fishing season, as they affirmed that its
ringing scared away the shoals of herring from the bay! It
has long been a favourite and popular idea that they were
driven away by the noise of gun-firing. The Swedes say that
the frequent firings of the British ships in the neighbourhood
of Gothenburg frightened the fish away from the place. In a
similar manner and with equal truth it was said that they
had been driven away from the Baltic by the firing of guns
at the battle of Copenhagen! "Ordinary philosophy is never
satisfied," says Dr. M'Culloch, "unless it can find a solution
for everything; and it is satisfied for this reason with imaginary ones." Thus in Long Island, one of the Hebrides, it
was asserted that the fish had been driven away by the kelp-
manufacture, some imaginary coincidence having been found
between their disappearance and the establishment of that
business. But the kelp fires did not drive them away from
other shores, which they frequent and abandon indifferently,
without regard to that work. A member of the House of
Commons, in a debate on a Tithe Bill in 1835, stated that a
clergyman, having obtained a living on the coast of Ireland,
signified his intention of taking the tithe of fish, which was,

however, considered to be so utterly repugnant to their privileges and feelings, that not a single herring had ever since visited that part of the shore !

The most prominent members of the *Clupediæ* are the common herring (*Clupea harengus*) ; the sprat, or garvie (*Clupea sprattus*) ; and the pilchard, or gipsy herring (*Clupea pilchardus*).

MEMBERS OF THE HERRING FAMILY.

1. Herring.   2. Sprat.   3. Pilchard.

The other members of this family are the whitebait, the anchovy, and the Alice and Twaite shad ; but these, although affording material for speculation to naturalists (see chapter on "Fish Growth"), are not of any commercial importance.

The fisheries for the common herring, the pilchard, and the sprat, are carried on, with a brief interval, all the year round ; but the great herring season is during the autumn—from August to October—when the sea is covered with boats in pursuit of that fine fish, and in some of its phases the herring-fishery assumes an aspect that is decidedly picturesque. Every little bay all round the island has its tiny fleet ; the mountain-

closed lochs of the Western Highlands have each a fishery ;
while at some of the more important fishing-stations there are
very large fleets assembled—as at Wick, Dunbar, Ardrishaig,
Stornoway, Peterhead, and Anstruther.   The chief curers have
places of business in these towns, where they keep a large
store of curing materials and a competent staff of coopers and
others to aid them in their business.   Such boats as do not
carry on a local fishery proceed from the smaller fishing-villages
to one or other of the centres of the herring trade.   In fact,
wherever an enterprising curer sets up his stand, there the
boats will gather round him ; and beside him will collect a
mob of all kinds of miscellaneous people—dealers in salt, sellers
of barrel-staves, vendors of "cutch," Prussian herring-buyers,
comely girls from the inland districts to gut, and men from the
Highlands anxious to officiate as " hired hands."   Itinerant
ministers and revivalists also come on the scene and preach
occasional sermons to the hundreds of devout Scotch people
who are assembled ; and thus arises many a prosperous little
town, or at least towns that might be prosperous were the
finny treasures of the sea always plentiful.   As the chief her-
ing season comes on a kind of madness seizes on all engaged,
ever so remotely, in the trade ; as for those more immediately
concerned, they seem to go completely " daft," especially the
younger hands.   The old men, too, come outside to view the
annual preparations, and talk, with revived enthusiasm, to
their sons and grandsons about what they did twenty years
agone ; the young men spread out the shoulder-of-mutton sails
of their boats to view and repair defects ; and the wives and
sweethearts, by patching and darning, contrive to make old
nets " look amaist as weel as new ;" boilers bubble with the
brown *catechu,* locally called " cutch," which is used as a
preservative for the nets and sails ; while all along the coasts
old boats are being cobbled up and new ones are being built
and launched.

The scene along the seabord from Buckhaven on the Firth of Forth to Buckie on the Firth of Moray is one of active preparation, and all concerned are hoping for a "lucky" fishing; "winsome" young lassies are praying for the success of their sweethearts' boats, because if the season turns out well they will be married women at its close. Curers look sanguine, and the owners of free boats seem happy. The little children too—those wonderful little children one always finds in a fishing village, striving so manfully to fill up "daddy's" old clothes—participate in the excitement: they have their winter's "shoon" and "Sunday breeks" in perspective. At the quaint village of Gamrie, at Macduff, or Buckie, the talk of old and young, on coach or rail, from morning to night, is of herrings. There are comparisons and calculations about "crans" and barrels, and "broke" and "splitbellies," and "full fish" and "lanks," and reminiscences of great hauls of former years, and much figurative talk about prices and freights, and the cost of telegraphic messages. Then, if the present fishery be dull, hopes are expressed that the next one may be better. "Ony fish this mornin'?" is the first salutation of one neighbour to another: the very infants talk about "herrin';" schoolboys steal them from the boats for the purpose of aiding their negotiations with the gooseberry woman: while wandering paupers are rewarded with one or two broken fish by good-natured sailors, when "the take" has been so satisfactory as to warrant such largess. At Wick the native population, augmented by four thousand strangers, wakens into renewed life; it is like Doncaster on the approach of the St. Leger. The summer-time of Wick's existence begins with the fishery: the shops are painted on their outsides and are replenished within; the milliner and the tailor exhibit their newest fashions; the hardware merchant flourishes his most attractive frying-pans; the grocer amplifies his stock; and so for a brief period all is *couleur de rose.*

They are not all practical fishermen who go down to the
sea for herring during the great autumnal fishing season. By
far the larger portion of those engaged in the capture of this
fish—particularly at the chief stations—are what are called
" hired hands," a mixture of the farmer, the mechanic, and the
sailor ; and this fact may account in some degree for a portion
of the accidents which are sure to occur in stormy seasons.
Many of these men are mere labourers at the herring-fishery,
and have little skill in handling a boat ; they are many of them
farmers in the Lewis, or small crofters in the Isle of Skye.
The real orthodox fisherman is a different being, and he is the
same everywhere. If you travel from Banff to Bayonne you
find that fishermen are unchangeable.

The men's work is all performed at sea, and, so far as the
capture of the herring is concerned, there is no display of
either skill or cunning. The legal mode of capturing the
herring is to take it by means of what is called a drift-net.
The herring-fishery, it must be borne in mind, is regulated by
Act of Parliament, by which the exact means and mode of
capture are explicitly laid down. A drift-net is an instrument
made of fine twine worked into a series of squares, each of
which is an inch, so as to allow plenty of room for the escape
of young herrings. Nets for herring are measured by the
barrel-bulk, and each barrel will hold two nets, each net being
fifty yards long and thirty-two feet deep. The larger fishing-
boats carry something like a mile of these nets ; some, at any
rate, carry a drift, which will extend two thousand yards in
length. These drifts are composed of many separate nets,
fastened together by means of what is called a back-rope, and
each separate net of the series is marked off by a buoy or
bladder which is attached to it, the whole being sunk in the
sea by means of a leaden or other weight, and fastened to the
boat by a longer or shorter trail-rope, according to the depth
in the water at which it is expected to find the herrings.

This formidable apparatus, which forms a great perforated wall, being let into the sea immediately after sunset, floats or drifts with the tide, so as to afford the herring an opportunity of striking against it, and so becoming captured—in fact they are drowned in the nets. The boats engaged in the drift-net fishing are of various sizes, and are strongly and carefully

VIEW OF LOCHFYNE.

built : the largest, being upwards of thirty-five feet keel, with a large drift of nets and good sail and mast, will cost something like a sum of £200.

The other mode of fishing for herrings, which has existed for about a quarter of a century, is illegal, although it is as nearly as possible the same as is legally used to capture the pilchard on the coast of Cornwall. In the west of Scotland, on Lochfyne in particular, where it is still to some extent practised, it is called " trawling ;" but the instrument of cap-

ture is in reality a " seine" net ; and, so far as the size of the
mesh is concerned, is all right. The mode of using this net I
shall presently describe ; in the meantime I may state that
the practice of " seining" has given cause to much disputation
and many quarrels, some of them resulting in violence and
bloodshed ; the whole dispute having given rise to the recent
Commission of Inquiry. It is worth while, I think, to abridge
the commissioners' account of the cause of quarrel, and the
arguments used on both sides of the question. The drift-net
men assert that immature herrings are caught by the trawl,
and that that mode of fishing breaks up the shoals, and that
these scatter and do not again unite, as also that the seine
destroys the spawn. A graver assertion is, that the trawled
herrings are not fit for curing in consequence of their being
injured in the capture ; likewise that the seine-net fishers are
given to brawling and mischief. The assertion is also made
that it is quite impossible for the two kinds of fishing to be
carried on together, especially in confined places like Lochfyne.
The real reason is, I think, brought in last—viz. that the
great quantities of fish taken on a sudden by the trawlers
affect the markets and derange the prices—all to the great
detriment of the drift-net men. The trawlers are quite able
to answer all these questions both individually and by a
general denial. They say that it is not their interest to con-
tract the width of the mesh, and that, in fact, the trawl-net
mesh is quite as large as the other. They assert that a seine-
net is not so much calculated to disturb a shoal of herrings
as the drift-net, which is of great length and at once obstructs
the shoal. They deny that they have interfered with the
spawning-beds, and also state that they have no particular
interest in catching foul fish, as they sell their herrings chiefly
in a fresh state, and say that their fish are most adapted for
the fresh market, likewise that they can be cured as easily as
herrings caught by the drift-nets. They emphatically deny

being brawlers, or that they wilfully injure the drift-nets; and they assert that both kinds of fishing can perfectly well be carried on simultaneously on the same fishing-ground. In fact the trawlers, in my opinion, have thoroughly made out their case; and the commissioners, I am very glad to record, have decided in their favour.

The pilchard is generally captured by means of the seine-net, and we never hear of its being injured thereby. It is also cured in large quantities, the same as the herring, although the *modus operandi* is somewhat different.

The pilchard was at one time, like the herring, thought to be a migratory fish, but it has been found, as in the case of the common herring, to be a native of our own seas. In some years the pilchard has been known to shed its spawn in May, but the usual time is October, and Mr. Couch thinks that fish does not breed twice in the same year. Their food, we are told by Mr. Couch, is small crustaceous animals, as their stomachs are frequently crammed with a small kind of shrimp, and the supply of this kind of food is thought to be enormous. When on the coast, the assemblage of pilchards assumes an arrangement like that of a great army, and the vast shoal is known to be made up by the coming together of smaller bodies of that fish, and these frequently separate and rejoin, and are constantly shifting their position. The pilchard is not now so numerous as it was a few years ago, but very large hauls are still occasionally obtained. According to a recent statement in the *Times*, the present pilchard season (1865) seems to have been a very bad one—" the worst that has been experienced for upwards of twenty years. The great majority of the boats have not nearly cleared their expenses."

Great excitement prevails on the coast of Cornwall during the pilchard season. Persons watch the water from the coast and signal to those who are in search of the fish the moment they perceive indications of a shoal. These watchers are

locally called "huers," and they are provided with signals of
white calico or branches of trees, with which to direct the
course of the boat, and to inform those in charge when they
are upon the fish—the shoal being best seen from the cliffs.
The pilchards are captured by the seine-net—that is, the shoal,
or spot of a shoal, that has risen, is completely surrounded by
a wall of netting, the principal boat and its satellites the volyer
and the lurker, with the "stop-nets," having so worked as
quite to overlap each other's wall of canvas. The place where
the joining of the two nets is formed is carefully watched, to
see that none of the fish escape at that place, and if it be too
open, the fish are beaten back with the oars of some of the
persons attending—about eighteen in all. In due time the
seine is worked or hauled into shallow water for the convenience of getting out the fish, and it may perhaps contain
pilchards sufficient to fill two thousand hogsheads. Generally
speaking, four or five seines will be at work together, giving
employment to a great number of the people, who may have
been watching for the chance during many days. When the
tide falls the men commence to bring ashore the fish, a tuck-
net worked inside of the seine being used for safety; and the
large shallow dipper boats required for bringing the fish to the
beach may be seen sunk to the water's edge with their burden,
as successive bucketfuls are taken out of the nets and emptied
into these conveyance vessels. To give the reader an idea of
quantity, as connected with pilchard-fishing, I may state that
it takes nearly three thousand fish to fill a hogshead. I have
heard of a shoal being captured that took a fortnight to bring
ashore. Ten thousand hogsheads of pilchards have been
known to be taken in one port in a day's time. The convenience of keeping the shoal in the water is obvious, as the
fish need not be withdrawn from it till it is convenient to
salt them. The fish are salted in curing-houses, great quantities of them being piled up into huge stacks, alternate layers

of salt and fish. During the process of curing a large quantity of useful oil exudes from the heaps. The salting process is called " bulking," and the fish are built up into stacks with great regularity, where they are allowed to remain for four weeks, after which they are washed and freed from the oil, then packed into hogsheads, and sent to Spain and Italy, to be extensively consumed during Lent, as well as at other fasting times. The hurry and bustle at any of the little Cornwall ports during the manipulation of a few shoals of pilchards must be seen, the excitement cannot be very well described.

The pilchard is, or rather it ought to be, the *Sardinia* of commerce, but its place is usurped by the sprat, or garvie as we call it in Scotland, and thousands of tin boxes of that fish are annually made up and sold as sardines. I have already alluded to the sprat, so far as its natural history is concerned. It is a fish that is very abundant in Scotland, especially in the Firth of Forth, where for many years there has been a good sprat-fishery. We do not now require to go to France for our sardines, as we can cure them at home in the French style. The sprat-fishery for sardine-making is still, however, a considerable maritime industry on the coast of France. In 1864 about 75,000 barrels of sprats were taken on the coast of Brittany, besides those sold fresh and the quantities done up in oil as sardines. The process of curing with oil is as follows :—The fish must be well washed in sea-water, after which they are sprinkled with clean salt. The next process is to cut off the heads of the fish, and take away the intestines, etc., after which they are again rinsed in the sea-water, and hung up or laid out to dry in order to beautify. After this they are placed for a very brief period in a pan of boiling oil, which completes the cure. Before being packed in the neat little tin boxes in which we find them, the sardines are laid down on a grating, in order to let the oil drain off—the finishing process being the ex-

posure of the box in a steam-chest for such a period as the
curer deems necessary. According to my informant, a thorough
cure is effected when the box appears convex on the two
sides, only it is necessary that this convexity should disappear
as the box becomes cool. Ten millions of boxes are annually
sent away from the coast of Brittany, and these are widely
distributed, not only in Europe, but in Australia and America
as well. I have elsewhere mentioned the use of cod-roe in the
French sprat-fishery. The quantity used costs about £80,000
annually, and is brought from Norway. Each boat engaged
in the sprat-fishery will use from twelve to twenty barrels!
Will not the consumption of such a quantity of roe tell by
and by on the cod-fishery?

Sprats, whether they be young herrings or no, are very
plentiful in the winter months, and afford a supply of wholesome food of the fish kind to many who are unable to procure
more expensive kinds. When the fishing for garvies (sprats)
was stopped a few years ago by order of the Board of White
Fisheries, there was quite a sensation in Edinburgh; and an
agitation was got up that has resulted in a partial resumption
of the fishing, which is of considerable value—about £50,000
in the Firth of Forth alone.

Commerce in herring is entirely different from commerce in
any other article, particularly in Scotland. In fact the fishery,
as at present conducted, is just another way of gambling. The
home "curers" and foreign buyers are the persons who at present
keep the herring-fishery from stagnating, and the goods (i.e. the
fish) are generally all bought and sold long before they are
captured. The way of dealing in herring is pretty much as
follows:—Owners of boats are engaged to fish by curers, the
bargains being usually that the curer will take two hundred
crans of herring—and a cran, it may be stated, is forty-five
gallons of ungutted fish; for these two hundred crans a certain
sum per cran is paid according to arrangement, the bargain

including as well a definite sum of ready money by way of
bounty, perhaps also an allowance of spirits, and the use of
ground for the drying of the nets.   On the other hand, the
boat-owner provides a boat, nets, buoys, and all the apparatus
of the fishery, and engages a crew to fish ; his crew may, perhaps, be relatives and part-owners sharing the venture with
him, but usually the crew consists of hired men who get so
much wages at the end of the season, and have no risk or
profit.   This is the plan followed by free and independent
fishermen who are really owners of their own boats and
apparatus.   It will thus be seen that the curer is bargaining
for two hundred crans of fish months before he knows that a
single herring will be captured ; for the bargain of next
season is always made at the close of the present one, and he
has to pay out at once a large sum by way of bounty, and
provide barrels, salt, and other necessaries for the cure before
he knows even if the catch of the season just expiring will all
be sold, or how the markets will pulsate next year.   On the
other hand, the fisherman has received his pay for his season's
fish, and very likely pocketed a sum of from ten to thirty
pounds as earnest-money for next year's work.   Then, again,
a certain number of curers who are men of capital will advance
money to young fishermen in order that they may purchase a
boat and the necessary quantity of netting to enable them to
engage in the fishery—thus thirling the boat to their service,
very probably fixing an advantageous price per cran for the
herrings to be fished and supplied.   Curers, again, who are
not capitalists, have to borrow from the buyers, because to
compete with their fellows they must be able to lend money
for the purchase of boats and nets, or to advance sums by way
of bounty to the free boats ; and thus a rotten unwholesome
system goes the round—fishermen, boat-builders, curers, and
merchants all hanging on each other, and evidencing that
there is as much gambling in herring-fishing as in horse-racing.

The whole system of commerce connected with this trade is decidedly unhealthy; and ought at once to be checked and re-constructed if there be any logical method of doing it.   At a port of three hundred boats a sum of £145 was paid by the curers for "arles," and spent in the public-houses !   More than £4000 was paid in bounties, and an advance of nearly £7000 made on the various contracts, and all this money was paid eight months before the fishing began.   When the season is a favourable one and plenty of fish are taken, then all goes well, and the evil day is postponed ; but if, as in one or two recent seasons, the take is poor, then there comes a crash.   One falls, and, like a row of bricks, the others all follow.   At the large fishing stations there are comparatively few of the boats that are thoroughly free : they are tied up in some way between the buyers and curers, or they are in pawn to some merchant who "backs" the nominal owner.   The principal, or at least the immediate sufferers by these arrangements are the hired men.

This "bounty," as it is called, is a most reprehensible feature of herring commerce, and although still the prevalent mode of doing business, has been loudly declaimed against by all who have the real good of the fishermen at heart.   Often enough men who have obtained boats and nets on credit, and hired persons to assist them during the fishery, are so unfor-tunate as not to catch enough of herrings to pay their expenses. The curers for whom they engaged to fish having retained most of the bounty money on account of boats and nets, consequently the hired servants have frequently in such cases to go home — sometimes to a great distance—penniless.   It would be much better if the old system of a share were re-introduced : in that case the hired men would at least participate to the extent of the fishing, whether it were good or bad.   Boat-owners try of course to get as good terms as possible, as well in the shape of price for herrings as in bounty and perquisites.   For an example of an engagement I may cite the case of a Burghhead boat, which bargained for 15s. per cran, 20s. of engaging money (arles), ten gallons of whisky, net-ground, net-driving—*i.e.* from the boat to the ground and back again—and £20 of cash in the shape of a bounty.*   At some places even larger sums are asked for and obtained—as much as £54 in bounty and perquisites.   My idea is that there ought to be no " engage-ments," no bounty, and no perquisites.   As each fishing comes round let the boats catch, and the curers buy day by day as the fish arrive at the quay.   This plan has already been adopted at some fishing-towns, and is an obvious improve-ment on the prevailing plan of gambling by means of " engagements " in advance.

In fact, this fishery is best described when it is called a lottery.   No person knows what the yield will be till the last moment : it may be abundant, or it may be a total failure. Agriculturists are aware long before the reaping season whether their crops are light or heavy, and they arrange ac-cordingly ; but if we are to believe the fisherman, his harvest is entirely a matter of "luck."   It is this belief in "luck" which is, in a great degree, the cause of our fisher-folk not keeping pace with the times : they are greatly behind in all matters of progress ; our fishing towns look as if they were, so to speak, stereotyped.   It is a woeful time for the fisher-folk when the herrings fail them ; for this great harvest of the sea, which needs no tillage of the husbandman, the fruits of which are reaped without either sowing seed or paying rent,

* " We understand that about 100 boats have been engaged to fish at Fraserburgh from Portsoy, Portknockie, Buckie, and Portgordon, and the other fishing villages.   The exact terms of engagement we subjoin as follows, from an authoritative source.   The terms are— 15s. per cran, with £15 bounty, £2 for lodgings, £1 as earnest-money, with cartage of nets, and net ground.   The cartage of nets and net ground costs £3 : 10s. to £4, so that the terms are equal to 15s. per cran, and £21 : 10s. to £22 in full of bounty."—*Banff Journal.*

is the chief industry that the bulk of the coast population
depend upon for a good sum of money. The fishing is the
bank, in which they have opened, and perhaps exhausted, a
cash-credit; for often enough the balance is on the wrong
side of the ledger, even after the fishing season has come and
gone. In other words, new boats have to be paid for out of
the fishing; new clothes, new houses, additional nets, and
even weddings, are all dependent on the herring-fishery. It is
notable that after a favourable season the weddings among the
fishing populations are very numerous. The anxiety for a
good season may be noted all along the British coasts, from
Newhaven to Yarmouth, or from Crail to Wick.

The highest prices are paid for the early fish, contracts
for these in a cured state being sometimes fixed as high as
forty-five shillings per barrel. These are at once despatched to
Germany, in the inland towns of which a prime salt herring
of the early cure is considered a great luxury, fetching sometimes the handsome price of one shilling! Great quantities
of cured herrings are sent to Stettin or other German ports,
and so eager are some of the merchants for an early supply
that in the beginning of the season they purchase quantities
unbranded, through the agency of the telegraph. On those
parts of the coast where the communication with large towns
is easy, considerable quantities of herring are purchased fresh,
for transmission to Birmingham, Manchester, and other inland
cities. Buyers attend for that purpose, and send them off
frequently in an open truck, with only a slight covering to
protect them from the sun. It is needless to say that a fresh
herring is looked upon as a luxury in such places, and a
demand exists that would exhaust any supply that could be
sent. During one day in last September what was thought
to be a hopeless glut of herrings arrived at Billingsgate; the
consignment was so vast as quite to alarm the salesmen of
that market; but their fears were groundless, as before noon

every herring was sold. From ten to twelve thousand tons of fresh herrings are sent from Dunbar alone, during the season, into inland districts, being distributed by means of the railway, and also by cadgers.

Many of the Scottish herring-curers are men of enterprise and intelligence. The late Mr. Methuen of Leith may be cited as an example of the class : he was of humble parentage, but had the good fortune, by perseverance and industry, to become the greatest herring-curer in the world. He raised his gigantic business on a small foundation, which his father and he laid at Burntisland in Fife. His business grew apace ; his yards overflowed into the streets, and his piles of barrels soon blocked up the passages. He gathered knowledge of his business from all who could give it him ; and in after years, when his trade had grown to be the greatest of its kind, he found this knowledge of great service to him. He was soon compelled, however, by the extension of his connection, to seek larger head-quarters than he could obtain at Burntisland. In 1833, therefore, he removed to Leith, the seaport of Edinburgh, where he continued to carry on his business till the time of his death. For thirty years he was at the head of the herring-trade in Britain, and was so energetic and reputable in his dealings as really to command success, in which, of course, he was materially aided by his rapidly-increasing capital. He created curing-stations, and so forced business. Wherever he saw an eligible spot, he marked it out as a place to cure in. His business widened and widened, till thousands of the Scottish fishing-boats were ready to obey his behests ; and, not contented with what he had achieved in his own country, he invaded England, and commenced stations along the east coast and on the Isle of Man, having some time before established business relations on the coast of Norway. Mr. Methuen took a warm interest in all questions connected with the herring-fishery, and may be said to have carried on business during the period when these fisheries were in their most prosperous condition ; in fact, he may be said to have seen the culmination of the trade.   He was foremost in action when an attempt was made to abolish the Fishery Board for Scotland.   His accurate acquaintance with the trade, and his knowledge of the natural history of the fish, and the precise nature of his statements as to the value of the Board, were the means of converting the Government of his time, so that the Board was maintained in its integrity.   Mr. Methuen's powers of observation were considerable ; he once reasoned out by a reference to some old letters the precise spot where a local shoal of herrings was to be found.   I have alluded to his plan of gathering knowledge from all with whom he come in contact ; he stored up such letters of his agents as contained facts for future use, and often found them of service.   At one of his stations in the far North the fishing had been unsuccessful for the greater part of the season, and there was no prospect of improvement, when he gave it his consideration.   Looking over his agent's letters at said place for some years back, he found, by a comparison of dates, that at a certain spot herrings were to be found.   He accordingly instructed his agent to send his boats to that spot.   The fishermen simply laughed at the idea of an individual sitting some hundreds of miles away and telling *them* where to get fish.   But as his orders were positive, they had to obey, and the consequence was that they returned the next morning loaded with herrings.

Having explained the relation of the curers to the trade, I must now speak of the cure—the greater number of the herrings caught on the coast of Scotland being pickled in salt; a result originally, no doubt, of the want of speedy modes of transit to large seats of population, where herrings would be largely consumed if they could arrive in a sufficiently fresh state to be palatable.   At stations about Wick the quantity of herrings disposed of fresh is comparatively small, so that by

far the larger portion of the daily catch has to be salted. This
process during a good season employs a very large number of
persons, chiefly as coopers and gutters; and, as the barrels have
to be branded, by way of certificate of the quality of their contents, it is necessary that the salting should be carefully done.

VIEW OF A CURING YARD.

As soon as the boats reach the harbour—and as the fishing is
appointed to be carried on after sunset they arrive very early
in the morning—the various crews commence to carry their
fish to the reception-troughs of the curers by whom they have
been engaged. A person in the interest of the curer checks
the number of crans brought in, and sprinkles the fish from
time to time with considerable quantities of salt. As soon as
a score or two of baskets have been emptied, the gutters set
earnestly to do their portion of the work, which is dirty and
disagreeable in the extreme. The gutters usually work in

companies of about five—one or two gutting, one or two carrying, and another packing. Basketfuls of the fish, so soon as they are gutted, are carried to the back of the yard, and plunged into a large tub, there to be roused and mixed up with salt ; then the adroit and active packer seizes a handful and arranges them with the greatest precision in a barrel, a handful of salt being thrown over each layer as it is put in, so that, in the short space of a few minutes, the large barrel is crammed full with many hundred fish, all gutted, roused, and packed in a period of not more than ten minutes. As the fish settle down in the barrel, more are added from day to day, till it is thoroughly full and ready for the brand. On the proper performance of these parts of the business, the quality of the cured fish very much depends. The late Sir Thomas Dick Lauder, who was at one time secretary to the Fishing Board, published plain instructions for taking and curing herrings ; he gives minute directions in all departments, and thus speaks of the important duties of the coopers :—" During the period of the curing, the cooper's first employment in the morning should be to examine every barrel packed on the previous day, in order to discover if any of them have lost the pickle, so that he may have all such barrels immediately re-packed, salted, and pickled. . . . . As already stated, the cooper in charge should see that the gutters are furnished every morning with sharp knives. He should be careful to strew salt among the herrings as they are turned into the gutting-boxes ; give a general but strict attention to the gutters, in order to insure that they do their work properly ; see that the herrings are properly sorted, and that all the broken and injured fish are removed ; and take care that the fish are sufficiently and effectually roused. Then he should see that every barrel is seasoned with water, and the hoops properly driven, before they are given to the packers. He should like-wise keep his eyes over the packers, to see that the tiers of herrings are regularly laid and salted, and that a cover is placed on every barrel immediately after it has been completely packed."

I have a very few words to say about the *brand :* whether or not each barrel of herrings should have stamped upon it a government mark indicative of its quality has been one of the most fertile subjects of controversy in connection with herring commerce. *Now* the brand—which was devised during the time the British government paid a bounty to the curer as an encouragement to fish for herrings—is voluntary, and has to be paid for, and in time, there can be no doubt, it will be altogether discontinued; and it would have been better perhaps had it never existed, although its continuance has been advocated by many excellent persons on the ground of its service to the fisheries. Other kinds of goods have been able to command a market without the interference of government—such as cotton and other textile fabrics, cheese, etc. Why then could not we sell our herrings on the faith of the curer? Government is not asked to brand our broadcloths, or our blankets, nor yet our steam-engines ; and I hope soon to see a total abolition of the brand on our herring-barrels ; but although I am an advocate for the total abolition of the brand I wish the present Fishery Board continued : there is ample employment for all the officers of that Board in acting as statisticians and police ; we can never obtain sufficient information about the capture and disposal of the fish, the fluctuations of the fishery, etc. etc.

The following detailed description of the "herring-harvest," as gathered in the Moray Frith, may be of interest to the general reader. It is reprinted, by permission, from a paper contributed by the author to the *Cornhill Magazine :—*

The boats usually start for the fishing-ground an hour or two before sunset, and are generally manned by four men and a boy, in addition to the owner or skipper. The nets, which

have been carried inland in the morning, in order that they
might be thoroughly dried, have been brought to the boat in a
cart or waggon.   On board there is a keg of water and a bag of
bread or hard biscuit ; and in addition to these simple necessaries, our boat contains a bottle of whisky which we have
presented by way of paying our footing.   The name of our
skipper is Francis Sinclair, and a very gallant-looking fellow
he is ; and as to his dress—why, his boots alone would ensure
the success of a Surrey melodrama ; and neither Truefit nor
Ross could satisfactorily imitate his beard and whiskers.
Having got safely on board—a rather difficult matter in a
crowded harbour, where the boats are elbowing each other for
room—we contrive, with some labour, to work our way out of
the narrow-necked harbour into the bay, along with the nine
hundred and ninety-nine boats that are to accompany us in
our night's avocation.   The heights of Pulteneytown, which
command the quays, are covered with spectators admiring
the pour-out of the herring fleet and wishing with all
their hearts " God speed " to the venturers : old salts who
have long retired from active seamanship are counting
their " takes " over again ; and the curer is mentally reckoning up the morrow's catch.   Janet and Jeanie are smiling a kindly good-bye to " faither," and hoping for the safe
return of Donald or Murdoch ; and crowds of people are
scattered on the heights, all taking various degrees of interest
in the scene, which is stirringly picturesque to the eye of the
tourist, and suggestive to the thoughtful observer.

Bounding gaily over the waves, which are crisping and
curling their crests under the influence of the land-breeze, our
shoulder-of-mutton sail filled with a good capful of wind, we
hug the rocky coast, passing the ruined tower known as " the
Old Man of Wick," which serves as a capital landmark for the
fleet.   Soon the red sun begins to dip into the golden west,
burnishing the waves with lustrous crimson and silver, and

against the darkening eastern sky the thousand sails of the herring-fleet blaze like sheets of flame. The shore becomes more and more indistinct, and the beetling cliffs assume fantastic and weird shapes, whilst the moaning waters rush into deep cavernous recesses with a wild and monotonous sough, that falls on the ear with a deeper and a deeper melancholy, broken only by the shrill wail of the herring-gull. A dull hot haze settles on the scene, through which the coppery rays of the sun penetrate, powerless to cast a shadow. The scene grows more and more picturesque as the glowing sails of the fleet fade into grey specks dimly seen. Anon the breeze freshens and our boat cleaves the water with redoubled speed : we seem to sail farther and farther into the gloom, until the boundary-line between sea and shore becomes lost to the sight.

We ought to have shot our nets before it became so dark, but our skipper, being anxious to hit upon the right place, so as to save a second shooting, tacked up and down, uncertain where to take up his station. We had studied the movements of certain "wise men" of the fishery—men who are always lucky, and who find out the fish when others fail ; but our crew became impatient when they began to smell the water, which had an oily gleam upon it indicative of herring, and sent out from the bows of the boat bright phosphorescent sparkles of light. The men several times thought they were right over the fish, but the skipper knew better. At last, after a lengthened cruise, our commander, who had been silent for half-an-hour, jumped up and called to action. "Up, men, and at 'em," was then the order of the night. The preparations for shooting the nets at once began by our lowering sail. Surrounding us on all sides was to be seen a moving world of boats ; many with their sails down, their nets floating in the water, and their crews at rest, indulging in fitful snatches of sleep. Other boats again were still flitting uneasily about ; their skippers, like our own, anxious to shoot in the best place, but as yet uncertain where to cast : they wait till they see indications of fish in other nets.   By and by we are ourselves ready, the sinker goes splash into the water, the "dog" (a large bladder, or inflated skin of some kind, to mark the far end of the train) is heaved overboard, and the nets, breadth after breadth, follow as fast as the men can pay them out (each division being marked by a large painted bladder), till the immense train sinks into the water, forming a perforated wall a mile long and many feet in depth ; the "dog" and the marking bladders floating and dipping in a long zigzag line, reminding one of the imaginary coils of the great sea-serpent.

Wrapped in the folds of a sail and rocked by the heaving waves we tried in vain to snatch a brief nap, though those who are accustomed to such beds can sleep well enough in a herring-boat.   The skipper, too, slept with one eye open ; for the boat being his property, and the risk all his, he required to look about him, as the nets are apt to become entangled with those belonging to other fishermen, or to be torn away by surrounding boats.   After three hours' quietude, beneath a beautiful sky, the stars—

"Those eternal orbs that beautify the night"—

began to pale their fires, and the grey dawn appearing indicated that it was time to take stock.   On reckoning up we found that we had floated gently with the tide till we were a long distance away from the harbour.   The skipper had a presentiment that there were fish in his nets ; indeed the bobbing down of a few of the bladders had made it almost a certainty ; at any rate we resolved to examine the drift, and see if there were any fish.   It was a moment of suspense, while, by means of the swing-rope, the boat was hauled up to the nets.   "Hurrah!" at last exclaimed Murdoch of the Isle of Skye, "there's a lot of fish, skipper, and no mistake."   Murdoch's news was true ; our nets were silvery with herrings—so laden, in fact, that it took a long time to haul them in. It was a beautiful sight to see the shimmering fish as they came up like a sheet of silver from the water, each uttering a weak death-chirp as it was flung to the bottom of the boat. Formerly the fish were left in the meshes of the nets till the boat arrived in the harbour; but now, as the net is hauled on board, they are at once shaken out. As our silvery treasure showers into the boat we roughly guess our capture at fifty crans—a capital night's work.

The herrings being all on board, our duty is now to "up sail" and get home : the herrings cannot be too soon among the salt. As we make for the harbour, we discern at once how rightly the term lottery has been applied to the herring-fishery. Boats which fished quite near our own were empty; while others again greatly exceeded our catch. "It is entirely chance work," said our skipper; "and although there may sometimes be millions of fish in the bay, the whole fleet may not divide a hundred crans between them." On some occasions, however, the shoal is hit so exactly that the fleet may bring into the harbour a quantity of fish that in the gross would be an ample fortune. So heavy are the "takes" occasionally, that we have known the nets of many boats to be torn away and lost through the sheer weight of the fish which were enmeshed in them.

The favouring breeze soon carried us to the quay, where the boats were already arriving in hundreds, and where we were warmly welcomed by the wife of our skipper, who bestowed on us, as the lucky cause of the miraculous draught, a very pleasant smile. When we arrived the cure was going on with startling rapidity. The night had been a golden one for the fishers—calm and beautiful, the water being merely rippled by the land-breeze. But it is not always so in the Bay of Wick : the herring-fleet has been more than once overtaken by a fierce storm, when valuable lives have been lost, and thousands of pounds' worth of netting and boats destroyed. On such occasions the gladdening sights of the herring-fishery are changed to wailing and sorrow. It is no wonder that the heavens are eagerly scanned as the boats marshal their way out of the harbour, and the speck on the distant horizon keenly watched as it grows into a mass of gloomy clouds. As the song says, " Caller herrin' " represent the lives of men ; and many a despairing wife and mother can tell a sad tale of the havoc created by the summer gales on our exposed northern coast.

From the heights of Pulteneytown, overlooking the quays and curers' stations, one has before him, as it were, an extended plain, covered with thousands and tens of thousands of barrels, interspersed at short distances with the busy scene of delivery, of packing, and of salting, and all the bustle and detail attendant on the cure. It is a scene difficult to describe, and has ever struck those witnessing it for the first time with wonder and surprise.

Having visited Wick in the very heat of the season, and for the express purpose of gaining correct information about this important branch of our national industry, I am enabled to offer a slight description of the place and its appurtenances. Travellers by the steamboat usually arrive at the very time the " herring-drave " is making for the harbour ; and a beautiful sight it is to see the magnificent fleet of boats belonging to the district, radiant in the light of the rising sun, all steadily steering to the one point, ready to add a large quota to the wealth of industrial Scotland. As we wend our way from the little jagged rock at which we are landed by the small boat attendant on the steamer, we obtain a glimpse of the one distinguishing feature of the town—the herring commerce. On all sides we are surrounded by herring. On our left hand countless basketfuls are being poured into the immense gutting-troughs, and on the right hand there are countless basketfuls being carried from the three or four hundred boats which are ranged on that particular side of the harbour; and behind the troughs more basketfuls are being carried to the packers. The very infants are seen studying the " gentle art ;" and countless rows of the breechless *gamins de Wick* are busy hooking up the silly " poddlies." All around the atmosphere is humid ; the sailors are dripping, the herring-gutters and packers are. dripping, and every thing and person appears wet and comfortless ; and as you pace along you are nearly ankle-deep in brine. Meantime the herrings are being shovelled about in the. large shallow troughs with immense wooden spades, and with very little ceremony. Brawny men pour them from the baskets on their shoulders into the aforesaid troughs, and other brawny men dash them about with more wooden spades, and then sprinkle salt over each new parcel as it is poured in, till there is a sufficient quantity to warrant the commencement of the important operation of gutting and packing. Men are rushing wildly about with note-books, making mysterious-looking entries. Carts are being filled with dripping nets ready to hurry them off to the fields to dry. The screeching of saws among billet-wood, and the plashing of the neighbouring water-wheel, add to the great babel of sound that deafens you on every side. Flying about, blood-bespattered and hideously picturesque, we observe the gutters ; and on all hands we may note thousands of herring-barrels, and piles of billet-wood ready to convert into staves. At first sight every person looks mad—some appear so from their costume, others from their manner—and the confusion seems inextricable ; but there is method in their madness, and even out of the chaos of Wick harbour comes regularity, as I have endeavoured to show.

So soon as a sufficient quantity of fish has been brought from the boats and emptied into the gutting-troughs, another of the great scenes commences—viz. the process of evisceration. This is performed by females, hundreds of whom annually find well-paid occupation at the gutting-troughs. It is a bloody business; and the gaily-dressed and dashing females whom we had observed lounging about the curing-yards, waiting for the arrival of the fish, are soon most wonderfully transmogrified. They of course put on a suit of apparel adapted to the business they have in hand—generally of oil-skin, and often much worn. Behold them, then, about ten or eleven o'clock in the forenoon, when the gutting scene is at its height, and after they have been at work for an hour or so: their hands, their necks, their busts, their

" Dreadful faces throng'd, and fiery arms "—

their every bit about them, fore and aft, are spotted and besprinkled o'er with little scarlet clots of gills and guts ; or as Southey says of Don Roderick, after the last and fatal fight—

" Their flanks incarnadined,
Their poitral smear'd with blood "—

See yonder trough, surrounded by a score of fierce eviscerators, two of them wearing the badge of widowhood! How deftly they ply the knife ! It is ever a bob down to seize a herring, and a bob up to throw it into the basket, and the operation is over. It is performed with lightning-like rapidity by a mere turn of the hand, and thirty or forty fish are operated upon before you have time to note sixty ticks of your watch. These ruthless widows seize upon the dead herrings with such a fierceness as almost to denote revenge for their husbands' deaths ; for they, alas ! fell victims to the herring lottery, and the widows scatter about the gills and guts as if they had no bowels of compassion.

In addition to herrings that are pickled and those sold in a fresh state, great quantities are made into what are called "bloaters," or transformed into "reds." At Yarmouth immense quantities of bloaters and reds are annually prepared for the English markets. The bloaters are very slightly cured and as slightly smoked, being prepared for immediate sale ; but the herrings brought into Yarmouth are cured in various ways : the bloaters are for quick sale and speedy consumption ; then there is a special cure for fish sent to the Mediterranean— " Straits-men" I think these are called ; then there are the black herrings, which have a really fine flavour. In fact the Yarmouth herrings are so cured as to be suitable to particular markets. It may interest the general reader to know that the name of " bloater" is derived from the herring beginning to swell or bloat during the process of curing. Small logs of oak are burned to produce the smoke, and the fish are all put on " spits" which are run through the gills. The " spitters" of Yarmouth are quite as dexterous as the gutters of Wick, a woman being able to spit a last per day. Like the gutters and packers of Wick, the spitters of Yarmouth work in gangs. The fish, after being hung and smoked, are packed in barrels, each containing seven hundred and fifty fish.

The Yarmouth boats do not return to harbour every morning, like the Scotch boats ; being decked vessels of some size, from fifty to eighty tons, costing about £1000, and having stowage for about fifty lasts of herrings, they are enabled to remain at sea for some days, usually from three to six, and of course they are able to use their small boats in the fishery, a man or two being left in charge of the large vessel, while the majority of the hands are out in the boats fishing. There has always been a busy herring-fishery at the port of Yarmouth. A century ago upwards of two hundred vessels were fitted out for the herring-fishery, and these afforded employment to a large number of people—as many as six thousand being employed in one way or the other in connection with the fishery. The Yarmouth boats or busses are not unlike the boats once used in Scotland, which have been already described. They carry from fifteen to twenty lasts of herrings (a last, counted fisherwise, is more than 13,000 her-

rings, but nominally it is 10,000 fish), and are manned with
some fourteen men or boys.

There has been a long-continued controversy in Scotland
as to the best kind of fishing-boats, certain parties arguing
that none but decked vessels ought to be used, which we
think would be a great mistake so long as the fishing is
carried on as at present. In the first place, there is no
harbour accommodation for a fleet of large decked vessels;
the present herring-boats, when not in use, are drawn up on
the beach, where they can readily be examined and repaired,
and can be easily pushed into the water when again required.
In the second place, these herring-boats rarely go far from
their fishing-port ; a voyage of from one to three hours carries
them to the fishing-place which they have selected—the chief
fisheries being just off the coast ; and as they have only to
spend a few hours on the fishing-ground before returning to
port, the present size of boat is in every way convenient for
the voyage.   And, in the third place, the open boats have this
advantage—viz. that it is easier to fish from one of them than
from a larger vessel—the great length of the present drift of
nets involving very severe labour, both in the letting of the
nets out from the boat and in hauling them in when laden with
fish.   So long, therefore, as the herring-fishery is a coast one,
the present style of boat is the best that can be employed.   If
it were necessary for the boats to go far out to sea, involving
a voyage of days, then it would be proper to have larger vessels,
because it is absolutely necessary that the herrings should be
cured within a few hours of their being captured.

The following figures as to the catch of 1862 and 1863, and
as to the number of boats and people employed, are from the
official returns of the fishing of these two years ; in fact I have
made a complete though brief abridgment of the whole papers,
which, at the time I write, are the latest published.   The
revenue derived under the Act for the branding of herrings,

passed in 1859, amounted to £5801 : 12 : 4 in 1862, being an
increase of £3157 : 0 : 4 over that of 1859 ; and in 1863 the
brand fees produced the sum of £4618 :16s. The returns of the
herring-fishing of 1863, as compared with that of 1862, which
was, however, an extraordinarily good year, are as follow :—

	Barrels.		Barrels.		Barrels.
1862.	Cured, 830,904	Branded,	346,712	Ex.,	494,910
1863.	Do. 654,816½	Do.	276,880½	Do.	407,761½

The quantity of herrings branded out of the fishing of 1862
was, as seen above, 346,712 barrels, a number greatly exceeding that of any previous year; which shows not only
that the fishing was very productive, but also the great demand for branded herrings, the reliance of the Continent upon
the brand (the chief herring trade there being in barrels that
have been branded), and the steady improvement in the cure
of the fish.   The fishing of 1863, when compared with those
of 1860 and 1861—fishings of which the total amounts are
nearer to that of 1863 than that of 1862—also show this in a
remarkable degree ; for we find from the returns that out of
a cure in 1863 less by 26,377 barrels than the cure of 1860,
there were branded 44,967 barrels more and exported 29,791
barrels more than in 1860 ; that out of a cure in 1863 less
by 14,012 barrels than the cure of 1861, there were branded
11,533 barrels more and exported 17,448 barrels more than in
1861.   A comparison of the rate per cent which the quantity
branded forms of the total quantity cured shows this still more
clearly.   In 1860 the rate was 55½ per cent; in 1861 it was
58⅓ per cent; in 1862, 59½ ; and in 1863 it was 62¼ per cent.

The quantity cured in 1862 exceeds, by upwards of 50,000
barrels, that of any previous year's fishing.   The districts in
which an increase of take was chiefly obtained were Buckie,
Banff, Fraserburgh, and Peterhead on the east coast, and
Stornoway and Inverary on the west.   The total increase at
these districts of the fishing of 1862 over that of 1861 being

184,023 barrels, and the increase of the whole of Scotland being 172,076 barrels, it would appear that, although there was a decided increase in these districts, the other fishing-places were scarcely up to the mark of the previous year. The fishing at Fraserburgh was remarkable as having yielded the highest average of any ever known in that district, being 226½ crans per boat. The season of 1862 was also remarkable for the decrease in the shoals of dogfish. This is shown from the entire and perfect condition of the herrings caught. In 1861, with a cure of 31,631 barrels at Fraserburgh, the broken fish were more than 4½ per cent; while in 1862, with a cure of 77,124 barrels, the broken were only a little over 2 per cent.

In 1863 there was an increase over 1862 in the districts of Lybster, Orkney, and Shetland, and the Isle of Man; but at Wick and some of the Moray Firth stations the fishing was almost the same; while it was greatly less at Eyemouth, Anstruther, Peterhead, Fraserburgh, Banff, Stornoway, and Inverary.

In 1862, at Wick, a fishing for herring with nets in the winter was tried for the first time, and was so far successful, herrings being caught having milt and roe, with the appearance that they might become full fish in three weeks or a month, and averaging 800 to the cran. This result goes far to prove that the herring is a fish of local habits, having no great range of emigration, and that it spawns twice in the course of the year. The winter fishing was repeated and extended in 1863. Trials were made for herring during the winter all along the south shores of the Moray Firth, and along the east coast as far as Montrose; and in some quarters this fishery was so extensively prosecuted as to lead to the fish being selected and branded for the Continental market.

The number of vessels fitted out in Scotland and the Isle of Man for the British herring-fishery 1862 was 281, employing 1149 men. The quantity of herrings cured in these vessels was 59,934 barrels, being an average of 213 barrels each vessel, generally made in two or three voyages. The number of boats in Scotland and the Isle of Man, whether decked or undecked, irrespective of the places to which they belong, employed in the herring-fishery of 1862, for one selected week in each district, was 9067, manned by 43,468 fishermen and boys, and employing 22,471 persons as coopers, gutters, packers, and labourers, making a total of persons employed 65,939. Of the total number of boats, 1122 fished at Wick, 960 at Loch Broom, 900 at Stornoway, 783 at Eyemouth, and 700 at Peterhead. The total number of boats employed in the shore-curing herring, and cod and ling fisheries in 1862 was 12,545, with an aggregate tonnage of 88,871, and valued at £272,960. The value of nets and lines belonging to these boats is estimated at £474,834. The boats are manned by 41,008 fishermen and boys, the curers and coopers employed amount to 2756, and the number of other persons employed is estimated at 50,098. In 1863 there was an increase of 47 boats, but a decrease of 150 fishermen and boys, while there was an increase of £34,369 in the estimated value of boats and nets.*

I have placed on the following page a complete journal of the daily catch of herrings at Wick for the season of 1862, in order to show the progress of the fishing.

* Since the above was written, the report by the commissioners for 1864 has been published, but the figures differ so slightly from those of 1863 that it is unnecessary to give them in detail, the total quantity of herrings cured being a decrease of 11,166¼ barrels, while, as regards boats and men employed, there was an increase of 140 boats, 126 fishermen and boys, and of £29,931 in the estimated value of boats and nets. The winter herring-fishery on the north-east coast about Wick, Lybster, and Helmsdale, was, contrary to expectation, quite unsuccessful. The probable cause was the very boisterous state of the weather, which prevented the boats from getting to sea. This year, therefore, affords no evidence either for or against the opinion that herrings exist in sufficient quantities to render a winter herring-fishery remunerative upon the coasts during the winter months.

Date.	Boats out.	Average crans.	Total daily catch.	General average.	Total catch for season.	Quality.	Weather.
July 3	20	2	40	0	40	Excellent	Mild.
,, 4	30	1	30	0	70	Do.	Wet.
,, 5	60	$\frac{1}{2}$	30	0	100	Do.	Damp and mild.
,, 8	50	$\frac{1}{2}$	25	0	125	Do.	Mild.
,, 9	70	0	10	0	135	Good	Gentle breeze.
,, 10	70	$1\frac{1}{2}$	105	0	240	Do.	Breezy.
,, 11	120	2	60	$\frac{1}{4}$	300	Do.	Cold and breezy.
,, 12	150	7	1,050	$1\frac{1}{4}$	1,350	Do.	Fine.
,, 15	180	1	180	$1\frac{1}{4}$	1,530	Mixed	Mild.
,, 16	170	1	170	$1\frac{1}{2}$	1,700	Good	Clear—strong tides.
,, 17	150	1	150	$1\frac{3}{4}$	1,850	Do.	Wet.
,, 18	100	1	100	2	1,950	Do.	Thick and wet.
,, 19	50	1	50	2	2,000	Do.	Rough.
,, 22	300	3	900	3	2,900	Do.	Mild.
,, 23	600	2	1,200	4	4,100	Excellent	Do.
,, 24	700	1	700	$4\frac{1}{2}$	4,800	Do.	Changeable.
,, 25	250	$\frac{1}{2}$	125	$4\frac{1}{2}$	4,925	Do.	Very rough.
,, 26	700	1	700	5	5,625	Do.	Mild.
,, 29	950	0	150	5	5,775	Do.	Mild and wet.
,, 30	900	$\frac{1}{2}$	450	6	6,225	Do.	Do.
,, 31	950	1	950	$6\frac{1}{2}$	7,175	Do.	Rough.
Aug. 1	250	2	500	7	7,675	Do.	Mild—heavy sea.
,, 2	1000	2	2,000	$8\frac{1}{2}$	9,675	Mixed	Mild and wet.
,, 5	150	1	150	9	9,825	Good	Rough.
,, 6	70	3	210	9	10,035	Spent	Do.
,, 7	1100	6	6,600	15	16,635	$\frac{1}{3}$ spent	Mild.
,, 8	1100	4	4,400	19	21,035	$\frac{1}{4}$ spent	Thick and rough.
,, 9	700	6	4,200	23	25,235	Do.	Do.
,, 12	1120	3	3,360	26	28,595	Good	Breezy.
,, 13	1120	8	8,960	34	37,555	Excellent	Thick, wet, and mild.
,, 14	1120	4	4,480	38	42,035	Do.	Do.
,, 15	1100	11	12,210	48	54,245	Do.	Do.
,, 16	1000	8	8,000	56	62,245	$\frac{1}{4}$ spent	Do.
,, 19	1000	0	50	56	62,295	Excellent	Strong gale.
,, 20	800	$\frac{1}{2}$	400	$56\frac{1}{2}$	62,695	Do.	Gentle breeze—cold.
,, 21	800	$\frac{1}{4}$	200	57	62,895	Do.	Do.
,, 22	900	$\frac{1}{2}$	450	57	63,345	Do.	Calm and clear.
,, 23	800	$\frac{1}{4}$	200	$57\frac{1}{2}$	63,545	Do.	Very wet and calm.
,, 26	1120	2	2,240	59	65,785	$\frac{1}{4}$ spent	Mild.
,, 27	1120	5	5,600	64	71,385	$\frac{1}{3}$ spent	Breezy.
,, 28	1120	1	1,120	65	72,505	Good	Clear and mild.
,, 29	1100	$\frac{3}{4}$	800	$65\frac{1}{2}$	73,305	Do.	Do.
,, 30	1000	$\frac{1}{2}$	500	66	73,805	Do.	Do.
Sept. 2	1050	$\frac{1}{2}$	525	$66\frac{1}{2}$	74,330	Excellent	Breezy.
,, 3	20	$\frac{1}{2}$	10	$66\frac{1}{2}$	74,340	Do.	Do.
,, 4	20	$\frac{1}{2}$	10	$66\frac{1}{2}$	74,350	Do.	Do.
,, 5	100	1	100	$66\frac{1}{2}$	74,450	Do.	Mild.
,, 6	600	$\frac{1}{4}$	150	67	74,600	Do.	Do.
,, 9	220	4	880	68	75,480	$\frac{1}{4}$ spent	Do.
,, 10	300	10	3,000	71	78,480	Good	Do.
,, 11	400	20	8,000	77	86,480	$\frac{1}{3}$ spent	Do.
,, 12	400	10	4,000	81	90,480	$\frac{1}{4}$ spent	Breezy.
,, 13	3	4	12	81	90,492	Good	Wind and rain.
,, 16	200	$\frac{3}{4}$	160	81	90,652	Do.	Mild.

The quantity of netting now employed in the herring-fishery is enormous, and is increasing from year to year. It has been strongly represented by Mr. Cleghorn, and others who hold his views, that the herring-fishery is on the decline; that if the fish were as plentiful as in former years, the increased amount of netting would capture an increased number of herrings. It is certain that, with a growing population and an increasing facility of transport, we are able to use a far larger quantity of sea produce now than we could do fifty years ago, when we were in the pre-Stephenson age. If, with our present facilities for the transport of fish to inland towns, Great Britain had been a Catholic instead of a Protestant country, having the example of the French fisheries before us, I have no hesitation in saying that by this time our fisheries would have been completely exhausted —that is, supposing no remedial steps had been taken to guard against such a contingency. Were we compelled to observe Lent with Catholic rigidity, and had there been numerous fasts or fish-days, as there used to be in England before the Reformation, the demand, judging from our present ratio, would have been greater than the sea could have borne. Interested parties may sneer at these opinions; but, notwithstanding, I maintain that the pitcher is going too often to the well, and that some day soon it will come back empty.

I have always been slow to believe in the inexhaustibility of the shoals, and can easily imagine the overfishing, which some people pooh-pooh so glibly, to be quite possible, especially when supplemented by the cod and other cannibals so constantly at work, and so well described by the Lochfyne Commission; not that I believe it possible to pick up or kill every fish of a shoal; but, as I have already hinted, so many are taken, and the economy of the shoal so disturbed, that in all probability it may change its ground or amalgamate with some other herring colony. I shall be met here by the old argument, that " the fecundity of fish is so enormous as to prevent their extinction," etc. etc. But the certainty of a fish yielding twenty thousand eggs is no surety for these being hatched, or if hatched, of their escaping the dangers of infancy, and reaching the market as table food. I watch the great shoals at Wick with much interest, and could wish to have been longer acquainted with them. How long time have the Wick shoals taken to grow to their present size ?—what size were the shoals when the fish had leave to grow without molestation ?—how large were the shoals when first discovered ?—and how long have they been fished ? are questions which I should like to have answered. As it is, I fear the great Wick fishery must come some day to an end. In the course of twenty-seven seasons as many as 1,275,027 barrels of herring have been caught off Wick (each barrel containing 700 fish) ; and in all probability as many more fish were killed by the nets, and never taken ashore. When the Wick fishery first began the fisherman could carry in a creel on his back the nets he required ; now he requires a cart and a good strong horse ! Leaving out one of the twenty-seven seasons (the first), and dividing the remaining twenty-six into two periods of thirteen each, we find the aggregate of the boats, the average crans to each, and the aggregate total for the

	Boats.	Average Crans.	Total Crans.
1st thirteen years,	10,202	941	735,318
2d „	13,522	519	539,719

During the first of these periods each boat carried about twenty-five nets, spun and worked in the county in a homely way ; during the second period each had from thirty to thirty-five nets, machine-made, the twine being very even and fine, and far larger and deeper, a great many of them being of cotton, and far superior in their catching power to those of the first period ; and yet, with 3320 additional boats carrying perhaps 200,000 more nets, larger, finer, and deeper than in the first period, we took 195,609 barrels fewer fish in the second than in the first thirteen years. During a late Wick fishing, a remarkable feature was the great disparity in the catch by individual boats. Although the average per boat over the whole fleet is set down as about eighty-three crans, yet half the boats do not average forty crans. As a rule, the boats that take the most fish are those with the longest, finest, and deepest drifts. In fact, the whole argument just amounts to this—that if the fish are as plentiful as ever, then double the quantity of netting *ought* to take double the quantity of herrings. During a late Wick season (1863), the entire fleet was only at sea twelve nights, and the average per night to each boat was only three crans. The *Northern Ensign,* a local journal, has over and over again asserted that the fish are as numerous as ever ; but that, in consequence of the crowd of boats, there is not room to capture them. In answer to this I may note, that on six different evenings of the season, when the boats out ranged from two to six hundred, the take did not average half a cran per boat. It may be likewise stated that 604 boats, in the year 1820, with a greatly less amount of netting, took as many fish as have been taken this season (1863) although the boats fishing were 480 above the season of 1820. The average capture per boat in 1820, with the limited netting, was 148 crans, whilst the average for 1863 was only 85 crans ! How is it possible to reconcile such great differences ?

I conclude this part of the herring question by one other illustration. In 1862 the aggregate sailings—*i.e.* number of voyages—of the Wick boats for the season was 28,755, and the total catch 92,004 barrels ; while this season (1863) the Wick boats have only taken 89,972 barrels in 32,630 voyages ; and all over the country, so far as I know—and I have made extensive inquiries—the tale is the same, a failure in the herring-fishery. Perhaps the best plan is at once to exhaust the figures of the subjeet while we are discussing it. As to the Wick July fishing, the following figures are illustrative of two different periods of five years each :—

Year.	Barrels.	Year.	Barrels.
1843	14,000	1859	2,500
1844	15,615	1860	12,850
1845	22,578	1861	5,821
1846	30,350	1862	7,173
1847	15,442	1863	8,517
	97,985		36,861

The figures of the greatest month of the fishery—viz. August—are as follow :—

Year.	Barrels.	Year.	Barrels.
1843	69,640	1859	80,853
1844	72,585	1860	86,120
1845	66,702	1861	73,580
1846	61,450	1862	65,321
1847	59,528	1863	46,000
	329,905		351,874

It will be seen from these figures that, even in the great herring month of August, notwithstanding the large increase of boats and nets, a decreased quantity has been taken during the last two years. To understand this better, the boats in the first period were 4345, and in the second period 5489, and in this last period the boats had vastly increased their netting, as many as 55,775 more nets having been added. Now, it stands to reason that if the herrings were as numerous as ever in the second period, the take should have been, through the mere increase of boats, not counting the addition to the amount of netting, 417,916 barrels.

The September fishing has only been prosecuted of late years, for the very good reason that in former times all the herring required were caught in July and August; during the last two years great efforts have been made to institute a September fishery, and a great force was brought to bear on the races of herring then coming to maturity, with what result the following figures will show :—

Year.	Barrels.	Year.	Barrels.
1843	4,100	1859	9,846
1844	2,000	1860	504
1845	2,880	1861	6,194
1846	900	1862	20,000
1847	9,100	1863	30,000
	18,980		66,544

The September fishery at Wick will have its day like the July and August fisheries.

One more table will finish these statistics; it represents the averages of the Wick fishery for two periods—one for seven years, ending in 1824; the other for the seven years ending with the season of 1863 :—

Years.	Boats.	Crans per Boat.	Years.	Boats.	Crans per Boat.
1818	482	136	1857	1100	73
1819	609	133	1858	1061	80
1820	604	148	1859	1094	79
1821	595	123	1860	1080	92
1822	595	91	1861	1180	87
1823	555	123	1862	1122	82
1824	625	$123\frac{1}{2}$	1863	1084	79
	4065	$877\frac{1}{2}$		7721	572

I shall not expend further argument on these figures, they speak too plainly to require illustration.

The state of the case as between the supply of fish and the extent of netting has been focussed into the annexed diagram, which shows at a glance how the question stands.

1818-1845. The drift of nets per boat contained 4500 square yards.

1857-1863. The drift of nets per boat contained 16,800 square yards.

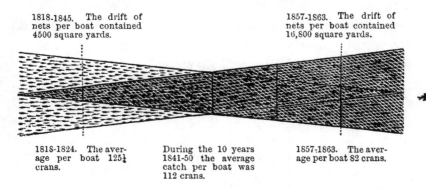

1818-1824. The average per boat 125¼ crans.

During the 10 years 1841-50 the average catch per boat was 112 crans.

1857-1863. The average per boat 82 crans.

Before concluding this chapter I wish to say a few words about a point of herring economy, which has been already alluded to in connection with the special commission appointed to inquire into the trawling system—viz. as to the natural enemies of the herring, the most ruthless of which are undoubtedly of the fish kind, and whose destructive power, some people assert, dwarfs into insignificance all that man can do against the fish :—" Consider," say the commissioners, " the destruction of large herring by cod and ling alone. It is a very common thing to find a codfish with six or seven large herrings, of which not one has remained long enough to be digested, in his stomach. If, in order to be safe, we allow a codfish only two herrings *per diem*, and let him feed on herrings for only seven months in the year, then we have 420 herring as his allowance during that time ; and fifty codfish will equal one fisherman in destructive power. But the quantity of cod and ling taken in 1861, and registered by the Fishery Board, was over 80,000 cwts. On an average thirty codfish go to one cwt. of dried fish. Hence, at least 2,400,000 will equal 48,000 fishermen. In other words, the cod and ling caught on the Scotch coasts in 1861, if they had been left in the water, would have caught as many herring as a number of fishermen *equal to all those in Scotland, and six thousand more,* in the same year; and as the cod and ling caught were certainly not one tithe part of those left behind, we may fairly estimate the destruction of herring by these voracious fish alone as at least ten times as great as that effected by all the fishermen put together." As to only one of the numerous land enemies of the herring, the late Mr. Wilson, in his *Tour round Scotland,* calculated that the gannets or solan geese frequenting one island alone—St. Kilda—picked out of the water for their food 214 millions of herrings every summer! The shoals that can withstand these destructive agencies must indeed be vast, especially when taken in connection with the millions of herrings that are accidentally killed by the nets, and never brought ashore for food purposes. The work accomplished by these natural enemies of the herring, which has been going on during all time, does not however affect my argument, that by the concentration on one shoal of a thousand boats per annum, with an annually-increasing net-power, we both so weaken and frighten the shoal that it becomes in time unproductive. As the late Mr. Methuen said in one of his addresses : " We have been told that we are to have dominion over the fish of the sea, but dominion does not mean extermination."

Although Scotland is the main seat of the herring-fishery, I should like to see statistics, similar to those collected in Scotland, taken at a few English ports for a period of years, in order that we might obtain additional data from which to arrive at a right conclusion as to the increase or decrease of the fishery for herring. It is possible to collect statistics of the cereal and root crops of the country ; it was done for all Scotland during three seasons, and it was well and quickly accomplished. What can be done for the land may also, I think, be done for the sea. I believe the present Board for

Scotland to be most useful in aiding the regulation of the fishery, and in collecting statistics of the catch ; their functions, however, might be considerably extended, and elevated to a higher order of usefulness, especially as regards the various questions in connection with the natural history of the fish.   The operations of the Board might likewise be extended for a few seasons to a dozen of the largest English fishing-ports, in order that we might obtain confirmation of what is so often rumoured, the falling off of our supplies of sea-food.   There are various obvious abuses also in connection with the economy of our fisheries that ought to be remedied, and which an active Board could remedy and keep right ; and a body of naturalists and economists might easily be kept up at a slight toll of say a guinea per boat.

CHAPTER VII.

———◆———

THE WHITE-FISH FISHERIES.

IT is among the white fish, as they are called, that we find the chief food-fishes of this kingdom—as the haddock, cod, whiting, ling, sole, flounder, turbot, and skate,—all of which, and about a dozen others (not including the mackerel), equally good for food, belong to two well-known fish families —Gadidæ and Pleuronectidæ—and give employment in their capture to the two best-known instruments of destruction, the line and the trawl.

It is exceedingly difficult to procure reliable statistics of the total quanity of fish taken in the British seas. These can only be obtained in a crude way from the fishermen, there being no tally kept by the salesman, except of a rough kind. I made some inquiries into the London fish supply at Billingsgate, but they were unsatisfactory, as there is no register kept there of the quantity sold. Each of the whole-sale men can give an idea of the total number or quantity of fish consigned to him ; but even if the whole body of sales-

men were to give such statistics, it would only, after all, represent a portion of the London supply, because much of the fish
required for the London commissariat is sent direct by railway
to private dealers.   But London, although it requires a very
large total of fish, seldom obtains all that its citizens could
eat, nor does it by any means get all that are captured, or
that are imported.   Manchester, Birmingham, Liverpool, and
other large towns in England ; and Glasgow, Edinburgh,
Dundee, and Aberdeen, in Scotland, require likewise to be
supplied.   And besides this home demand, we send considerable quantities of our white fish to the Continent,
especially in a dried or prepared state.   The fishermen of
the Shetland Isles, for instance, cure largely for the Spanish
and other Continental markets.   Finnan haddocks and pickled
cod can be so prepared as to bear shipment to a long distance,
and kippered salmon are found on sale everywhere, as are
also pickled and smoked herrings.

The natural history of our white fish, as I have already
said, is but imperfectly known.   As an instance of the very
limited knowledge we possess of the natural history of even
our most favourite fishes, I may state that at a meeting of
the British Association a few years ago, a member who read
an interesting paper *On the Sea Fisheries of Ireland*, introduced specimens of a substance which the Irish fishermen
considered to be spawn of the turbot; stating that wherever this substance was found trawling was forbidden ; the
supposed spawn being in reality a kind of sponge, with no
other relation to fish except as being indicative of beds of
mollusca, the abundance of which marks that fish are plentiful.
It follows that the stoppage of the trawl on the grounds
where this kind of squid is found is the result of sheer ignorance, and causes the loss in all likelihood of great quantities
of the best white fish.   It is not easy to say when the Gadidæ
are in proper season.   Some of the members of that family

are used for table purposes all the year round; and as different salmon rivers have their different close-times, so undoubtedly will the white fish of different seas or firths have different spawning seasons. In reference, for instance, to so important a fish as the turbot, we are very vaguely told by Yarrell that it spawns in the spring-time, but have no indication of the particular month during which that important operation takes place, or how long the young fish take to grow. Even a naturalist so well informed as the late Mr. Wilson was of opinion that the turbot was a travelling fish, which migrated from place to place.

The combined ignorance of naturalists and fishermen has much to do with the scarcity of white fish which is now beginning to be experienced; and unless some plan be hit upon to prevent overfishing, we may some fine morning experience the same astonishment as a country gentleman's cook, who had given directions to the gamekeeper to supply the kitchen regularly with a certain quantity of grouse. For a number of years she found no lack, but in the end the purveyor threw down the prescribed number, and told her she need look for no more from him, for on that day the last grouse had been shot. "There they are," said the gamekeeper, "and it has taken six of us with a gun apiece to get them, and after all we have only achieved the labour which was gone through by one man some years ago." The cook had unfortunately never considered the relation between guns and grouse.

The Gadidæ family is numerous, and its members are valuable for table purposes; three of the fishes of that genus are particularly in request—viz. whiting, cod, and haddock. These are the three most frequently eaten in a fresh state; there are others of the family which are extensively captured for the purpose of being dried and salted, among which are the ling, the tusk, etc. The haddock (*Morrhua aylefinus*)

has ever been a favourite fish, and the quantities of it which
are annually consumed are really wonderful. Vast numbers
used to be taken in the Firth of Forth, but from recent inquiries at Newhaven I am led to believe that the supply has
considerably decreased of late years, and that the local fishermen have to proceed to considerable distances in order to procure any quantity.

In reference to the question, " Where are the haddocks ?" which is asked on another page, it is right to say
that this prime fish has more than once become scarce.
I have been reminded of a time, in 1790, when three of these
fish were sold for 7s. 6d. in the Edinburgh market ; but
although there have been from time to time sudden disappear-
ances of the haddock from particular fishing-grounds, as indeed there have been of all fish, that is a different, a totally
different matter from what the fisher folk and the public have
now to complain off—viz. a yearly decreasing supply.   Mr.
Grieve, of the Café Royal, Edinburgh, tells me that this season (August 1865), he is paying ninepence each for these fish,
and is very glad to get them even at that price. I took part in
a newspaper controversy about the scarcity of the haddock, and
I found plenty of opponents ready to maintain that there was
no scarcity, but that any quantity could be captured. In some
degree that is the truth, but what is the hook-power required
now to capture, "any quantity," and how long does it take to
obtain a given number, as compared with former times, when
that fish was supposed to be more plentiful? Why do we require, for instance, to send to Norway and other distant places
for haddocks and other white fish? the only answer I can
imagine is that we cannot get enough at home. As to the
general scarcity of white fish, the late Mr. Methuen, the fish-
curer, wrote a year or two ago :—"This morning I am told
that an Edinburgh fishmonger has bought all the cod brought
into Newhaven at 5s. to 7s. each. I recollect when I cured

thousands of cod at 3d. and 4d. each ; they were caught between Burntisland and Kincardine, on which ground not a
cod is now to be got ; and at the great cod emporium of Cellardyke, the cod-fishing, instead of three score for a boat's fishing,
has dwindled down to about half-a-dozen cod."

THE GADIDÆ FAMILY.

The old belief in the migratory habits of fish comes again
into notice in connection with the haddock.   Pennant having
taught us that the haddock appeared periodically in great
quantities about mid-winter, that theory is still believed, although the appearance of this fish in shoals may be easily
explained, from the local habits of most of the denizens of the
great deep.   It is said that "in stormy weather, the haddock
refuses every kind of bait, and seeks refuge among marine
plants in the deepest parts of the ocean, where it remains until the violence of the elements is somewhat subsided."   This
fish does not grow to any great size ; it usually averages about
five pounds.   I prefer it as a table fish to the cod ; the very
best haddocks are taken on the coast of Ireland.   The scarcity

U

of fresh haddocks may in some degree be accounted for by the immense quantities which are converted into "Finnan haddies" —a well-known breakfast luxury no longer confined to Scotland. It is difficult to procure genuine Finnans, smoked in the original way by means of peat-reek ; like everything else for which there is a great demand, Finnan haddocks are now "manufactured" in quantity ; and, to make the trade a profitable one, they are cured by the hundred in smoking-houses built for the purpose, and are smoked by burning wood or sawdust, which, however, does not give them the proper *gout*. In fact the wood-smoked Finnans, except that they are fish, have no more the right flavour than Scotch marmalade would have were it manufactured from turnips instead of bitter oranges.   Fifty years ago it was different ; then the haddocks were smoked in small quantities in the fishing villages between Aberdeen and Stonehaven, and entirely over a peat fire.   The peat-reek imparted to them that peculiar flavour which gained them a reputation.   The fisher-wives along the north-east coast used to pack small quantities of these delicately-cured fish into a basket, and give them to the guard of the " Defiance" coach, which ran between Aberdeen and Edinburgh, and the guard brought them to town, confiding them for sale to a brother who dealt in provisions ; and it is known that out of the various transactions which thus arose, individually small though they must have been, the two made, in the course of time, a handsome profit.   The fame of the smoked fish rapidly spread, so that cargoes used to be brought by steamboat, and Finnans are now carrried by railway to all parts of the country with great celerity, the demand being so great as to induce men to foist on the public any kind of cure they can manage to accomplish ; indeed smoked codlings are extensively sold for Finnan haddocks. Good smoked haddocks of the Moray Firth or Aberdeen cure can seldom now be had, even in Edinburgh, under the price of sixpence per pound weight.

The common cod (*Morrhua vulgaris*) is, as the name implies, one of our best-known fishes, and it was at one time very plentiful and cheap. It is found in the deep waters of all our northern seas, but has never been known in the Mediterranean. It has been largely captured on the coasts of Scotland, and, as is elsewhere mentioned, it occurs in profusion on the shores of Newfoundland, where its plentifulness led to a great fishery being established. The cod is extremely voracious, and eats up most greedily the smaller inhabitants of the seas ; it grows to a large size, and is very prolific in the perpetuation of its kind. A cod-roe has more than once been found to be half the gross weight of the fish, and specimens of the female have been caught with upwards of eight millions of eggs ; but of course it cannot be expected that in the great waste of waters all the ova will be fertilised, or that any but a small percentage of the fish will ever arrive at maturity. This fish spawns in mid-winter, but there are no very reliable data to show when it becomes reproductive. My own opinion has already been expressed that the cod is an animal of slow growth, and I would venture to say that it is at least three years old before it is endowed with any breeding power. I may call attention here to one of the causes that must tend to render the fish scarce. As if the natural enemies of the young fish were not sufficient to aid in its extirpation, and the loss of the ova from causes over which man has no control not enough in the way of destruction, there is a commerce in cod-roe, and enormous quantities of it, as I have mentioned in the preceding chapter, are used in France as ground-bait for the sardine fishery ! The roe of this fish is also frequently made use of at table ; a cod-roe of from two to four pounds in weight can unfortunately be bought for a mere trifle, but it ought to cost a good few pounds instead of a few pence. I have elsewhere stated that the quantity of eggs yielded by a female cod is more than three millions

supposing only a third of them to come to life—that is one
million—and that a tenth part of that number, viz. one hundred
thousand, becomes in some shape—that is, either as codling or
cod—fit for table uses, what should be the value of the cod-
roe that is carelessly consumed at table ?   If each fish be
taken as of the value of sixpence, the amount would be £2500.
But supposing that only twenty full-grown codfish resulted
from the three millions of eggs ; these, at two and sixpence
each, would represent the sum of fifty shillings as the possible
produce of one dish, which, in the shape of cod-roe, cost
only about as many farthings !

Cuvier tells us that " almost all the parts of the cod are
adapted for the nourishment of man and animals, or for some
other purposes of domestic economy.   The tongue, for instance,
whether fresh or salted, is a great delicacy ; the gills are carefully preserved, to be employed as baits in fishing ; the liver,
which is large and good for eating, also furnishes an enormous
quantity of oil, which is an excellent substitute for that of the
whale, and applicable to all the same purposes ; the swim-
ming-bladder furnishes an isinglass not inferior to that yielded
by the sturgeon ; the head, in the places where the cod is
taken, supplies the fishermen and their families with food.
The Norwegians give it with marine plants to their cows, for
the purpose of producing a greater proportion of milk.   The
vertebræ, the ribs, and the bones in general, are given to their
cattle by the Icelanders, and by the Kamtschatkadales to their
dogs.   These same parts, properly dried, are also employed as
fuel in the desolate steppes of the shores of the Icy Sea.
Even their intestines and their eggs contribute to the luxury
of the table."   I may just mention another most useful product of the codfish.   Cod-liver oil is now well known in
materia medica under the name of *oleum jecoris aselli*.   The
best is made without boiling, by applying to the livers a slight
degree of heat, straining through thin flannel or similar

texture. When carefully prepared, it is quite pure, nearly
inodorous, and of a crystalline transparency. The specific
gravity at temperature 64° is about ·920°. It seems to
have been first used medicinally by Dr. Percival in 1782 for
the cure of chronic rheumatism ; afterwards by Dr. Bardsly
in 1807. It has now become a popular remedy in all the
slow-wasting diseases, particularly in scrofulous affections of
the joints and bones, and in consumption of the lungs. The
result of an extended trial of this medicine in the hospital at
London for the treatment of consumptive patients shows that
about 70 per cent gain strength and weight, and improve in
health, while taking the cod-liver oil ; and this good effect
with a great many is permanent. Skate-liver oil is also
coming into use for medicinal purposes, and I have no doubt
that the oil obtained from some of our other fishes will also
be found useful in a medicinal point of view.

The codfish is best when eaten fresh, but vast quantities
are sent to market in a dried or cured state : the great seat
of the cod-fishery for curing purposes is at Newfoundland.
But considerable numbers of cod and ling are likewise cured
on the coasts of Scotland. The mode of cure is quite simple.
The fish must be cured as soon as possible after it has been
caught. A few having been brought on shore, they are at
once split up from head to tail, and by copious washings
thoroughly cleansed from all particles of blood. A piece of
the backbone being cut away, they are then drained, and afterwards laid down in long vats, covered with salt, heavy weights
being placed upon them to keep them thoroughly under the
action of the pickle. By and by the fish are taken out of the
vat, and are once more drained, being at the same time carefully washed and brushed to prevent the collection of any
kind of impurity. Next the fish are *pined* by exposure to the
sun and air ; in other words, they are bleached by being
spread out individually on the sandy beach, or upon such rocks

or stones as may be convenient.   After this process has been
gone through the fish are then collected into little heaps, which
are technically called *steeples*.   When the *bloom*, or whitish
appearance which after a time they assume, comes out on the
dried fish the process is finished, and they are then quite
ready for market.   The consumption of dried cod or ling is
very large, and extends over the whole globe ; vast quantities
are prepared for the religious communities of Continental
Europe, who make use of it on the fast-days instituted by the
Roman Catholic Church.

Besides the common cod, there are the dorse (*M. callarias*),
and the poor or power cod (*M. minuta*), also the bib or pout
(*M. lusca*).

The whiting (*Merlangus vulgaris*) is another of our delicious table-fishes, which is found in comparative plenty on the
British coasts.   This fish is by some thought to be superior to
all the other Gadidæ.   Very little is known of its natural history.   It deposits its spawn in March, and the eggs are not
long in hatching—about forty days, I think, varying, however,
with the temperature of the season.   Before and after shedding
its milt or roe the whiting is out of condition, and should not
be taken for a couple of months.   The whiting prefers a sandy
bottom, and is usually found a few miles from the shore, its
food being much the same as that of other fishes of the family
to which it belongs.   It is a smallish fish, usually about twelve.
inches long, and on the average two pounds in weight.

I need scarcely refer to the other members of the Gadidæ :
they are numerous and useful, but, generally speaking, their
characteristics are common and have been sufficiently detailed.*   I will now, therefore, say a few words about the

* A correspondent has favoured me with the following brief account
of the *sillock-fishing* as carried on in Shetland :—" Sillocks are the young
of the saith, and they make their appearance in the beginning of
August about the small isles, and are of the size of parrs in Tweed.

Pleuronectidæ. There are upwards of a dozen kinds of flat fish that are popular for table purposes. One of these is a very large fish known as the holibut (*Hippoglopus vulgaris*), which has been found in the northern seas to attain occasionally a weight of from three to four hundred pounds. One of this species of fish of extraordinary size was brought to the Edinburgh market in April 1828 ; it was seven feet and a half long, and upwards of three feet broad, and it weighed three hundred and twenty pounds ! The flavour of the holibut is not very delicate, although it has been frequently mistaken for turbot by those not conversant with fish history.

They continue about said isles for a few weeks, and in the months of September and October, and sometimes longer, they hover about the small isles, when the fishermen catch them for the sake of their liver, which contains oil. One boat of twelve feet of keel will sometimes catch as many as thirty bushels in a part of a day, and this year (1864), owing to the high price of oil, each bushel was worth about 1s. 6d. The fish itself is taken to the dung-hill when the take is not great, but when there is a great take the liver is taken out and the fish thrown into the sea. There are no Acts of Parliament against using the net ; but after some time the sillocks leave the isles and draw to the shore, where there are any edge-places. It is allowed that the island of Whalsey is about the best place in Shetland for the fish to draw to, but whenever they come there, the proprietor, Mr. Bruce, will not allow " pocking," as a week would finish them all ; but the people must all fish with the rod, so that each man may get as many as keep him a day or two. The " pocking" sets them all out, but the fish don't mind the rod ; it is very picturesque to see perhaps fifty men sitting round the basin with their rods, and the sillocks covering about a rood of the sea, varying from three to six feet deep, and so close together that you would think they could not get room to stir. They will continue plentiful till the end of April, at which time they take to the deep sea ; and when they make their apearance the following year they are about four times larger, and are then called piltocks. But these are only taken by the rod. Mr. Bruce just says, If you pock, you cannot be my tenant ; so they must either give up the one or the other, and by that way of doing every household has as many of these small fish as they can make use of during the winter."

The true turbot (*Rhombus maximus*) is the especial delight of aldermanic epicures, and fabulous sums are said to have been given at different times by rich persons in order to secure a turbot for their dinner-table. This fine fish is, or rather used to be, largely taken on our own coasts ; but now we have to rely upon more distant fishing-grounds for a large portion of our supply. The old complaint of our ignorance of fish habits must be again reiterated here, for it is not long since it was supposed that the turbot was a migratory fish that might be caught at one place to-day and at another to-morrow. The late Mr. Wilson, who ought to have known better, said, in writing about this fish :—" The English markets are largely supplied from the various sand-banks which lie between our eastern coasts and Holland. The Dutch turbot-fishery begins about the end of March, a few leagues to the south of Scheveling. The fish *proceed* north-wards as the season advances, and in April and May are found in great shoals upon the banks called the Broad Forties. Early in June they surround the island of Heligoland, where the fishery continues to the middle of August, and then terminates for the year. At the beginning of the season the trawl-net is chiefly used ; but on the occurrence of warm weather the fish retire to deeper water, and to banks of rougher ground, where the long line is indispensable."

The turbot was well known in ancient gastronomy : the luxurious Italians used it extensively, and christened it the sea-pheasant from its fine flavour. In the gastronomic days of ancient Rome the wealthy patricians were very extravagant in the use of all kinds of fish ; so much so that it was said by a satirist that

> " Great turbots and the soup-dish led
>   To shame at last and want of bread."

The turbot is very common on the English and Scottish coasts,

and is known also on the shores of Greece and Italy. This
fish is taken chiefly by means of the trawl-net, but in some
places it is fished for by well-baited lines. We derive
large quantities of our turbot from Holland, so much as
£100,000 having been paid to the Dutch in one year
for the quantity of these fish which were brought to
London, and on which, at one time, a duty of £6 per boat

THE PLEURONECTIDÆ FAMILY.

1. Flounder.   2. Turbot.   3. Plaice.   4. Sole.   5. Dab.

was exigible. This fish spawns during the autumn, and is
in fine condition for table use during the spring and early
summer. Yarrell says the turbot spawns in the spring ; but,
with due respect, I think he is wrong ; I would not, however,
be positive about this, for there will no doubt be individuals
of the turbot kind, as there are of all other kinds, that will
spawn all the year round. The turbot is a great flat fish. In
Scotland, from its shape, it is called " the bannock-fluke." It
is about twenty inches long, and broad in proportion ; and a
prime fish of this species will weigh from four to eight pounds.

The best-known fish of the Pleuronectidæ is the sole (*Solea
vulgaris*), which is largely distributed in all our seas, and
used in immense quantities in London and elsewhere. The
sole is too well known to require any description at my
hands. It is caught by means of the trawl-net, and is in
good season for a great number of months. Soles of a
moderate weight are best for the table. I prefer such as
weigh from three to five pounds per pair. I have been told,
by those who ought to know best, that the deeper the water
from which it is taken the better the sole. It is quite a
ground fish, and inhabits the sandy places round the coast,
feeding on the minor crustacea, and on the spawn and young
of various kinds of fish. Good supplies of this popular fish
are taken on the west coast of England, and they are said to
be very plentiful in the Irish seas ; indeed all kinds of fish
are said to inhabit the waters that surround the Emerald Isle.
There can be no doubt of this, at any rate, that the fishing
on the Irish coasts has never been so vigorously prosecuted
as on the coasts of Scotland and England—so that there has
been a greater chance for the best kinds of white fish to
thrive and multiply. Seaside visitors would do well to go on
board some of the trawlers and observe the mode of capture.
There is no more interesting way of passing a seaside holiday
than to watch or take a slight share in the industry of the
neighbourhood where one may be located.

The smaller varieties of the flat fish—such as Muller's
top-knot, the flounder, whiff, dab, plaice, etc.—I need not
particularly notice, except to say that immense quantities of
them are annually consumed in London and other cities. Mr.
Mayhew, in some of his investigations, found out that upwards of 33,000,000 of plaice were annually required to aid the
London commissariat ! But that is nothing. Three times
that quantity of soles are needed—one would fancy this to
be a statistic of shoe-leather—the exact figure given by Mr.

Mayhew is 97,520,000 ! This is not in the least exaggerated. I discussed these figures with a Billingsgate salesman a few months ago, and he thinks them quite within the mark.

I have already alluded to the natural history of the mackerel, and shall now say a word or two about the fishery, which is keenly prosecuted. The great point in mackerel-fishing is to get the fish into the market in its freshest state ; and to achieve this several boats will join in the fishery, and one of their number will come into harbour as speedily as possible with the united take. The mackerel is caught in England chiefly by means of the seine-net, and much in the same way as the pilchard. A great number of this fish are however captured by means of well-baited lines, and in some places a drift-net is used. Any kind of bait almost will do for the mackerel-hooks—a bit of red cloth, a slice of one of its own kind, or any clear shiny substance. Mackerel are not quite so plentiful as they used to be.

As to when the Gadidæ and other white fish are in their proper season it is difficult to say. Their times of sickness are not so marked as to prevent many of the varieties from being used all the year round. Different countries must have different seasons. We know, for instance, that it is proper to have the close-time of one salmon river at a different date from that of some other stream that may be farther south or farther north ; and I may state here, that during a visit which I made to the Tay in December last, beautiful clean salmon were then running. There are also exceptional spawning seasons in the case of individual fish, so that we are quite safe in affirming that the sole and turbot are in season all the year round. The following tabular view of the dates when our principal fishes are in season does not refer to any particular locality, but has been compiled to show that fish are to be obtained nearly all the year round from some part of the coast :—

FISH TABLE.

S denotes that the fish is in season ; F in finest season ; and O out of season.

	Jan.	Feb.	March.	April.	May.	June.	July.	Aug.	Sept.	Oct.	Nov.	Dec.
Brill . . .	S	S	S	S	S	S	S	S	S	S	S	S
Carp . . .	S	S	S	S	S	S	S	S	S	S	S	S
Cockles . .	S	S	S	S	O	O	O	O	S	S	S	S
Cod . . .	F	S	S	O	O	O	O	O	S	S	F	F
Crabs . .	O	O	O	S	F	F	F	F	F	S	S	S
Dabs . . .	S	S	S	S	S	S	S	S	O	O	O	O
Dace . . .	F	F	O	O	O	S	S	S	F	F	F	S
Eels . . .	S	S	S	O	O	O	O	S	F	F	F	S
Flounders .	S	S	S	S	S	S	S	S	S	S	S	S
Gurnets . .	O	O	O	O	S	S	S	S	S	O	O	O
Haddocks .	F	S	O	O	S	S	S	S	S	F	F	F
Holibut . .	S	F	F	S	S	F	F	S	S	S	S	S
Herrings .	S	S	O	O	S	S	F	F	S	S	S	S
Ling . . .	S	S	F	S	O	O	O	O	O	S	S	S
Lobsters . .	O	O	O	S	F	F	F	S	S	S	S	S
Mackerel .	O	O	O	S	S	S	S	S	S	S	O	O
Mullet . .	O	O	O	S	S	S	S	O	O	O	O	O
Mussels* .	S	S	S	S	O	O	O	O	S	S	S	S
Oysters . .	S	S	F	F	O	O	O	O	S	S	S	S
Plaice . .	S	O	O	O	S	S	S	S	S	S	S	S
Prawns . .	O	O	S	F	F	F	F	S	O	O	O	O
Salmon . .	O	S	S	F	F	F	S	S	O	O	O	O
Shrimps . .	S	S	S	S	S	S	S	S	S	S	S	S
Skate . .	F	F	F	F	F	F	S	S	O	O	S	S
Smelts . .	S	S	S	S	S	O	O	O	O	O	S	S
Soles . . .	S	S	S	S	S	S	S	S	S	S	S	S
Sprats . .	S	O	O	O	O	O	O	O	O	O	S	S
Thornback .	O	O	O	O	O	O	S	S	S	S	S	O
Trout . .	O	S	F	F	F	F	S	S	O	O	O	O
Turbot . .	S	S	S	S	S	S	S	S	S	S	S	S
Whitings .	F	F	O	O	O	S	S	S	S	F	F	F

There is no organisation in Scotland for carrying on the white fisheries, as there is in the case of the oyster or herring

* In the Firth of Forth mussels are collected all the year round, but they invariably fall off in condition during a prevalence of easterly winds. .

fisheries. So far as our most plentiful table fish are concerned, the supply seems utterly dependent on chance or the
will of individuals. A man (or company) owning a boat goes
to sea just when he pleases. In Scotland, where a great
quantity of the best white fish are caught, this is particularly
the case, and the consequence is that at the season of the
year when the principal white and flat fish are in their
primest condition, they are not to be procured ; the general
answer to all inquiries as to the scarcity being, " The men are
away at the herring." This is true ; the best boats and the
strongest and most intelligent fishermen have removed for a
time to distant fishing-towns to engage in the capture of the
herring, which forms, during the summer months, a noted
industrial feature on the coasts of Scotland, and allures to the
scene all the best fishermen, in the hope that they may gain
a prize in the great herring-lottery, prizes in which are not
uncommon, as some boats will take fish to the extent of two
hundred barrels in the course of a week or two. Only a few
decrepit old men are left to try their luck with the cod and
haddock lines; the result being, as I have stated above, a
scarcity of white and flat fish, which is beginning to be felt
in greatly enhanced prices. An intelligent Newhaven fishwife recently informed me that the price of white fish in
Edinburgh—a city close to the sea—has been more than
quadrupled within the last thirty years. She remembers
when the primest haddocks were sold at about one penny per
pound weight, and in her time herrings have been so plentiful that no person would purchase them. We shall not soon
look again on such times.

The cod and haddock fishery is a laborious occupation.
At Buckie, a quaint fishing-town on the Moray Firth, which
I will by and by describe, it is one of the staple occupations
of the people. At that little port there are generally about
thirty or forty large boats engaged in the fishery, as well as a

number of smaller craft used to fish inshore. These boats, which measure from thirty to forty feet, are, with the necessary hooks and lines, of the value of about £100. Each boat is generally the property of a joint-stock company, and has a crew of eight or nine individuals, who all claim an equal share in the fish captured. The Buckie men often go a long distance, forty or fifty miles, to a populous fishing-place, and are absent from home for a period of fifteen or twenty hours. At many of the fishing villages from which herring or cod boats depart, there is no proper harbour, and at such places the sight of the departing fleet is a most animated one, as all hands, women included, have to lend their aid in order to expedite the launching of the little fleet, as the men who are to fish must be kept dry and comfortable. Even at places where there is a harbour, it is often not used, many of the boats being drawn up for convenience on what is called the boat-shore. At Cockenzie, near Edinburgh, several of the boats are still drawn up in this rude way, and the women not only assist in launching and drawing up the boats, but they sell the produce taken by each crew by auction to the highest bidder—the purchasers usually being buyers on speculation, who send off the fish by train to Edinburgh, Manchester, or London.

From the little ports of the Moray Firth, the men, as I have said, have to go long distances to fish for cod and ling. As they have none but open boats, it will easily be understood that they live hard upon such occasions. They are sometimes absent from home for about a week at a stretch, and as the weather is often very inclement the men suffer severely. The fish are not so easily procured as in former years, so that the remuneration for the labour undergone is totally inadequate. A large traffic in living codfish used to be carried on from Scotland; quick vessels furnished with wells took the cod alive as far as Gravesend, whence they were

sent on to London as required.   Although the railways have
put an end to a good deal of this style of transport, some cargoes of cod have been carried alive all the way from the
Rockall fishery to Gravesend.   But the percentage of waste
is necessarily enormous : however, it *pays* to do this, and one
result of the Rockall discovery has been the starting of a joint-
stock company to work one of the large North Sea fisheries.
The cod-bank at the Faroe Islands is now about exhausted ;
but the gigantic cod-fishery which has been carried on for two
centuries on the banks of Newfoundland still continues to be
prosecuted with great enterprise, although, according to reliable information, not with the success which characterised
the fishery some years ago.   In a few years more it will be
quite possible to make a decided impression even on the codbanks of Newfoundland.   The Great Dogger Bank fishery has
now become affected by overfishing, and the Rockall Bank
fails to yield anything like the large "takes" with which it
rewarded those who first despoiled it of its finny treasures.
A gentleman who dabbles a little in fishing speculations writes
me—" In 1862, I sent a fine smack to Rockall, and fish were
in great plenty—some very large ; but the weather is usually
so bad, and the bank so exposed to the heavy seas of the
North Atlantic, that the best and largest vessels fail to fish
with profit in consequence of the wear and tear and delay.
This will account in some degree for the cessation of enterprise as regards the Rockall fishery."   A writer in the
Quarterly Review, a few years ago, said of the Dogger Bank :—
" No better proof that its stores are failing could be given
than the fact that, although the ground, counting the Long
Bank and the north-west flat in its vicinity, covers 11,800
square miles, and that in fine weather it is fished by the
London companies with from fifteen to twenty dozen of long
lines, extending ten or twelve miles, and containing from
9000 to 12,000 hooks, it is not yet at all common to take

even as many as fourscore of fish of a night—a poverty which
can be better appreciated when we learn that 600 fish for 800
hooks is the catch for deep-sea fishing about Kinsale." I cannot say much about the white-fish fisheries of Ireland from personal knowledge, but I have been informed on good authority
that the coast fisheries of that country are not half worked, and
consequently are not in such an exhausted state as those of
Scotland and England. The west coast of Ireland, from Galway Bay to Erris Head north, and north-west to Donegal Bay,
is said to contain all the best kinds of table fish in great
quantities—mackerel being plentiful in their season, as are
cod, hake, ling, and others of the Gadidæ. As for turbot, they
can be had everywhere, and have been so plentiful as to be
used for bait on the long lines set for haddock, etc. Lobsters
and other shell-fish can likewise be procured in any quantity.
If the accounts given of the abundance of white fish on the
Irish coasts are to be relied upon, there must be a rare field
there for the opening up of new fishing enterprises.

Prolific as our coast fisheries have been, and still are,
comparatively speaking, the North Sea is at present the grand
reservoir from which we obtain our white fish. Indeed, it has
been the great fish-preserve of the surrounding peoples since
ever there was a demand for this kind of food. All the best-
known fishing banks are to be found in the German Ocean—
Faroe, Loffoden, Shetland, and others nearer home—and its
waters, filling up an area of 140,000 square miles, teem with
the best kinds of fish, and give employment to thousands of
people, as well in their capture and cure as in the building of
the ships, and the development of the commerce which is
incidental to all large enterprises.

It will doubtless be interesting to my readers to know
something about the general machinery of fish-capture, so far
as regards the British sea-fisheries. The modern cod-smack,
clipper-built for speed, with large wells for carrying her live

fish, costs £1500. She usually carries from nine to eleven men and boys, including the captain. Her average expense per week is £20 during the long-line season in the North Sea ; but it exceeds this much if unfortunate in losing lines. Fishing has of late been a most uncertain venture. The line is chiefly used for the purpose of taking cod and haddock. The number of lines taken to sea in an open boat depends upon the number of men belonging to the particular vessel. Each man has a line of 50 fathoms (300 feet) in length ; and attached to each of these lines are 100 " snoods," with hooks already baited with mussels, pieces of herring or whiting. Each line is laid " clear" in a shallow basket or "scull"—that is, it is so arranged as to run freely as the boat shoots ahead. The 50-fathom line, with 100 hooks, is in Scotland termed a "taes." If there are eight men in a boat the length of line will be 400 fathoms (2400 feet), with 800 hooks (the lines being tied to each other before setting). On arriving at the fishing-ground the fishermen heave overboard a cork buoy, with a flag-staff fixed to it about six feet in height. The buoy is kept stationary by a line, called the "pow-end," reaching to the bottom of the water, and having a stone or small anchor fastened to the lower end. To the pow-end is also fastened the fishing-line, which is then "paid" out as fast as the boat sails, which may be from four to five knots an hour. Should the wind be unfavourable for the direction in which the crew wish to set the line they use the oars. When the line or taes is all out the end is dropped, and the boat returns to the buoy. The pow-end is hauled up with the anchor and fishing-line attached to it. The fishermen then haul in the line with whatever fish may be on it. Eight hundred fish might be taken (and often have been) by eight men in a few hours by this operation ; but many fishermen now say that they consider themselves very fortunate when they get a fish on every five hooks on an eight-taes line.

Many a time too the fish are all eaten off the line by "dogs" and other enemies, so that only a few fragments and a skeleton or two remain to show that fish have been caught. The fishermen of deck-welled cod-bangers use both hand-lines and long-lines such as have been described. The cod-bangers' tackling is of course stronger than that used in open boats. The long-lines are called "grut-lines," or great-lines. Every deck-welled cod-banger carries a small boat on deck for working the great-lines in moderate weather. This boat is also provided with a well, in which the fish are kept alive till they arrive at the banger, when they are transferred from the small boat's well to that of the larger vessel.

Hungry codfish will seize any kind of bait, and great-lines are usually baited with bits of whiting, herring, haddock, or almost any kind of fish. For hand-lines the fishermen prefer mussels or white whelks. White whelks are caught by a line on which is fastened a number of pieces of carrion or cod-heads. This line is laid along the bottom where whelks are known to abound. The whelks attach themselves to the cod-heads, and are pulled up, put into net bags, something like onion-nets, and placed in the well of the vessel, where they are kept alive till required for use. Another kind of bait used by the boat fishermen for hand-lines is that of the lug-worm. The "lug" is a sand-worm, from four to five inches long, and about the thickness of a man's finger. The head part of the worm is of a dark brown fleshy substance, and is the part used as bait, the rest of the worm being nothing but sand. The "lug" is dug from the sand with a small spade or three-pronged fork.

The principal fishing-grounds in the North Sea where cod-bangers are employed are the Dogger Bank, Well Bank, and Dutch Bank. The fishing-ground of the open-boat fishermen is on the coasts of Fife, Midlothian, and Berwickshire; for haddocks, cod, ling, etc., it is around the island of May and the Bell Rock, Marrbank, Murray Bank, and Montrose Pits, etc.

The Scottish fishing-boats, with a few exceptions, are all open ; but whilst the open boats are a subject of dispute, they are an undoubted convenience to the men. The boats, as a general rule, seldom go far from home except to the seat of some particular fishery, and being low in the build the nets are easily paid out and hauled in when they are so fortunate as to obtain a good haul of fish. The Scottish fishery is mostly what may be called a local or shore fishery, as the boats go out and come home, with a few exceptions, once in the twenty-four hours. A few boats with a half deck have been introduced of late years, and in these the fishermen can make a much longer voyage ; but, as a rule, the Scottish fishermen have not, like their English brethren, a comfortable decked lugger in which to prosecute their labours. In the event of a storm the open Scottish boats are poorly off, as some of their harbours are at such times totally inaccessible, and the boats being unable, from their frail construction, to run out to sea, are frequently driven upon the rocky coasts and wrecked, the men being drowned or killed among the rocks. It is gratifying to think that a good number of harbours of refuge have lately been constructed, and that in particular an extensive one is being at present erected at Wick, the seat of the great herring fishery. I have more than once, while conducting inquiries into the fishing industries of the United Kingdom, seen the storm break upon the herring-fleet while it was engaged in the fishery. Such scenes are terribly sublime, as boat after boat is engulphed by the ravening waters, or is dashed against the rocky pillars of the shore, and the men sucked into the deep by the powerful waves. The sea is free to all, without tax and without rent, but the price paid in human life is a terrible equivalent :—" It is only they who go down to the sea in ships who see the works of the Lord and His wonders in the deep."

There has been a large amount of exaggeration as to the injury done to the white-fish fishery by the trawls. Fishermen who have neither the capital nor the enterprise to engage in trawling themselves are sure to abuse those who do; but the trawl is so formidable as to have induced various French writers to advocate its prohibition. They describe this instrument of the fishery as terrible in its effects, leaving, when it is used, deep furrows in the bottom of the sea, and crushing alike the fry and the spawn; but there is a very evident exaggeration in this charge, because as a general rule the beam-trawl cannot be worked with safety except on a sandy or muddy bottom, and, so far as we know, fish prefer to spawn on ground that is slightly rocky or weedy, so that the spawn may have something to adhere to, which it evidently requires in order to escape destruction; and when a quantity of spawn is discerned on a bit of sea-weed or rock, we always find that, from some viscid property of which it is possessed, it adheres to its resting-place with great tenacity. The trawl-net, however destructive its agency, cannot, I fear, be dispensed with; and, used at proper seasons and at proper places, is the best engine of capture we can have for the kinds of fish which it is employed to secure. The trawl is very largely used by English fishermen, but it is only of late years that the trawlers have come so far north as Sunderland and Berwick, and it is the fishermen of these places who have got up the cry about that net being so injurious to the fisheries. In Scotland there are no resident trawlers, the fisheries being chiefly of the nature of a coasting industry, where the men, as a general rule, only go out to sea for a few hours and then return with their capture. Having been frequently on board of the trawling ships, I may perhaps be allowed to set down a few figures indicative of the power of the great beam-net.

A trawler, then, is a vessel of about 35 tons burden, and usually carries 7 persons—viz. 5 men and 2 apprentices—as a crew to work her.* The trawl-rope is 120 fathoms in length and 6 inches in circumference, and to this rope are attached the different parts of the trawling apparatus—viz. the beam, the trawl-heads, bag-net, ground-rope, and span or bridle.

* A Barking trawler usually carries 5 men and 3 boys, and costs when in full work £12 per week. A Hull trawler costs much less, and the owner has less risk ; because the crew, from the captain downwards, share in the catch. The Barking men refuse to enter into this arrangement, which probably helps to account for the decay of the Barking fishery, for that of Hull is comparatively prosperous. The co-operative system prevails among a few of the fisher people of England. In an account of a Yorkshire fishing-place recently published in *Once a Week*, the following statistics of the cost of boats, etc., are given :—

" Each yawl, varying in tonnage from 28 to 45 tons, costs from £600 to £650, and is divided into shares ; of its earnings 3s. 6d. in the pound are paid to the owner or owners, 10s. are devoted to the current expenses, and the remainder is divided among the men who find the bait. When a new boat is required, several persons—gentlemen speculators, harbour-masters, etc., and boatmen—take certain shares of it, which vary in amount from a half-quarter to a half of the cost ; application is then made to a builder, sail-maker, anchor-maker, and other tradesmen ; and the vessel, in due time, is paid for, equipped, and given over to the owners. Each lugger-yawl carries two masts, and is provided with three sets of sails to suit various states of weather. The foresail contains 200 or 250 yards, the mizen 100, and the mizen-topsail 40 yards ; the lesser sizes being severally of 100, 60, and 50 yards. The jib is very small. On the average the yawl is of 40 tons, and measures 51 feet keel, or 55 feet over all, and is of 17 or 18 feet beam ; drawing 6½ feet water aft, and 5 feet forward. The amount of ballast varies from 20 to 30 tons. The yawl is provided with 120 nets, each of which costs £30. Half of this number are left on shore, and changed at the end of every 12 weeks. The crew is composed of 7 men and 2 boys. For instance, the 'Wear,' commanded by Colling, a first-rate seaman, carries two others, like himself part-owners, 4 men receiving, besides their food, £1, and 1 boy at 18s., and another at 11s.

The trawler is furnished with a capstan for hauling in this heavy machine. The beam, a spar of heavy elm wood, is 38 feet in length, and 2 feet in circumference at the middle, and is made to taper to the ends. Two trawl-heads (oval rings, 4 feet by 2½ feet) are fixed to the beam, one at each end. The upper part of the bag-net, which is about 100 feet long, is fastened to the beam, while the lower part is attached to the ground-rope. The ends of the ground-rope are fastened

a week; each fisherman, who is a net-owner, receives 24s. a week. The expenses in wages and wear and tear are calculated at from £12 to £15 weekly. The herrings are valued at £2 per 1000 on an average. Sometimes 23,000 fish are caught in a single haul, occasionally as many as 60,000, but 40,000 are considered a good catch. To remunerate the crew, £50 or £60 a week ought to be obtained. Each net is 10 fathoms long, and is sunk 9 fathoms during the fishing, the upper part being floated by a long series of barrels, which are fitted at intervals of 15 fathoms. The warps used for laying out the nets in each vessel measure 2200 yards. Two men take up the nets, two empty the fish out of them, and one boy stows the nets while his fellow stows the warps, which are raised by a windlass worked by the men. Each net weighs about 28 pounds. In order to preserve the nets and sails, it is necessary at frequent intervals to cover them with tanning, which is prepared in large coppers. These coppers cost £40."

On the Gulf of St. Lawrence the engagements of fishermen are as follows :—

" The fishermen are brought to the fishing-station at the expense of the firm engaging them. They are furnished with a good fishing-boat, thoroughly fitted, and are besides supplied with fresh bait as long as it can be got, and they require it, but on payment of a sum of $6 to $8 ; and for each 100 codfish delivered on the stage they receive the sum of 5s. 6d., one half in money and the other half in goods and provisions. At these prices, and fish being abundant, fishermen earn $5, $10, $15, and even $20 a day ; and after an absence of from 6 to 9 weeks, bring home from $80 to $120, and sometimes more. But they have to board themselves ; and if the fish is not abundant, their account of the provisions lent to their families before their departure, their own board, the purchase of their lines, take up the greatest part of their earnings, and they very often return to Magdelen Islands with empty pockets."

Great quantities of all kinds of fish are found in the St. Lawrence.

to the trawl-beds, and being quite slack, the mouth of the
bag-net forms a semicircle when dragged over the ground.
The whole apparatus is fastened to the trawl-rope by means
of the span or bridle, which is a rope double the length of the
beam, and of a thickness equal to the trawl-rope.   Each end
of the span is fastened to the beam, and to the loop thus
formed the trawl-rope is attached.   The ground-rope is usually
an old rope, much weaker than the trawl-rope, so that, in the
event of the net coming in contact with any obstruction in
the water, the ground-rope may break and allow the rest of
the gear to be saved.   Were the warp to break instead of the
ground-rope, the whole apparatus, which is of considerable
value, would be left at the bottom.   The trawler, as I noted
while the net was in the water, usually sails at the rate of
2 or 2½ knots an hour.   The best depth of water for trawling
is from 20 to 30 fathoms, with a bottom of mud or sand.   At
times, however, the nets are sunk much deeper than this, but
that is about the depth of water over the great Silver Pits, 90
miles off the Humber, where a large number of the Hull
trawlers go to fish.   When they are caught, the fish (chiefly
soles and other flat fish) are then packed in baskets called pads,
and are preserved in ice until brought to market.   To take
twelve or fourteen pads a day is considered excellent fishing.
Besides these ground-fish the trawl often encloses haddocks,
cod, and other round fish, when such happen to be feeding on
the bottom.   It sometimes happens that the beam falls to the
ground, and, the ground-rope lying on the top of the bag-net,
no fish can get in.   This accident, which, however, seldom
occurs, is called a back fall.   Mr. Vivian of Hull, in a letter
to the editor of a Manchester newspaper, gave two years ago a
very graphic account of the trawl-fishing, and stated that 99
out of every 100 turbot and brills, nine-tenths of all the haddocks, and a large proportion of all the skate, which are daily
sold in the wholesale fishmarkets of this country are caught

by the system of trawling. Trawling is without doubt the most efficient mode of getting the white fish at the bottom of the ocean ; and were it made penal, London and the large towns would at times be entirely without fish. As a matter of course, trawling must exhaust the shoals at particular places. A fleet of upwards of 100 smacks, each with a beam nearly 40 feet long, trawling night and day, disturbs, frightens, or captures whatever fish are to be found in that locality, entrapping, besides, shell-fish, anchors, stores that have been sunken with ships ages ago ; even a wedge of gold has been brought up by this insatiable instrument. The only remedy is to widen the field of action.

It is best, however, in a case of dispute, as in this trawl question, to allow those interested to speak for themselves. I have gone over an immense mass of the evidence taken by a recent commission appointed by Parliament to make inquiry on the subject, and will set some parts of it before my readers, so that, if a little trouble be taken in weighing the *pros* and *cons* of the matter, they may be able to form their own judgment on this vexed question. A Cullercoats fisherman is very strong against the beam-trawl. He is certain that thirty years ago we could get double the quantity of fish, during the fishing season, that we obtain now, and that the supply has fallen away little by little ; and he says that even ten years ago it was almost as good as it was thirty years ago. Some years hence England will cry out for want of fish if trawling be allowed to go on. The price of fish has doubled, he says, of late years. "When I was a young man, there were nine in family of us, and my wife could purchase haddock for twopence which would serve for our dinners. Now she could not obtain the same quantity for less than ninepence or tenpence. Of recent years the number of fishermen and fishing-boats has greatly increased. I do not think the fishermen of the present day are better off than

those when I was a young man." The fishermen at Cullercoats, when they trawl, use the small trawl, and fish in shallow
water. Under these circumstances they do no injury. The
trawlers, with the large trawl, says a Mr. Nicholson who was
examined, not only sweep away the lines of the fishermen, but
also destroy the fish. At Cullercoats a man engaged in the
line-fishing gets all the fish on his own lines, and his wife
goes to town and disposes of them. The beam-trawling
commenced about six years ago. The number of boats and
the fishing population still go on steadily increasing. Beam-
trawling does two kinds of harm : in the first place, it
sweeps away the fishermen's lines ; and next, it destroys the
spawn. "There may be a remedy for a fisherman losing his
lines, but I never heard of it. I am aware that they could
recover damages, but the difficulty is to get hold of the
offending parties. The only remedy I can suggest is to do
away with the trawl-fishing altogether." This witness stated
that ten years ago he used to take sixty or seventy codfish
per day, and that now he cannot get one. The trawlers,
being able to fish in all weathers, beat the local fishermen out
of the field.

Templeman, a South Shields fisherman, says that when
engaged in trawling he has drawn up three and a half
tons of fish-spawn ! He also says in his evidence that in
trawling one-half of the fish are dead and so hashed as to be
unfit for market. Has seen a ton and a half of herring-
spawn offered for sale as manure. The take of fish upon the
Dogger Bank has decreased very much. The fishermen
cannot catch one quarter part there now that they used to do.
The number of trawl-boats on the Dogger Bank has increased
about 10 per cent within the last year, and yet they are
getting about a quarter less fish. Some of them can scarcely
make a living now at all. They have impoverished all other
places, and now they have come here, and in a short time

there will not be a fish left. It is the same with the other
fish-banks, and that accounts for the trawlers now coming to
this neighbourhood. They have destroyed the Hartlepool
and Sunderland ground, and now they have come to a small
patch off here, and they will sweep it clean too. A trawl-
boat will sometimes catch five tons a day; but on the
average a ton and a half; but as a great deal of that has to
be thrown overboard, they only bring about ten cwt. to
market. The boats belonging to Cullercoats, carrying the
same number of hands as the trawlers, only catch upon the
average about five stones. The fish caught in the trawl are
not fit for the market, as the insides are broke and the galls
burst and running through them. "If I had my way, I
would pass an Act of Parliament to do away with trawling,
and oblige every man to fish with hooks and lines. I think
that would increase the quantity of fish for the country,
because the young fish would not take the hooks. I am not
aware that if the small boats get five stones a day it would at
all diminish the supply of fish for the market; but if the
trawling is allowed to continue that very soon will."

Thomas Bolam, on being examined, said: "I have followed
the herring-fishing for twenty-one years, and the white-fishing
six years. In the course of those six years I have found that
the supply of white fish has gradually diminished both in the
number and size of the fish. In twenty years' experience
in the herring-fishing I find a fearful diminution in the total
quantity caught. The shoals of herring are now only about
one-third the size they were when I first commenced the fishing. At that time we used to get 14,000 or 15,000; now the
length of 4000 or 5000 is thought a good take. I attribute
the falling-off to the existence of the trawling system."

Many other fishermen gave similar evidence. A fisherman named Bulmer, residing at Hartlepool, said that the white
fish were not only scarcer, but that they were deteriorating in

size as well. The falling off in quantity has decidedly been accompanied by a smaller size, more particularly in haddocks. Haddocks, twenty years ago, were caught from five pounds to six pounds in weight; now they hardly average three pounds. There is scarcely a single cod to be caught now, and formerly our boats got them scores together, and had to trail them out in rows, and could only sell them for about 10s. a score; now they realise at Christmas 5s. and 6s. each. " Of turbot-fishing I am sorry to speak. It pains me to think of the injuries we have sustained in this particular fishing by trawlers. At present we dare not cast our nets, as they are sure to be lost. I lost two ' fleets' of turbot-nets worth £25. About twenty-six years ago I have caught two hundred turbot in one day : now there are none to be got." Another resident gave similar evidence, and thought that if trawling was persisted in their noble bay would soon be fallow ground. John Purvis of Whitburn also says that haddocks have decreased in size as well as in quantity—thinks they are at least a third smaller now as compared with former years. Considers that the trawling system has caused the diminution of fish which has taken place during the last four years. David Archibald of Croster had bought trawled fish not for food, as they were only fit to be used as bait.

Having given a fair sample of the evidence against the trawling system, it will be but just that we now hear the other side of the case. It is unfortunate, of course, that we cannot obtain really impartial evidence on this vexed question, as the party complaining is the party said to have had their fishery prospects ruined by the use of the beam-trawl, whilst the trawlers, of course, won't hear a bad word said of the engine by which they gain their living. A Torbay fisherman, accustomed to trawling for the last twenty-six years, flatly contradicts much that has been said against the trawl-net. He asserts that he never took or saw any spawn taken, and that only about half a hundredweight in each two tons of the fish taken is unfit for the market. He does not think the fish are decreasing either in quantity or size.

John Clements, a trawl-net fisherman from Hull, was one of the men examined at Sunderland; his evidence was as follows:—" I have followed trawling for twenty-six years. I have fished down here for ten years. There was no diminution of fish at Hull; but we land it easier here, and in a better condition for the market. I never noticed any spawn in the nets, but I have got a basket or two of small fish, which, when not fit for food, we throw away. In the ten years which I have come down here I have found an increase in the quantity and take. I think trawling increases the fish, as the trawl-net turns up the food of the fish, worms and slugs, and the fish follow the net like a swarm of crows after a harrow. I do not think that we disturb the spawn in that way. This morning there were two or three haddocks broken out of sixteen or seventeen baskets, each basket containing seven or eight stones. The trawl-net fish do not fetch such a good price as the line fish, but it is from the quantity and not the quality. We have added to the enjoyment of the people of this town by the good supply of fish we have given them. Twenty years ago a month's catch was about £50, and now it is from £80 to £120; and this is not from the better price, but the greater quantity which we are enabled to get by going farther out to sea with the larger boats. In the winter time I fish on Dogger Bank, and in summer inshore. I never came across any of the long-line nets. I have found herring-spawn in haddocks; but I have never found any in the net. We catch a good deal of sand here. It comes in as soon as we stop; but it falls through before we get the net to the surface of the water. The farther off we go the more haddocks we get; and the nearer we come to the shore the more soles we get. I have caught a good deal of cod. In one instance I caught one hundred and eight cods in a haul. That was forty miles off Flambro' Head. My nets have been examined officially only once in twelve years. The shorter the haul the better the fish ; but I have had the fish in splendid condition with a large haul. I have never had any fish damaged by having the gall-bladder burst. A gall-bladder may be burst, but we would not see it unless we opened the fish."

A Hull trawler spoke to the following effect :—" I never saw any spawn in the net. It is impossible for spawn to be caught in the net. There is often unmarketable fish, but it is only when there is a strong breeze and a difficulty in getting the gear on board. We generally get seven or eight hampers in a haul, and one basket would perhaps be unfit for the market. The hooked fish is a more saleable fish, as it has got the scales and slime on it, and the trawl fish has not got the slime on it, and the scales are sometimes rubbed off." Some haddocks were here produced which the witness said were a fair specimen. The scales were on them, and on one being opened the inside was found to be in a unbroken state.

The following is a summary of the evidence given by William Dawson, a very intelligent fisherman of Newbiggin, who spoke from fifty years' experience :—" He had fished cod, ling, turbot, and several kinds of shell-fish, but not oysters. He was still engaged as a fisherman. He fished with a line for soles. The number of fishermen and boats had increased. In 1808 there were eight boats, and there are now about thirty boats. Fifty years ago the boats were about one-third the size. The boats carried just about the same lines as now. The boats now carry about three times as much net as they did. The number of white fish is falling off a great deal. In 1812 every boat brought in more white fish than they could carry. We do not go much more frequently to sea now. In the size of the fish now there is not much difference—a little

smaller. The haddock and herring fisheries had decreased.
He had not noticed much difference in the size, only in the
quantity. There was a greater number of boats engaged now
in the herring-fishing—the number of herring having decreased
within the last ten or twelve years. Little mackerel was
caught there. Large quantities of mackerel were off this
coast at times, but they had no nets to take them. Although
a good many sprats were seen, they did not try to catch
them. The cause of the falling off in the quantity of fish he
considered was their being destroyed farther south. No
trawling vessels came here till last summer. They went
about twelve miles from land, and trawled in the fishing-
ground. The lines of the fishing-boats were parallel, and
about a quarter of a mile apart. When there was a south-
east storm they got plenty of fish, but it was not so now.
With a north-east storm they had plenty of fish. In his
recollection, fifty years back, there was plenty of fish with a
south-east storm. There had been no interference with their
nets, and no one had regulated the times of fishing. There
might be some advantage if the government made a law to
prevent either the English or French fishing from Saturday
morning to Monday night. That would give time for the
fish to draw together. That alluded to herring. They
should not allow the trawl-boats to fish on the coasts. The
French boats often came within three miles of the land.
Herring are caught within three miles of the shore. The
French boats shifted with the herring along the coast, and
have caught a great quantity. There should be a rule that
herring-nets should not be shot before sunset. When the
Queen's cutters came the French boats made off to more
than three miles from the land. Lobsters had diminished,
but not the crabs. He believed they had caught too many
lobsters. The boat's crew is not so well off now as thirty
years ago. Lodgings were better. They do not earn so

much money now. In the course of a year (about 1825) he
made £126, and a few years back he made only £78. The
average for the last five years at the white fishing was about
£50.   Other £50 might be made at the herring-fishing.
The buoys of the lines were large enough for the trawlers to
see them, and they could see where the nets were. They
destroyed both the fish and the lines. A line boat with
fittings costs about £40, and a herring-boat with nets not less
than £100. The men bought the boats with money saved.
Little fish was destroyed on their lines, except what was
eaten by the dog-fish. There were herring there in January
and February, but were not caught. Their boats fished between Tynemouth and Dunstanborough castles. He could
remember when there were no French boats on the coast;
they first came about 1824. The French boats fish on the
Sundays. Their boats did not. A young man ought to earn
£100 a year. It would cost a full third to keep his boat and
tackling up. The boats lasted about fourteen years."

I need not go on repeating similar evidence, but the
witnesses were nearly all agreed that the beam-trawl did not
do the injury to the fisheries that was charged against it,
especially as regards injury to spawn. I may perhaps, by
way of conclusion to this contradictory evidence, be allowed
to quote from the *Times* a portion of a letter on trawling,
written by a "Billingsgate Salesman:"—"Seven years'
experience in Billingsgate, and my lifetime previous spent
among the fishermen in a seaport-town, may enable me to
offer a few remarks, which through your able abilities may be
sifted, and perhaps leave a portion of matter which you may
consider of some value and turn to some account. My
personal interest is not only in trawl-fishing, but hook and
line, seined-net, drift-net, and other kinds; for, being a commission agent, it is all fish that comes to my net. I cannot
speak of the qualities of trawl-net fishing, either for or against,

not having been connected with that branch of the trade, but
after a remark or two on the information received by Mr.
Fenwick, and which is conveyed in your columns from
certain gentlemen professing to have a knowledge of the trade,
I will give you my information as briefly as possible. The
fact is this—it never will be possible to catch what we consider trawl-fish in sufficient quantities to meet the demand
but by the trawl, the principal kinds being turbot, brill, soles,
and plaice. A small quantity may be taken by other means,
but more by accident than otherwise. As for trawl-fish being
mutilated and putrid before landing, how does it happen that
so many spotless and pure fish, out of the above kinds, are
not only sold in London but all over the country, and exhibited
on the tables both of rich and poor? Yourself and every
nobleman can speak on this point ; and when informed that
they are all caught by the trawl (a fact undeniable), you will
consider it wrong on the part of any one to mislead the public
on a matter of so much importance. Advise him to fathom
the secrets of the ocean, and discover a better mode to obtain
them."

A great deal of obloquy has been thrown on the trawl,
because it *hashes* the fish ; but the destruction of young fish
—that is, fish unfit for human food because of their being
young—is not peculiar to the trawl. When the lines are
thrown out for cod the fishermen cannot command that only
full-grown fish are to seize upon the bait : the tender codling,
the unfledged haddock, the greedy mackerel *will* bite—the consequence being that thousands of sea-fish are annually killed
that are unfit for food, and that have never had an opportunity of adding to their kind. But this mischance is incidental to all our fisheries, no matter what the engine of capture
may be, whether net or line. Look how we slaughter our
grilses, without giving them the opportunity of breeding! The
herring-fishing is a notable example of this mode of doing

business : the very time that these animals come together to perpetuate their species is the time chosen by man to kill them.   Of course if they are to be used as food, they must be killed at some time, and the proper time to capture them forms one of those fishing mysteries which we have not as yet been able to solve.   We protect the salmon with many laws at the most interesting time of its life, and why we should not be able to devise a close-time for the cod, tur- bot, haddock, and sole of particular coasts—for each portion of the coast has its particular season—is what I cannot under- stand, and can only account for the anomaly on the ground of salmon being private property.

The labour of the Scottish fishermen is greatly augmented by the want of good harbours for their boats.   Time and op- portunity serving, the men of the fisher class are really in- dustrious, and this want of proper harbourage is a hardship to them.   It is curious to notice the little quarry-holes that on some parts of the Moray Firth serve as a refuge for the boats.   There is the harbour of Whitehills, for instance : it could not be of any possible use in the event of a stiff gale arising, for in my opinion the boats would never get into it, but would be dashed to pieces on the neighbouring rocks.   I have witnessed one or two storms on the north-east coast of Scotland, and shall never forget the scenes of misery these tumults of the great deep occasioned.   Even lately (October 1864) there was a storm raging along these coasts that left most impressive death-marks at nearly all the fishing places on the Moray Firth.   I was not an eye-witness of this last gale, but I have gathered from various sources, oral and writ- ten, one or two passages descriptive of its violence and the loss of life it occasioned.

At Portessie, one of the Moray Firth villages, a boat called the Shamrock, containing a crew of nine men, was numbered among the lost.   It had sailed on a Wednesday morning in

October 1864, for the fishing-ground known as "the Bank,"
about twenty miles off.   John Smith, the principal owner
of the boat, an old man, was not at the time able to go
to sea ; but he had seven sons, and five of these, with
four near relatives, sailed in the ill-fated Shamrock from
Portessie harbour on that fatal morning.   The Shamrock was
accompanied by some other boats belonging to the same place,
and the little fleet left as early as three A.M.,. keeping together
more or less until they reached the fishing-ground.   On arriving at the Bank the Shamrock, it appears, had separated from
the others, the crew preferring to go some distance in order to
cast their lines ; and she had not been seen by the other boats
after parting from them.   About seven o'clock on the following morning, some of the people of Whitehills, on going round
to the spot known as Craigenroan, a quarter of a mile to the
westward, were alarmed at seeing a boat lying high and dry
among the rocks, as if it had been tossed up at high tide and
left perched there on the receding of the waters.   The mast,
some oars, and other articles, were seen lying here and there
beside her, strewn among the rocks, and there were holes seen
in her sides—evidence only too conclusive that the boat was
a wreck.   A closer inspection discovered her mark and number—"B.F., 743," and then was also seen the name and unmistakable designation, "Shamrock, Pt. Essie—J. Smith."
On examination it was conjectured, from the way in which
the mast had been wrenched off, that the boat had foundered,
either some distance at sea, or among inshore breakers, right-
ing again as she was beaten up on the rocks, where, as we have
said, she was found sitting high and dry on her keel.   It
was at once felt that all the crew had perished, and
the bodies of the men were eagerly sought for by their
friends and relatives.   On Friday, the lifeless body of John
Smith, "Bodie," was found washed up on the beach.   On the
same day the corpse of his son, à young man who was to have

been married in a week—and whose house, like that of a friend and namesake, was being furnished at home—was cast ashore at Whitehills, and one of the first to recognise the body was the father of the betrothed. Another body was got at the mouth of the little burn at the further end of the Boyndie Links. This also was on Friday it was found to be the remains of one of the five brothers —namely John, aged twenty-five, the namesake alluded to, who was to have been married on the morrow. The body of another of the five brothers—namely William—was found floating in the bay, off Banff Harbour, lashed to a buoy, to which the poor fellow had attached himself, probably in the boat, for safety. At one time the body was seen in this position at Whitehills, suspended from the buoy, and so close to the shore that had a grappling-iron been at hand it might have been secured. It would have been of no avail, however, as the vital spark had long since fled ; but the passage of the body, drawn back with the tide and carried round to Banff, served to reconcile certain apparently conflicting evidences as to the history of the wreck, or rather as to the spot where it occurred.

On the occasion of this storm there was deep wailing at Buckie, for in that town there was more than one woman who was widowed by the tempest. Of necessity a fisherman's wife is extremely masculine in character. Her occupation makes her so, because she requires a strength of body which no other female attains, and of which the majority of men cannot boast. The long distances she has frequently to travel in all weathers with her burden, weighing many stones, make it essential for her to possess a sturdy frame, and be capable of great physical endurance. Accordingly, most of the fishwives who carry on the sale of their husbands' fish possess a strength with which no prudent man would venture to come into conflict. Then the nature of their calling makes them bold in manners,

and in speech rough and ready.   Having to encounter daily
all sorts of people, and drive hard bargains, their wits, though
not refined, are sharpened to a keen edge, and they are more
than a match for any "chaff" directed towards them either by
purchaser or passer-by.   So long, however, as they are civilly
and properly treated, they are civil and fair-spoken in return,
and can, when occasion serves, both flatter and please in a
manner by no means offensive.   Altogether, the Scottish
fishwife is an honest, out-spoken, good-hearted creature, rough
as the occupation she follows, but generally good-natured and
what the Scotch call "canty."   She does not even want feeling, though, it may be, her avocation gives her little opportunity to show it.   But who is so often called upon to endure
the strongest emotions of fear, suspense, and sorrow, as the
fisherman's wife ?   Every time the wind blows, and the sea
rises, when the boats of her husband or kinsfolk are "out,"
she knows no peace till they are in safety ; and not seldom has
she been doomed to stand on the shore and look at the white
foaming sea in which the little boat, containing all she held
dear, was battling with the billows, with the problem of its
destruction or salvation all unsolved.

   To return to the history of the storm.   No less than
twenty-seven boats belonging to Buckie had left for the
fishing, some of them as early as two o'clock in the morning.   Some hours previous to the boats leaving, there were
indications of the coming storm.   A heavy surf was rolling on the coast, but almost unaccompanied by wind, only
slight airs now and again coming from the north, but the
barometer had fallen considerably during the night.   With
these indications of bad weather, the men on duty at the
Coast Guard station hailed the Portessie men when on their
way to join their boats at Buckie harbour, and warned them
of the likelihood of a storm overtaking them.   Little heed,
however, appears to have been given to this warning, and the

boats left the harbour with more than usual difficulty, the sea at the entrance being so rough. The boats pursued a north-east course, but from the absence of a breeze the oars had to be resorted to, and nearly twelve hours elapsed before they got to the fishing rendezvous. In ordinary circumstances, with a good wind, the boats would have reached the fishing-ground in about three hours, and would have returned by the next tide—about mid-day. About six P.M. the storm broke upon the fishermen with great violence. The majority of the boats kept close together, and as the first of the gale was suc-ceeded by comparative calm, the crews, imagining that they had seen the worst of the storm, began to finish their fishing. This would have occupied about an hour, but, before it was half accomplished, the wind, veering rather more to the north, blew a perfect hurricane, and the sea became so disturbed that it was hardly possible to manage the boats. The sails, which had been hoisted when the wind first sprang up, were reduced, some of them by as many as six reefs, but the experience and energy of the hardy fishermen seemed scarce sufficient to battle successfully for existence among the warring elements. Some of the crews in this strait made for the Banff coast ; others made up their minds to endeavour to ride out the storm, and a good number ran for Cromarty, or the ports on the opposite side of the Firth. The attainment of either of these three alternatives was a work of peril, for there is no harbour of refuge on either side of the Firth to which boats may with safety run from a storm ; and the broken water is about as plentiful and dangerous in the centre of the Firth as it is along the shore. While the brave fishermen were encountering the severest perils attending their calling, the anxiety and suspense of their relations were heartrending. The storm in its intensity, though its coming had been fore-shadowed, was not felt on shore till about nine P.M. on Wednesday evening. From that hour, however, the wind, now from the east, and again from the north, came in terrific gusts, and the whole bay at Buckie boiled and moaned as it had been seldom known to do before.

Long before the storm was at its height, the wives and sweethearts of those at sea had become alarmed for their safety ; they could well remember the desolation that a similar tempest, which occurred on the 16th August 1848, caused in their households. They left their homes to wander along the sea-beach, and peer through the storm for any sign of the approach of the boats containing their relatives. A huge fire was kindled on the top of the braes in the hope that its glare might attract those at sea, and beacon them to a safe shore. During the early part of the night the suspense and fear of the whole inhabitants of Buckie were extreme, and while this anxiety was being endured the boats that had first left the fishing-ground were nearing the land. Some of the boats for a considerable time were allowed to run before the wind, the crews not knowing whither they went, as they were not within sight of lights. When at length they got within sight of the lights very great caution had to be exercised, and a little confusion was occasioned by the unusual number of fires exhibited. Shortly after eleven o'clock a boat was seen approaching Buckie harbour, and getting a favourable opportunity of crossing the bar, it entered the harbour in safety. Two other boats followed, but these had much greater difficulty in gaining the port. The tide was at its height about two o'clock A.M., when a fourth boat approached. At the entrance to the harbour she shipped a sea, and it was thought by all on the shore that she had been upset. The same wave, however, carried the boat a considerable distance into the harbour, and as she continued in an upright position she was soon pulled to the beach, and her crew landed in safety. When the tide was fully in, it stood about twenty feet above its ordinary point, the waves breaking almost on the foundations of the Coast Guard watch-house. On the pier the water fell so heavily that it was often some feet deep, and the spray from the waves mounted to a height of about forty feet above the lighthouse. The people kept watching on the shore till daybreak, but no sign of any of the other boats was visible, and as no known casualty had occurred to the boats that made for Buckie and Portgordon, keen hopes were entertained that the remainder of the boats had found shelter on the opposite side of the Firth, or would be able to ride out the storm. The anxiety in Buckie continued during Thursday, and was rather intensified towards the afternoon when the wind, veering round to W.N.W., again heightened almost to the pitch it had reached during the previous night. Several people from the villages on both sides of Buckie came into that town in the afternoon to ascertain whether the post should bring tidings from their missing friends. With great consideration the captain of one of the boats that got into Cromarty wrote by first post to say that no casualty had occurred within his knowledge, and that a number of boats (some eight or nine) had entered Cromarty in safety, and others were approaching the harbour.

I was a witness to some of the effects of the previous great storms that had raged in the Moray Firth about the close of the year 1857. A number of fishing-boats and their crews were lost at that time, Buckie again coming in for a large share of the desolation. I have preserved a few scraps descriptive of the storm, cut, I think, from the *Banffshire Journal ;* and these, supplemented by what I gathered personally from the descriptions of those engaged in the contest, will give my readers a good idea of the scene at Buckie. Premising that before the storm attained its culminating point one or two of the boats had got safely into the harbour, I may state that as the sea increased in anger and the waves lashed the shore in ever-augmenting fury, the excitement of those on

land became terrible. People seemed disposed to run everywhere, and no one knew where to run. It was nearly an
hour—sixty minutes of terrible suspense—after the two first
boats came into the harbour ere any others came in sight. By
and by, however, they began to appear, most of them evidently making for the sands opposite and east of the new
town of Buckie, some for Craigenroan, a place of shelter
east of Portessie. The attention of the Buckie people was
chiefly centred in the arrivals at their own shore, as other
boats were scarcely seen ; and while their own boats were
every now and then, from two to three o'clock, dropping in at
home, there was the chance that those running for Craigenroan belonged to other towns. At two o'clock the storm had
about culminated, and as the boats came each in sight (they
were only seen a short way off land) there was a shriek
from those assembled on the shore, while the utmost anxiety
prevailed till they were each ashore and the men landed,
every one providing themselves with ropes and whatever could be supposed likely to be useful in putting forth
efforts to save life. The crowd ran from one point to
another along the coast to whatever place it was likely the
boats would strike, and most enthusiastic were the exertions
made by one and all to get the imperilled men out of jeo-
pardy, so soon as ever they came within reach. The boats,
as they arrived, were secured with mooring-ropes, and a
hand or two left to take care of each, while the spare men
spread themselves along the beach to assist in saving the
lives and property of their fellows in distress. Four boats
got safely in. Alas for the fifth! About half-past two
o'clock this fifth boat, like the others, without a stitch of
canvas, came in sight pretty far west, and was expected
to land in "The Neuk," opposite New Buckie. Tossed
mountain high at one moment, and the next down between
the gigantic waves, she came along in much the same circum-

stances as the others.   Hundreds soon gathered at the point
she was expected to reach.   The boats had come so near the
shore that the men on board were perfectly well recognised
by their friends, among whom there were wives in the greatest
anxiety to rescue their husbands from the angry deep, fathers
to rescue their sons, brother to welcome brother, etc.   But how
sad was the scene beggars all description, for within a hundred yards of the shore a tremendous sea struck the boat on
her broadside, and turned her right over, as quick as a man
would turn his hand, the crew of course being all cast into the
water.   The crowd on shore held up their hands appalled, and
cried and shrieked, many of them in perfect distraction.   The
scene was heartrending in the extreme ; but the first manifes-
tations of grief and alarm by and by toned down to mournful
wailings, although, as was to be expected, the excitement and
confusion were very great.   Three of the men were never seen,
having at once sunk to rise no more.   Two seemed to get on
the bottom of the boat, but one of them very shortly disappeared.   The other one, however, stood up on his feet, and
put his hands to his waistcoat near the buttons, from which
act it was supposed he was preparing to strip and be in readiness to swim.   The situation was heightened by the interest of
those on shore in seeing him in this perilous position, and the
grief of his friends was intensely unspeakable when they saw
the first heavy sea wash him away from the footing he had
gained, and, in its rolling fury, hide him perhaps for ever from
human eyes.   The remaining three of the eight who were on
board (the crew numbered eleven, but three had not gone to
sea that day) also disappeared for a little, but in a short time
they were seen floating about on spars and pieces of the masts ;
and hope still existed that rescue might be extended to them.
They were driven from one point to another with fearful
velocity, and indeed were only now and again visible.   Anxiety
was felt in every breast still more acutely than ever, as these

three were wafted nearer and nearer the shore ; and so sorely
did they struggle, that, even against every probability, hope
whispered that their safety was possible.   For full twenty
minutes they floated about in this situation, latterly coming
within about twenty yards of where the people were standing
—so near that, had the sea been ordinarily calm, hundreds
were there who would have considered it no difficult task to
rush into the water and give them their hand.   One man
cried to his brother to put his hair away from his eyes, when,
by the motion the latter made, it was evident he heard quite
distinctly.   Two or three different times he obeyed, putting
up his hand, and rubbing his hair over his forehead.   An
anxious wife actually rushed into the tide nearly to the neck,
in an endeavour to rescue her husband, but her heroic
effort was completely unavailing.   The tide was ebbing at the
time, but the waves, in terrible force, rushed far up on the
beach, and swept back again with fearful power.   No one
could keep his footing in the water.   Attempts were made
to join hands and thus extend help to the unfortunate men,
but, besides the weight of the water itself, the backwash of
the waves hurled the gravel beach from below their feet, so
that to stand on it was impossible ; and even while these
vain efforts were being made at rescue, the men, worn out in
the raging surf, sank, one after another, amid the cries and
shrieks of their despairing relatives.

The number of men drowned on the north-east coast—*i.e.*
at Wick, Helmsdale, and Peterhead—during the great storm
of 1848, was one hundred, and the value of the boats and the
nets that were lost upon that remarkable occasion was at least
£7000.   The gale broke upon the coast on the 19th of August,
just as the fishing was being busily prosecuted.   Most of the
boats ran for shelter to the nearest haven, and it is melancholy
to know that many of them foundered at the very entrance to
their harbour.   The whole of the mischief was done in the

brief period of three hours.   In that period many a poor woman was made miserable, and many a hearth rendered cheerless.   It is gratifying to think that since the date of the great storm considerable improvement has been made in the Scottish fishery harbours, and that at Wick a great harbour of refuge is now in progress.   The weather prophecies now published by the Board of Trade, and telegraphed to all important seaports, are also of great use to the fisher-folk, as are the large barometers which have been erected in nearly every fishing village.   These are the elements of science which will ultimately chase away superstition from our sea-coast villages, if indeed we can honestly call the poetic fancies of these fisher-folks superstitions.   We cannot wonder that, as the dark remembrance of some great bereavement escapes from the chambers of their memory, they see forms in the flying clouds, or hear voices in the air, that cannot be seen or heard by landsmen unaccustomed to the treacherous waters of the great deep.

Large quantities of fish offal are used by the farmers as manure.   The intestines of the herring are regularly sold for the purpose of being thrown upon the land, and I have heard of as many as three hundred barrels of haddock offal being sold from one curing-yard.   It is thought by some economists that the commoner kinds of fish might be largely captured and converted into fish guano.   I have not studied that part of the fishing question very deeply, but I am disposed to doubt the propriety of employing fishing vessels to capture coarse fish for manure, as I do not think it will pay to do so. In former years fish were extensively used as manure, but that was during seasons when the capture was so large as to produce a glut.   I reprint, in the shape of an appendix to this volume, an account of the fish-guano manufactory at Concarneau in Finisterre, as well as some information about the fish-manure of Norway.

CHAPTER VIII.

———◆———

THE NATURAL AND ECONOMIC HISTORY OF
THE OYSTER.

Proper Time for Oyster-Fishing to Begin—Description of the Oyster—Contro-
versies about its Natural History—Spatting of the Oyster—Growth of the
Oyster—Quantity of Spawn Emitted by the Oyster—Social History of
the Oyster—Great Men who were Fond of Oysters—Oyster-Breeding in
France—Lake Fusaro—Beef's Discovery of Artificial Culture—Oyster-
Farming in the Bay of Biscay—The Celebrated Green Oysters—Marennes
—Dr. Kemmerer's Plan—Lessons to be gleaned from the French Piscicul-
turists—How to Manage an Oyster-Farm—Whitstable—Cultivation of
Natives—The Colne Oyster-Trade—Scottish Oysters—The Pandores—
Extent of Oyster-Ground in the Firth of Forth—Dredging—Extent of
American Oyster-Beds.

AUGUST is a month that has red-letter days for those who
delight in the luxuries of eating. Do we not in that
month begin the carnival of "St. Grouse?" and do we not
hear in the bye-streets of London the pleasant sounds of
"Please to remember the Grotto?" It is the month that ushers
in the ever-welcome oyster. In nearly every small street
and alley early in August may be heard resounding the words
"Only once a year!" and groups of merry children building
their grottoes remind us that the long days are passing, that
autumn is at hand, and that in a few brief months the Christmas barrel of oysters will be travelling "inland" on the
rapid railway, passing in its course the friendly and welcome
exchange hamper of country produce, containing the choice

pheasant and the plump turkey. But September, and not August, is the right month for the inauguration of the oyster season, although, by ancient custom, perhaps originating in the impatience of our *gourmets*, the proper date has been anti-cipated, and oyster-eating has become general even so early as the 5th of August. It is wrong, however, to partake of oysters thus early—as wrong as it was three centuries ago to eat them on St. James's day, although the superstition of the period gave weight to the act ; as in those days there existed a proverb that persons who ate oysters on the 25th of July would have plenty of money all the rest of the year.

In those remote times the knowledge of sea-produce was exceedingly limited, as people could only guess the proper season for indulging in what we call "shell-fish ;" and al-though it is not easy, from the difficulty of obtaining access to sea animals, to obtain accurate information about their growth and habits, yet it is pleasing to think that we know a great deal more of those interesting creatures than our fore-fathers ever did. Our worthy ancestors, for instance, were quite content to swallow their oysters without inquiring very minutely about how they were bred; the oyster-shell was opened simply that its contents might be devoured along with the necessary quantity of bread and butter and brown stout. They did not think of the delicacy as a subject of natural history—with them it was simply a delicious condiment. But in the present day that style of eating has been alto-gether reformed : people like to know what they eat; and from the investigations of M. Coste and other naturalists we now know as much about the oyster, and the mollusca in general, as we do about the crustacea.

Generally speaking, many curious opinions have been held about shell-fish. At one time they were thought to be only masses of oily or other matter scarcely alive and in-sensible to pain. Who could suppose, it was asked, that a portion of blubber like the oyster, that could only have been first eaten by some very courageous individual, could have any feeling? But we know better now, and although the organisation of the mollusca is not of a high order, it is perfect of its kind, and has within it indications of organs that in beings of a higher type serve a loftier purpose, and point out the beginnings of nature, showing how she works her way from the simplest imaginings of animal life to the complex human machine. The oyster has no doubt in its degree its joys and sorrows, and throbs with life and pleasure, as animals do that have a higher organic structure.

Zoologically the oyster is known as *Ostræa edulis.* Its outward appearance is familiar to even very landward people, and no human engineer could have invented so admirable a home for the pulpy and headless mass of jelly that is contained within the rough-looking shell. The oyster is a curiously-constructed animal; but I fear that, comparatively speaking, very few of my readers have ever seen a perfect one, as oysters are very much mutilated, being generally deprived of their beards before they are sent to table, and otherwise hurt, both accidentally in the opening and by use and wont, as in the case of the beard. Its mouth—it has no jaws or teeth—is a kind of trunk or snout, with four lips, and leafy coverings or gills are spread over the body to act as lungs, and keep from the action of the water the air which the animal requires for its existence. This covering is divided into two lobes with ciliated edges. Four leaves or membranous plates act as capillary funnels, open at the farthest extremities. Behind the gills there is a large whitish fatty part enclosing the stomach and intestines. The vessels of circulation play into muscular cavities, which act the part of the heart. The stomach is situated near the mouth. The oyster has no feet, but can move by opening and closing its shell, and it secures food by means of its beard, which acts as a kind of rake. In fact the internal structure of the oyster, while it is excellently adapted to that animal's mode of life, is exceedingly simple.

It is not my purpose in the present work to enter into the minutiæ of oyster life. Indeed, there have been so many controversies about the natural history of this animal as to render it impossible to narrate in the brief space I can devote to it a tenth part of what has been written or spoken about the life and habits of the "breedy creature." Every stage of its growth has been made the stand-point for a wrangle of some kind. As an example of the keenness with which each stage of oyster life is now being discussed, I may mention that in the summer of 1864 a most amusing squabble broke out in the pages of the *Field* newspaper on an immaterial point of oyster life, which is worth noting here as an example of what can be said on either side of a question. The controversy hinged upon whether an oyster while on the bed lay on the flat or convex side. Mr. Frank Buckland, who originated the dispute, maintained that the right, proper, and natural position of the oyster, when at the bottom of the sea, is with the flat shell downwards. Mr. James Lowe, a gentleman who takes great interest in pisciculture, and who has explored the oyster-beds of France, held the opinion that the oyster is never in its proper position except when the flat shell is uppermost. Of course, the natural position of the oyster is of no practical importance whatever ; and I know, from personal observation of the beds at Newhaven and Cockenzie, that oysters lie both ways,—indeed, with a dozen or two of dredges tearing over the beds it is impossible but that they must lie quite higgledy-piggledy, so to speak. A great deal that is incidentally interesting was brought up in the discussion to which I have been referring. There have been several other disputes about points in the natural history of the oysters—one in particular as to whether that animal is provided with organs of vision. Various opinions have been enunciated as to whether an oyster has eyes, and one author asserts that it has so many as twenty-four, which again is denied, and the assertion made that the so-called eyes project-ing from the border of the mantle have no optical power what-ever; but be that as it may, I have no doubt whatever that the oyster has a power of knowing the light from the dark.

Without wishing to dogmatise on any point of oyster life, I think I can bring before my readers in a brief way a few interesting facts in the natural history of the edible oyster.

As is well known, there is a period every year during which the oyster is not fished; and the reason why our English oyster-beds have not been ruined or exhausted by overfishing arises, among other causes, from this fact of there being a definite close-time assigned to the breeding of the mollusc. It would be well if the larger varieties of sea pro-duce were equally protected; for it is sickening to observe the countless numbers of unseasonable fish that are from time to time brought to Billingsgate and other markets, and greedily purchased. The fact that oysters are supplied only during certain months in the year, and that the public have a general corresponding notion that they are totally unfit for wholesome eating during May, June, July, and August (those four wretched months which have not the letter "r" in their names), has been greatly in their favour. Had there been no period of rest, it is almost quite certain that oysters would long ago—I allude to the days when there was no system of cultivation—have become extinct, so great is the demand for this dainty mollusc.

Oysters begin to sicken about the end of April, so that it is well that their grand rest commences in May. The shedding of the spawn continues during the whole of the hot months— not but that during that period there may be found supplies of healthy oysters, but, as a general rule, it is better that there should be a total cessation of the trade during the summer season, because were the beds disturbed by a search for the healthy oysters the spawn would be scattered and destroyed.

Oysters do not leave their ova, like many other marine creatures, but incubate them in the folds of their mantle, and among the laminæ of their lungs. There the ova remain surrounded by mucous matter, which is necessary to their development, and within which they pass through the embryo state. The mass of ova, or "spat" as it is familiarly called, undergoes various changes in its colour, meanwhile losing its fluidity. This state indicates the near termination of the development and the sending forth of the embryo to an independent existence, for by this time the young oysters can live without the protection of the maternal organs. An eminent French pisciculturist says that the animated matter escaping from the adults on breeding-banks is like a thick mist being dispersed by the winds—the *spat* is so scattered by the waves that only an imperceptible portion remains near the parent stock. All the rest is dissipated over the sea space ; and if these myriads of animalculæ, tossed by the waves, do not meet with solid bodies to which they can attach themselves, their destruction is certain, for if they do not fall victims to the larger animals which prey upon them, they are unfortunate in not fixing upon the proper place for their thorough development.

Thus we see that the spawn of the oyster is well matured before it leaves the protection of the parental shell ; and by the aid of the microscope the young animal can be seen with its shell perfect and its holding-on apparatus, which is also a kind of swimming-pad, ready to clutch the first " coigne of vantage" that the current may carry it against. My theory is, that the parent oyster goes on *brewing* its spawn for some time—I have· seen it oozing from the same animal for some days—and it is supposed that the spawn swims about with the current for a short period before it falls, being in the meantime devoured by countless sea animals of all kinds.

The operation of nursing, brewing, and exuding the spat from the parental shell will occupy a considerable period— say from two to four weeks. It is quite certain that the close-time for oysters is necessary and advantageous, for we seldom find this mollusc, as we do the herring and other fish, full of eggs, so that most of the operations connected with its reproduction go on in the months during which there is no dredging. As I have indicated, immense quantities of the spawn of oysters are annually devoured by other molluscs, and by fish and crustaceans of various sizes ; it is well, therefore, that it is so bountifully supplied. On occasions of visiting the beds I have seen the dredge covered with this spawn ; and no pen could number the thousands of millions of oysters thus prevented from ripening into life. Economists ought to note this fact with respect to fish generally, for the enormous destruction of spawn of all kinds must exercise a very serious influence on our fish supplies. I may also note that the state of the weather has a serious influence on the spawn and on the adult oyster-power of spawning. A cold season is very unfavourable, and a decidedly cold day will kill the spat.

Some people have asserted that the oyster can reproduce its kind in twenty weeks, and that in ten months it is full-grown. Both of these assertions are pure nonsense. At the age of three months an oyster is not much bigger than a pea; and the age at which reproduction begins has never been accurately ascertained, but it is thought to be three years. I give here one or two illustrations of oyster-growth in order to show the ratio of increase. The smallest, about the dimensions of a pin's head, may be called a fortnight old. The next

size represents the oyster as it appears when three months
old.   The other sizes are drawn at the ages of five, eight,
and twelve months respectively.   Oysters are usually four
years old before they are sent to the
London market.. At the age of five years
the oyster is, I think, in its prime ; and
some of our most intelligent fishermen
think its average duration of life to be
ten years.

In these days of oyster-farming the
time at which the oyster becomes reproductive may be easily
fixed, and it will no doubt be found to vary in different
localities.   At some places it becomes saleable—chiefly, however, for fattening — in the course of two years ; at other
places it is three or four years before it becomes a saleable
commodity ; but on the average it will be quite safe to assume that at four years the oyster is both ripe for sale and
able for the reproduction of its kind.   Let us hope that the
breeders will take care to have at least one brood from each
batch before they offer any for sale.   Oyster-farmers should
keep before them the folly of the salmon-fishers, who kill
their grilse—i.e. the virgin fish—before they have an opportunity of perpetuating their race.

Another point on which naturalists differ is as to the
quantity of spawn from each oyster.   Some enumerate the
young by thousands, others by millions.   It is certain enough
that the number of young is prodigious—so great, in fact, as
to prevent their all being contained in the parent shell at one
time ; but I do not believe that an oyster yields its young
" in millions"—perhaps half a million is on the average the
amount of spat which each oyster can "brew" in one season.
I have examined oyster-spawn (taken direct from the oyster)
by means of a powerful microscope, and find it to be a liquid
of some little consistency, in which the young oysters, like

the points of a hair, swim actively about, in great numbers, as many as a thousand having been counted in a very minute globule of spat. The spawn, as found floating on the water, is greenish in appearance, and each little splash may be likened to an oyster nebula, which resolves itself, when examined by a powerful glass, into a thousand distinct animals.

The oyster, it is now pretty well determined, is hermaphrodite, and it is very prolific, as has been already observed, but the enormous fecundity of the animal is largely detracted from by bad breeding seasons ; for, unless the spawning season be mild, soft, and warm, there is usually a very partial fall of spat, and of course quite a scarcity of brood ; and even if one be the proprietor of a large bed of oysters, there is no security for the spawn which is emitted from the oysters on that bed falling upon it, or within the bounds of one's own property even ; it is often enough the case that the spawn falls at a considerable distance from the place where it has been emitted. Thus the spawn from the Whitstable and Faversham Oyster Companies' beds—and these contain millions of oysters in various stages of progress—falls usually on a large piece of ground between Whitstable and the Isle of Thanet, formerly common property, but lately *given* by Act of Parliament to a company recently formed for the breeding of oysters. The saving of the spawn cannot be effected unless it falls on proper ground—*i.e.* ground with a shelly bottom is best, for the infant animal is sure to perish if it fall among mud or upon sand ; the infant oyster must obtain a holding-on place as the first condition of its own existence.

Oysters have not on the aggregate spawned extensively during late years. The greatest fall of spawn ever known in England occurred in 1827, and it is thought by practical men, as well as naturalists, that they do not spawn at all in cold seasons, and in Britain not always in warm seasons ; and Mr.

Buckland, I believe, assumes that the more favourable spawning on the French coast of the Bay of Biscay is caused by the greater, because more direct, influence of the Gulf Stream on the waters there than in the English Channel, but this idea is also disputed. If the oyster does not spawn every year it would require to emit an enormous quantity in those favourable years when it does spawn, so as to keep up the supply. On being exuded from the parental shell, the spawn of the oyster at once rises to the surface, where its vitality is easily affected, and it is often killed in certain places by snow-water or ice. A genial warmth of sunshine and water is considered highly favourable to its proper development during the few days it floats about on the surface. It is thought that not more than one oyster out of each million arrives at maturity. It is curious to note that some oysters have immense shells with very little " meat " in them. I recently saw in a popular tavern (date Sept. 29, 1864), several oysters much larger externally than crown-pieces with the " meat " about the size of a sixpence : these were Firth of Forth oysters from Cockenzie. It is not easy to determine from the external size of the animal the amount of " meat " it will yield—apparently, " the bigger the oyster the smaller the meat." In the early part of the season we get only the very small oysters in Edinburgh— the reason assigned being that all the best dredgers are " away at the herring," and that the persons left behind at the oyster-beds are only able to skim them, so that, for a period of about six weeks, we merely obtain the small fry that are lying on the top. It is quite certain that as the season advances the oysters obtained are larger and of more decided flavour. In the " natives " obtained at Whitstable the shell and the meat are pretty much in keeping as to size, and this is an advantage.

The Abbé Diquemarc, who has keenly observed the habits of the principal mollusca, assures us that oysters, when free, are perfectly able to transport themselves from one place to another, by simply causing the sea-water to enter and emerge suddenly from between their valves ; and these they use with extreme rapidity and great force.   By means of the operation now described, the oyster is enabled to defend itself from its enemies among the minor crustacea, particularly the small crabs, which endeavour to enter the shell when it is half open. " Some naturalists," the Abbé says, "go the length of allowing the oyster to have great foresight," which he illustrates by an allusion to the habits of those found at the sea-side.   " These oysters," he says, " exposed to the daily change of tides, appear to be aware that they are likely to be exposed to dryness at certain recurring periods, and so they preserve water in their shells to supply their wants when the tide is at ebb. This peculiarity renders them more easy of transportation to remote distances than those members of the family which are caught at a considerable distance from the shore."

But oysters have their social as well as their natural and economic history.   The name of the courageous individual who ate the first oyster has not been recorded, but there is a legend concerning him to the following effect :—Once upon a time—it must be a prodigiously long time ago, however —a man of melancholy mood, who was walking by the shores of a picturesque estuary, listening to the monotonous murmur of the sad sea-waves, espied a very old and ugly oyster, all coated over with parasites and sea-weeds.   It was so unprepossessing that he kicked it with his foot, and the animal, astonished at receiving such rude treatment on its own domain, gaped wide with indignation.   Seeing the beautiful cream-coloured layers that shone within the shelly covering, and fancying the interior of the shell itself to be beautiful, he lifted up the aged "native" for further examination, inserting his finger and thumb within the shells.   The irate mollusc, thinking no doubt that this was meant as a further insult, snapped his pearly door close upon the finger of the intruder, causing him some little pain. After releasing his wounded digit, the inquisitive gentleman very naturally put it in his mouth. "Delightful!" exclaimed he, opening wide his eyes. "What is this?" and again he sucked his thumb. Then the great truth flashed upon him, that he had found out a new delight—had in fact accidentally achieved the most important discovery ever made up to that date! He proceeded at once to the verification of his thought. Taking up a stone, he forced open the doors of the oyster, and gingerly tried a piece of the mollusc itself. Delicious was the result; and so, there and then, with no other condiment than the juice of the animal, with no reaming brown stout or pale chablis to wash down the repast, no nicely-cut, well-buttered brown bread, did that solitary anonymous man inaugurate the oyster banquet. Another way of the story is that the man who ate the first oyster was compelled to do so for a punishment :—

> "The man had sure a palate covered o'er
> With brass, or steel, that on the rocky shore
> First broke the oozy oyster's pearly coat,
> And risk'd the living morsel down his throat."

Ever since the apocryphal period of this legend, men have gone on eating oysters. Poets, princes, pontiffs, orators, statesmen, and wits have gluttonised over the oyster-bed. Oysters were at one time, it is true, in danger of being forgotten. From the fourth century to about the fifteenth they were not much in use; but from that date to the present time the demand has never slackened. Going back to the times which we now regard as classic, we are told—as I will by and by relate in more detail when I come to describe the art of oyster-farming—that we owe the original idea of pisciculture to a certain Sergius Orata, who invented an oyster-pond in which to breed oysters, not for his own table, but for profit. We

have all read of the feasts and fish-dinners of the classic
Italians. These were on a scale, as has been already indicated,
far surpassing our modern banquets at Greenwich and
Blackwall, even though the charge for these be, as was recently complained in the *Times*, two and three guineas for
each person. Talking of fish-dinners reminds me of a description I have read of a dish produced in China containing
juvenile crabs. On the cover being removed the crablets
jump out on the table and are greedily seized and eaten by
the guests who are assembled. The dish is filled with vinegar,
which imparts great liveliness to the young creatures. The
shell is soft and gelatinous, and the *morceau* is highly palatable. Lucullus had sea-water brought to his villa in canals
from the coast of Campania, in which he bred fish in such
abundance for the use of his guests that not less than
£35,000 worth was sold at his death. Vitellius ate oysters
all day long, and some people insinuate that he could
eat as many as a thousand at one sitting—a happiness too
great for belief! Callisthenes, the philosopher of Olynthus,
was also a passionate oyster-eater, and so was Caligula, the
Roman tyrant. The wise Seneca dallied over his few hundreds
every week, and the great Cicero nourished his eloquence with
the dainty. The Latin poets sang the praises of the oyster,
and the fast men of ancient Rome enjoyed the poetry during
their carouse, just as modern fellows, not at all classic, enjoy
a song over their oysters in the parlour of a London or provincial tavern.

In all countries there are records of the excessive fondness
of great men for oysters. Cervantes was an oyster-lover, and
he satirised the oyster-dealers of Spain. Louis XI., careful
lest scholarship should become deficient in France, feasted the
learned doctors of the Sorbonne, once a year, on oysters ; and
another Louis invested his cook with an order of nobility as
a reward for his oyster-cookery. Napoleon, also, was an

oyster-lover ; so was Rousseau ; and Marshall Turgot used to eat a hundred or two, just to whet his appetite for breakfast. Invitations to a dish of oysters were common in the literary and artistic circles of Paris at the latter end of last century. The Encyclopedists were particularly fond of oysters. Helvetius, Diderot, the Abbé Raynal, Voltaire, and others, were confirmed oyster-men. Before the Revolution, the violent politicians were in the habit of constantly frequenting the Parisian oyster-shops ; and Danton, Robespierre, and others, were fond of the oyster in their days of innocence. The great Napoleon, on the eve of his battles, used to partake of the bivalve ; and Cambaceres was famous for his shell-fish banquets. Even at this day the consumption of oysters in Paris is enormous. According to recent statistics the quantity eaten there is one million per day !

Among our British celebrities, Alexander Pope was an oyster-eater of taste, and so was Dean Swift, who was fond of lobsters as well. Thomson, of *The Seasons*, who knew all good things, knew how good a thing an oyster was. The learned Dr. Richard Bentley could never pass an oyster-shop without having a few ; and there have been hundreds of subsequent Englishmen who, without coming up to Bentley in other respects, have resembled him in this. The Scottish philosophers, too, of the last century—Hume, Dugald Stewart, Cullen, etc.—used frequently to indulge in the "whiskered pandores" of their day and generation. "Oyster-ploys," as they were called, were frequently held in the quaint and dingy taverns of the Old Town of Edinburgh. These Edinburgh oyster-taverns of the olden time were usually situated under-ground, in the cellar-floor ; and, even in the course of the long winter evenings, the carriages of the quality folks would be found rattling up, and setting down fashionable ladies, to partake of oysters and porter, plenteously but rudely served. What oysters have been to the intellect of Edinburgh in later times, who needs to be told that has heard of Christopher North and read the *Noctes Ambrosianæ* ?

The Americans become still more social over their oysters than we do, and their extensive seabord affords them a very large supply, although I regret to learn that, in consequence of overfishing and of carrying away the fish at improper seasons, the oyster-banks of that great country are in danger of becoming exhausted. In City Island the whole population participates in the oyster-trade, and there is an oyster-bed in Long Island Sound which is 115 miles long.

The oyster can be cooked in many ways, but the pure animal is the best of all, and gulping him up in his own juice is the best way to eat him. The oyster, I maintain, may be eaten raw, day by day, every day of the 214 days that it is in season, and never do hurt. It never produces indigestion—never does the flavour pall. The man who ends the day with an oyster in his mouth rises with a clean tongue in the morning, and a clear head as well.

The secret of there being only a holding-on place required for the spat of the oyster to insure an immensely-increased supply having been penetrated by the French people—and no doubt they are in some degree indebted to our oyster-beds on the Colne and at Whitstable for their idea—the plan of systematic oyster-culture was easy enough, as I will immediately show. A few initiatory experiments, in fact, speedily settled that oysters could be grown in any quantity. Strong pillars of wood were driven into the mud and sand ; arms were added ; the whole was interlaced with branches of trees, and various boughs besides were hung over the beds on ropes and chains, whilst others were sunk in the water and kept down by a weight. A few boat-loads of oysters being laid down, the spat had no distance to travel in search of a home, but found a resting-place almost at the moment of being exuded ; and, as the fairy legends say, " it grew and it grew," till, in the fulness of time, it became a marketable commodity.

But the history of this modern phase of oyster-farming, as practised on the foreshores of France, is so interesting as to demand at my hands a rather detailed notice, for it is one of the most noteworthy circumstances connected with the revived art of fish-culture, that it has resulted in placing upon the shores of France upwards of 7000 fish-farms for the cultivation of the oyster alone.

It is no exaggeration to say, that about fifteen years ago there was scarcely an oyster of native growth in France ; the beds—and I cite the case of France as a warning to people at home, I mean as regards our Scottish oyster-beds—had become so exhausted from overdredging as to be unproductive, so far as their money value was concerned, and to be totally unable to recover themselves so far as their power of reproductiveness was at stake. And the people were consequently in despair at the loss of this favourite adjunct of their banquets, and had to resort to other countries for such small supplies as they could obtain. As an illustration of the overdredging that had prevailed, it may be stated that oyster-farms which formerly employed 1400 men, with 200 boats, and yielded an annual revenue of 400,000 francs, had become so reduced as to require only 100 men and 20 boats. Places where at one time there had been as many as fifteen oyster-banks, and great prosperity among the fisher class, had become, at the period I allude to, almost oysterless. St. Brieuc, Rochelle, Marennes, Rochefort, etc., had all suffered so much that those interested in the fisheries were no longer able to stock the beds, thus proving that, notwithstanding the great fecundity of these sea animals, it is quite possible to overfish them, and thoroughly exhaust their reproductive power. It was under these circumstances that M. Coste instituted that plan of

oyster-culture which has been so much noticed of late in the
scientific journals, and which appears to have been inspired
by the plan of the mussel-farms in the Bay of Aiguillon, and
the oyster-parcs of Lake Fusaro, so far at least as the principle
of cultivation is concerned.   At the instigation of the French
Government, he made a voyage of exploration round the coasts
of France and Italy, in order to inquire into the condition of
the sea-fisheries, which were, it was thought, in a declining
condition.   It was his "mission," and he fulfilled it very well,
to see how these marine fisheries could be artificially aided, as
the fresh-water fisheries had been aided through the re-discovery by Joseph Remy of the long-forgotten plan of pisciculture, as already detailed in a preceding portion of this work.

The breeding of oysters was a business pursued with great
assiduity during what I have called the gastronomic age of
Italy, the period when Lucullus kept a stock of fish valued at
£50,000 sterling, and Sergius Orata invented the art of oyster-
culture.   There is not a great deal known about this ancient
gentleman, except that he was an epicure of most refined taste
(the "master of luxury" he was called in his own day), and
some writers of the period thought him a very greedy person,
a kind of dealer in shell-fish.   It was thought also that he
was a housebroker or person who bought or built houses, and
having improved them, sold them to considerable advantage.
He received, however, an excellent character, while standing
his trial for using the public waters of Lake Lucrinus for his
own private use, from his advocate Lucinus Crassus, who said
that the revenue officer who prevented Orata was mistaken if
he thought that gentleman would dispense with his oysters,
even if he was driven from the Lake of Lucrinus, for, rather
than not enjoy his molluscous luxury, he would grow them on
the tops of his houses.

Lake Fusaro, of which I give a kind of bird's-eye view, is
highly interesting to all who take an interest in the prosperity

of the fisheries, as the first seat of oyster-culture. It is the Avernus of Virgil, and is a black volcanic-looking pool of water, about a league in circumference, which lies between the site of the Lucrine Lake—the lake used by Orata—and the ruins of the town of Cumæ. It is still extant, being even now, as I have said, devoted to the highly profitable art of oyster-farming, yielding, as has often been published, from

LAKE FUSARO.

The accompanying engraving gives a general view of Lake Fusaro (the Avernus of the ancients), showing here and there the stakes surrounding the artificial banks, the single and double ranges of stakes on which the faggots are suspended, and at one extremity the labyrinths, in the face of which is a canal of from 2½ to 3 metres broad and 1½ metres deep joining the lake to the sea. A small lake, believed to be the ancient Cocytus, communicates with this canal. The pavilion in the lake is the ordinary residence of the persons in charge of the fishery.

this source an annual revenue of about £1200. This classic sheet of water was at one time surrounded by the villas of the wealthy Italians, who frequented the place for the joint benefit of the sea-water baths and the shell-fish commissariat, which had been established in the two lakes (Avernus and Lucrine). The place, which, before then, was overshadowed by thick plantations, had been consecrated by the superstitious to the use of the infernal gods.

The mode of oyster-breeding at this place, then as now, was to erect artificial pyramids of stones in the water, surrounded by stakes of wood, in order to intercept the spawn, the oyster being laid down on the stones. I have shown these modes in the accompanying engravings. Faggots of branches were also used to collect the spawn, which, as I have already said, requires, within forty-eight hours of its emission, to

OYSTER-PYRAMID.

secure a holding-on place or be lost for ever. The plan of the Fusaro oyster-breeders struck M. Coste as being eminently practical and suitable for imitation on the coasts of France : he had one of the stakes pulled up, and was gratified to find it covered with oysters of all ages and sizes. The Lake Fusaro system of cultivation was therefore, at the instigation of Professor Coste, strongly recommended for imitation by the French Government to the French people, as being the most suitable to follow, and experiments were at once entered upon with a view to prove whether it would be as practicable to cultivate oysters as easily among the agitated waves of the open sea as in the quiet waters of Fusaro. In order to settle this point, it was determined to renew the old oyster-beds in

the Bay of St. Brieuc, and notwithstanding the fact that the
water there is exceedingly deep and the winds very violent,
immediate and almost miraculous success was the result.
The fascines laid down soon became covered with seed, and
branches were speedily exhibited at Paris, and other places,
containing thousands of young oysters. The experiments in
oyster-culture tried at St. Brieuc were commenced early in the
spring of 1859, on part of a space of 3000 acres that

OYSTER-FASCINES.

was deemed suitable for the reception of spat. A quantity of
breeding oysters, approaching to three millions, was laid down
either on the old beds or on newly-constructed longitudinal
banks; these were sown thick on a bottom composed chiefly of
immense quantities of old shells—the "middens" of Cancale
in fact, where the shell accumulation had become a nuisance—
so that there was a more than ordinary good chance for the
spat finding at once a proper holding-on place. Then again,
over some of the new banks, fascines made of boughs tightly
tied together were sunk and chained over the beds, so as to
intercept such portions of the spawn as were likely, upon
rising, to be carried away by the force of the tide. In less
than six months the success of the operation in the Bay of St.
Brieuc was assured; for, at the proper season, a great fall of

spawn had occurred, and the bottom shells were covered with
the spat, while the fascines were so thickly coated with young
oysters that an estimate of 20,000 for each fascine was not
thought an exaggeration.

In a piscicultural report for 1860, we obtain, in connection with the St. Brieuc experiments, an idea of the cost of
oyster-breeding, which I translate for the benefit of people at
home :—" The total expenses for forming a bank were 221
francs ; and if the 300 fascines laid down upon it be multiplied
by 20,000 (the number of oysters they contain), 6,000,000 will
be obtained, which, if sold at twenty francs a thousand, will
produce 120,000 francs. If, however, the number of oysters on
a fascine were to be reckoned at only 10,000, the sum of 60,000
francs would be received, which, for an éxpenditure of only
221 francs, would give a larger profit than any other branch
of industry."

Twelve months, however, before the date of the experiments
I have been describing at St. Brieuc, the artificial culture of
oysters had successfully commenced on another part of the
coast—namely, the Ile de Re off the shore of the lower Charente
(near la Rochelle), in the Bay of Biscay, which may now be
designated the capital of French oysterdom, having more *parcs*
and *claires* than Marennes, Arcachon, Concarneau, Cancale,
and all the rest of the coast put together, and which, before it
became celebrated for its oyster-growing, was only known in
common with other places in France for its successful culture
of the vine.   It is curious to note the rapid growth of the
industry of oyster-culture on the Ile de Re.   It was begun so
recently as 1858, and there are now upwards of 4000 parks and
claires upon its shores, and the people may be seen as busy in
their fish-parks as the market-gardeners of Kent in their straw-
berry-beds.   Oyster-farming on the Ile was inaugurated by a
stone-mason having the curious name of Beef.

This shrewd fellow, who was a keen observer of nature,

and had seen the oyster-spat grow to maturity, began thinking of oyster-culture simultaneously with Professor Coste, and
wondering if it could be carried out on those portions of the
public foreshore that were left dry by the ebb of the waters.
He determined to try the experiment on a small scale, so as
to obtain a practical solution of his " idea," and, with this
view, he enclosed a small portion of the foreshore of the island
by building a rough dyke about eighteen inches in height. In
this park he laid down a few bushels of growing oysters, placing amongst them a quantity of large stones, which he gathered
out of the surrounding mud. This initiatory experiment was
so successful, that in the course of a year he was able to sell
£6 worth of oysters from his stock. This result was of
course very encouraging to the enterprising mason, and the
money was just in a sense found money, for the oysters went
on growing while he was at work at his own proper business
as a mason. Elated by the profit of his experiment, he proceeded to double the proportions of his park, and by that
means more than doubled his oyster commerce, for, in 1861,
he was able to dispose of upwards of £20 worth, and
this without impoverishing, in the least degree, his breeding stock. He continued to increase the dimensions of
his farm, so that by 1862 his sales had increased to £40.
As might have been expected, Beef's neighbours had been
carefully watching his experiments, uttering occasional sneers
no doubt at his enthusiasm, but, for all that, quite ready to
go and do likewise whenever the success of the industrious mason's experiments became sufficiently developed to
show that they were profitable as well as practical. After
Beef had demonstrated the practicability of oyster-farming,
the extension of the system over the foreshores of the island,
between Point de Rivedoux and Point de Lome, was rapid
and effective; so much so that two hundred beds were conceded by the Government previous to 1859, while an addi-

tional five hundred beds were speedily laid down, and in 1860 large quantities of brood were sold to the oyster-farmers at Marennes, for the purpose of being manufactured into green oysters in their claires on the banks of the river Seudre. The first sales after cultivation had become general amounted to £126, and the next season the sum reached in sales was upwards of £500, and these moneys, be it observed, were for very young oysters; because, from an examination of the dates, it will at once be seen that the brood had not had time to grow to any great size. So rapid indeed has been the progress of oyster-culture at the Ile de Re that what were formerly a series of enormous and unproductive mud-banks, occupying a stretch of shore about four leagues in length, are now so transformed, and the whole place so changed, that it seems the work of a miracle. Various gentlemen who have inspected these farms for the cultivation of oysters speak with great hopefulness about the success of the experiment. Mr. Ashworth, so well known for his success as a salmon fisher and breeder in Ireland, tells me that oyster-farming on the shores of the French coast is one of the greatest industrial facts of the present age, and thinks that oyster-farming will in the end be even more profitable than salmon-breeding. There is only one drawback connected with these and all other sea-farms in France : the farmers, we regret to say, are only "tenants at will," * and liable at any moment to be ejected ; but notwithstanding this disadvantage the work of oyster-culture still goes bravely forward, and it is calculated, in spite of the bad spatting of the last three years, that there is a stock of oysters in the beds on

* Mr. Ashworth, in a communication to Mr. Barry, one of the Commissioners of Irish Fisheries, says: " No charge is made for the oyster-parks, but each plot is marked and defined on a map, and the produce is considered to be the private property of the person who establishes it. They vary in size twenty or thirty yards square, the stone or tiles are placed in rows about five feet apart, with the ends open so as to admit of the wash of the tide in and out."

the Ile de Re—accumulated in only six years—of the value
of upwards of £100,000.

Much hard work had no doubt to be endured before such
a scene of industry could be thoroughly organised.   When the
great success of Beef's experiments had been proclaimed in the
neighbourhood a li+tle army of about a thousand labourers

OYSTER-PARKS.

came down from the interior of the country and took possession, along with the native fishermen, of the shores, portions of
which were conceded to them by the French Government at
a nominal rent of about a franc a week, for the purpose of being cultivated as oyster parks and claires.   The most arduous
duty of these men consisted in clearing off the mud, which
lay on the shore in large quantities, and which is fatal to the
oyster in its early stages ; but this had to be done before the
shores could be turned to the purpose for which they were
wished.   After this preliminary business had been accom-

plished, the rocks had to be blasted in order to find stones for
the construction of the park-walls ; then these had to be
built, and the ground had also to be paved in a rough and
ready kind of way ; foot-roads had also to be arranged for the
convenience of the farmers, and carriage-ways had likewise to
be made to admit of the progress of vehicles through the different farms.   Ditches had to be contrived to carry off the
mud ; the parks had to be stocked with breeding oysters, and
to be kept carefully free from the various kinds of sea animals
that prey upon the oyster ; and many other daily duties had
to be performed that demanded the minute attention of the
owners.   But all obstacles were in time overcome, and some
of the breeders have been so very successful of late years
as to be offered a sum of £100 for the brood attached
to twelve of their rows of stones, the cost of laying these
down being about two hundred francs !   To construct an
oyster-bed thirty yards square costs about £12 of English money, and it has been calculated that the return
from some of the beds has been as high as 1000 per
cent !   The whole industry of the Ile is wonderful when it
is considered that it has been all organised in a period of
seven years.   Except a few privately-kept oysters, there was
no oyster establishment on the island previous to 1858.

The following authentic statistics, collected by Mr. Thomas
Ashworth, of the oyster industry of the island of Re, when
only in the fourth year of culture, may prove interesting to
my readers :—

Parks for collecting spawn and breeding -	2,424
Fattening-ponds (claires) - - - -	839
Supposed number of oysters in parks -	74,242,038
Aggregate number in the claires -	1,026,282
Revenue of the parks - - -	1,086,230 francs.
Revenue of the claires - - -	40,015 ,,
Hectares of ground in parks and claires -	146
Proprietors of beds - - - -	1,700

Some gentlemen from the island of Jersey who visited Re report that an incredible quantity of oysters has been produced on that shore, which a few years ago was of no value, so that this branch of industry now realises an extraordinary revenue, and spreads comfort among a large number of families who were previously in a state of comparative

OYSTER-CLAIRES.

indigence. But more interesting even than the material prosperity that has attended the introduction of this industry into the island of Re is the moral success that has accrued to the experiment. Excellent laws have been enacted by the oyster-farmers themselves for the government of the colony. A kind of parliament has been devised for carrying on arguments as to oyster-culture, and to enable the four communities, into which the population has been divided, to communicate to each other such information as may be found useful for the general good of all engaged in oyster-farming.

Three delegates from each of the communities are elected to conduct the general business, and to communicate with the Department of Marine when necessary.

A small payment is made by every farmer as a contribution to the general expense, while each division of the community employs a special watchman to guard the crops, and see that all goes on with propriety and good faith ; and although each of the oyster-farmers of the Ile de Re cultivates his own park or claire for his own sole profit and advantage, they most willingly obey the general laws that have been enacted for the good of the community.   It is pleasant to note this.   We cannot help being gratified at the happy moral results of this wonderful industry, and it will readily be supposed that with both vine-culture (for the islanders have fine vineyards) and oyster-culture to attend to, these farmers are kept very busy.   Indeed, the growing commerce—the export of the oysters, and the import of other commodities for the benefit of so industrious a population—incidental to such an immense growth of shell-fish as can be carried on in the 4000 parks and claires which stud the foreground of Re must be arduous ; but as the labour is highly remunerative, the labourers have great cause for thankfulness.   It is right, however, to state that, with all the care that can be exercised, there is still an enormous amount of waste consequent on the artificial system of culture ; the present calculation is, that even with the best possible mode of culture the average of reproduction is as yet only fourteenfold ; but it is hoped by those interested that a much larger ratio of increase will be speedily attained.   This is desirable, as prices have gone on steadily increasing since the time that Beef first experimented.   In 1859 the sales were effected at about the rate of fifteen shillings per bushel, for the lowest qualities—the highest being double that price ; these were for fattening in the claires, and when sold again they brought from two to three pounds per bushel.

One of the most lucrative branches of foreign oyster-farming may be now described—*i.e.* the manufacture of the celebrated green oysters.   The greening of oysters, many of which
are brought from the Ile de Re parks, is extensively carried on
at Marennes, on the banks of the river Seudre, and this particular branch of oyster industry, which extends for leagues
along the river, and is also sanctioned by free grants from
the state, has some features that are quite distinct from
those we have been considering, as the green oyster is of
considerably more value than the common white oyster.   The
peculiar colour and taste of the green oyster are imparted to
it by the vegetable substances which grow in the beds where
it is manipulated.   This statement, however, is scarcely an
answer to the question of "why," or rather "how," do the
oysters become green?   Some people maintain that the oyster
green is a disease of the liver-complaint kind, whilst there
are others who attribute the green colour to a parasite that
overgrows the mollusc.   But the mode of culture adopted
is in itself a sufficient answer to the question.   The industry carried on at Marennes consists chiefly of the fattening in claires, and the oysters operated upon are at one
period of their lives as white as those which are grown at
any other place ; indeed it is only after being steeped for
a year or two in the muddy ponds of the river Seudre that
they attain their much-prized green hue.   The enclosed ponds
for the manufacture of these oysters—and, according to all
epicurean authority, the green oyster becomes " *the* oyster
par excellence"—require to be water-tight, for they are not
submerged by the sea, except during very high tides.   Each
claire is about one.hundred feet square.   The walls for re-
taining the waters require therefore to be very strong ; they
are composed of low but broad banks of earth, five or six feet
thick at the base and about three feet in height.   These walls
are also useful as forming a promenade on which the watchers

or workers can walk to and fro and view the different ponds. The flood-gates for the admission of the tide require also to be thoroughly watertight and to fit with great precision, as the stock of oysters must always be kept covered with water; but a too frequent flow of the tide over the ponds is not desirable, hence the walls, which serve the double purpose of both keeping in and keeping out the water. A trench or ditch is cut in the inside of each pond for the better collection of the green slime left at each flow of the tide, and many tidal inundations are necessary before the claire is thoroughly prepared for the reception of its stock. When all these matters of construction and slime-collecting have been attended to, the oysters are then scattered over the ground, and left to fatten. When placed in these greening claires they are usually from twelve to sixteen months old, and they must remain for a period of two years at least before they can be properly greened, and if left a year longer they are all the better ; for I maintain that an oyster should be at least about four years old before it is sent to table. In a privately-printed pamphlet on the French oyster-fisheries, sent to me by Mr. Ashworth, it is stated that oysters deposited in the claires for feeding possess the same powers of reproduction as those kept in the breeding-ponds. "Their progeny is deposited in the same profusion, but that progeny not coming in contact with any solid body, it inevitably perishes, unless it can attach itself to the vertical sides of some erection." A very great deal of attention must be devoted to the oysters while they are in the greening-pond, and they must be occasionally shifted from one pond to another to ensure perfect success. Many of the oyster-farmers of Marennes have two or three claires suitable for their purpose. The trade in these green oysters is very large, and they are found to be both palatable and safe, the greening matter being furnished by the sea. Some of the breeders or rather manufacturers of green oysters, anxious to be soon rich, content themselves with placing adult oysters only in these claires, and these become green in a very short time, and thus enable the operator to have several crops in a year without very much trouble. The claires of Marennes furnish about fifty millions of green oysters per annum, and these are sold at very remunerative prices, yielding an annual revenue of something like two and a half millions of francs.

As to the kind of ground most suitable for oyster-growth, Dr. Kemmerer, of St. Martin's (Ile de Re), an enthusiast in oyster-culture, gives us a great many useful hints. I have summarised a portion of his information :—The artificial culture of the oyster may be considered to have solved an important question—namely, that the oyster continues fruitful after it is transplanted from its natural abode in the deep sea to the shores. This removal retards but never hinders fecundation. The sea oyster, however, is the most prolific, as the water at a considerable depth is always tranquil, which is a favourable point in oyster-growth ; but the shore oyster-banks will also be very productive, having two chances of replenishment—namely, from the parent oysters in the *parcs*, and from those currents that may float seed from banks in the sea. Muddy ground is excellent for the *growth* of oysters ; they grow in such localities very quickly, and become saleable in a comparatively short space of time. Dry rocky ground is not so suitable for the young oyster, as it does not find a sufficiency of food upon it, and consequently languishes and dies. Marl is the most esteemed, and on it the oyster is said to become perfect in form and excellent in flavour. In the marl the young oyster finds plenty of food, constant heat, and perfect quiet. Wherever there is mud and sun there will be found the little molluscs, crustacea, and swimming infusoria, which are the food of the oyster. The culture of the oyster in the mud-ponds and in the marl—a culture which ought some day to become general—changes completely its qualities; the albumen becomes fatty, yellow or green, oily, and of an exquisite flavour. The animal and phosphorus matter increases, as does the osmozone. This oyster, when fed, becomes exquisite food. In effecting the culture of the sea-shores and of the marl-ponds, I am pursuing a practical principle of great importance, by the conversion of millions of shore oysters, squandered without profit, into food for public consumption. The green oyster, to this day, has only been regarded as a luxury for the tables of the rich; but, as I have indicated, there are an immense number of farms or ponds on the Seudre, and I would like to see it used as food by everyone.

The French oyster-farmers are happy and prosperous. The wives assist their husbands in all the lighter labours, such as separating and arranging the oysters previous to their being placed on the claires. It is also their duty to sell the oysters; and for this purpose they leave their home about the end of August and proceed to a particular town, there to await and dispose of such quantities of shell-fish as their husbands may forward to them. In this they resemble the fisherwomen of other countries. The Scotch fishwives do all the business connected with the trade carried on by their husbands; it is the husbands' duty to capture the fish only, and the moment they come ashore their duties cease, and those of their wives and daughters begin with the sale and barter of the fish.

Before going farther, it may be stated that the best mode of receiving the spawn of the oyster has not been determined. M. Coste, whose advice is well worthy of being followed, recommended the adoption of fascines of brushwood to be fixed over the natural oyster-beds in order to intercept the young ones; others again, as we have just seen, have adopted the *parcs*, and have successfully caught the spawn on dykes constructed for that purpose; but Dr. Kemmerer has invented a tile, which he covers with some kind of composition that can,

when occasion requires, be easily peeled off, so that the crop
of oysters that may be gathered upon it can be transferred
from place to place with the greatest possible ease, and this
plan is useful for the transference of the oyster from the collecting *parc* to the fattening *claire*. The annexed drawing
will give an idea of the Doctor's invention. The composition
and the adhering oyster may all be stripped off in one piece,
and the tile may be coated for future use. Tiles are exceedingly useful in aiding the oyster-breeder to avoid the natural

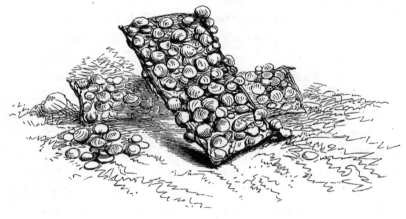

OYSTER-TILES.

enemies of the oyster, which are very numerous, especially at
the periods when it is young and tender. The oysters may be
peeled off the tiles when they are six or seven months old.
Spat-collectors of wood have also been tried with considerable
success. Hitherto these tiles have been very successful, although it is thought by experienced breeders that no bottom
for oysters is so good as the natural one of " cultch," as the old
oyster-shells are called, but the tile is often of service in catching the "floatsome," as the dredgers call the spawn, and to secure
that should be one of the first objects of the oyster-farmer.

    We glean from these proceedings of the French piscicul-
turists the most valuable lessons for the improvement and

conduct of our British oyster-parks. If, as seems to be pretty certain, each 'matured oyster yields about two millions of young per annum; and if the greater proportion of these can be saved by being afforded a permanent resting-place, it is clear that, by laying down a few thousand breeders, we may, in the course of a year or two, have, at any place we wish, a large and reproductive oyster-farm. With reference to the question of growth, Coste tells us that stakes which had been fixed for a period of thirty months in the lake of Fusaro were quite loaded with oysters when they came to be removed. These were found to embrace a growth of three seasons. Those of the first year's spawning were ready for the market; the second year's brood were a good deal smaller; whilst the remainder were not larger than a lentil. To attain miraculous crops similar to those once achieved in the Bay of St. Brieuc, or at the Ile de Re, little more is required than to lay down the spawn in a nice rocky bay, or in a place paved for the purpose, and having as little mud about it as possible. A place that had a good stream of water flowing into it is the most desirable, so that the flock might procure food of a varied and nutritious kind. A couple of hundred stakes driven into the soft places of the shore, between high and low water mark, and these well supplied with branches held together by galvanised iron wire (common rope would soon become rotten), would, in conjunction with the rocky ground, afford capital holding-on places, so that any quantity of spawn might, in time, be developed into fine "natives," or "whiskered pandores." There are hundreds of places on the English and Irish coasts where such farms could be advantageously laid down.

As showing the productiveness of some of the French oyster-beds, it may be stated that 350,000 oysters were obtained in the space of an hour from the Plessix bed, which is half a mile from the port of Auray; and, within a month or two after the opening of those beds, upwards of twenty millions were brought into port, giving employment to 1200 fishermen. The gentlemen from Jersey who explored the French oyster-beds saw in the bay of Arcachon, at Testé, many beds which were highly productive. One man had laid down 500,000 oysters, and these he estimated had increased in three years to seven millions! I may just be allowed to give here one other illustration of oyster-growth; the figures appertain to the Ile de Re : " The inspectors recently counted 600 full-grown oysters to the square metre, and seeing that 630,000 square metres are now under cultivation, it follows that the oysters on this tract of desert mud are worth from six to eight millions of francs, the total crop being (at the time spoken of) 378,000,000 of oysters !"

A large oyster-farm requires a great deal of careful attention, and several people are necessary to keep it in order. If the farm be planted in a bay where the water is very shallow, there is great danger of the stock suffering from frost; and again, if the brood be laid down in very deep water, the oysters do not fatten or grow rapidly enough for profit. In dredging, the whole of the oysters, as they are hauled on board, should be carefully examined and picked; all below a certain size ought to be returned to the water till their beards have grown large enough. In winter, if the beds be in shallow water, the tender brood must be placed in a pit for protection from the frost; which of course takes up a great deal of time. Dead oysters ought to be carefully removed from the beds. The proprietors of private "layings" are generally careful on this point, and put themselves to great trouble every spring to lift or overhaul all their stock in order to remove the dead or diseased. Mussels must be carefully rooted out from the beds; otherwise they would in a short time render them valueless. The layings for example, of Mr. David Plunkett, in Killery Bay, for which he had a licence from the Irish

Board of Fisheries, were overrun by mussels, and so rendered
almost valueless. The weeding and tending of an oyster-bed
requires, therefore, much labour, and involves either a part-
nership of several people—which is usual enough, as at
Whitstable—or at least the employment of several dredgermen and labourers. But, for all that, an oyster-farm may be
made a most lucrative concern. As a guide to the working
of a very large oyster-farm—say a concern of £70,000 a year or
thereabout—I shall give immediately some data of the Whitstable Free Dredgers' Company ; but I wish first to say that
the organisation which is constantly at work for supplying
the great metropolis with oysters is more perfect than can be
said of any other branch of the fish trade. In oyster-culture
we approach in some degree to the French, although we do
not, as they do, except as regards the new company, begin
at the beginning and plant the seed. All that we have
yet achieved is the art of nursing the young " brood,"
and of dividing and keeping separate the different kinds
of oysters. This is done in parks or farms on various portions of the coasts of Kent and Essex, and the whole process, from beginning to end, may be viewed at Whitstable,
where there is a large oyster-ground and a fine fleet of boats
kept for the purpose of dredging and planting. I have
already stated that the Whitstable oyster-beds are held as by
a joint-stock company, into which, however, there is no other
way of entrance than by birth, as none but the free dredge-
men of the town can hold shares. When a man dies his
interest in the company dies with him, but his widow—if he
was a married man—obtains a pension. The sales from
the public and private beds of Whitstable sometimes attain
a total of £200,000 per annum. The business of the company is managed by twelve directors, who are known as
" the Jury." The stock of oysters held in the private layings
of the company is said to be of the value of £200,000. The

extent of the public and other oyster-ground at Whitstable is about twenty-seven square miles.

The oyster-farm of Whitstable is a co-operation in the best sense of the term, and has been in existence for a long period. The layings at Whitstable occupy about a mile and a half square, and the oyster-beds there have been so very prosperous as to have attained the name of the " happy fishing-grounds." At Whitstable, Faversham, and adjoining grounds, not counting a large surface granted to a newly-formed company, a space of twenty-seven square miles, as I have mentioned above, is taken up in oyster-farms, and the industry carried on in this space of ground involves the annual earning and expenditure of a very large sum of money. Over 3000 people are employed in the various industries connected with the fishery, who earn capital wages all the year round—the sum paid for labour by the different companies being set down at over £160,000 per annum ; and in addition to this expenditure for wages, there is likewise a large sum of money annually expended for the repairing and purchasing of boats, sails, dredges, and other implements used in oyster-fishing. At Whitstable the course of work is as follows :—The business of the company is to feed oysters for the London and other markets ; for this purpose they buy brood or spat, and lay it down in their beds to grow. When the company's own oysters produce a spat—that is, when the spawn, or "floatsome" as the dredgers call it, emitted from their own beds falls upon their own ground—it is of great benefit to them, as it saves purchases of brood to the extent of what has fallen ; but this falling of the spat is in a great degree accidental, for no rule can be laid down as to whether the oysters will spawn in any particular year, or where the spawn may be carried to. No artificial contrivances of the kind known in France have yet been used at Whitstable for the saving of the spawn. I will now explain, before going further, the ratio of oyster-growth.

While in the spat state it is calculated that a bushel measure
will contain 25,000•oysters. When the spawn is two years
old it is called brood, and while in this condition a bushel
measure will hold 5500. In the next stage of growth, oysters
are called ware, and it takes about 2000 of them to fill the
bushel. In the final or oyster stage a bushel contains about
1500 individuals. Very large sums have been paid in some
years by the Whitstable company for brood with which to
stock their grounds, great quantities being collected from
the Essex side, there being a number of people who derive a
comfortable income from collecting oyster-brood on the public
foreshores, and disposing of it to persons who have private
nurseries, or oyster-layings as these are locally called. The
grounds of Pont are particularly fruitful in spat, and yield
large quantities to all that require it. Pont is an open space
of water, sixteen miles long by three broad, free to all ; about
one hundred and fifty boats, each with crews of three or four
men, find constant employment upon it, in obtaining young
oysters, which they sell to the neighbouring oyster-farmers,
although it is certain that the brood thus freely obtained must
have floated out of beds belonging to the purchasers. The price
of brood is often as high as forty shillings per bushel, and it
is the sum obtained over this cost price that must be looked
to for the paying of wages and the realisation of profit. Oysters
have risen in price very much of late years, and brood has
also, in consequence of the scarcity of spat, been proportion-
ally high.

.Whitstable oyster-beds are "worked" with great industry,
and it is the process of "working" that gives employment to
so many people, and improves the Whitstable oysters so much
beyond those found on the natural beds, which are known as
"Commons," in contradistinction to the bred oysters of Whitstable and other grounds, which are called "Natives." These
latter are justly considered to be of superior flavour, although

no particular reason can be given for their being so, and indeed in many instances they are not natives at all—that is in the sense of being spatted on the ground-—but are, on the contrary, a grand mixture of all kinds of oysters, brood being brought from Prestonpans and Newhaven in the Firth of Forth, and from many other places, to augment the stock. The so-called "native" oysters—and the name is usually applied to all that are bred in the estuary of the Thames—are very large in flesh, succulent and delicate in flavour, and fetch a much higher price than any other oyster. The beds of natives are all situated on the London clay, or on similar formations. There can, however, be no doubt that the difference in flavour and quantity of flesh is obtained by the Thames system of transplanting and working that is vigorously carried on over all the beds. Every year the whole extent of the layings is gone over and examined by means of the dredge; successive portions are dredged over day by day, till it may be said that almost every individual oyster is examined. On the occasion of these examinations, the brood is detached from the cultch, double oysters are separated, and all kinds of enemies—and these are very numerous—are seized upon and killed. It requires about eight men per acre to work the beds effectually. During three days a week, dredging for what is called the "planting" is carried on; that is, the transference of the oysters from one place to another, as may be thought suitable for their growth, and also the removing of dead ones, the clearing away of mussels, and so on. On the other three days of the week it becomes the duty of the men to dredge for the London market, when only so many are lifted as are required. A bell is carried round and rung every morning to rouse the dredgers whose turn it is for duty, and who at a given signal start to do their portion of the work. As to this working of the oyster-beds, an eminent authority has said it is utterly useless to enclose a piece of ground and simply plant it; it is utterly useless to throw a lot of oysters down amongst every state of filth. You must keep constantly dredging, not only the bed itself, but the public beds outside, so as to keep the bottom fit for the reception and growth of the young oysters, and free of its multitudinous natural enemies.

It may as well be explained here also, that what are called native beds are all cultivated beds; the natural beds are uncultivated, and are generally public and free to all comers. The Colne beds, however, are an exception: they are natural beds, but are held by the city of Colchester as property. Whenever a new bed is discovered anywhere nowadays, the run upon it is so great that it is at once despoiled of its shelly treasures; and the native beds would soon become exhausted if they were not systematically conducted on sound commercial principles, and regularly replenished with brood.

As regards the oyster-cultivation of the river Colne, some interesting statistics have been recently made public at Colchester by Councillor Hawkins. That gentleman tells us that oyster-brood increases fourfold in three years. The quantity of oysters in a London bushel is as follows:—First year, *spat*, number not ascertainable; second year, *brood*, 6400; third year, *ware*, 2400; fourth year, *oysters*, 1600; therefore, four wash of brood (*i.e.* four pecks), purchased at say 5s. per wash, increase by growth and corresponding value to 42s. per bushel, or a sum of eight guineas. The Whitstable dredgers, it is said, drew £60,000 for their oysters in 1860—viz. £10,000 for "commons," and £50,000 for "natives;" but out of this sum they had of course to pay for "brood." The gross amount received by the Colne Fishery Company for oysters sold during the last ten years, ending at July 1862, appears by the treasurer's account to have been £83,000; the average annual produce of the Colne Fishery Company having been 4374 bushels for that period. However, the quantity obtained from the river Colne by the com-

pany bears but a small proportion to the yield from private
layings, which are in general only a few acres in extent.
"The private layings," however, we are told, "cannot fairly
be made the measure of productiveness for a large fishery;
as they may be compared to a garden in a high state of cultivation, while the fishery generally is better represented by a
large tract of land but partially reclaimed from a state of
nature." The difference in cost of working a big fishery
and a little one seems to be great. One of the owners of a
private laying states that, when the expense of dredging or
lifting the oysters exceeded 4s. per bushel, he gave up working, while in the Colne Fishery dredgermen are never paid
less than 12s., and sometimes as high as 40s. a bushel. The
Colne Company is managed by a jury of twelve, appointed by
the water-bailiff, who is under the jurisdiction of the corpora-
tion of Colchester. Whenever it is time to begin the season's
operations, the jury meet and take stock of the oysters on
hand, fix the price at which sales are to be made, and regulate
the charge for dredging, which is paid by the wash. Under
direction of the jury, the foreman of the company sets the
daily stint to the men; and so the work, which is very light,
goes pleasantly forward from season to season.

As showing in a tabular form the ratio of oyster-repro-
duction, I here subjoin, from the Irish Oyster Blue Book,
edited by Mr. Barry, a "Table showing the estimated annual
rate of development and increase of value, calculated at fourfold, during a period of four years, of a breeding oyster-bed of
the extent of one acre, situated in the Thamas estuary, capable
of producing a good quality of 'natives,' and stocked with
1000 bushels of oysters, of 1600 each:"—

FIRST YEAR.

256 bushels containing each 25,000 oysters, 1st year's
 spawn, in 1st year of growth, spat at 20s. per
 bushel £256

SECOND YEAR.

1000 bushels, containing each 6400 oysters, 1st year's
   spawn, in 2d year of growth, brood at 25s. per
   bushel £1,250
256 bushels, containing each 25,000 oysters, 2d year's
   spawn, in 1st year of growth, spat at 20s. per
   bushel 256
                             ———— £1,506

THIRD YEAR.

2667 bushels, containing each 2400 oysters, 1st year's
   spawn, in 3d year of growth, ware at 30s. per
   bushel £4,000
1000 bushels, containing each 6400 oysters, 2d year's
   spawn, in 2d year of growth, brood at 25s. per
   bushel 1,250
256 bushels, containing each 25,000 oysters, 3d year's
   spawn, in 1st year of growth, spat at 20s. per
   bushel 256
                             ———— 5,502

FOURTH YEAR.

4000 bushels containing each 1600 oysters, 1st year's
   spawn, in 4th year of growth, oysters at 35s. per
   bushel £7,000
2667 bushels containing each 2400 oysters, 2d year's
   spawn, in 3d year of growth, ware at 30s. per
   bushel 4,000
1000 bushels containing each 6400 oysters, 3d year's
   spawn, in 2d year of growth, brood at 25s. per
   bushel 2,500
256 bushels containing each 25,000 oysters, 4th year's
   spawn, in 1st year of growth, spat at 20s. per
   bushel 256
                             ———— 13,756

At Faversham, Queenborough, and Rochester, there is a
large commerce carried on in this particular shell-fish. In
others of the "parks" at these places, "natives" are grown in
perfection. The company of the burghers of Queenborough
grow the fine Milton oyster so well known to the connoisseur,
and the company's beds are well attended to. I may note the
Faversham Company, said to be the oldest among the Thames

companies, having been in existence for a few centuries. All
of these companies grow the "natives," and I may explain that
the portion of the beds set apart for the rearing of "natives"
is as sacred as the waxen cells devoted to the growth of queen
bees, and the coarser denizens of the mid-channel are not
allowed to be mixed therewith. The management of all the
Kent and Essex oyster companies is pretty much the same,
but there are also gentlemen who trade solely upon their own
account ; there is Mr. Allston, for instance, a London oyster-
merchant, who keeps his own fleet of vessels, and does a very
large business in this particular shell-fish.

The demand for native and other oysters by the Londoners alone is something wonderful, and constitutes of
itself a large branch of commerce—as the numerous gaily-
lit shell-fish shops of the Strand and Haymarket will
testify. These emporiums for the sale of oysters and
stout are mostly fed through Billingsgate, which is the
chief piscatorial bourse of the great metropolis. It is
not easy to arrive at correct statistics of what London
requires in the way of oysters ; but, if we set the number
down as being nearly 800,000,000 we shall not be very far
wrong. To provide these, the dredgermen or fisher people at
Colchester, and other places on the Essex and Kent coasts,
prowl about the sea-shore and pick up all the little oysters
they can find—these ranging from the size of a threepenny-
piece to a shilling ; and persons and companies having layings purchase them to be nursed and fattened for the table,
as already described. At other places the spawn itself is
collected, by picking it from the pieces of stone, or the old
oyster-shells to which it may have adhered ; and it is
nourished in pits, as at Burnham, for the purpose of being
sold to the Whitstable people, who carefully lay that brood
in their grounds. A good idea of the oyster-traffic may be
obtained from the fact that, in some years, the Whitstable

men have paid £30,000 for brood, in order to keep up the
stock of their far-famed oysters. Mr. Hawkins says that he
knows a man who is proprietor of only three acres of oyster-
layings, and yet from that confined area he annually sells
from 1500 to 2000 wash of the best native oysters.

The chief centre in England for the distribution of oysters
is Billingsgate, and the countless .thousands of bushels of
this molluscous dainty which find their way through
"Oyster Street" to this Fish Exchange mark the everlasting demand. Oysters are sold by the bushel, and every
measure is made to pay a toll of fourpence, and another.
sum of a like amount for carriage to the shore. All oysters sold at Billingsgate are liable to this eightpenny tax.
The London oysters—and I regret to say it, for there is
nothing finer than a genuine oyster—are sophisticated in the
cellars of the buyers, by being stuffed with oatmeal till the
flavour is all but lost in the fat. The flavour of oysters—like
the flavour of all other animals—depends on their feeding.
The fine *goût* of the highly-relished Prestonpans oysters is
said to be derived from the fact of their feeding on the refuse
liquor which flows from the saltpans of that neighbourhood.
I have eaten of fine oysters taken from a bank that was visited
by a rather questionable stream of water ; they were very
large, fat, and of exquisite flavour, the shell being more than
usually well filled with "meat." What the London oysters gain
in fat by artificial feeding they assuredly lose in flavour. The
harbour of Kinsale (a receptacle for much filth) used to be
remarkable for the size and flavour of its oysters. The beds
occupied the whole harbour, and the oysters there were at
one time very plentiful, and far exceeded the Cork oysters in
fame (and they have long been famous) ; but they were so
overfished as to be long since used up, much to the loss
of the Irish people, who are particularly fond of oysters,
and delight in their "Pooldoodies" and "Red-banks" as

much as the English and Scotch do in their "Natives" and "Pandores."

The far-famed Scottish oysters obtained near Edinburgh, and once so cheap, are becoming scarce and dear, and the scalps or beds are being so rapidly overfished that, in a short time, if the devastation be not at once stopped, the pandore and Newhaven oysters will soon be but names. Some of the greediest of the dredgermen actually capture the brood, and, barrelling it up, send it away to Holland and other places, to supply the artificial beds now being constructed off that coast. English buyers also come and pick up all they can procure for the Manchester and other markets. Thus there is an inducement, in the shape of a good price, to the Newhaven men to spoliate the beds—another illustration of "killing the goose for the golden egg." The growth of the railway system has also extended the Newhaven men's market. Before the railway period very few boats went out at the same time to dredge; then oysters were very plentiful —so plentiful, in fact, that three men in a boat could, with ease, procure 3000 oysters in a couple of hours; but now, so great is the change in the productiveness of the scalps, that three men consider it an excellent day's work to procure about the fifth part of that quantity. The Newhaven oyster-beds lie between Inchkeith and Newhaven, and belong to the city of Edinburgh, and were given in charge to the free fishermen of that village, on certain conditions, which are at present systematically disregarded. The rental paid by the Newhaven men to the city is £10 per annum, and a sum of £25 per annum is paid by the same parties for the use of the oyster-beds belonging to the Duke of Buccleuch, which are also situated in the Firth of Forth, just off the port of Granton; and besides these there are one or two beds in the Firth of Forth of considerable size belonging to the crown, which have been also worked by the Newhaven men. The beds are of great extent, and years ago used to yield for the consumption of the city of Edinburgh from ʻsix to eight thousand oysters a day, but I question very much if we shall obtain anything like that quantity during this present season. The proprietor of the most popular Edinburgh tavern experiences the greatest difficulty in obtaining oysters ; and I take this opportunity of informing the Lord Provost of that city that, in the course of a year or two; " Auld Reekie" will, most probably, unless the authorities actively bestir themselves in the matter, have to obtain her oysters from Colchester or Whitstable.   Last season (1864-65), thousands of barrels full of young oysters were disposed off to English and foreign fishermen at the rate of about 20s. a barrel.   This, surely, is a state of things dreadful for Scotchmen to contemplate.   In former and more energetic times, the municipal authorities of the modern Athens used to venture on a voyage of exploration to view their scalps, and afterwards hold a feast of shells, as they do yet at *some* oyster towns on the annual opening of the fishery.[*]

[*] Since the above observations were penned it is satisfactory to know that the Town Council of Edinburgh have begun an investigation into the state of their oyster-scalps.   An official report has been made to the following effect :—" The sub-committee of the Lord Provost's committee beg to report that, from the inquiries made by them, there can be no doubt whatever that the city's scalps, by the improper way in which they have been dredged, are at present nearly worthless, vast quantities of the seeding brood of oysters having been dredged and sold for exportation to England and other places ; that, in these circumstances, the sub-committee are of opinion that, if possible, the lease which the Free Fishermen have obtained should be reduced, so as the town may have henceforth complete control, and with that view the agents should be instructed to take the opinion of counsel ; but if that cannot be done, that immediate steps should be taken, by a conference with the Duke of Buccleuch, Sir George Suttie, the Earl of Morton, and the Commissioners of Woods and Forrests—to whom, along with the city, all the scalps in the Forth belong—to have the whole oysters in the Forth placed under one management for their joint behoof.   At present the rules made by any one of the proprietors become wholly

The "pandore" oysters are principally obtained at the village of Prestonpans and the neighbouring one of Cockenzie. Dredging for oysters is a principal part of the occupation of the Cockenzie fishermen.   There are few lovers of this dainty

OYSTER-DREDGING AT COCKENZIE.

mollusc who have not heard of the "whiskered pandores." The pandore oyster is so called because of being found in the

inoperative from the fact that when improper oysters are brought ashore, the fishermen at once declare that they are taken from other scalps than those of the party challenging ; and, particularly, that they have been taken from what they call neutral ground, which belongs to the Government, and for that they pay no rent.   It is proper to say that the respectable portion of the Society of Free Fishermen profess their readiness to aid in restoring the city scalps to a proper condition, and in keeping them right hereafter ; and they produce a letter from their agents, Messrs. Gardiner, to that effect, along with a copy of a minute of the society."

neighbourhood of the saltpans. It is a large fine-flavoured oyster, as good as any "native" that ever was brought to table, the Pooldoodies of Burran not excepted. The men of Cockenzie derive a good portion of their annual income from the oyster traffic. The pursuit of the oyster, indeed, forms a phase of fisher life there as distinct as at Whitstable. The times for going out to dredge are at high tide and low tide. The boats used are the smaller-sized ones employed in the white fishery. The dredge somewhat resembles in shape a common clasp-purse ; it is formed of net-work, attached to a strong iron frame, which serves to keep the mouth of the instrument open, and acts also as a sinker, giving it a proper pressure as it travels along the oyster-beds. When the boat arrives over the oyster-scalps, the dredge is let down by a rope attached to the upper ring, and is worked by one man, except in cases where the boat has to be sailed swiftly, when two are employed. Of course, in the absence of wind recourse is had to the oars. The tension upon the rope is the signal for hauling the dredge on board, when the entire contents are emptied into the boat, and the dredge returned to the water. These contents, not including the oysters, are of a most heterogeneous kind—stones, sea-weed, star-fish, young lobsters, crabs, actinæ—all of which are usually returned to the water, some of them being considered as the most fattening ground-bait for the codfish. The whelks, clams, mussels, and cockles, and occasionally the crabs, are used by the fishermen as bait for their white-fish lines. Once, in a conversation with a veteran dredger as to what strange things *might* come in the dredge, he replied, "Well, master, I don't know what sort o' curiosities we sometimes get ; but I have seen gentlemen like yourself go out with us a-dredgin', and take away big baskets full o' things as was neither good for eating or looking at. The Lord knows what they did with them." During the whole time that this dredging is being carried on, the crew keep up a wild monotonous song, or rather chant, in which they believe much virtue to lie. They assert that it charms the oysters into the dredge.

> " The herring loves the merry moonlight,
>   The mackerel loves the wind ;
> But the oyster loves the dredger's song,
>   For he comes of a gentle kind."

Talking is strictly forbidden, so that all the required conversation is carried on after the manner of the *recitative* of an opera or oratorio. An enthusiastic London *litterateur* and musician, being on a visit to Scotland, determined to carry back with him, among other natural curiosities, the words and music of the oyster-dredging song. But, after being exposed to the piercing east wind for six hours, and jotting down the words and music of the dredgers, he found it all to end in nothing ; the same words were never used, the words were ever changing. The oyster-scalps are gone over by the men much in the way that a field is ploughed by an agricultural labourer, the boat going and returning until sufficient oysters are secured, or a shift is made to another bed.

The geographical distribution of oysters is most lavish ; wherever there is a seabord there will they be found. The old stories of ancient mariners, who sailed the seas before the days of cheap literature, will be recalled, and their boasted knowledge of the wonders of the fish world—of oysters that grew on trees, and oysters so large that they required to be carved just like a round of beef or quarter of lamb. All these tales were formerly considered so many romances. Who believed Uncle Jack when he gravely told his wondering nephews about oysters as large as a soup-plate being found on the coast of Coromandel? But, nevertheless, Uncle Jack's stories have been found to be true : there *are* large oysters which require carving, and oysters *have* been plucked off trees. There are wonderful tales about oysters that have been taken on the

coast of Africa—plucked too from the very trees that our
good, but ignorant, forefathers did not believe in. The ancient
Romans, who knew all the secrets of good living, had the
oysters of all countries brought to their fish-stews, in order
that they might experiment upon them and fatten them for
table purposes. Although they gave the palm to those from
Britain, they had a great many varieties from Africa, and had
ingenious modes of transporting them to great distances which
have been lost to modern pisciculturists.

Many other parts of America besides the New York district are famous for oysters ; and in some parts of the American Continent they grow to a very large size. So important,
in fact, do the Americans consider the oyster, that it has been
the subject of innumerable "messages" by Governors, Vice-
Presidents, heads of departments, etc.—the last we have seen
being that of Governor Wise to the Legislature of Virginia.
According to that gentleman's estimate, Virginia possesses an
area of about 1,680,000 acres of oyster-beds, containing about
784,000,000 of bushels of that one mollusc. It is estimated by
some naturalists that the oyster spawns at least 3,000,000 annually ; yet, notwithstanding this enormous productive power,
and the vast extent of oyster-beds in this one state, there is
danger, the governor tells us, of the oyster being exterminated,
unless measures are taken to prevent their being dredged at improper seasons of the year. Governor Wise proposes to confine
the oyster-catching business to citizens of the state exclusively, and to charge three cents a bushel for all the oysters
taken, which he estimates would yield an annual revenue of
480,000 dollars. The governor is of opinion that the oyster-
banks so regulated will pay a better bonus to the state than
paper-money banks, and regards them as a richer source of
profit than either gold, iron, or copper mines. Another of the
American States may be mentioned for its oyster wealth.
The seabord of Georgia is famed for its immense supplies of

that mollusc, great breakwaters being formed by oysters, which keep off the sea from the land ; in fact all over America the oyster is to be found in great abundance.   In New York and other cities evidences are to be seen on all sides of the love of the people for this favourite mollusc.   Oyster-saloons abound in all the principal streets, and each one appears to do more business than its neighbour.   In these saloons—most of which, though handsomely fitted up, are situated underground in the basement of some of the great mercantile establishments for which the chief cities of the Union are famed—the cooking of oysters is carried on at all hours, and in all modes.   A writer who has described the traffic says : " Oysters pickled, stewed, baked, roasted, fried, and scolloped ; oysters made into soups, patties, and puddings ; oysters with condiments and without condiments ; oysters for breakfast, dinner, and supper ; oysters without stint or limit—fresh as the pure air, and almost as abundant—are daily offered to the palates of the Manhattanese, and appreciated with all the gratitude which such a bounty of nature ought to inspire."   So much for America.

CHAPTER IX.

———◆———

OUR SHELL-FISH FISHERIES.

Productive Power of Shell-Fish—Varieties of the Crustacean Family—Study
of the Minor Shell-Fishes—Demand for Shell-Fish—Lobsters—A Lobster
Store-Pond Described — Natural History of the Lobster and other
Crustacea—March of the Land-Crabs—Prawns and Shrimps, how they
are caught and cured—Scottish Pearl-Fisheries—Account of the Scottish
Pearl-Fishery—A Mussel-Farm—How to grow Bait.

SHELL-FISH is the popular name bestowed by unscientific
persons on the crustacea and mollusca, and no other
designation could so well cover the multitudinous variety of
forms which are embraced in these extensive divisions of the
animal kingdom. Fanciful disquisitions on shell-fish and on
marine zoology have been intruded on the public of late till
they have become somewhat tiresome ; but as our knowledge
of the natural history of all kinds of sea animals, and particularly of oysters, lobsters, crabs, etc., is decidedly on the
increase, there is yet room for all that I have to say on the
subject of these dainties ; and there are still unexplored
wonders of animal life in the fathomless sea that deserve
the deepest study.

The economic and productive phases of our shell-fish
fisheries have never yet, in my opinion, been sufficiently
discussed, and when I state that the power of multiplication
possessed by all kinds of crustacea and mollusca is even
greater, if that be possible, than that possessed by finned

fishes, it will be obvious that there is much in their natural history that must prove interesting even to the most general reader. Each oyster, as we have seen, gives birth to almost incredible quantities of young. Lobsters also have an amazing fecundity, and yield an immense number of eggs—each female producing from twelve to twenty thousand in a season; and the crab is likewise most prolific. I lately purchased a crab weighing within an ounce of two pounds, and it contained a mass of minute eggs equal in size to a man's hand; these were so minute that a very small portion of them, picked off with the point of a pin, when placed on a bit of glass, and counted by the aid of a powerful microscope, numbered over sixty, each appearing of the size of a red currant, and not at all unlike that fruit: so far as I could guess the eggs were not nearly ripe. I also examined about the same time a quantity of shrimp eggs; and it is curious that, while there are the cock and hen lobster, I never saw any difference in the sex of the shrimps: all that I handled, amounting to hundreds, were females, and all of them were laden with spawn, the eggs being so minute as to resemble grains of the finest sand.

Although the crustacean family counts its varieties by thousands, and contains members of all sizes, from minute animalculæ to gigantic American crabs and lobsters, and ranges from the simplest to the most complex forms, yet the edible varieties are not at all numerous. The largest of these are the lobster (*Astacus marinus*) and the crab (*Cancer pagurus*); and river and sea cray-fish may also be seen in considerable quantities in London shell-fish shops; and as for common shrimps (*Crangon vulgaris*) and prawns (*Palœmon serratis*), they are eaten in myriads. The violet or marching crab of the West Indies, and the robber crab common to the islands of the Pacific, are also esteemed as great delicacies of the table, but are unknown in this country except by reputation.

Leaving old and grave people to study the animal economy

of the larger crustacea, the juveniles may with advantage take
a peep at the periwinkles, the whelks, or other mollusca.
These are found in immense profusion on the little stones
between high and low water mark, and on almost every rock
on the British coast.   Although to the common observer the
oyster seems but a repulsive mass of blubber, and the periwinkle a creature of the lowest possible organisation, nothing
can be further from the reality.   There is throughout this
class of animals a wonderful adaptibility of means to ends.
The turbinated shell of the periwinkle, with its finely-closed
door, gives no token of the powers bestowed upon the animal,
both as provision for locomotion (this class of travellers
wherever they go carry their house along with them) and
for reaping the tender rock-grass upon which they feed.   They
have eyes in their horns, and their sense of vision is quick.
Their curiously-constructed foot enables them to progress in
any direction they please, and their wonderful tongue either
acts as a screw or a saw.   In fact, simple as the organisation
of these animals appears to be, it is not less curious in its own
way than the structure of other beings which are thought to
be more complicated.   In good truth, the common periwinkle
(*Littorina vulgaris*) is both worth studying and eating, vulgar
as some people may think it.

Immense quantities of all the edible molluscs are annually
collected by women and children in order to supply the large
inland cities.   Great sacks full of periwinkles, whelks, etc.,
are sent on by railway to Manchester, Glasgow, London, etc.;
whilst on portions of the Scottish sea-coast the larger kinds
are assiduously collected by the fishermen's wives and prepared as bait for the long hand-lines which are used in capturing the codfish or other Gadidæ.   As an evidence of how
abundant the sea-harvest is, I may mention that from a spot
so far north as Orkney hundreds of bags of periwinkles are
weekly sent to London by the Aberdeen steamer.

From personal inquiry made by the writer a few months
ago it was estimated that for the commissariat of London
alone there were required two millions and a half of crabs and
lobsters! May we not, therefore, take for granted that the
other populous towns of the British empire will consume an
equally large number? The people of Liverpool, Manchester,
Edinburgh, Glasgow, and Dublin are as fond of shell-fish as
the denizens of the great metropolis ; at any rate, they eat all
they can get, and never get enough. The machinery for supplying this ever-increasing demand for lobsters, crabs, and
oysters is exceedingly simple. On most parts of the British
coast there are people who make it their business to provide
those luxuries of the table for all who wish them. The capital
required for this branch of the fisheries is not large, and the
fishermen and their families attend to the capture of the crab
and lobster in the intervals of other business. The Scotch
laird's advice to his son to "be always stickin' in the ither
tree, it will be growin' when ye are sleepin'," holds good in
lobster-fishing. The pots may be baited and left till such
time as the victim enters, whilst the men in the meantime
take a short cruise in search of bait, or try a cast of their
haddock-lines a mile or two from the shore ; or the fishing can
be watched over, and when the lobsters are numerous, the
pots be lifted every half hour or so. The taking of shell-fish
also affords occupation to the old men and youngsters of the
fishing villages, and these folks may be seen in the fine days
assiduously waiting on the lobster-traps and crab-cages, which
are not unlike overgrown rat-traps, and are constructed of
netting fastened over a wooden framework, baited with any
kind of fish offal, or garbage, the stench of which may be
strong enough to attract the attention of those minor monsters
of the deep. A great number of these lobster-pots are sunk
at, perhaps, a depth of twelve or twenty fathoms at an appropriate place, being held together by a strong line, and all

marked with a peculiarly-cut piece of cork, so that each fisherman may recognise his own lot. The knowing youngsters of our fishing communities can also secure their prey by using a long stick. Mr. Cancer Pagurus is watched as he bustles out for his evening promenade, and, on being deftly pitched upon his back by means of a pole, he indignantly seizes upon it with all his might, and the stick being shaken a little has the desirable effect of causing Mr. Crab to cling thereto with great tenacity, which is, of course, the very thing desired by the grinning "human" at the other end, as whenever he feels his prey secure he dexterously hauls him on board, unhooks the crusty gentleman with a jerk, and adds him to the accumulating heap at the bottom of the old boat. The monkeys in the West Indies are, however, still more ingenious than the "fisher loons" of Arran or Skye. Those wise animals, when they take a notion of dining on a crab, proceed to the rocks, and slyly insinuating their tail into one of the holes where the crustacea take refuge, that appendage is at once seized upon by the crab, who is thereby drawn from his hiding-place, and, being speedily dashed to pieces on the hard stone, affords a fine feast to his captor. On the granite-bound coast of Scotland the sport of crab-hunting may be enjoyed to perfection and the wonders of the deep be studied at the same time. A long pole with a small crook at the end will be found useful to draw the crab from his nest, or great fun may be enjoyed by tying during low-water a piece of bait to a string and attaching a stone to the other end of the cord. The crab seizes upon this bait whenever the tide flows, and drags it to its hole, so that when the ebb of the tide recurs the stone at the end of the cord marks the hiding-place of the animal, who thus falls an easy prey to his captor. The natives are the best instructors in these arts, and seaside visitors cannot do better than engage the services of some strong fisher youth to act as guide in such perambulations as they may make on the beach.   There are few seaside places where the natives cannot guide strangers to rock pools and picturesque nooks teeming with materials for studying the wonders of the shore.

Lobsters are collected and sent to London from all parts of the Scottish shore.   I have seen on the Sutherland and other coasts the perforated chests floating in the water filled with them.   They were kept till called for by the welled smacks, which generally made the circuit of the coasts once a week, taking up all the lobsters or crabs they could get, and carrying them alive to London.   From the Durness shores alone as many as from six to eight thousand lobsters have been collected in the course of a single summer, and sold, big or little, at threepence each to the buyers.   The lobsters taken on the north-east coast of Scotland and at Orkney are now packed in seaweed and sent in boxes to London by railway. The lobsters have been more plentiful, it is thought, in the Orkney Islands of late years ; a larger trade has been done in them since the railway was opened from Aberdeen—at all events, more of the animals have been caught, and the prices are double what they used to be in the time of the welled smacks alluded to above.   The fisher-folks of Orkney confess that the trade in lobsters pays them well.

All kinds of crustaceans can be kept alive at the place of capture till " wanted " —that is, till the welled vessel which carries them to London or Liverpool arrives—by simply storing them in a large perforated wooden box anchored in a convenient place.   Nor must it be supposed that the acute London dealers allow too many lobsters to be brought to market at once ; the supply is governed by the demand, and the stock kept in large store-boxes at convenient places down the river, where the sea-water is strong and the liquid filth of London harmless.   But these old-fashioned store-boxes will, no doubt, be speedily superseded by the construction of artificial store-ponds on a large scale, similar to that erected by Mr. Richard Scovell at Hamble, near Southampton. That gentleman informs me that his pond has been of good service to him. It is about fifty yards square, and is lined with brick, having a bottom of concrete, and was excavated at a cost of about £1200. It will store with great ease 50,000 lobsters, and the animals may remain in the pond as long as six weeks, with little chance of being damaged. Lobsters, however, do not breed in this state of confinement, nor have they been seen to undergo a change of shell. There is, of course, an apparatus of pipes and sluices for the purpose of supplying the pond with water. The stock is recruited from the coasts of France and Ireland ; and to keep up the supply Mr. Scovell has in his service two or three vessels of considerable size, which visit the various fisheries and bring the lobsters to Hamble in their capacious wells, each of which is large enough to contain from 5000 to 10,000 animals.

The west and north-west coasts of Ireland abound with fine lobsters, and welled vessels bring thence supplies for the London market, and it is said that a supply of 10,000 a week can easily be obtained. Immense quantities are also procured on the west coast of Scotland. A year or two ago I saw on board the *Islesman* steamboat at Greenock a cargo of 30,000 lobsters, obtained chiefly on the coasts of Lewis and Skye. The value of these to the captors would be upwards of £1000, and in the English fishmarkets the lot would bring at least four times that sum. As showing how enormous the food wealth of the sea still is, notwithstanding the quantity taken out of it, I may cite here a few brief particulars of a little experiment of a charitable nature which was tried by a gentleman who took a warm interest in the Highland fishermen, and the results of which he himself lately made public. Commiserating the wretchedness which he had witnessed among many, who, although anxious to labour, were unable to procure work, and at the same time feeling that the usual method of assisting them was based on a mistaken principle, this gentleman undertook the establishment of a fishery upon a small scale at his own expense. He therefore expended a sum of £600, with which he procured eight boats, completely equipped, and a small smack of sixteen tons. The crews, consisting of thirty men, he furnished with all the necessary fishing materials, paying the men weekly wages ranging from nine to thirteen shillings, part of the sum being in meal. The result of this experiment was, that these eight boats sent to the London market in a few months as many lobsters as reimbursed the original cost of the fishing plant. The men and their families were thus rescued from a state of semi-starvation, and are now living in comfort, with plenty surrounding their dwellings ; and have, besides, the satisfaction of knowing that their present independent condition has been achieved principally by means of their own well-sustained industry.

A very large share of our lobsters is derived from Norway, as many as 30,000 sometimes arriving from the fjords in a single day. The Norway lobsters are much esteemed, and we pay the Norwegians something like £20,000 a year for this one article of commerce. They are brought over in welled steam-vessels, and are kept in the wooden reservoirs already alluded to, some of which may be seen at Hole Haven, on the Essex side of the Thames. Once upon a time, some forty years ago, one of these wooden lobster-stores was run into by a Russian frigate, whereby some 20,000 lobsters were set adrift to sprawl in the muddy waters of the Thames. In order that the great mass of animals confined in these places may be kept upon their best behaviour, a species of cruelty has to be perpetrated to prevent their tearing each other to pieces : the great claw is, therefore, rendered paralytic by means of a wooden peg being driven into a lower joint.

I have no intention of describing the whole members of the crustacea ; they are much too numerous to admit of that, ranging as they do from the comparatively giant-like crab and lobster down to the millions of minute insects which at some places confer a phosphorescent appearance on the waters of the sea. My limits will necessarily confine me to a few of the principal members of the family—the edible crustacea, in fact ; and these I shall endeavour to speak about in such plain language as I think my readers will understand, leaving out as much of the fashionable " scientific slang" as I possibly can.

The more we study the varied crustacea of the British shores, the more we are struck with their wonderful formation, and the peculiar habits of their members. I once heard a clergyman at a lecture describe a lobster in brief but fitting terms as a standing romance of the sea—an animal whose clothing is a shell, which it casts away once a year in order that it may put on a larger suit—an animal whose flesh is in its tail and legs, and whose hair is in the inside of its breast, whose stomach is in its head, and which is changed every year for a new one, and which new one begins its life by devouring the old! an animal which carries its eggs within its body till they become fruitful, and then carries them outwardly under its tail ; an animal which can throw off its legs when they become troublesome, and can in a brief time replace them with others ; and lastly, an animal with very sharp eyes placed in movable horns. The picture is not at all overdrawn. It is a wondrous creature this lobster, and I may be allowed a brief space in which to describe the curious provision of nature which allows for an increase of growth, or provides for the renewal of a broken limb, and which applies generally to the edible crustacea.

The habits of the principal crustacea are now pretty well understood, and their mode of growth is so peculiar as to render a close inspection of their habits a most interesting study. As has been stated, a good-sized lobster will yield about 20,000 eggs, and these are hatched, being so nearly ripe before they are abandoned by the mother, with great rapidity— it is said in forty-eight hours—and grow quickly, although the young lobster passes through many changes before it is fit to be presented at table. During the early periods of growth it casts its shell frequently. This wonderful provision for an increase of size in the lobster has been minutely studied during its period of moulting. Mr. Jonathan Couch says the additional size which is gained at each period of exuviation is perfectly surprising, and it is wonderful to see the complete covering of the animal cast off like a suit of old clothes, while it hides, naked and soft, in a convenient hole, awaiting the growth of its new crust. In fact, it is difficult to believe that the great soft animal ever inhabited the cast-off habitation which is lying beside it, because the lobster looks, and really is, so much larger. The lobster, crab, etc., change their shells about every six weeks during the first year of their age, every two months during the second year, and then the changing of the shell becomes less frequent, being reduced to four times a year. It is supposed that this animal becomes reproductive at the age of five years. In France the lobster-fishery is to some extent " regulated." A close-time exists, and size is the one element of capture that is most studied. All the small lobsters are thrown back to the water. There is no difficulty in observing the process of exuviation. A friend of mine had a crab which moulted in a small crystal basin. I presume that at some period in the life of the crab or lobster growth will cease, and the annual moulting become unnecessary ; at any rate, I have seen crabs and other crustaceans taken from an island in the Firth of Forth which were covered with parasites evidently two or three years old.

To describe minutely the exuviation of a lobster, crab, or

shrimp would in itself form an interesting chapter of this work, and it is only of late years that many points of the process have been witnessed and for the first time described. Not long ago, for instance, it was doubtful whether or not the hermit-crabs (*Anomoura*) shed their skin ; and, that fact being settled, it became a question whether they shed the skin of their tail ! There was a considerable amount of controversy on this delicate point, till the "strange and unexpected discovery" was made by Mr. Harper. That gentleman was fortunate enough to catch a hermit-crab in the very act, and was able to secure the caudal appendage which had just been thrown off. Other matters of controversy have been instituted in reference to the growth of various members of the crustacea ; indeed, the young of the crab in an early stage have before now been described by naturalists as distinct species, so great is the metamorphosis they undergo before they assume their final shape—just as the sprat in good time changes in all probability to the herring. Another point of controversy at one period existed in reference to the power of crustaceans to replace their broken limbs, or occasionally to dispense at their own good pleasure with a limb, when it is out of order, with the absolute certainty of replacing it.

When the female crustacea retire in order to undergo their exuviation they are watched, or rather guarded, by the males ; and if one male be taken away, in a short time another will be found to have taken his place. I do not think there is any particular season for moulting ; the period differs in different places, according to the temperature of the water and other circumstances, so that we might have shell-fish (and white-fish too) all the year round were a little attention paid to the different seasons of exuviation and egg-laying.

The mode in which a hen lobster lays her eggs is curious : she lodges a quantity of them under her tail, and bears them about for a considerable period ; indeed, till they are so nearly hatched as only to require a very brief time to mature them. When the eggs are first exuded from the ovary they are very small, but before they are committed to the sand or water they increase considerably in size and become as large as good-sized shot. Lobsters may be found with eggs, or "in berry" as it is called, all the year round ; and when the hen is in process of depositing her eggs she is not good for food, the flesh being poor, watery, and destitute of flavour.

When the British crustacea are in their soft state they are not considered as being good for food ; but, curiously enough, the land-crabs are most esteemed while in that condition. The epicure who has not tasted "soft crabs" should hasten to make himself acquainted with one of the most delicious luxuries of the table. The eccentric land-crab, which lives far inland among the rocks, or in the clefts of trees, or burrows in holes in the earth, makes in the spring-time an annual pilgrimage to the sea in order to deposit its spawn, and the young, guided by an unerring instinct, return to the land in order to live in the rocks or burrow in the earth like their progenitors. In the fish-world we have something nearly akin to this. We have the salmon, that spends one half its life in the sea, and the other half in the fresh water ; it proceeds to the sea to attain size and strength, and returns to the river in order to perpetuate its kind. The eel, again, just does the reverse of all this : it goes down to the sea to spawn, and then proceeds up the river to live ; and at certain seasons it may be seen in myriad quantities making its way up stream. The march of the land-crabs is a singular and interesting sight : they congregate into one great army, and travel in two or three divisions, generally by night, to the sea ; they proceed straight forward, and seldom deviate from their path unless to avoid crossing a river. These marching crabs eat up all the luxuriant vegetation on their route : their path is marked by desolation. The moment they arrive at the water the operation of spawning is commenced by allowing the waves to wash gently over their bodies. A few days of this kind of bathing assists the process of oviposition, and knots of spawn similar to lumps of herring-roe are gradually washed into the water, which in a short time finishes the operation. Countless thousands of these eggs are annually devoured by various fishes and monsters of the deep that lie in wait for them during the spawning season. After their brief seaside sojourn, the old crabs undergo their moult, and at this period thousands of them sicken and die, and large numbers of them are captured for table use, soft crabs being highly esteemed by all lovers of good things. By the time they have recovered from their moult the army of juveniles from the seaside begins to make its appearance in order to join the old stock in the mountains ; and thus the legion of land-crabs is annually recruited by a fresh batch, which in their turn perform the annual migration to the sea much as their parents have done before them.

Before leaving the crabs and lobsters, it is worthy of remark that an experienced dealer can tell at once the locality whence any particular lobster is obtained—whether from the west of Ireland, the Orkney Islands, or the coast of Brittany. The shelly inhabitants of different localities are distinctly marked. Indeed fish are peculiarly local in their habits, although the vulgar idea has hitherto been that all kinds of sea animals herd indiscriminately together ; that the crab and the lobster crept about the bottom rocks, whilst the waving skate or the swaggering lingfish dashed about in mid-water, the prowling "dogs" busily preying on the shoals of herring supposed to be swimming near ; the brilliant shrimp flashing through the crowd like a meteor, the elegant saithe keeping them company ; the whole being overshadowed by a few whales, and kept in awe by a dozen or so of sharks ! Nothing can be more different than the reality of the water-world, which is colonised quite as systematically as the earth.

Particular shoals of herring, for instance, gather off particular
counties ; the Lochfyne herring, as I have mentioned in the
account of the herring-fishery, differs from the herring of the
Caithness coast or that of the Firth of Forth; and any 'cute
fishmonger can tell a Tweed salmon from a Tay one.   The
herring at certain periods move in gigantic shoals, the chief
members of the Gadidæ congregate on vast sand-banks, and
the whales occasionally roam about in schools ; while the
Pleuronectidæ occupy sandy places in the bottom of the sea.
We have all heard of the great codbanks of Newfoundland,
of the fish community at Rockall ; then is there not the
Nymph Bank, near Dublin, celebrated for its haddocks?
have we not also the Faroe fishing-ground, the Dogger Bank,
and other places with a numerous fish population?   There
are wonderful diversities of life in the bosom of the deep ;
and there is beautiful scenery of hill and plain, vegetable
and rock, and mountain and valley.   There are shallows and
depths suited to different aspects of life, and there is life of
all kinds teeming in that mighty world of waters, and the
fishes live

> " A cold sweet silver life, wrapped in round waves,
>   Quickened with touches of transporting fear."

The prawn and the shrimp are ploughed in innumerable
quantities from the shallow waters that lave the shore.   The
shrimper may be seen any day at work, pushing his little net
before him.   To reach the more distant sandbanks he requires
a boat; but on these he captures his prey with greater facility,
and richer hauls reward his labour than when he plies his
putting-net close inshore.   The shrimper, when he captures
a sufficient quantity, proceeds to boil them ; and till they
undergo that process they are not edible.   The shrimp is
" the ' Undine' of the waters," and seems possessed by some
aquatic devil, it darts about with such intense velocity.   Like
the lobster and the crab, the prawn periodically changes its

skin; and its exertions to throw off its old clothes are really
as wonderful as those of its larger relatives of the lobster and
crab family. There are a great many species of shrimp in
addition to the common one; as, for instance, banded, spinous,
sculptured, three-spined, and two-spined. Young prawns,
too, are often taken in the ".putting-nets" and sold for
shrimps. Prawns are caught in some places in pots resembling
those used for the taking of lobsters. The prawn exuviates
very frequently; in fact it has no sooner recovered from one
illness than it has to undergo another. Although the prawn
and the shrimp are exceedingly common on the British coasts,
when we consider the millions of these "sea insects," as they
have been called, which are annually consumed at the breakfast tables and in the tea-gardens of London alone (not to
speak of those which are greedily devoured in our watering-
places, or the few which are allowed to reach the more inland
towns of the country), we cannot but wonder where they all
come from, or who provides them; and the problem can only
be solved by taking into account the fact that we are surrounded by hundreds of miles of a productive seabord, and
that thousands of seafaring people, and others as well, make
it their business to supply such luxuries to all who can
pay for them. It is even found profitable to send these
delicacies to England all the way from the remote fisheries of
Scotland.

The art of "shrimping" is well understood all round the
English coasts. The mode of capturing this particular member
of the crustacea is by what is called a shrimp-net, formed of a
frame of wood and twine into a long bag, which is used as a
kind of minature trawl-net; each shrimping-boat being provided with one or two of these instruments, which, scraping
along the sand, compel the shrimp to enter. Each boat is
provided with a "well," or store, to contain the proceeds of the
nets, and on arrival at home the shrimps are immediately

boiled for the London or other markets. The shrimpers are
rather ill-used by the trade. Of the many thousand gallons
sent daily to London, they only get an infinitesimal portion of
the money produce. The retail price in London is four shillings per gallon, out of which the producer is understood to get
only threepence ! I have been told that the railways charge at
the extraordinary rate of £9 a ton for the carriage of this
delicacy to London. It is an interesting sight to watch the
shrimpers at their work, and such of my readers as can obtain a
brief holiday should run down to Leigh, or some nearer fishing
place, where they can see the art of shrimping carried on in
all its picturesque beauty.

The fresh-water cray-fish, a very delicate kind of miniature
lobster, abundantly numerous in all our larger streams, and
exceedingly plentiful in France, may often be seen on the
counters of our fishmongers; as also the sea cray-fish, which is
much larger in size, having been known to attain the weight
of ten or twelve pounds, but it is coarser in the flavour than
either the crab or lobster. The river cray-fish, which lodges
in holes in the banks of our streams, is caught simply by
means of a split stick with a bit of bait inserted at the end.
The fresh-water cray-fish has afforded a better opportunity for
studying the structure of the crustacea than any of the salt-
water species, as its habits can be more easily observed.
The sea cray-fish is not at all plentiful in the British
Islands, although we have a limited supply in some of our
markets.

There has hitherto been a fixed period for the annual
sacrifice to crustacean gastronomy. As my readers are already
aware, there is a well-known time for the supplying of oysters,
which is fixed by law, and which begins in August and ends
in April. During the r-less months oysters are less wholesome
than in the colder weather. The season for lobsters begins about
March, and is supposed to close with September, so that in

the round of the year we have always some kind of shell-fish delicacy to feast upon.   Were a little more attention devoted to the economy of our fisheries, we might have lobsters and crabs upon our tables all the year round.   In my opinion lobsters are as good for food in the winter time as during the months in which they are most in demand.   It may be hoped that we shall get to understand all this much better by and by, for at present we are sadly ignorant of the natural economy of these, and indeed all other denizens of the deep.

A new branch of shell-fishing has been lately revived in Scotland.   I allude to the pearl-fisheries which are now being carried on in our large streams, and which, if prudently conducted, may become a source of considerable wealth to the Scottish people.

The pearl is found in a species of shell-fish which is a variety of the mussel, not an oyster, as is commonly supposed. The pearl has been pronounced the most beautiful of all our gems, coming, as it does, finished and perfect, direct from the laboratory of nature, and consequently owing nothing to the cunning of man except its discovery—

> " Ocean's gem, the purest
> Of Nature's works ! what days of weary journeyings,
> What sleepless nights, what toils on land and sea,
> Are borne by men to gain thee !"

In the Eastern seas professional divers are employed to go down into the depths of the ocean in order to obtain them—a dangerous occupation, at one time only followed by condemned criminals.   The best-known fishery for pearls is that at Ceylon, which was a very lucrative concern, at one time, in the hands of the industrious Dutch.

Pearls are of remote antiquity.   In the time of Pliny they held the highest rank among all gems, and the Romans esteemed and largely used them—the ladies ornamenting, with lavish extravagance, all parts of their dress with them ;

and so extravagant did they become in their use of these gems
by way of personal ornament, that Seneca, the wise moralist,
reproaches a patrician by saying that his lady wore all the
wealth of his house in her ears, it being at that time the
fashion for a lady to have three or four of these valuable gems
hung in each ear-drop. As to the value of these drops from
the deep, we may instance Cleopatra's banquet to Mark

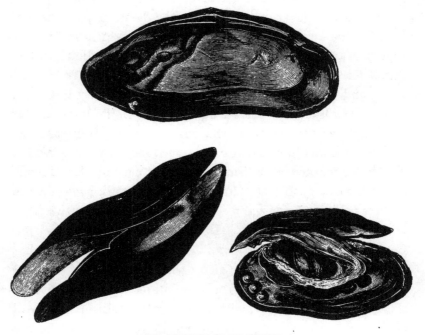

THE SCOTTISH PEARL-MUSSEL.

Antony, when, according to vulgar belief, she took a pearl
from her ear, worth £80,000 of our money, and dissolving it
in vinegar, swallowed it! The pearl which Cæsar presented
to the mother of Marcus Brutus is said to have been of the
value of £48,000. Then we are told that Clodius, the son of
the tragedian, once swallowed a pearl worth £8000. Actors'
sons of the present day have been known to do extravagant
things ; but few of them, I suspect, could achieve a feat like

this.   In the East, too, in those early days, the pearl was held in the highest esteem.   We read of one gem, still to be seen in Persia, I believe, that had a market price set upon it equal to £100,000 of our money; and there is another pearl mentioned as obtained in 1587 from the island of Margarita which weighed 250 carats, the value of which was named as being $150,000; and there are many other instances on record of the value of pearls to which I need not make further reference.

When our government took up the Eastern pearl-fishery in 1797, the annual produce was £144,000, which in the following year was increased by £50,000, but immediately afterwards fell off, most probably from overfishing.   It revived again, and in the beginning of the present century the pearl ground was leased to private adventurers at the large rent of £120,000 per annum, with the wise understanding that the bed or bank was to be divided into portions, only one of which was to be worked at a time, so that a part of the mussels might have a good rest.   From various causes, however, the Ceylon fisheries have again failed, and for a year or two have been totally unproductive.   In a privately-printed work on Ceylon, by James Steuart, Esq. of Colpetty, which the author has kindly forwarded to me along with a quantity of Oriental pearl-oyster shells, there is a very interesting description of the Ceylon pearl-fishery, with notes on the natural history of the oyster.   In reference to the recent failure of the fishery for gems in the Gulf of Manaar, Mr. Steuart has supplied me with the following interesting note :—

   " The Gulf of Manaar pearl-fisheries having again ceased to be productive, the government of Ceylon appear to be impressed with a belief that further information is needed respecting the habits of the pearl-oyster, and that it may be desirable to obtain the services of a naturalist to study and report on the best means of insuring a continuous revenue from pearls.

" The natural history of the edible oyster is now so well understood that its culture on artificial beds is in successful progress in many places on the coasts of both England and France; but it is one thing to breed and fatten edible oysters for the palate, and another to breed the pearly mollusc of Ceylon to produce pearl.

" That which is commonly called the pearl-oyster of the Gulf of Manaar is classed by naturalists with the mussel in consequence of its shells being united by a broad hinge and its having a strong fibrous byssus with which it attaches itself to the shells of others, to rocks, and to other substances. It had long been believed that the fish in question had not the power of locomotion, nor of detaching its byssus from the substances to which it adhered ; but in the year 1851 it was satisfactorily ascertained that when it had become detached it possessed the power of extending its body from within its shells and of creeping up the inner side of a glass globe containing sea-water. It was, however, left to the late Dr. Kelaart, when employed by government as a naturalist to study the habits of the fish, to discover that, although it could not detach its byssus from the rock to which it adhered, it had the power of casting off from its body its entire byssus and of proceeding to some other spot, and there, by forming a new byssus, of attaching itself to any substance near to it. It is therefore now believed that the Manaar pearl-fish has the power of changing its position, and this may account for the disappearance of large quantities from the sandy places on which the brood sometimes settles ; but it is by no means so clear that these fish are able to drag their shells after them over the rugged surface of coral rocks.

" I have already stated that the produce of the pearl-fish of the Gulf of Manaar varies in richness of colour, in the size of the pearl, and the quantity of its yield, according to the nature of the ground on which it rests, or of the food which that ground supplies. In some cases the pearl produced barely repays the cost of fishing. It would therefore appear to be desirable that the component parts of the surface of the most productive banks should be subjected to chemical analysis. And as the natural history of the mussel and the scollop does not appear to be so well ascertained as that of the edible oyster, it might be attended by some useful result if a prize were offered for the best treatise on these European bivalves as being the nearest approach to the pearly mollusc of Ceylon. With the information thus obtained, it might not be necessary to incur the expense of sending a naturalist to Ceylon."

During the past two or three summers the early industry of pearl-seeking has been very successfully revived in Scotland, chiefly through the exertions of Mr. Moritz Unger, a dealer in gems residing in Edinburgh. That gentleman having, in the way of his trade, occasionally fallen in with pearls said to be obtained in Scottish rivers, was so struck with their great beauty that he determined to set about their collection in a more systematic way. At that time there was in Scotland only one professed fisher for pearls, who lived at Killin, and whose stock was principally bought up by the late Marquis of Breadalbane. Mr. Unger, having in view the extension of the trade, travelled over the whole country, and announced his intention of buying, at a fixed scale of prices, all the pearls he could obtain—taking possession, in the meantime, of such gems as he could get from the peasantry, and paying them a liberal price. The consequence is, that now, instead of there being but one professed pearl-seeker in Scotland, there are hundreds who cling to pearl-fishing as their sole occupation, and, being sober and industrious men, they make a good living by it.

The Scotch pearls were, in the middle ages, celebrated all over Europe for their size and beauty. Just one hundred years ago—between the years 1761 and 1764—pearls to the value of £10,000 were sent to London from the rivers Tay and

Isla ; but the trade carried on in the corresponding years of this century is far more than double that amount. Mr. Unger estimates the pearls found last summer (1864) to be of the value to the finders of about £10,000 ; whereas, on his first tour, he bought up, four years ago, all that were to be had for the sum of £40. Single specimens have recently been found worth as much as £60.

From the middle of last century till about 1860 the Scottish pearl-fisheries were quite neglected, and large pearls were found only as it were by accident in occasional dry seasons, when the rivers were scant of water, and the mussels were consequently accessible without much trouble. It was left for Mr. Unger to discern the capabilities of the Scottish pearl as an ornamental gem of great value ; and it is now a fact that the beautiful pink-hued pearls of our Scottish streams are admired even beyond the Oriental pearls of Ceylon. The Empress Eugenie, Queen Victoria, and other royal ladies, as well as many of the nobility, have been making large purchases of these Scottish gems. In some rural districts the peasantry are making little fortunes by pearl-seeking for only a few hours a day. Many of the undemonstrative weavers and cobblers, whose residence is near a pearl-producing stream, contrive, in the early morning, or after the usual day's work, to step out and gather a few hundreds of the pearl-containing mussels, in which they are almost sure to find a few gems of more or less value. The pearl-fisher requires no capital to set him up in his trade ; he needs no costly instruments, but has only to wade into the stream, put forth his hand, and gather what he finds.

An intelligent pearl-fisher, who resides near the river Doon, has sent me the following graphic account of what he calls " the pearl fever : "—" For many years back the boys were in the habit of amusing themselves in the summer-time, when the water was shallow, by gathering mussels and search-

ing them for pearls, having heard somehow that money could
be obtained for them; but they often enough found that,
however difficult it might be to secure the pearl, it was still
more difficult to get it converted into cash—threepence, sixpence, or a shilling, being the ordinary run of prices, buyers
and sellers being alike ignorant of the commodity in which
they were dealing. It was not until the middle of the summer
of 1863 that the fever of pearl-seeking broke out thoroughly
on the banks of the classic Doon. The weather had been un-
commonly dry for some time, and the river had in many places
become extremely shallow; some of the women and children
had been employing their spare time in gathering mussels
and opening them, and few of those who had given it a trial
failed to become the possessors of one or more pearls. Just
then Mr. Unger made his appearance, and bought up all he
could get at prices which perfectly startled the people; and,
as a consequence, young and old, male and female, rushed like
ducks to the water, and waded, dived, and swam, till the
excitement became so intense as to be called by many the
'pearl fever.' The banks of the river for some time presented
an extraordinary scene. Here a solitary female, very lightly
clad indeed, is seen wading up to the breast, and as she stoops
to pick up a mussel, her head is of necessity immersed in the
water. Having got hold of a shell she throws it on to the opposite bank and stoops for another, and in this manner secures
as many as her apron will hold, and carries them home to find
that, very likely, she has more blanks than prizes among them.
There, in a shallow part of the stream, a swarm of boys are
trying their fortune; there is a great degree of impatience
in their mode of fishing, for each shell is opened and examined so soon as it is lifted. A little above them are two
scantily-clad females earnestly at work; one of them is
actually stone blind, but she gropes with her naked feet for a
shell, then picks it up with her hand, carefully opens it with

a stout knife, and with her thumb feels every part of its interior. She has been pretty successful, and her tidy dress
when she is resting from her labour betokens the good use
she makes of the proceeds of her fishing. The spectator may
next pass through the crowds of men, women, and boys
similarly employed, where the grassy banks are reddened by
the constant tread of many feet, and the smell of heaps upon
heaps of putrid mussels tells the magnitude of the slaughter.
The eye is then attracted by the sight of a man on crutches
making for the river. He soon gets seated on the right bank
of the stream, where his better half, in water almost beyond
her depth, is gathering from the bottom of the muddy and all
but stagnant part of the river a quantity of shells for him to
examine. Nor were the labours of this couple unrewarded ;
by their united exertions they earned in a few weeks somewhat above £8, and so little idea had they of the value of the
pearls, that on one occasion when they expected about 15s. for
a few they had despatched to the collector, they were agreeably surprised at the receipt of three times the amount by
return of post. It was found that the fishing was most successful where the river was deep and its motion sluggish. To
get at the mussels in such places, large iron rakes, with long
teeth and handles about twenty feet in length, were procured,
and by means of these some of the deepest parts of the river
were dragged and some valuable pearls secured; many of
which were disposed of at £1 each, others at 25s., and one at
£2 ; while a great number ranged from 7s. 6d. to 15s. each.
But by far the greater portion were either entirely useless, or
on account of their smallness, bad shape, or colour, were parted
with for a mere trifle. Some idea of the extent of the pearl-
fishery in 1863 of this one river may be gathered from the
fact that Mr. Unger paid to those engaged in it a sum exceeding £150 for each month the fishing lasted ; and a goodly
number of pearls were disposed of to private individuals in

the vicinity for their own special use, besides those that found their way into the markets. During the continuance of the fishery the general cry was that so much exposure of the body was likely to introduce a variety of diseases such as had not hitherto been known in the place ; but no such effects made their appearance. And though there were exceptional cases where the extra cash (for it was like found money) obtained for the pearls was worse than wasted, there are many who can point to a new suit of clothes or a good lever watch, when asked what they had to show as the reward of the many cold drenchings they got while dredging the Doon for pearls."

In 1863 a controversy arose as to which rivers produced the best pearls, and it was then argued that only in those streams issuing from lochs was a continuous supply of the pearl-mussel to be found, and although there are a few pearl streams which take their rise in some little spring and gather volume as they flow, yet their number, as far as is known, is only four—viz. the Ugie, Ythan, Don, and Isla—and even these are now (1865) very nearly exhausted. Many of the finest gems have been found in the Doon, Teith, Forth, Earn, Tay, Lyon, Spey, Conan, etc. etc. Until this summer (1865) it has been supposed that the lochs are the natural reservoirs of the pearl-mussel, and when in 1860-1 a portion of Loch Venachar was laid dry for the purpose of building a sluice for the Glasgow Waterworks, innumerable shells were found, from which the labourers gathered a great many very fine pearls. The above theory was thereby so much confirmed that Mr. Unger was induced in 1864 to try further experiments on Lochs Venachar, Achray, and Lubnaig, by means of dredging, which, considering the rough mode of procedure, was so successful, especially on a place called Lynn Achore, at the east end of Loch Venachar, that he at last considered himself justified in incurring considerable expense. Accordingly he procured this summer (1865) one of Siebes' diving apparatus, and bringing down one of the best divers from London, proceeded to search the bottoms of several lochs on a systematic plan. Many obstacles were thrown in Mr. Unger's way by the proprietors, and although he was particularly anxious to experiment on Loch Tay, the present Earl of Breadalbane would not grant permission for him to do so. But with the consent of the Earl of Moray the first regular trial was made on Loch Venachar, and it was ascertained beyond a doubt that shells were to be found in all the sandy shallow parts of the loch; not however in beds, as people were led to suppose from dredging experiments, but only here and there in clusters of a dozen or so, except at the mouth of the loch, where they were more extensive and in larger quantities. The diver also went down in various parts of the loch to the depth of a hundred feet, where it was found to be quite impracticable to search for anything so small as a pearl-mussel on account of the thick muddy bottom. Mr. Unger, nothing daunted by this partial failure, went to Sir Robert Menzies, who not only consented at once to his trying Loch Rannoch, but generously placed all available boats and utensils, besides the service of several men, at his disposal; after a week's trial, however, Mr. Unger was reluctantly compelled for the present to desist from any further experiments.

Pearls are found in many of the Irish and Welsh rivers, and Mr. Unger now receives constant accessions to his stock from the north of Ireland. The Conway was noted for pearls in the days of Camden. The pearl-mussels are called by the Welsh "Deluge shells," and are thought by the ignorant to have been left by the Flood. The river Irt, in Cumberland, was also at one time a famous stream for pearls; and during last century several pearls were found in the streams of Ireland, particularly in the counties of Tyrone and Donegal. We read of specimens that fetched sums varying from £4 to £80.

If my readers be curious to know how many shells will

have to be opened before this toil is rewarded with a find of
pearls, let them be told that, on the average, the searcher
never opens a hundred mussels without being made happy
with a few of the gems. It is remarked that they are more
certain to have pearls when they are taken from the stony
places of the river. Thousands of mussels have been found in
the sand, but these have rarely if ever contained a single pearl ;
whilst the shells again that are found in soft and muddy bottoms have plenty of gems, but they are poor in quality and
bad in colour. No pearls are ever found in a young shell,
and all such may at once be rejected. A skilful operator
opens the mussel with a shell, in order to avoid scratching
the pearl ; the opened fish is thrown into the water, and it is
either the mussels or the insects gathering about them that are
greedily devoured by the salmon and other fish, so that those
proprietors of streams who were becoming uneasy as to the
effects of the pearl-fishery on the salmon may set their
minds at rest. Although at one time none of the London
dealers in gems would look at a Scotch pearl, it is an interesting fact that now the fame of the Scottish fisheries has so
extended as to bring buyers from France and other Continental countries ; and, as boats and dredges are now being introduced, it is thought that any moderate demand may be
supplied. Great quantities of pearls have been sent to the
collector through the post-office.

An Ayrshire paper says of the Doon fishery :—" That owing to the wholesale slaughter of the mussels last season, the
pearl-fishing this summer (1864) in the river Doon has been
neither so exciting nor remunerative. Few have paid much
attention to it ; but even amongst those few rather more than
£100 has been obtained for pearls since the month of May,
there being more than one individual who has earned at least
£13 during that period, having followed their avocation daily,
whilst the pearl-fishing was engaged in as a *profitable* recrea-

tion. As a whole the pearls of the river Doon are of an inferior quality, £2 being about the highest price at which any of them have been sold ; these weighed from eight to twelve grains, but were far from being very bright in colour. ' It is all a matter of chance,' say some of the pearl-fishers ; ' you may fish a whole day and not make sixpence, and one worth a pound may be, yea has been, found in the second shell." Such things have frequently happened, but the earnest plodding fisher has always been handsomely paid for his work. Though on an average a pearl is found in every thirty shells, only one pearl in every ten is fit for the market. It will thus be seen that one hundred and thirty shells have to be gathered, opened, and examined, and one hundred and thirty lives sacrificed, in order to secure one marketable pearl.*

It is not unlikely that the present mania for pearl-gathering may very speedily exhaust the supply of mussels. The energy with which the fishing is carried on undoubtedly points to a very speedy diminution of a shell-fish which was

* The following information as to the colour and structure of the pearl may interest the general reader :—

Sir Robert Reading, in a letter to the Royal Society dated October 13, 1688, in speaking of Irish pearls, states that pearls, if once dark, will never clear upon any alteration in the health or age of the mussel. This Mr. Unger stoutly contradicts ; he shows by many specimens that some of the finest Scotch pearls are perfectly dark inside. The theory put forth by Sir Everard Home, that the peculiar lustre so much valued in the pearl arises from the centre, is thereby upset. There is no doubt Sir David Brewster is correct in his statement on that point in the *Edinburgh Encyclopædia.* Some writers assert that irregular pearls may be rounded. This of course is erroneous : they are, as everybody knows, formed in layers like an onion, and these layers being cut across would be exposed in such a manner that even the highest polish would not hide them. It is, however, quite possible in many instances to improve a bad-coloured pearl by removing one or more of the coats ; and in this way many a pearl of comparatively trifling value has been turned into a gem of rare beauty. The best way to distinguish a real pearl from an imitation one is to take a sharp knife and gently try to scrape it : if imitation

never very plentiful, and it would be a very good plan to try
the system of culture on hurdles which has been found so successful for the growth of the edible mussel of the Bay of
Aiguillon, to be now described.

Considering the importance attached by fishermen to the
easy attainment of a cheap supply of bait, it is surprising
that no attempt has been made in this country to economise
and regulate the various mussel-beds which abound on the
Scottish and English coasts. The mussel is very largely used
for bait, and fishermen have to go far, and pay dear, for what
they require—their wives and families being also employed
to gather as many as they can possibly procure on the accessible places of the coast, but usually the bait has to be purchased and carried from long distances. I propose to show
our fisher-people how these matters are managed in France,
and how they may obviate the labour and expense connected
with bait buying or gathering, by growing such a crop of
mussels as would not only suffice for an abundant supply of
bait, but produce a large quantity for sale as well.

Mussel-culture has been carried on with immense success
on a certain part of the coast of France for a period of no less
than seven centuries! So long ago as the year of grace 1135
an Irish barque was wrecked in the Bay of Aiguillon. The
cargo and one of the crew were saved by the humanity of the
fishermen inhabiting the coast. The name of the one man
who was thus saved from shipwreck was Walton, and he
gave to the people, in gratitude for saving his life, the germ
of a marvellous fish-breeding idea. He invented artificial

the knife will glide over the surface without making any impression, it
being glass, and a real pearl will not be injured by a gentle hand.
Pieces of shells are, however, extensively used and sold as pearls. They
are cut into shapes closely resembling half pearls, and mounted in various ways, so that many professed judges have been deceived. These are
easily to be distinguished by their iridescent lustre from the true pearl,
which has but one distinct tint.

mussel-culture.   An exile from Erin, Walton was ingenious enough to create a " hurdle," which, intercepting the spat of the mussels, served as a place for them to grow.   In a sense, the origin of this mussel-farm was accidental.   The bay where this industry is now flourishing was, at the time of the ship-wreck, and is at present, a vast expanse of mud, frequented by sea-fowl, and it was while devising a kind of net or trap for the capture of these that he obtained the germ of his future idea of mussel-culture. The net or bag-trap which he em-ployed in catching the night birds which floated on the water was fixed in the mud by means of toler-

MUSSEL-STAKES.

ably strong supports, and he soon found out that the parts of his net which were sunk in the water had intercepted large quantities of mussel-spat, which in time grew into the finest possible mussels, larger in size and finer in quality than those grown upon the neighbouring mud. From less to more this simple discovery progressed into a regular industry, which at present forms almost the sole oc-cupation of the inhabitants of the neighbouring shores.   The system pursued is that invented by Walton about the middle of the twelfth century, and has been handed down from generation to generation in all its original simplicity and ingenuity.   The apparatus for the growth of the mussel, with which the bay is now almost covered, is called a *bouchot*, and is of very simple construction.   A number of strong piles or stakes, each 12 feet in length and 6 inches in diameter, are driven into the mud to the depth of 6 feet, at a distance of about 2 feet from each other, and are ranged in two converging rows, so as to form a V, the sharp point of which is always turned towards the sea, that the stakes may offer the least possible resistance to the waves. These two rows form the framework of the *bouchot*. Strong branches of trees are

A MUSSEL-FARM.

then twisted and interwoven into the upper part of the stakes, which are 6 feet in height, until the whole length of the row is, by this species of basket-work on a large scale, formed into a strong fence or palisade. A space of a few inches is left between the bottom of the fence and the surface of the mud, to allow the water to pass freely between the stakes when the tide ebbs and flows. The sides of the *bouchot* are from 200 to 250 metres long, and each *bouchot*, therefore, forms a fence of about 450 metres, 6 feet high. There are now some 500 of these *bouchots* or breeding-grounds in the Bay of Aiguillon, making a fence of 225,000 metres, extending over a space of 8 kilometres, or 5 miles, from the point of St. Clemens to the mouth of the river of Marans.

The Bay of Aiguillon, as has already been observed, is a vast field of mud, and, when left dry at low water, it is impassable on foot. To enable him to traverse it at low water, the *boucholeur* uses a canoe. This canoe, formed of plain planks of wood, is about nine feet in length and eighteen inches in breadth and depth, the fore-end being something like the usual shape of the bow of a boat. The *boucholeur* places himself at the stern of the canoe, rests his right knee on the bottom of the boat, leans his body forward, and, seizing the two sides of the canoe with his hands, throws out his left leg, which is encased in a strong boot, backwards to serve as an oar. In this position he pushes his left leg in and out of the mud, and thus propels his light boat along the surface to whatever part of the field he wishes to visit. Notwithstanding the windings and twistings of the confused maze formed on the surface of the bay by the *bouchots*, long habit enables the *boucholeur*, even in the darkest night, to distinguish his neighbour's establishment in the crowd. The *boucholeur* uses his canoe not only in transporting his mussels from the *bouchot* to the shore, and attending to the various operations of the mussel-field, but also in conveying to the proper spot the stakes and hurdles necessary for the construction and repair of the *bouchots*. The furrows left by the canoe in the mud might, in the summer time, by hardening in the sun, render the propulsion of his canoe across the field a very arduous task to the *boucholeur*. Nature has, however, provided an admirable remedy for this possible evil. A small crustacean, the *corophie*, appears in great numbers in the mud-field about the end of the month of April, and during the summer months levels and overturns many leagues of these furrows, and mixes the mud with water, in searching after the innumerable multitudes of worms (annelidæ) of all species that infest the mud. The corophies, which are remarkably fond of these marine worms, pursue them in every direction through the mud ; and, by their vigorous efforts to discover their prey, prevent the furrows from forming an obstacle to the progress of the *boucholeur*. This crustacean disappears suddenly, in a single night, towards the end of October.

The cultivation of mussels is carried on by the inhabitants of the communes of Esnandes, Chavron, and Marsilly. Many of the *boucholeurs* possess several *bouchots*, while the poorest of them have only a share of one *bouchot*, cultivating it, together with the other owners, and dividing the profits among them, according to their shares. The *bouchots* are arranged in four divisions, according to their position in the bay, and are distinguished as *bouchots du bas* or *d'aval*, *bouchots batard*, *bouchots milieu*, and *bouchots d'avant*. The *bouchots du bas*, placed farthest from the shore, and only uncovered during spring tides, are not formed of fences as the *bouchots* proper, but consist simply of a row of stakes, planted about one boat distant from each other, and in the most favourable position for the preservation of the *naissain*, or young of the mussels. Upon these isolated stakes the spat is allowed to collect, which is afterwards to be transplanted for the purpose of peopling barren or poorly-furnished palisades in those divisions which, planted nearer the shore, are more frequently uncovered by the tide.

The various operations of mussel-cultivation are designated by agricultural terms—such as sowing, planting, transplanting, etc. Towards the end of April the seed (*semence*) fixed during February and March to the stakes of the *bouchot du bas* is about the size of a grain of flax, and is then called *naissain*. By the month of July it attains the size of a bean, and is called *renouvelain*, and is then ready for transplantation to a less favourable state of existence upon the *bouchot batard*, where the action of the tide would probably have retarded its growth if transplanted earlier. In the month of July, then, the *boucholeurs* direct their canoes towards the isolated stakes, bearing the *semence*, now developed into the *renouvelain*, which they detach by means of a hook fixed to the end of a pole. Care is taken to gather such a quantity as they are able to transplant during low water—the only time when this operation can be carried on. The *semence*, placed in baskets, is transported by means of the canoe to the fences of the *bouchot batard*. The operation of fixing the *renouvelain* upon the palisades of the *bouchot batard* is called *la batrisse*. The *semence*, enclosed in bags of old net, is placed in all the empty spaces along the palisades until the hurdles are quite covered, sufficient space being left between the bags to admit of the growth of the young mussels. The bags soon rot and fall to pieces, leaving the young mussels adhering to the sides of the *bouchot*. The mussels by and by attain a large size, and grow so close to each other that the whole fence looks like a wall blackened by fire.

When the mussels grow so large that they touch and overlap each other, the cultivator thins the too-crowded ranks of the *bouchots batard*, in order to make way for a younger generation of mussels. The mussels thus obtained are transplanted and placed on the empty or partially-covered hurdles, and transplanted to the *bouchot milieu*, which is uncovered during neap-tides. This operation is performed in the manner already described, only the larger size of the mussels renders the use of a net to enclose them unnecessary. The labour of transplanting is continued so long as there remain upon the *bouchot du bas* any *renouvelain* fit for being placed on the *bouchots* nearer the shore. The work must be carried on at all times of the day and night during low water, as that is the only period that the *bouchots* are uncovered. There is also the labour of replacing and covering with mussels any of the palisades that may have sunk or been broken.

After about a year's sojourn on these artificial beds the mussels are fit for the market. Before being ready for sale, they are transplanted to the *buchots d'avant,* which are placed close to the shore to admit of the mussels being easily gathered by the hand when ready for the market. A very perceptible difference in quality is seen in the mussels grown on different parts of the bay—those of the upper division possessing the finest flavour, while those of the lower divisions are much inferior, a circumstance caused no doubt by their suffering much more from the influence of the wind.

The mussel has become, by its abundance and cheapness, the daily food of the poorer classes, and sells well throughout the year. It is, however, only in season from the month of July till the end of January, and it is during that period that the most important operations of the farmer are carried on, and that the great part of the harvest is sent to the market. During the spawning season, which lasts from the end of February to the end of April, they lose their good flavour and become meagre and tough.

At the foot of the cliffs, along the shores, the *boucholeurs* dig large holes for the purpose of storing their implements of labour. When a supply of mussels is required for a neighbouring market the *boucholeurs* bring them in their canoes to the landing-place, whence they are conveyed by the wives to these stores, where they are cleared and packed in hampers and baskets, which are placed upon the backs of horses or in carts, and driven during the night to the place of destination, which is reached in good time for the opening of the market in the morning. About 140 horses and 90 carts are employed for the purpose of thus supplying the neighbouring towns and villages.

A well-peopled *bouchot* usually yields, according to the length of its sides, from 400 to 500 loads of mussels—that is at the rate of a load per metre. A load weighs 150 kilogrammes (about 3 cwts.), and sells for 5 francs. A single *bouchot*, therefore, bears about 60,000 or 75,000 kilogrammes annually in weight, of the value of from 2000 to 2500 francs. The whole harvest of these *bouchots* would therefore weigh from 30 to 35 millions of kilogrammes, which would yield a revenue of something like a million francs.

I hope this plan of mussel-culture will speedily be adopted on our own coasts ; it would be a saving of both time and money to the fishermen, who cannot do without bait in large quantities, seeing that the number of hooks required for the line-fishing has so largely increased during late years. The procuring of the necessary quantity of mussels is sometimes impossible ; and when that is the case the men cannot proceed to the fishing, but have to remain at home in forced idleness till the bait can be obtained. This plan of growing the mussels might be easily adopted by our fisher-folks, whom it is now my province to describe.

CHAPTER X.

—◆—

THE FISHER-FOLK.

The Fisher-People the same everywhere—Growth of a Fishing Village—Marrying and giving in Marriage—The Fisher-Folks' Dance—Newhaven near Edinburgh—Newhaven Fishwives—A Fishwife's mode of doing Business—Superstitions—Fisherrow—Dunbar—Buckhaven—Cost of a Boat and its Gear—Scene of the *Antiquary*: Auchmithie—Smoking Haddocks—The Round of Fisher Life—"Finnan Haddies"—Fittie and its quaint Inhabitants—Across to Dieppe—Bay of the Departed—The Eel-Breeders of Comacchio—The French Fishwives—Narrative of a Fishwife—Buckie—Nicknames of the Fisher-Folk—Effects of a Storm on the Coast.

A BOOK professing to describe the harvest of the sea must of necessity have a chapter about the quaint people who gather in the harvest, otherwise it would be like playing "Hamlet" without the hero.

I have a considerable acquaintance with the fisher-folk; and while engaged in collecting information about the fisheries, and in investigating the natural history of the herring and other food-fishes, have visited most of the Scottish fishing villages and many of the English ones, nor have I neglected Normandy, Brittany, and Picardy; and wherever I went I found the fisher-folk to be the same, no matter whether they talked a French *patois* or a Scottish dialect, such as one may hear at Buckie on the Moray Firth, or in the *Rue de Pollet* of Dieppe. The manners, customs, mode of life, and even the dress and superstitions, are nearly the same on the coast of France as they are on the coast of Fife, and used-up gentlemen in search of seaside sensations could scarcely do better than take a tour among the Scottish fisher-folks, in order to view the wonders of the fishing season, its curious industry, and the quaint people.

There are scenes on the coast worthy of any sketch-book ; there are also curious seaside resorts that have not yet been vulgarised by hordes of summer visitors — infant fishing villages, set down by accident in the most romantic spots, occupied by hardy men and rosy women, who have children " paidling " in the water or building castles upon the sand. Such seascapes—for they look more like pictures than realities —may be witnessed from the deck of the steamboat on the way to Inverness or Ultima Thule.   Looking from the steamer —if one cannot see the coast in any other way—at one of these embyro communities, one may readily guess, from the fond attitude of the youthful pair who are leaning on the old boat, that another cottage will speedily require to be added to the two now existing.   In a few years there will be another ; in course of time the four may be eight, the eight sixteen ; and lo ! in a generation there is built a large village, with its adult population gaining wealth by mining in the silvery quarries of the sea; and by and by we will see with a pleased eye groups of youngsters splashing in the water or gathering seaware on the shore, and old men pottering about the rocks setting lobster-pots, doing business in the crustaceous delicacies of the season.   And on glorious afternoons, when the atmosphere is pure, and the briny perfume delicious to inhale —when the water glances merrily in the sunlight, and the sails of the dancing boats are just filled by a capful of wind— the people will be out to view the scene and note the growing industry of the place ; and, as the old song says—

> " O weel may the boatie row,
>   And better may she speed ;
> And muckle luck attend the boat
>   That wins the bairnies' bread."

In good time the little community will have its annals of births, marriages, and deaths ; its chronicles of storms, its records of disasters, and its glimpses of prosperity ; and in two hundred years its origin may be lost, and the inhabitants of the original village represented by descendants in the sixth generation. At any rate, boats will increase, curers of herrings and merchants who buy fish will visit the village and circulate their money, and so the place will thrive. If a pier should be built, and a railway branch out to it, who knows but it may become a great port.

I first became acquainted with the fisher-folk by assisting at a fisherman's marriage. Marrying and giving in marriage involves an occasional festival among the fisher-folks of New-haven of drinking and dancing—and all the fisher-folks are fond of the dance. In the more populous fishing towns there are usually a dozen or two of marriages to celebrate at the close of each herring season ; and as these weddings are what are called in Scotland penny weddings—*i.e.* weddings at which each guest pays a small sum for his entertainment—there is no difficulty in obtaining admission to the ceremony and customary rejoicings. Young men often wait till the close of the annual fishing before they venture into the matrimonial noose ; and I have seen at Newhaven as many as eight marriages in one evening. It has been said that a " lucky" day, or rather night, is usually chosen for the ceremony, for " luck" is the ruling deity of the fishermen ; but as regards the marriage customs of the fisher-class, it was ex-plained to me that marriages were always held on a Friday (usually thought to be an unlucky day), from no superstitious feeling or notion, as was sometimes considered by strangers, but simply that the fishermen might have the last day of the week (Saturday) and the Sunday to enjoy themselves with their friends and acquaintances, instead of, if their weddings took place on Monday or Tuesday, breaking up the whole week afterwards. I considered this a sort of feasible and reasonable explanation of the matter. On such occasions as those of marriage there is great bustle and animation. The guests are invited two days beforehand by the happy couple *in propriis personis*, and means are taken to remind their friends again of the ceremony on the joyous day. At the proper time the parties meet—the lad in his best blue suit, and the lass and all the other maidens dressed in white—and walk to the manse or church, as the case may be, or the minister is " trysted " to come to the bride's father's residence. There is a great dinner provided for the happy occasion, usually served at a small inn or public-house when there is a very large party. All the delicacies which can be thought of are procured : fish, flesh, and fowl ; porter, ale, and whisky, are all to be had at these banquets, not forgetting the universal dish of skate, which is produced at all fisher marriages. After dinner comes the collection, when the best man, or some one of the company, goes round and gets a shilling or a sixpence from each. This is the mode of celebrating a penny wedding, and all are welcome who like to attend, the bidding being general. The evening winds up, so far as the young folks are concerned, with unlimited dancing. In fact dancing at one time used to be the favourite recreation of the fisher-folk. In a dull season they would dance for " luck," in a plentiful season for joy— anything served as an excuse for a dance.* On the wedding-

* I have culled the following account of a fisherman's wedding-dance from an excellent provincial journal. The solemnisation of a marriage is a great event in the village, and when one occurs it is customary to invite nearly all the adult population to attend. The ceremony is mostly always performed in the church, and it not unfrequently happens that at some of the marriages the whole lower part of the church is well packed with the marriage-train. The Collieston weddings are remarkable for the hilarity which ensues after the company return from the ceremony. After a sumptuous dinner the

night the old folks sit and enjoy themselves with a bowl of
punch and a smoke, talking of old times and old fishing
adventures, storms, miraculous hauls, etc. ; in short, like old
military or naval veterans, they have a strong *penchant* " to
fight their battles o'er again." The fun grows fast and furious
with all concerned, till the tired body gives warning that it is
time to desist, and by and by all retire, and life in the fishing
village resumes its old jog-trot.

It would take up too much space, and weary the reader
besides, were I to give in detail an account of all the fishing
places I have visited during the last ten years. My purpose
will be amply served by a glance at a few of the Scottish
fishing villages, which, with the information I can interpolate
about the fisher-folks of the coast of France, and the eel-
breeders of Comacchio, not to mention those of Northumberland
and Yorkshire, will be quite sufficient to give the general

company adjourn to the links to a place which is smooth and level,
and which lies at no very great distance from the Coast-Guard station at
the end of the sands of Forvie, and there, to the inspiriting strains of
the violin, dance the ancient, picturesque, and intricate " Lang Reel o'
Collieston "—a reel danced by their forefathers and each succeeding
generation from time immemorial. To those who are fond of " tripping
the light fantastic toe," and who never had the fortune to see it danced,
it would doubtless be interesting were we to give a description of this
" The Lang Reel o' Collieston ;" but, although fond of that sort of
exercise, we do not boast professional skill, and consequently are
unacquainted with the technical names of the various movements in this
particular department of the worship of Terpsichore. We may, however,
mention that, as indicated by its name, the *lang reel* o' Collieston is a
lang reel in a double sense. It is of long duration and lengthy in its
dimensions, for all the wedding party join in dancing the " lang reel." It
is commenced by the bride and her " best man," and pair after pair link
into its links as the dance proceeds, until all have linked themselves
into it, and then pair after pair drop off, as in some country-dances,
until none are left dancing but the bride and " best man" who commenced it. As may be supposed, this extended saltatory effort is rather
trying for the bride ; and we heard one sonsy wife of forty declare, in

reader a tolerable idea of this interesting class of people; and to suit my own convenience I will begin at the place where I witnessed the marriage, for Newhaven, near Edinburgh—" Our Lady's Port of Grace" as it was originally named—is the most accessible of all fishing villages; and, although it is not the primitive place now that it was some thirty years ago, having been considerably spoiled in its picturesqueness by the encroachments of the modern architect, and the intrusion of summer pleasure-seekers, it is still unique as the abode of a peculiar people who keep up the social distinctiveness of the place. How Newhaven and similar fishing colonies originated there is no record; it is said, however, that this particular community was founded by King James III., who was extremely anxious to extend the industrial resources of his kingdom by the prosecution of the fisheries, and that to aid him in this design he brought over a colony of foreigners to

recapitulating the share she had on her wedding-day, that "the back of her legs didna cour (recover) the lang reel for a month afterwards." The dance movement is very curious. The dancers " reel, set, and cross, and cleek," and change places in such a way as to take them by degrees from the head of the dance to the foot, and back to the head again, and so on, the whole being like the links of a chain when reeling. When the couples are dancing, the lang reel o' Collieston looks like a series of common Highland reels, and it is in the reeling that the peculiarity and intricacy of indescribableness of the dance exists. This reel is quite indispensable at marriages, and after it has been danced other reels and dances are enjoyed and kept up with very great spirit— natural and imbibed; and to see the lang reel o' Collieston danced on the greensward under the blue canopy of heaven, on a sweet afternoon in summer, is a treat worth going many miles to enjoy. Not only would the eye enjoy a rare feast, but what with the sweet music of the violin, the merry song of the lark in mid-heaven right overhead, the ringing guffaws of the juvenile spectators, the clapping of hands, and the loud *hoochs* or whoops of the dancing fishermen, all commingling and commingled with the murmur of billows breaking among the rocks, the ear would have a banquet of no ordinary kind nor of everyday occurrence.—*Banffshire Journal*.

practise and teach the art. Some fishing villages are known to have originated in the shipwreck of a foreign vessel, when the people saved from destruction squatted on the nearest shore and grew in the fulness of time into a community.

NEWHAVEN FISHWIVES.

Newhaven is most celebrated for its "fishwives," who were declared by King George IV. to be the handsomest women he had ever seen, and were looked upon by Queen Victoria with eyes of wonder and admiration. The Newhaven fishwife must not be confounded by those who are unacquainted in the locality with the squalid fish-hawkers of Dublin; nor, although they can use strong language occasionally, are they to be taken as examples of the *genus* peculiar to Billingsgate. The

Newhaven women are more like the buxom *dames* of the
market of Paris, though their glory of late years has been
somewhat dulled. There is this, however, to be said of them,
that they are as much of the past as the present; in dress and
manners they are the same now as they were a hundred years
ago ; they take a pride in conserving all their traditions and
characteristics, so that their customs appear unchangeable,
and are never, at any rate, influenced by the alterations which
art, science, and literature produce on the country at large.
Before the railway era, the Newhaven fishwife was a great
fact, and could be met with in Edinburgh in her picturesque
costume of short but voluminous and gaudy petticoats, shouting " Caller herrings !" or " Wha'll buy my caller cod ?" with
all the energy that a strong pair of lungs could supply.   Then,
in the evening, there entered the city the oyster-wench, with
her prolonged musical aria of " Wha'll o' caller ou ? "   But the
spread of fishmongers' shops and the increase of oyster-taverns
is doing away with this picturesque branch of the business.
Thirty years ago nearly the whole of the fishermen of the
Firth of Forth, in view of the Edinburgh market, made for
Newhaven with their cargoes of white fish ; and these, at that
time, were all bought up by the women, who carried them on
their backs to Edinburgh in creels, and then hawked them
through the city.   The sight of a bevy of fishwives in the
streets of the Modern Athens, although comparatively rare,
may still occasionally be enjoyed ; but the railways have
lightened their labours, and we do not find them climbing the
Whale Brae with a hundredweight, or two hundredweight,
perhaps, of fish, to be sold in driblets, for a few pence, all
through Edinburgh.

The industry of fishwives is proverbial, their chief maxim
being, that "the woman that canna work for a man is no
worth ane ; ' and accordingly they undertake the task of disposing of the merchandise, and acting as Chancellor of the

Exchequer.* Their husbands have only to catch the fish, their labour being finished as soon as the boats touch the quay. The Newhaven fishwife's mode of doing business is well known. She is always supposed to ask double or triple what she will take; and, on occasions of bargaining, she is sure, in allusion to the hazardous nature of the gudeman's occupation, to tell her customers that "fish are no fish the day, they're just men's lives." The style of higgling adopted when dealing with the fisher-folk, if attempted in other kinds of commerce,

* In the fishing villages on the Firths of Forth and Tay, as well as elsewhere in Scotland, the government is gynecocracy. In the course of the late war, and during the alarm of invasion, a fleet of transports entered the Firth of Forth, under the convoy of some ships of war which would reply to no signals. A general alarm was excited, in consequence of which all the fishers who were enrolled as sea-fencibles got on board the gunboats, which they were to man as occasion should require, and sailed to oppose the supposed enemy. The foreigners proved to be Russians, with whom we were then at peace. The county gentlemen of Mid-Lothian, pleased with the zeal displayed by the sea-fencibles at a critical moment, passed a vote for presenting the community of fishers with a silver punch-bowl, to be used on occasions of festivity. But the fisherwomen, on hearing what was intended, put in their claim to have some separate share in the intended honorary reward. The men, they said, were their husbands; it was they who would have been sufferers if their husbands had been killed, and it was by their permission and injunctions that they embarked on board the gunboats for the public service. They therefore claimed to share the reward in some manner which should distinguish the female patriotism which they had shown on the occasion. The gentlemen of the county willingly admitted the claim ; and, without diminishing the value of their compliment to the men, they made the females a present of a valuable brooch, to fasten the plaid of the queen of the fisherwomen for the time.

It may be further remarked, that these Nereids are punctillious among themselves, and observe different ranks according to the commodities they deal in. One experienced dame was heard to characterise a younger damsel as " a puir silly thing, who had no ambition, and would never," she prophesied, " rise above the *mussel-line* of business."—*Note to Antiquary.*

gives rise to the well-known Scottish reproach of " D'ye tak' me for a fishwife ?"   The style of bargain-making carried on by the fishwives may be illustrated by the following little scene :—

A servant girl having just beckoned to one of them is answered by the usual interrogatory, " What's yer wull the day, my bonnie lass ?" and the " mistress" being introduced, the following conversation takes place :—

" Come awa, mem, an' see what bonnie fish I hae the day."

" Have you any haddocks ?"

" Ay hae I, mem, an' as bonnie fish as ever ye clappit yer twa een on."

" What's the price of these four small ones ?"

" What's yer wull, mem ?"

" I wish these small ones."

" What d'ye say, mem ? sma' haddies ! they's no sma' fish, an they're the bonniest I hae in a' ma creel."

" Well, never mind, what do you ask for them ?"

" Weel, mem, its been awfu' wather o' late, an' the men canna get fish ; ye'll no grudge me twentypence for thae four ?"

" Twentypence !"

" Ay, mem, what for no ?"

" They are too dear, I'll give—"

" What d'ye say, mem ? ower dear ! I wish ye kent it : but what'll ye gie me for thae four ?"

" I'll give you a sixpence."

" Ye'll gie me a what ?"

" A sixpence."

" I daur say ye wull, ma bonny leddy, but ye'll no get thae four fish for twa sixpences this day."

" I'll not give more."

" Weel, mem, gude day" (making preparations to go); " I'll tak' eighteenpence an' be dune wi't."

" No ; I'll give you twopence each for them."

And so the chaffering goes on, till ultimately the fishwife
will take tenpence for the lot, and this plan of asking double
what will be taken, which is common with them all and
sometimes succeeds with simple housewives, will be repeated
from door to door, till the supply be exhausted. The mode
of doing business with a fishwife is admirably illustrated in
the *Antiquary*. When Monkbarns bargains for "the bannock-
fluke" and "the cock-padle," Maggie Mucklebackit asks
four and sixpence, and ends, after a little negotiation and
much finesse, in accepting half-a-crown and a dram; the latter
commodity being worth siller just then, in consequence of the
stoppage of the distilleries.

The fishwives while selling their fish will often say something quaint to the customer with whom they are dealing. I
will give one instance of this, which, though somewhat ludi-
crous, is characteristic, and have no doubt the words were
spoken from the poor woman's heart. "A fishwife who was cry-
ing her "caller cod" in George Street, Edinburgh, was stopped
by a cook at the head of one of the area stairs. A cod was
wanted that day for the dinner of the family, but the cook
and the fishwife could not trade, disagreeing about the price.
The night had been stormy, and instead of the fishwife flying
into a passion, as is their general custom when bargaining for
their fish if opposed in getting their price, the poor woman
shed tears, and said to the cook, 'Tak' it or want it; ye may
think it dear, but it's a' that's left to me for a faither o' four
bairns.'"

Notwithstanding, however, their lying and cheating in
the streets during the week when selling their fish, there
are no human beings in Scotland more regular in their
attendance at church. To go to their church on a Sunday,
and see the women all sitting with their smooth glossy hair
and snow-white caps, staring with open eyes and mouth
at the minister, as he exhorts them from the pulpit as to

what they should do, one would think them the most innocent and simple creatures in existence. But offer one of them
a penny less than she feels inclined to take for a haddock, and
he is a lucky fellow who escapes without its tail coming across
his whiskers. Of late our fishwives have been considering
themselves of some importance. When the Queen came first
to Edinburgh, she happened to take notice of them, and every
printshop window is now stuck full of pictures of Newhaven
fishwives in their quaint costume of short petticoats of flaming
red and yellow colours.*

The sketch of fisher-life in the *Antiquary* applies as well
to the fisher-folk of to-day as to those of sixty years since.
This is demonstrable at Newhaven; which, though fortunate
in having a pier as a rendezvous for its boats, thus admitting
of a vast saving of time and labour, is yet far behind inland
villages in point of sanitary arrangements. There is in the
"town" an everlasting scent of new tar, and a permanent
smell of decaying fish, for the dainty visitors who go down to
the village from Edinburgh to partake of the fish-dinners for
which it is so celebrated. Up the narrow closes, redolent of

---

* "The Scottish fishwomen, or "fishwives" of Newhaven and Fisherrow, as they are usually designated, wear a dress of a peculiar and
appropriate fashion, consisting of a long blue. duffle jacket, with wide
sleeves, a blue petticoat usually tucked up so as to form a pocket, and
in order to show off their ample under petticoats of bright-coloured
woollen stripe, reaching to the calf of the leg. It may be remarked
that the upper petticoats are of a striped sort of stuff technically called,
we believe, drugget, and are always of different colours. As the women
carry their load of fish on their backs in creels, supported by a broad
leather belt resting forwards on the forehead, a thick napkin is their
usual headdress, although often a muslin cap, or mutch, with a very
broad frill, edged with lace, and turned back on the head, is seen peeping from under the napkin. A variety of kerchiefs or small shawls
similar to that on the head encircle the neck and bosom, which, with
thick worsted stockings, and a pair of stout shoes, complete the
costume."

" bark," we see hanging on the outside stairs the paraphernalia
of the fisherman—his " properties," as an actor would call
them ; nets, bladders, lines, and oilskin unmentionables, with
dozens of pairs of those particularly blue stockings that seem
to be the universal wear of both mothers and maidens.   On
the stair itself sit, if it be seasonable weather, the wife and
daughters, repairing the nets and baiting the lines—gossiping
of course with opposite neighbours, who are engaged in a
precisely similar pursuit ; and to day, as half a century ago,
the fishermen sit beside their hauled-up boats, in their white
canvas trousers and their Guernsey shirts, smoking their
short pipes, while their wives and daughters are so employed,
seeming to have no idea of anything in the shape of labour
being a duty of theirs when ashore.   In the flowing gutter
which trickles down the centre of the old village we have
the young idea developing itself in plenty of noise, and adding
another layer to the incrustation of dirt which it seems to be
the sole business of these children to collect on their bodies.
These juvenile fisher-folk have already learned from the mud-
larks of the Thames the practice of sporting on the sands
before the hotel windows in the expectation of being rewarded with a few halfpence.   " What's the use of asking for
siller before they've gotten their denner?" we once heard one
of these precocious youths say to another, who was proposing
to solicit a bawbee from a party of strangers.

To see the people of Newhaven, both men and women,
one would be apt to think that their social condition was one
of great hardship and discomfort; but one has only to enter
their dwellings in order to be disabused of this notion, and to
be convinced of the reverse of this, for there are few houses
among the working population of Scotland which can compare
with the well-decked and well-plenished dwellings of these
fishermen.   Within doors all is neat and tidy.   When at the
marriage I have mentioned, I thought the house I was invited

to was the cleanest and the cosiest-looking house I had ever seen. Never did I see before so many plates and bowls in any private dwelling ; and on all of them, cups and saucers not excepted, fish, with their fins spread wide out, were painted in glowing colours ; and in their dwellings and domestic arrangements the Newhaven fishwives are the cleanest women in Scotland, and the comfort of their husbands when they return from their labours on the wild and dangerous deep seems to be the fishwife's chief delight. I may also mention that none of the young women of Newhaven will take a husband out of their own community, that they are as rigid in this matrimonial observance as if they were all Jewesses.*

The following anecdotic illustration of the state of information in Newhaven sixty years since is highly characteristic :—

A fisherman, named Adam L——, having been reproved pretty severely for his want of Scripture knowledge, was resolved to baulk the minister on his next catechetical visitation. The day appointed he kept out of sight for some time ; but at length, getting top-heavy with some of his companions, he was compelled, after several falls, in one of which he met

---

* " There fishermen and fishermen's daughters marry and are given in marriage to each other with a sacredness only second to the strictness of intermarriage observed among the Jews. On making inquiry we find that occasionally one of these buxom young damsels chooses a husband for herself elsewhere than from among her own community ; but we understand that when this occurs the bride loses caste, and has to follow the future fortunes of the bridegroom, whatever these may turn out to be. Speaking of marriages, the present great scarcity both of beef and mutton, and the consequent high price of these articles of food, seems in no way to terrify the denizens of Newhaven, for there the matrimonial knot is being briskly tied. While chatting with some of the fishermen just the other day we heard that two of these celebrations had taken place the night before, and that other four weddings were expected to come off during this week ; and we both heard and saw the fag end of the musical and dancing jollification, which was held in a public-house on these two recent occasions, and which was kept up

with an accident that somewhat disfigured his countenance, to take shelter in his own cottage. The minister arrived, and was informed by Jenny, the wife, that her husband was absent at the fishing. The Doctor then inquired if she had carefully perused the catechism he had left on his last visit, and being answered in the affirmative, proceeded to follow up his conversation with a question or two. "Weel, Jenny," said the minister, "can ye tell me the cause o' Adam's fall?" By no means versed in the history of the great progenitor of the human race, and her mind being exclusively occupied by her own Adam, Janet replied, with some warmth, "'Deed, sir, it was naething else but drink!" at the same time calling upon her husband, "Adam, ye may as weel rise, for the Doctor kens brawly what's the matter; some clashin' deevils o' neebours hae telt him a' aboot it!"

The remains of many old superstitions are still to be found about Newhaven. I could easily fill a page or two of this volume with illustrative anecdotes of sayings and doings that are abhorrent to the fisher mind. The following are given as the merest sample of the number that might be collected.

until far on in the next afternoon. We can see little to tempt the young women of Newhaven to enter into the marriage state, for it seems only to increase their bodily labour. This circumstance, however, would appear to be no obstacle in the way, but rather to spur them on; and we recollect of once actually hearing, when a girl rather delicate for a Newhaven young woman was about to be married, another girl, a strapping lass of about eighteen, thus express herself :—" Jenny Flucker takin' a man! she's a gude cheek; hoo is she tae keep him? the puir man'll hae tae sell his fish as weel as catch them." When upon this subject of intermarriages among the Newhaven people it is proper to mention that we heard contradictory accounts regarding the point; some saying that no such custom existed, or at least that no such rule was enforced by the community, while another account was that only one marriage out of the community had, so far as had come to the knowledge of our informant, taken place during the last eight or nine years."—*North Briton.*

They have several times "gone the round" of the newspapers but are none the worse for that :—

If an uninitiated greenhorn of a landsman chanced to be on board of a Newhaven boat, and, in the ignorance and simplicity of his heart, talked about " salmon," the whole crew— at least a few years ago—would start, grasp the nearest *iron thowell,* and exclaim, " Cauld iron !" " cauld iron !" in order to avert the calamity which such a rash use of the appellation was calculated to induce ; and the said uninitiated gentleman would very likely have been addressed in some such courteous terms as " O ye igrant brute, cud ye no ca'd it redfish ?" Woe to the unfortunate wight—be he Episcopalian or Presbyterian, Churchman or Dissenter—who being afloat talks about " the minister :" there is a kind of undefined terror visible on every countenance if haply this unlucky word is spoken ; and I would advise my readers, should they hereafter have occasion, when water-borne, to speak of a clergyman, to call him " the man in the black coat;" the thing will be equally well understood, and can give offence to none. I warn them, moreover, to be guarded and circumspect should the idea of a cat or a pig flit across their minds ; and should necessity demand the utterance of their names, let the one be called "Theebet" and the other " Sandy ; " so shall they be landed on *terra firma* in safety, and neither their ears nor their feelings be insulted by piscatory *wit.* In the same category must be placed every four-footed beast, from the elephant moving amongst the jungles of Hindostan to the mouse that burrows under the cottage hearth-stone. Some quadrupeds, however, are more " unlucky" than others; dogs are detestable, hogs horrible, and hares hideous ! It would appear that Friday, for certain operations, is the most unfortunate ; for others the most auspicious day in the week. On that day no sane fisherman would commence a Greenland voyage, or proceed to the herring-ground, and on no other day of the week would he be married.

2 F

In illustration of the peculiar dread and antipathy of fishermen to swine, I give the following extract from a volume
published by a schoolmaster, entitled *An Historical Account
of St. Monance.* The town is divided into two divisions, the
one called Nethertown and the other Overtown—the former
being inhabited entirely by fishermen, and the latter by agriculturists and petty tradesmen:—" The inhabitants of the
Nethertown entertained a most deadly hatred towards swine,
as ominous of evil, insomuch that not one was kept amongst
them ; and if their eyes haplessly lighted upon one in any
quarter, they abandoned their mission and fled from it as they
would from a lion, and their occupation was suspended till the
ebbing and flowing of the tide had effectually removed the
spell. The same devils were kept, however, in the Uppertown,
frequently affording much annoyance to their neighbours below, on account of their casual intrusions, producing much
damage by suspension of labour. At last, becoming quite
exasperated, the decision of their oracle was to go in a body
and destroy not the animals (for they dared not hurt them),
but all who bred and fostered such demons, looking on them
with a jealous eye, on account of their traffic. Armed with
boat-hooks, they ascended the hill in formidable procession,
and dreadful had been the consequence had they not been
discovered. But the Uppertown, profiting by previous remonstrance, immediately let loose their swine, whose grunt
and squeak chilled the most heroic blood of the enemy, who,
on beholding them, turned and fled down the hill with tenfold
speed, more exasperated than ever, secreting themselves till
the flux and reflux of the tide had undone the enchantment.
. . . According to the most authentic tradition, not an
animal of the kind existed in the whole territories of St. Monance for nearly a century ; and, even at the present day, though
they are fed and eaten, the fisher people are extremely averse
to looking on them or speaking of them by that name ; but,

when necessitated to mention the animal, it is called 'the beast,' or 'the brute,' and, in case the real name of the animal should accidentally be mentioned, the spell is undone by a less tedious process—the exclamation of 'cauld iron' by the person affected being perfectly sufficient to counteract the evil influence. Cauld iron, touched or expressed, is understood to be the first antidote against enchantment."

At Fisherrow, a few miles east from Newhaven, there is another fishing community, who also do business in Edinburgh, and whose manners and customs are quite as superstitious as those of the folks I have been describing. "The Fisher-raw wives," in the pre-railway times, had a much longer walk with their fish than the Newhaven women ; neither were they held in such esteem, the latter looking upon themselves as the salt of their profession. Dr. Carlyle of Inveresk, whose memoirs were recently published, in writing of the Fisherrow women of his time, says :—" When the boats come in late to the harbour in the forenoon, so as to leave them no more than time to reach Edinburgh before dinner, it is not unusal for them to perform their journey of five miles by relays, three of them being employed in carrying one basket, and shifting it from one to another every hundred yards, by which means they have been known to arrive at the fishmarket in less than three quarters of an hour. It is a well-known fact, that three of these women went from Dunbar to Edinburgh, a distance of twenty-seven miles, with each of them a load of herrings on her back of 200 pounds, in five hours." Fatiguing journeys with heavy loads of fish are now saved to the wives of both villages, as dealers attend the arrival of the boats, and buy up all the sea produce that is for sale. In former times there used to be great battles between the men of Newhaven and the men of Fisherrow, principally about their rights to certain oyster-scalps. The Montagues and Capulets were not more deadly in their hatreds than these rival fishermen. Now the oyster-grounds are so well defined that battles upon that question are never fought.

Fisherrow has long been distinguished for its race of hardy and industrious fishermen, of whom there are about two hundred in all. They go to the herring-fishing at Caithness, at North Sunderland, at Berwick, North Berwick, and Dunbar, and about sixty men go to Yarmouth, on the east coast of England, a distance of about 300 miles. Ten boats, with a complement of eight men each, go to the deep-sea white-fishing, and two or three boats to the oyster-dredging.

The white-fishing of Fisherrow has long been a staple source of income. At what time a colony of fishermen was established at that village is unknown. They are most likely coeval with the place itself. When the Reverend Dr. Carlyle, minister of the parish of Inveresk, wrote (about 1790) there were forty-nine fishermen and ninety fishwives, but since that time the numbers of both have of course much increased.

The system of merchandise followed by the fishwives in the old days of creel-hawking, and even yet to a considerable extent, was very simple. Having procured a supply of fish, which having bestowed in a basket of a form fitted to the back, they used to trudge off to market under a load which most men would have had difficulty in carrying, and which would have made even the strongest stagger. Many of them still proceed to the market, and display their commodities ; but the majority, perhaps, perambulate the streets of the city, emitting cries which, to some persons, are more loud than agreeable, and which a stranger would never imagine to have the most distant connection with fish. Occasionally, too, they may be seen pulling the door-bell of some house where they are in the habit of disposing of their merchandise, with the blunt inquiry, " Ony haddies the day ?" *

While treating of the peculiarities of these people, I may

* Some of this information about Fisherrow is from *Chambers' Journal*.

record the following characteristic anecdote:—" A clergyman, in whose parish a pretty large fishing-village is situated, in his visitations among the families of the fish-carriers found that the majority of them had never partaken of the sacrament. Interrogating them regarding the reason of this neglect, they candidly admitted to him that their trade necessarily led them so much to cheat and tell lies, that they felt themselves unqualified to join in that religious duty." It is but justice, however, to add that, when confidence is reposed in them, nothing can be more fair and upright than the dealings of the fisher class ; and, as dealers in a commodity of very fluctuating value, they cannot perhaps be justly blamed for endeavouring to sell it to the best advantage.

At Prestonpans, and the neighbouring village of Cockenzie, the modern system, as I may call it, for Scotland, of selling the fish wholesale, may be seen in daily operation. When the boats arrive at the boat-shore, the wives of those engaged in the fishing are in readiness to obtain the fish, and carry them from the boats to the place of sale. They are at once divided into lots, and put up to auction, the skipper's wife acting as the George Robins of the company, and the price obtained being divided among the crew, who are also, generally speaking, owners of the boat. Buyers, or their agents, from Edinburgh, Glasgow, Liverpool, Manchester, etc., are always ready to purchase, and in a few hours the scaly produce of the Firth of Forth is being whisked along the railway at the rate of twenty miles an hour. This system, which is certainly a great improvement on the old creel-hawking plan, is a faint imitation of what is done in England, where the owners of fishing-smacks consign their produce to a wholesale agent at Billingsgate, who sells it by auction in lots to the retail dealers and costermongers.

Farther along on the Scottish east coast is North Berwick, now a bathing resort, and a fishing town as well ; and farther

east still is Dunbar, the seat of an important herring-fishery
—grown from a fishing village into a country town, in which
a mixture of agricultural and fishing interests gives the place
a somewhat heterogeneous aspect ; and between St. Abb's Head
and Berwick-on-Tweed is situated Eyemouth, a fishing-village
pure and simple, with all that wonderful filth scattered about
which is a sanitary peculiarity of such towns.   The population
of Eyemouth is in keeping with the outward appearance of
the place.   As a whole, they are a rough uncultivated people,
and more drunken in their habits than the fishermen of the
neighbouring villages.   Coldingham shore,. for instance, is
only three miles distant, and has a population of about one
hundred fishermen, of a very respectable class, sober, well
dressed, and "well-to-do."   A year or two ago an outburst of
what is called "revivalism" took place at Eyemouth, and
seemed greatly to affect it.   The change produced for a time
was unmistakable.   These rude unlettered fishermen ceased
to visit the public-houses, refrained from the use of oaths, and
instead sang psalms and said prayers.   But this wave of revivalism, which passed over other villages besides Eyemouth,
has rolled away back, and in some instances left the people
worse than it found them ; and I may perhaps be allowed to
cite the fish-tithe riots as a proof of what I say.   These riots,
for which the rioters were tried before the High Court of
Justiciary at Edinburgh, and some of them punished, arose
out of a demand by the minister for his tithe of fish.

   Crossing the Firth of Forth, the cost of Fife, from Burntisland to "the East Neuk," will be found studded at intervals
with quaint fishing-villages ; and the quaintest among .the
quaint is Buckhaven.   Buckhaven, or, as it is locally named,
Buckhyne, as seen from the sea, is a picturesque group of
houses sown broadcast on a low cliff.   Indeed, most fishing
villages seem thrown together without any kind of plan.   The
local architects had never thought of building their villages in

rows or streets; as the fisher-folks themselves say, their houses are "a' heids and thraws," that is, set down here and there without regard to architectural arrangement. The origin of Buckhaven is rather obscure : it is supposed to have been founded by the crew of a Brabant vessel, wrecked on that portion of the Fife coast in the reign of Philip II. The population are, like most of their class, a peculiar people, living entirely among themselves ; and any stranger settling among them is viewed with such suspicion that years will often elapse before he is adopted as one of the community. One of the old Scottish chap-books is devoted to a satire of the Buckhaven people. These old chap-books are now rare, and to obtain them involves a considerable amount of trouble. Thirty years ago the chapmen were still carrying them about in their packs; now it is pleasing to think they have been superseded by the admirable cheap periodicals which are so numerous and so easy to purchase. The title of the chap-book referred to above is, *The History of Buckhaven in Fifeshire, containing the Witty and Entertaining Exploits of Wise Willie and Witty Eppie, the Ale-wife, with a description of their College, Coats of Arms, etc.* It would be a strong breach of etiquette to mention the title of this book to any of the Buckhaven people ; it is difficult to understand how they should feel so sore on the point, as the pamphlet in question is a collection of very vulgar witicisms tinged with such a dash of obscenity as prevents their being quoted here. The industrious fishermen of Buckhaven are moral, sober, and comparatively wealthy. Indeed, many of the Scottish fisher-folk are what are called "warm" people ; and there are not in our fishing villages such violent alternations of poverty and prosperity as are to be found in places devoted entirely to manufacturing industry. There is usually on the average of the year a steady income, the people seldom suffering from "a hunger and a burst," like weavers or other handicraftsmen.

As denoting the prosperous state of the people of Buckhaven, it may be stated that most of the families there have saved money ; and, indeed, some of them are comparatively wealthy, having a bank account, as well as considerable capital in boats, nets, and lines.   Fishermen, being much away from home, at the herring-fishery or out at the deep-sea fishing, have no temptation to spend their earnings or waste their time in the tavern.   Indeed, in some Scottish fishing villages there is not even a single public-house.   The Buckhaven men delight in their boats, which are mostly " Firth-built,"—*i. e.* built at Leith, on the Firth of Forth.   Many of the boats used by the Scottish fishermen are built at that port : they are all constructed with overlapping planks ; and the hull alone of a boat thirty-eight feet in length will cost a sum of £60.   Each boat, before it can be used for the herring or deep-sea fishery must be equipped with a set of nets and lines ; say, a train of thirty-five nets, at a cost of £4 each, making a sum of £140 ; which, with the price of the hull, makes the cost £200, leaving the masts and sails, as well as inshore and deep-sea lines and many other *etceteras,* to be provided for before the total cost can be summed up.   The hundred boats which belong to the men of Buckhaven consequently represent a considerable amount of capital.   Each boat with its appurtenances has generally more than one owner; in other words, it is held in shares.   This is rather an advantage than otherwise, as every vessel requires a crew of four men at any rate, so that each boat is usally manned by two or three of its owners —a pledge that it will be looked carefully after and not be exposed to needless danger.   With all the youngsters of a fishing village it is a point of ambition to obtain a share of a boat as soon as ever they can ; so that they save hard from their allowances as extra hands, in order to attain as early as possible to the dignity of proprietorship.   We look in vain, except at such wonderful places as Rochdale, to find manufacturing

CHAP. X.]   CO-OPERATION AMONG THE FISHERS.   441

operatives in a similar financial position to these Buckhaven men; in fact, our fishermen have been practising the plan of co-operation for years without knowing it, and without making it known. The co-operative system seems to prevail among the English fisher-folk as well. At Filey, on the Yorkshire coast, many of the large fishing yawls—these vessels average about 40 tons each—are built by little companies and worked on the sharing principle : so much to the men who find the bait, and so much to each man who provides a net ; and a few shillings per pound of the weekly earnings of the ship go to the owners. In France there are various ways of engaging the boats and conducting the fisheries. There are some men who fish on their own account, who have their own boat, sail, and nets, etc., and who find their own bait, whether at the sardine-fishery or when prosecuting any other branch of the sea fisheries. Of course these boat-owners hire what assistance they require, and pay for it. There are other men again who hire a boat and work it on the sharing plan, each man getting so much, the remainder being left for the owner. A third class of persons are those who work off their advances : these are a class of men so poor as to be obliged to pawn their labour to the boat-owners long before it is required. We can parallel this at home in the herring-fishery, where the advance of money to the men has become something very like a curse to all concerned.

The joint-stock fishing system has been prevalent in Scotland, with various modifications, for a very long period. Ship-carpenters at one time used to speculate in the fisheries, and build boats in order to give fishermen a share in them, and persons who had nets would lend them out on condition of getting a share in the speculation. The two or three fisher-men chiefly concerned would assume a few landsmen as assistants. At the end of the season the proceeds of the fishing were divided; the proprietors of the boat drew each one deal, every man half a deal, and every net was awarded half a deal. The landsmen, being counted as boys, only drew a quarter of a deal.

The retired Buckhaven fishermen can give interesting information about the money value of the fisheries. One, who was a young fellow five-and-twenty years ago, told me the herring-fishery was a kind of lottery, but that, on an average of years, each boat would take annually something like a hundred crans—the produce, in all cases where the crew were part owners, after deducting a fifth part or so to keep up the boat, being equally divided. "When I was a younker, sir," said this person, "there was lots o' herrin', an' we had a fine winter fishin' as well, an' sprats in plenty. As to white fish, they were abundant five-an'-twenty year ago. Haddocks now are scarce to be had; being an inshore fish, they've been a' ta'en, in my opinion. Line-fishin' was very profitable from 1830 to 1840. I've seen as many as a hunder thoosand fish o' ae kind or anither ta'en by the Buckhyne boats in a week —that is, countin' baith inshore boats an' them awa at the Dogger Bank. The lot brocht four hunder pound; but a' kinds of fish are now sae scarce that it taks mair than dooble the labour to mak the same money that was made then."

In the pre-railway era, most of the fishermen along the east coast of Fife (at Buckhaven, Cellardyke, St. Monance, and Pittenweem), as also the fishermen along the south coast (North Bewick, Dunbar, Eyemouth, and Burnmouth), used to carry their catchings of white fish to villages up the Firth of Forth, and dispose of them to cadgers and creel-hawkers, who had the retail trade of Edinburgh and Leith in their own hands. These persons distributed themselves over the country in order to dispose of their fish, and some of them would return with farm-produce in its place. The profits realised from thus retailing the produce of fishermen belonging to distant villages enabled those who resided on firths bordering the large towns and cities quietly to lie on their oars. Railways having given facilities to the east coast of Fife fishers, as well as those on the opposite coast, to send their produce to market from their own respective villages, and a new class of traders having arisen—viz. fishmongers having retail shops—the creel-hawking trade is now fast declining, and as a following result so also must be the material wealth of the villages that were in a great measure dependent upon it. In fact, railways have quite revolutionised the fish trade. There are a few females, formerly creel-hawkers, who continue still to act as retailers of fish. But many of them have taken shops, and others stalls in retail markets, and attend the wholesale market regularly to purchase their supplies. These retail dealers in fish do remarkably well ; but those who still continue to hawk about a few haddocks or whitings when they can be procured find that creel-hawking is but a precarious trade.

I will now carry the reader with me to a very quaint place indeed, the scene of Sir Walter Scott's novel of *The Antiquary* —Auchmithie ; and then on to Fittie, at Aberdeen—another fishing quarter of great originality : we will go in the steamer.

Steamboat travelling has been in some degree superseded by the railway carriage ; but to tourists going to Inverness or Thurso the steamer has its attractions. It is preferable to the railroad when the time occupied in the journey is not an object. On board a fine steamboat one has opportunities to study character, and there are always a few characters on board a coasting steam-vessel. And going north from Edinburgh the coast is interesting. The steamer may pass the Anster or Dunbar herring-fleet.

> " Up the waters steerin',
> The boats are thick and thrang;
> Aboon the Bass they're bearin',
> They'll shoot their nets ere lang.

" The morn, like siller glancin',
    They'll haul them han' to han' ;
  Syne doon the water dancin',
    Come hame wi' sixty cran."

The passengers can see the Bell Rock lighthouse, and think of
the old legend of the pirate who took away the floating bell
that had been erected by a pious abbot on the Inchcape Rock
as a warning to mariners, and who was promptly punished for
his sin by being shipwrecked on the very rock from which he
had carried off the bell. After leaving Aberdeen, the Bullers
of Buchan are among the wonders of the shore, and the sea
soughs at times with mournful cadence in the great caverns
carved out by the waves on the precipitous coast, or it foams
and lashes with majestic fury, seeking to add to its dominions.
All the way, till the Old Man of Wick is descried, guarding
the entrance of Pulteneytown harbour, there are ruined castles,
and ancient spires, and curious towers perched on high sea-
cliffs ; or there are frowning hills and screaming sea-birds to
add to the poetry of the scene. And along these storm-washed
coasts there are wonders of nature that show the strong arm
of the water, and mark out works that human ingenuity could
never have achieved. Loch Katrine and the Pass of Glencoe
have been the fashion ever since Sir Walter Scott *made* Scotland ; but there are other places besides these that are worth
visiting.

The supposed scene of Sir Walter Scott's novel of *The
Antiquary*, on the coast of Forfarshire, presents a conjunction
of scenic and industrial features which commends it to notice.
At Auchmithie, which is distant a few miles from Arbroath,
there is often some cause for excitement; and a real storm or
a real drowning is something vastly different from the ship-
wreck in the drama of *The Tempest*, or the death of the Colleen
Bawn. The beetling cliffs barricading the sea from the land
may be traversed by the tourist to the music of the ever-

lasting waves, the dashing ‧of .which oṅly makes thé deep solitude more solemn ;‧ the sea-gull sweeps around with its shrill cry, and playful whales gambol iṅ the placid waters. ‧:

The village of Auchmithie, which is wildly grand and romantic, stands on the top of the cliffs, and as the road to it is steep a great amount of labour devolves on the fishermen in carrying down their lines and nets, and carrying up their produce, etc. One customary feature observed by strangers on entering Auchmithie is, that when met by female children they invariably stoop down, making a very low curtsey, and for this piece of polite condescension they expect that a few halfpence will be thrown to them. If you pass on without noticing them they will not ask for anything, but once throw them a few halfpence and a pocketful will be required to satisfy their importunities. There are two roads leading to Auchmithie from Arbroath, one along the sea-coast, the other through the country. The distance is about 3½ miles in a north-east direction, and the country road is the best ; and approaching the village in that direction it has a very fair aspect. Two rows of low-built slate-roofed houses, and a school and chapel, stand a few yards off by themselves. On the north side of the village is a stately farm-house, surrounded by trees, and on the south side a Coast-Guard station, clean, white-washed, and with a flagstaff, giving the whole a regular and picturesque appearance. Entering the village of Auchmithie from the west, and walking through to the ex- treme east end, the imagination gets staggered to think how any class of men could have selected such a wild and rugged part of the coast for pursuing the fishing trade—a trade above all others that requires a safe harbour where boats can be launched and put to sea at a moment's warning if any signals of distress be given. The bight of Auchmithie is an indentation into rocky cliffs several hundred feet in perpendicular height. About the middle of the bight there is a steep ravine

or gully with a small stream, and at the bottom of this ravine
there is a small piece of level ground where a fish-curing house
is erected, and where also the fishermen pull up their boats that
they may be safe from easterly gales. There are in all about
seventeen boats' crews at Auchmithie. Winding roads with
steps lead down the side of the steep brae to the beach. There
are a few half-tide rocks in the bight that may help to break
the fury of waves raised by easterly winds ; but there is no
harbour or pier for the boats to land at or receive shelter from,
and this the fishermen complain of, as they have to pay £2
a year for the privilege of each boat. The beach is steep, and
strewed with large pebbles, excellently adapted, they say, for
drying fish upon.

The visitor, in addition to studying the quaint people,
may explore one of the vast caves which only a few years ago
were the nightly refuge of the smuggler. Brandy Cove and
Gaylet Pot are worth inspection, and inspire a mingled feeling
of terror and grandeur. The visitor may also take a look at
the "Spindle"—a large detached piece of the cliffs, shaped
something like a corn-stack, or a boy's top with the apex
uppermost. When the tide is full this rock is surrounded
with water, and appears like an island. Fisher-life may be
witnessed here in all its unvarnished simplicity. Indeed
nothing could well be more primitive than their habits and
mode of life. I have seen the women of Auchmithie "kilt
their coats" and rush into the water in order to aid in shoving
off the boats, and on the return of the little fleet carry the
men ashore on their brawny shoulders with the greatest ease
and all the *nonchalance* imaginable, no matter who might be
looking at them. Their peculiar way of smoking their haddocks may be taken as a very good example of their other
modes of industry. Instead of splitting the fish after cleaning
them, as the regular curers do, they smoke them in their round
shape. They use a barrel without top or bottom as a substitute

for a curing-house. The barrel being inserted a little distance in the ground, an old kail-pot or kettle, filled with sawdust, is placed at the bottom, and the inside is then filled with as many fish as can conveniently be hung in it. The sawdust is then set fire to, and a piece of canvas thrown over the top of the barrel : by this means the females of Auchmithie smoke their haddocks in a round state, and very excellent they are when the fish are caught in season. The daily routine of fisher-life at Auchmithie is simple and unvarying ; year by year, and all the year round, it changes only from one branch of the fishery to another. The season, of course, brings about its joys and sorrows : sad deaths, which overshadow the village with gloom ; or marriages, when the people may venture to hold some simple *fête*, but only to send them back with renewed vigour to their occupations. Time, as it sweeps over them, only indicates a period when the deep-sea hand-lines must be laid aside for the herring-drift, or when the men must take a toilsome journey in search of bait for their lines. Their scene of labour is on the sea, ever on the sea ; and, trusting themselves on the mighty waters, they pursue their simple craft with persevering industry, never heeding that they are scorched by the suns of summer or benumbed by the frosts of winter. There is, of course, an appropriate season for the capture of each particular kind of fish. There are days when the men fish inshore for haddocks ; and there are times when, with their frail vessels, the fishermen sail long distances to procure larger fish in the deep seas, and when they must remain in their open boats for a few days and nights. But the El-dorado of all the coast tribe is " the herring." This abounding and delightful fish, which can be taken at one place or another from January to December, yields a six weeks' fishing in the autumn of the year, to which, as has already been stated, all the fisher-folk look forward with hope, as a period of money-making, and which, so far as the young people are concerned, is generally expected to end, like the third volume of a love-story, in matrimony.

Taking a jump from Auchmithie, it is desirable to pause a moment at the small fishing village of Findon, in the parish of Banchory-Devenick, in Kincardineshire, in order to say a few words about a branch of industry in connection with the fisheries that is peculiar to Scotland. Yarmouth is famed for its "bloaters," a preparation of herrings slightly smoked, well known o_ve_r England; and in Scotland, as has already been mentioned in a previous chapter, there is that unparagoned dainty, the "Finnan haddock," the best accompaniment that can be got to the other substantial components of a Scottish breakfast. Indeed, the Finnan haddock is celebrated as a breakfast luxury all over the world, although it is so delicate in its flavour, and requires such nicety in the cure, that it cannot be enjoyed in perfection at any great distance from the sea-coast. George IV., who had certainly, whatever may have been his other virtues, a kingly genius in the matter of relishes for the palate (does not the world owe to him the discovery of the exquisite propriety of the sequence of port wine after cheese?), used to have genuine Finnan haddocks always on his breakfast-table, selected at Aberdeen and sent express by coach every day for his Majesty's use. Great houses of brick have now been erected at various places on the Moray Firth and elsewhere; and in these immense quantities of haddocks and other fish are smoked for the market by means of burning billets of green wood. Formerly the fisher-folk used to smoke a few haddocks in their cottages over their peat-fires for family use. I have already described how the fame of the Finnan haddock arose. The trade soon grew so large that it required a collection to be made in the fishing districts in order to get together the requisite quantity; so that what was once a mere local effort has now become a prominent branch of the fish trade. But it is seldom that the home-smoked fish can be

obtained, with its delicate flavour of peat-reek. The manufactured Finnan or yellow haddock, smoked in a huge ware-
house, is more plentiful, of course, but it has lost the old relish.
It is pleasant to see the clean fireside and the clear peat-fire in
the comfortably-furnished cottage, with the children sitting
round the ingle on the long winter evenings, listening to the
tales and traditions of the coast, the fish hanging all over the
reeking peats, acquiring the while that delicate yellow tinge so
refreshing to the eyes of all lovers of a choice dish.

Footdee, or "Fittie" as it is locally called, is a quaint
suburb of Aberdeen, figuring not a little, and always with a
kind of comic quaintness, in the traditions of that northern
city, and in the stories which the inhabitants tell of each
other. They tell there of one Aberdeen man, who, being in
London for the first time, and visiting St. Paul's, was surprised
by his astonishment at its dimensions into an unusual burst
of candour. "My stars!" he said, "this maks a perfect feel
(fool) o' the kirk o' Fittie." Part of the quaint interest thus
attached to this particular suburb by the Aberdonians themselves arises from its containing a little colony or nest of
fisher-folk, of immemorial antiquity. There are about a hundred families living in Fittie, or Footdee Square, close to
the sea, where the Dee has its mouth. This community, like
all others made up of fishing-folk, is a peculiar one, and
differs of course from those of other working-people in its
neighbourhood. In many things the Footdee people are like
the gipsies. They rarely marry, except with their own class;
and those born in a community of fishers seldom leave it, and
very seldom engage in any other avocation than that of their
fathers. The squares of houses at Footdee are peculiarly
constructed. There are neither doors nor windows in the
outside walls, although these look to all the points of the
compass ; and none live within the square but the fishermen
and their families, so that they are as completely isolated and

secluded from public gaze as are a regiment of soldiers within
the dead walls of a barrack. The Rev. Mr. Spence, of Free
St. Clement's, lately completed plans of the entire "toun,"
giving the number and the names of the tenants in every
house; and from these exhaustive plans it appears that the
total population of the two squares was 584—giving about
nine inmates for each of these two-roomed houses. But the
case is even worse than this average indicates. "In the
South Square only eight of the houses are occupied by single
families; and in the North Square only three, the others being
occupied by at least two families each—one room apiece—
and four *single* rooms in the North Square contain *two* families
each! There are thirty-six married couples and nineteen
widows in the twenty-eight houses; and the number of distinct families in them is fifty-four." The Fittie men seem
poorer than the generality of their brethren. They purchase
the crazy old boats of other fishermen, and with these, except
in very fine weather, they dare not venture very far from "the
seething harbour-bar;" and the moment they come home
with a quantity of fish the men consider their labours over,
the duty of turning the fish into cash devolving, as in all other
fishing communities, on the women. The young girls, or
"queans," as they are called in Fittie, carry the fish to market,
and the women sit there and sell them; and it is thought that
it is the officious desire of their wives to be the treasurers of
their earnings that keeps the fishermen from being more enterprising. The women enslave the men to their will, and
keep them chained under petticoat government. Did the
women remain at home in their domestic sphere, looking
after the children and their husbands' comforts, the men
would then pluck up spirit and exert themselves to make
money in order to keep their families at home comfortable
and respectable. Just now there are many fishermen who
will not go to sea as long as they imagine their wives have

got a penny left from the last hawking excursion. There is
no necessity for the females labouring at out-door work. There
are few trades in this country where industrious men have a
better chance to make money than fishermen have, especially
when they are equipped with proper machinery for their calling.   At Arbroath, Auchmithie, and Footdee (Fittie), the
fishing population are at the very bottom of the scale for
enterprising habits and social progress.   When the wind
is in any way from the eastward, or in fact blowing hard
from any direction, the fishermen at these places are very
chary about going to sea unless dire necessity urges them.

The people of "Fittie" are progressing in morals and
civilisation.   One of the local journalists who took the trouble
to visit the place lately, in order to describe truthfully what
he saw, says :—" They have the reputation of being a very
peculiar people, and so in many respects they are ; but they
have also the reputation of being a dirtily-inclined and de-
graded people, and this we can certify from personal inspection they are not.   We have visited both squares, and found
the interior of the houses as clean, sweet, and wholesome as
could well be desired.   Their white-washed walls and ceiling,
their well-rubbed furniture, clean bedding, and freshly-sanded
floors, present a picture of tidiness such as is seldom to be
met with among classes of the population reckoned higher in
the social scale.   And this external order is only the index
of a still more important change in the habits and character
of our fisher-toun, the population of which, all who know it
agree in testifying, has within the past few years undergone
a remarkable change for the better in a moral point of view.'
Especially is this noticed in the care of their children, whose
education might, in some cases, bring a tinge of shame to the
cheek of well-to-do town's folks.   Go down to the fisher
squares, and lay hold of some little fellow hardly able to
waddle about without assistance in his thick made-down

moleskins, and you will find he has the Shorter Catechism at his tongue-end. Ask any employer of labour in the neighbourhood of the shore where he gets his best apprentices, and he will tell you that for industry and integrity he finds no lads who surpass those from the fisher squares. Inquire about the families of the fishermen who have lost their lives while following their perilous occupation, and you will find that they have been divided among other families in the square, and treated by the heads of these families as affectionately as if they had been their own."

As regards the constant intermarrying of the fisher class, and the working habits of their women, I have read an Italian fable to the following effect:—" A man of distinction, in rambling one day through a fishing-village, accosted one of the fishermen with the remark that he wondered greatly that men of his line of life should chiefly confine themselves, in their matrimonial connections, to women of their own caste, and not take them from other classes of society, where a greater security would be obtained for their wives keeping a house properly, and rearing a family more in accordance with the refinement and courtesies of life. To this the fisherman replied, that to him, and men of his laborious profession, such wives as they usually took were as indispensable to their vocation as their boat and nets. Their wives took their fish to market, obtained bait for their lines, mended their nets, and performed a thousand different and necessary things, which husbands could not do for themselves, and which women taken from any other of the labouring classes of society would be unable to do. ' The labour and drudgery of our wives,' continued he, ' is a necessary part of our peculiar craft, and cannot by any means be dispensed with, without entailing irreparable injury upon our social interests.' MORAL.—This is one among many instances, where the solid and the useful must take precedence of the showy and the elegant."

As I have already mentioned, the fishers are intensely superstitious. No matter where we view them, they are as much given to signs and omens at Portel near Boulogne as at Portessie near Banff. For instance, whilst standing or walking they don't like to be numbered. Rude boys will sometimes annoy them by shouting—

> " Ane, twa, three ;
> What a lot o' fisher mannies I see !"

It is also considered very offensive to ask fisher-people, whilst on their way to their boats, where they are going to-day ; and they do not like to see, considering it unlucky, the impression of a very flat foot upon the sand ; neither, as I have already explained, can they go to work if on leaving their homes in the morning a pig should cross their path. This is considered a particularly unlucky omen, and at once drives them home. Before a storm, it is usually thought, there is some kind of warning vouchsafed to them ; they see, in their mind's eye doubtless, a comrade wafted home-ward in a sheet of flame, or the wraith of some one beckons them with solemn gesture landward, as if saying, " Go not upon the waters." When an accident happens from an open boat, and any person is drowned, that boat is never again used, but is laid up high and dry, and allowed to rot away— rather a costly superstition. Then, again, some fisher-people perform a kind of " rite " before going to the herring-fishery, in drinking to a " white lug "—that is, that when they " pree " or examine a corner or lug of their nets, they may find it glitter with the silvery sheen of the fish, a sure sign of a heavy draught.

But the fishermen of other coasts are quite as quaint, superstitious, and peculiar as those of our own. The residents in the *Faubourg de Pollet* of Dieppe are just as much alive to the signs and tokens of the hour as the dwellers in the square of Fittie, or those who inhabit the fishing quarter of Boulogne.

It is a pity that the guide-books say so little about these and
similar places.   The fishing quarter of Boulogne is not unlike
Newhaven : there is the same " ancient and fish-like smell,"
the same kind of women with a very short petticoat, the only
difference being that our Scottish fishwives wear comfortable

A FRENCH FISHWOMAN.

shoes and stockings.   We can see too the dripping nets hung
up to dry from the windows of the tumble-down-like houses,
and the *gamins* of Boulogne lounge about the gutter's side on
the large side stones, or run up and down the long series of
steps just the same as the fisher-folks' children do at home.
    It is only, however, by penetrating into the quaint villages
situated on the coasts of Normandy and Brittany, that we

can gain a knowledge of the manners and customs of those persons who are daily engaged in prosecuting the fisheries. The clergymen of their districts, as may be supposed, have great power over them, and all along the French coast the fisher-people have churches of their own, and they are constantly praying for "luck," or leaving propitiatory gifts upon the altars, as well as going pilgrimages in order that their wishes may be realised. A dream is thought of such great consequence among these people, that the women will hold a conference, early in the day, in order to its interpretation. Each little village has its storied traditions, many of them of great interest, and some of them very romantic. I can only briefly allude, however, to one of these little stories. Some of my readers may have heard of the Bay of the Departed on the coast of Brittany, where, in the dead hour of night, the boatmen are summoned by some unseen power to launch their boats and ferry over to a sacred island the souls of men who had been drowned in the surging waters. The fishermen tell that, on the occasion of those midnight freights, the boat is so crowded with invisible passengers as to sink quite low in the water, and the wails and cries of the shipwrecked are heard as the melancholy voyage progresses. On their arrival at the Island of Sein, invisible beings are said to number the invisible passengers, and the wondering awe-struck crew then return to await the next supernatural summons to boat over the ghosts to the storied isle, which was in long back days the chief haunt of the Druidesses in Brittany. A similar story may be heard at Guildo on the same coast. Small skiffs, phantom ones it is currently believed, may be seen when the moon is bright darting out from under the castle cliffs, manned by phantom figures, ferrying over the treacherous sands the spirits whose bodies lie engulphed in the neighbourhood. Not one of the native population, so strong is the dread of the scene, will pass the spot after nightfall, and strange stories are told of phantom lights and woeful demons that lure the unsuspecting wayfarer to a treacherous death.

The Parisian fishwives are clean and buxom women, like their sisters of Newhaven, and they are quite as celebrated if not so picturesque in their costume. About a century and a half ago—and I need not go further back—there were a great number of fishwives in Paris, there being not less than 4000 oyster-women, who pursued their business with much dexterity, and were able to cheat their customers as well, if not better than any modern fishwife. One of their best tricks was to swallow many of the finest oysters under the pretence of their not being fresh. Among the Parisian fishwives of the last century we are able to pick out Madame Picard, who was famed for her poetical talent, and was personally known to many of the eminent Frenchmen of the last century. Her poems were collected and published in a little volume, and ultimately by marriage this fishwife became a lady, having married a very wealthy silk merchant. The fishwives of Paris have long been historical: they have figured prominently in all the great events connected with the history of that city. A deputation from these market-women, gorgeously dressed in silk and lace, and bedecked with diamonds and other precious stones, frequently took part in public affairs. Mirabeau was a great favourite of the Parisian fishwives; at his death they attended his funeral and wore mourning for him. These Poissardes took an active part in the revolution of 1789, and did deeds of horror and charity that one has a difficulty in reconciling. It was no uncommon sight, for instance, to see the fishwives carrying about on poles the heads of obnoxious persons who had been murdered by the mob.

As I am on the subject of the foreign fisher-folk, I may as well say a few words more about the quaint eel-breeders of Comacchio, to whom I have already had occasion to allude. According to M. Coste, the social life of the people at Comacchio, who are engaged in the work of eel-culture, is very curious; but I think the industrial phase is so much mixed up with the social as to render the two inseparable. The community is in a sense—that is, so far as discipline is concerned —a military one, and strict laws are laid down for the conduct of the fishery. A large number of the men live in barracks, and observe the monkish rule of passive obedience. Each of the islands of the lagoon may be described as a small farm, having a chief cultivator, a few servants, a plentiful supply of the necessary implements of labour, its living-house, and its store for the harvest. It appears so natural to the people to suppose these stations to be farms, that they have from the very earliest times described the various basins as fields, just as if they were composed of earth instead of water ; and of these places there are no less than four hundred, the most important of them belonging to the state, the rest being private property. The government of the whole lagoon is exclusively in the hands of the farmer-general or his representative, who rents the fisheries from the Pope. There is a large body of men employed by him, who are divided into brigades, and whose business lies in the construction of the dykes, and in the management of the floodgates during the seeding of the lagoon, and the organisation of the labyrinths during the fishing-season. This cultivating brigade numbers about three hundred men ; the police brigade consists of one hundred and twenty persons ; and besides these there is an administrative brigade of one hundred individuals. A great deal of work has to be done by the persons employed, whether at the various farms, in the offices, or in the kitchen, for at Comacchio a large portion of the fish is cooked for the market. Upon each farm there are about twelve labourers, who live in a barrack under severe discipline, having all things in common. There is a master who exercises absolute power in his own domain; he is paid a salary of four scudi seventy-five baiocchi per month, with two and a half pounds of fish per day, and during summer-time, when the fish are scarce, he gets an additional allowance of money. The rate of wages at this place appears exceedingly small when contrasted with the payment of English labour. The wages of the learners or apprentices are exceedingly modest; they are remunerated with the "sair-won penny-fee" of 26s. per annum, in addition to their food! But then the poor people of Comacchio—the widow, the orphan, the aged and the infirm labourer—are all maintained at the expense of the community.

But it is right to mention also that a greater than a mere salaried interest in the labours incidental to the working of these fish-farms is kept up by the greater portion of the *employes* having a share of or commission on the produce, which in good years amounts to as much as twelve Roman ecus for each man. The captain is, of course, responsible in every way for his farm, both that the labour be properly carried on, and also for the moral conduct of the men under his charge, to whom he is bound to set a good example, as well of neatness in dress as activity in business.

Exiled in the valley which they cultivate, each family finds it necessary to devote its attention to those domestic offices so necessary for economy and comfort. The *vallanti* take in turn, as our soldiers do, the duty of cooking. They place the fish which they receive as a part of their wages in a common stock, to which is added such provision as the messenger may have brought from the town. When the cook has prepared the repast, they all sit down to table in one company, from the head man to the most humble servant; but although they mix thus promiscuously together, military etiquette is strictly observed—the foreman occupies the place of honour, having the under-foreman and the secretary by his side, next come the vallanti, and then the apprentices and cleaners. A benediction is then pronounced, after which the foreman serves out to each man his proper modicum of food, taking care to respect those rights of precedence which have been indicated. Eels, cooked upon the gridiron, form the staple of the repast, and the dinner is washed down with a little bosco-eli-esco wine. After dinner is over, the labourers return to their work. When evening arrives some remain awake all night, seated in arm-chairs, and others lie down in hard beds similar to those of the barracks. None of the *employes* of the valley are allowed to be absent from duty without a written permission, and heavy fines are exacted on any occasion of this rule being infringed. The discipline of each valley is the same, and one cannot conceive of a more monotonous life than that led by these humble fishermen, which season after season is ever the same, and goes on for years in one dull unvarying round. An unexpected tourist excites quite a commotion among the simple people, and they have great hopes that as the place becomes known to the outer world their prison life will ultimately be ameliorated.

The fish season is opened with great solemnity of prayer, and many of those other ceremonies of the church peculiar to Roman Catholic communities — one of which is the consecration of the lagoon. The labyrinths, which have been constructed from hurdles in each watery field (see plan in "Fish Culture") are crowded with fish, so that there is comparatively little trouble in the capture, and the salter waters of the sea being let in, the migratory instinct of the animal is excited, so that it becomes an easy prey to the fishermen. Upon the occasion of taking a great haul of fish in any particular valley, a gun is fired to announce the glad tidings to the other islanders, and next day a feast is held to celebrate the capture, which must, however, be of a certain amount.

The town of Comacchio is chiefly a long street of one-storied houses, situated on the principal island of the lagoon. There is a cathedral in the town, but it is entirely destitute of any architectural character, and there is a tower, from the top of which a good view of the lagoon and its various islands may be obtained; but in an industrial point of view the chief feature of the place is the great kitchen where the cure of the fish is carried on, one of the peculiarities of Comacchio being that a large portion of the eels are cooked before being sent to market. The kitchen where the eels are cooked is a large room containing a number of fireplaces ranged along one side. These fireplaces are about five feet square, and in front of each of them are hung six or seven spits on which the eels are impaled and roasted. The fire is placed on a low grate, and immediately below the spits is a trough or duct to catch the grease that drops from the eels while cooking. Before being roasted the fish undergo an operation. A workman seated before a block of wood, with a small hatchet in his hand, seizes the eels one by one and with great dexterity cuts off the head and tail, which are given to the poor, divides the body of the eel into several pieces of equal length according to its size, and throws them into a basket at his side. Each piece at the same time is slightly notched to facilitate the work of the next operator, who with equal skill and quickness puts the bits on the spit. It is only the large eels, however, that are decapitated and divided, the smaller ones are simply notched and stuck on the spit. The spits thus filled are next handed to the women in front of the fire. Two women are necessary for each fireplace : one regulates the fire ; the second looks after the roasting of the eels, which is the most important part of the labour, carefully shifting the spits from a higher to a lower position in front of the fire until the fish are properly done, when the spits are taken off by the woman, who places them aside for the next operation. This woman also attends to the grease that collects in the trough below the spits, and puts it in jars for future use. Besides these fireplaces, there are a number of furnaces fitted with large circular frying-pans,

which are exclusively attended to by men. All the fish for
which the spit is unsuitable are fried in these pans with a
mixture of the grease dropped from the eels and olive-oil.
They are exposed to the air for some time, even during very
warm weather, before being cooked. This operation renders
them fitter for preservation. The eels roasted on spits, and the
fish cooked in the frying-pans, are placed in baskets of open-
work to *dreep* and cool. They are then packed in barrels of
large and small sizes. The packing is carefully and regularly
done similar to the method of packing herrings. A mixture of
vinegar and salt is poured into the barrel before it is closed
up. The vinegar must be of the strongest, and the salt
employed is grey rock-salt instead of white salt. Previous
to exportation the barrels are branded with different letters
according to the nature of the fish contained in them.

Another method of preserving the fish is by salting. In
the room devoted to this operation is a raised quadrangular
space inclined so as to have a flow into a kind of ditch or
trough, similar to that which receives the grease from the eels
in the kitchen. On this raised space a layer of grey rock-salt
is spread, and upon this salt the eels are disposed, laid at full
length and closely squeezed together. Another layer of salt
is spread upon the eels, and then another layer of eels is
disposed crosswise on the first row, and so on until the pile is
sufficiently high. A layer of salt is spread on the top, which
is crowned by a board heavy with weights to press the fish
close together and prevent the air from penetrating into the
pile. The brine that exudes from the heap of fish and salt
flows into the trough already mentioned. When the fish are
considered to be well impregnated with the salt, which requires a period of twelve or fifteen days according to the size
of the eels, the fish are taken down and packed in barrels, the
same as the cooked eels, but without any liquid. There is a
third mode of preparation, which consists in first immersing

them for some time in the brine obtained from the above process of salting and then drying them. It is found necessary
to put them into this liquid when alive, as otherwise the
entrails would not absorb enough of salt to preserve them.
In order to render the operation still more effective, powdered
salt is introduced into the intestines by a wooden rod. After
this they are washed in lukewarm water, and then hung up to
dry below the ceiling of the kitchen or in a room somewhat
smoky. The eels dried in this manner become of a bronze
colour and are called smoked, a name which is also applied
to all the fish prepared by the drying process, although smoke
has nothing to do with the process. When the fish are destined for speedy consumption they are only half-dried. A
barrel of pickled eels contains one hundred and fifty pounds
weight, and costs a little more than ninety-seven francs. The
fish of Comacchio are sent to all parts of Italy, and in Venice,
Rome, and Naples they are greatly in demand.

As I have already indicated, the income obtained at
Comacchio from this one fish is something wonderful; labour
being so cheap, the profits are of course proportionately large.
The population of the lagoon is about seven thousand individuals, and, as I have endeavoured to show, their mode of
life is exceedingly primitive, the one grand idea being the
fishery, of the ingenuity and productiveness of which the
population are very proud.

The short and simple annals of the fisher-folk are all
tinged with melancholy—there is a skeleton in every closet.
There is no household but has to mourn the loss of a father
or a son. Annals of storms and chronicles of deaths form the
talk of the aged in all the fishing villages. The following narrative is a sample of hundreds of other sad tales that might
be collected from the coast people of Scotland. It was related
to a friend by a woman at Musselburgh :—" Weel, ye see, sir,
I hae'na ony great story till tell. At the time I lost my guid-

man I was livin' doon by at the Pans (Prestonpans, a fishing village). The herrin' season was ower aboot a month, and my guidman had laid by a guid pickle siller, and we had skytched oot a lot o' plans for the futur'. We had nae bairns o' oor ain, although we had been married for mony years ; but we had been lang thinkin' o' takin' in a wee orphint till bring up as oor ain ; and noo that the siller was geyan' plenty, we settled that Mairon M'Farlane should come hame till us by the beginnin' o' November. My guidman was thinkin' aboot buyin' a new boat, although his auld ane was no sae muckle the waur for wear. I was thinkin' aboot askin' the guidman for a new Sunday's goon ; in fac', we were biggin' castles in the air a' on the foundation o' the herrin' siller ; but hech, sir, it's ower true that man—ay, and woman tae—purposes, but the Great Almighty disposes. The wee orphint wasna till find a new faither and mither in my guidman and me ; the auld boat wasna till mak' room for a new ane ; and my braw Sunday goon, which, gin I had had my choice, would hae been a bricht sky-blue ane, was changed intae black—black as nicht, black as sorrow and as death could mak' it. There was a fine fishin' o' the haddies, and the siller in the bank was growing bigger ilka week, for the wather was at its best, and the fish plentifu'. Aweel, on the nicht o' the seventeent o' November, after I had put a' the lines in order, and gien Archibald his supper, aff he gangs frae the herbour wi' his boat, and four as nice young chiels as ye ever set an ee on for a crew. An' there wasna muckle fear o' dirty wather, although the sun had gaen doon rayther redder than we could hae wished. Some o' the new married, and some o' the lasses that were sune tae be married, used tae gang doon tae the herbour, and see their guidmen and their sweethearts awa'. I was lang by wi' that sort o' thing ; no that my love was less, but my confidence was mair, seein' that it had been tried and faund true through the lang period o' fourteen years. As I was

tidyin' up the hoose afore gangin' till my bed, I heard the
men in the boats cryin' till ane anither, as they were workin'
oot intae the firth. Tae bed I gaed, and lookin' at the low o'
the fire, as it keepit flichterin' up and deein' awa', sune set me
soond asleep. What daftlike things folks think, see, and dae
in their sleep. I dreamt that nicht that I was walkin' alang
the sands till meet my guidman, wha had landed his boat at
Morrison's Haven. The sun was shinin' beautifu', and the
waves were comin' tumlin' up the sand, sparklin' and lauchin'
in the sunlicht, dancin' as if they never did ony ill. I saw
my guidman at the distance, and I put my best fit forrit till
meet him. I was as near him as tae see his face distinckly,
and was aboot tae cry oot, 'Archibald, what sort o' fishin' hae
ye had?' when a' on a suddint a great muckle hand cam' doon
frae the sky, and puttin' its finger and thoom roond my guidman, lifted him clean oot o' my sicht jist in a meenit. The
fricht o' the dream waukened me, and I turned on my side
and lookit at whaur the fire ought tae be, but it was a' black-
ness. The hoose was shakin' as if the great muckle hand had
gruppit it by the gavel, and was shakin' it like a wunnelstraw.
Hech, sir, ye leeve up in a toon o' lands, and dinna ken what
a storm is. Aiblins ye get up in the mornin' and see a tree or
twa lyin' across the road, and a lum tummilt ower the rufe, and
a kittlin' or twa smoort aneath an auld barrel ; but bless ye,
sir, that's no a storm sic as we folk on the seaside ken o'.
Na, na ! The sky—sky ! there's nae sky, a' is as black as
black can be ; ye may put your hand oot and fill your nieve
wi' the darkness, exceppin' the times when the lichtnin' flashes
doon like a twisted threid o' purple gowd ; and then ye can
see the waves lookin' ower ane anither's heads, and gnashin'
their teeth, as ye micht think, and cryin' oot in their anger for
puir folk's lives. Siccan a nicht it was when I waukened.
My guidman had been oot in mony a storm afore, sae I comforted mysel' wi' thinkin' that he would gey and likely mak

for North Berwick or Dunbar when he saw the wather airtin'
for coorse. I wasna frightened, yet I couldna sleep for the
roarin' o' the wind. Mornin' cam'. I gaed doon till the shore,
and a' the wives and sweethearts o' the Pans gaed wi' me.
There was a heavy fog on the sea, sae thick that neither
Inchkeith nor the Law were to be seen. Naething was there
but the sea and the muckle waves lowpin' up and dashin'
themselves tae death on the rocks and the sands. Eastwards
and westwards we lookit, an' better lookit, but naething was
till be seen but the fog and the angry roaring sea—no a boat,
no a sail was visible on a' the wild waters. Weel, we had a
lang confab on the shore as tae what our guidmen and our
sweethearts micht aiblins hae dune. It was settled amang us
without a doot that they had gane intill North Berwick or
Dunbar, and sae we expeckit that in the afternoon they would
maybe tak' the road and come hame till comfort us. After
denner we—that is, the wives and sweethearts—took the gait
and went as far as Gosfort Sands till meet our guidmen and
the lads. The rain was pourin' doon like mad ; but what was
that till us ? we were lookin' for what was a' the world till our
bosoms, and through wind and weet we went tae find it, and
we nayther felt the cauld blast nor the showers. Cauldly and
greyly the short day fell upon the Berwick Law. Darker and
darker grew the gloamin', but nae word o' them we loo'd afore
a' the world. The nicht closed in at lang and last, and no a
soond o' the welcome voices. Eh, sir, aften and aften hae I
said, and sang ower till mysel', the bonny words o' poetry that
says—

> ' His very foot has music in't,
> As he comes up the stair.'

But Archibald's feet were never mair till come pap, pappin,
in at the door. Twa sorrowfu' and lang lang days passed awa',
and the big waves, as if mockin' our sorrow, flang the spars o'
the boats up amang the rocks, and there was weepin' and

wailin' when we saw them, or in the grand words o' the Book, there was 'lamentation and sorrow and woe.' We kent then that we micht look across the sea, but ower the waters would never blink the een that made sunshine around our hearths ; ower the waters would never come the voices that were mair delightfu' than the music o' the simmer winds when the leaves gang dancing till their sang. My story, sir, is dune. I hae nae mair tae tell. Sufficient and suffice it till say, that there was great grief at the Pans—Rachel weepin' for her weans, and wouldna be comforted. The windows were darkened, and the air was heavy wi' sighin' and sabbin'."

Resuming our tour, I may hint to the reader that it is well worth while, by way of variety, to see the fishing population of the various towns on the Moray Firth. Taking the south side as the best point of advantage, it may be safely said that from Gamrie to Portgordon there may be found many studies of character, and bits of land-, or rather sea-scape, that cannot be found anywhere else. Portsoy, Cullen, Portessie, Buckie, Portgordon, are every one of them places where all the specialities of fisher life may be studied. Buckie, from its size, may be named as a kind of metropolis among these ports ; and it differs from some of them inasmuch as it contains, in addition to its fisher-folk, a mercantile popu-lation as well. The town is divided and subdivided by means of its natural situation. There is Buckie-east-the-burn, New Buckie, Nether Buckie, Buckie-below-the-brae, Buckie-aboon-the-brae, and, of course, Buckie-west-the-burn. A curious system of "nicknames" prevails among the fisher-people, and most notably among those on the Moray Firth, and in some of the Scottish weaving villages as well. In all communications with the people their "to" (*i.e.* addi-tional), or, as the local pronunciation has it, "tee" names, must be used. At a public dinner a few months ago several of the Buckie fishermen were present ; and it was noticeable that the gentlemen of the press were careful, in their reports of the proceedings, to couple with the real names of the men the appellations by which they were best known—as "Mr. Peter Cowie, 'langlegs,' proposed the health, etc." So, upon all occasions of registering births, marriages, or deaths, the "tee" name must be recorded. If a fisherman be summoned to answer in a court of justice, he is called not only by his proper name, but by his nickname as well. In many of the fishing villages, where the population is only a few hundreds, there will not, perhaps, be half a dozen surnames, and the whole of the inhabitants therefore will be related "through-ither," as such intermixture is called in Scotland. The variety of nicknames, therefore, is wonderful, but necessary in order to the identification of the different members of the few families who inhabit the fishing villages. The different divisions of Buckie, for instance, are inhabited by different clans ; on the west side of the river or burn there are none but Reids and Stewarts, while on the east side we have only Cowies and Murrays. Cowie is a very common name on the shores of the Moray Firth ; at Whitehills, and other villages, there are many bearing that surname, and to distinguish one from the other, such nicknames as Shavie, Pinchie, Howdie, Doddlies, etc., are employed. In some families the nickname has come to be as hereditary as the surname ; and when Shavie senior crosses "that bourne," etc., Shavie junior will still perpetuate the family "tee" name. All kinds of circumstances are indicated by these names—personal blemishes, peculiarities of manner, etc. There is, in consequence, Gley'd Sandy Cowie, Gley'd Sandy Cowie, dumpie, and Big Gley'd Sandy Cowie ; there is Souples, Goup-the-Lift, Lang-nose, Brandy, Stottie, Hawkie, etc. Every name in church or state is represented —kings, barons, bishops, doctors, parsons, and deacons ; and others, in countless variety, that have neither rhyme nor reason to account for them.

As an instance of the many awkward *contretemps* which occur through the multiplicity of similar names in the northern fishing villages, the following may be recorded :—In a certain town lived two married men, each of them yclept Adam Flucker, and their individuality was preserved by those who knew them entitling them as Fleukie (Flounder) Flucker, and Haddie (Haddock) Flucker. Fleukie was blessed with a large family, with probable increase of the same, and cursed with a wife who ruled him like a despot. Haddie had possessed for many years a treasure of a wife, but prospect of a family there was none. Now these things were unknown to the carrier, who had newly entered on his office. From the store of an inland town he had received two packages, one for Haddie (a fashionable petticoat of the gaudiest red), and the other for Fleukie (a stout wooden cradle), to supply the place of a similar article worn out by long service. The carrier, in simplicity of ignorance, reversed the destination of the packages, which, of course, were returned to the inland merchant with threats of vengeance and vows never to patronise his store again.

Let the reader take, as an example of the quaint ways and absurd superstitions of the Moray Firth fisher-folk, the following little episode, which took place in the Small-Debt Court at Buckie, at the instance of a man who had been hired to assist at the herring-fishery, and who was pursuing his employer for his wages :—

On the case being called, the pursuer stated that he had been dismissed by the defender from his employment without just cause, indeed without any cause at all ; and the defender, on being asked what he had to say, at once admitted the dismissal, and to the great astonishment of the Sheriff, confessed that he had nothing to assign as a reason for it, except the fact that the pursuer's name was " Ross."

" Ye see, my Lord, I did engage him, though I was weel

tauld by my neibors that I sudna dee't, and that I cudna expect
te hae ony luck wi' him, as it was weel kent that 'Ross' was an
unlucky name. I thocht this was nonsense, but I ken better
noo. He gaed te sea wi' us for a week, and I canna say but
that he did's wark weel eneuch ; but we never gat a scale.
Sae the next week, I began to think there beet te be something in fat my neibors said ; sae upo' the Monday I wadna
tak' him oot, and left him ashore, and that very night we had
a gran' *shot;* and ye ken yersel', my Lord, that it wad hae been
ower superstishus to keep him after that, and sae I wad hae
naething mair te dae wi' him, and pat him aboot's business."

The Sheriff was much amused with this novel application
of the word "superstitious ;" but, in spite of that application,
he had no difficulty in at once deciding against the defender,
with expenses, taking occasion while doing so to read him a
severe lecture upon his ignorance and folly. The lecture,
however, has not been of much use, for I have ascertained
that the "freit" in question is still as rife as ever, and that
there is scarcely an individual among the communities of
white-fishers on the Banffshire coast who, if he can avoid it,
will have any transaction with any one bearing the obnoxious
name of "Ross."

I should now like to give my readers a specimen of
the patois or dialect spoken by the Moray Firth fisher-folk,
although it is somewhat difficult to do it effectively on paper ;
but I will try, taking a little dialogue between the fishermen
and the curer about a herring-fishing engagement as the best
mode of giving an idea of the language and pronunciation of
the Buckie bodies :—

SCENE—*A Curer's Office.* PRESENT—*The* CURER *and the
three* "SHAVIES."

Curer—Well, Shavie, ye've had a pretty good fishing this
year.

Shavie senior—Ou ay, it's been geyan gweed.

Shavie tertius—Fat did ye say, man ? gweed—it's nae been better than last.

Curer—Well, laddie, what was wrong with last year's fishing ?

Bowed Shavie—Weel awat, man, it was naething till brag o', an' fat's mair, I lost my beets at it ; ye'll be gaun till gie's a new pair neist fishin'.

Shavie senior—Ay, that was whan he *k*-nockit his *k*-nee again the boat-shore and brak his cweet.

Curer—Well, but lads, what about next fishing ?

Shavie senior—Ou, is't neist fishin' ye're wantin' till speak o' ?

Curer—Yes ; will you engage ?

Shavie junior—Fat are ye gaun till offer ?

Curer—Same as last.

Bowed Shavie—Fat d'ye say, man ?

Curer—Fourteen shillings a cran and fifteen pound bounty.

Shavie senior—Na, na, Maister Cowie ; that winna dee ava, man.

Bowed Shavie—We can get mair nor that at Fitehills.

Shavie junior—I'll be fuppit, lathie, if I dinna hae mair siller an' mair boonty tee.

Curer—Well, make me an offer.

Shavie senior—Ou ay, man ; we'll tak' saxteen shillin' the cran an' a boonty o' twunty pound, an' a pickle cutch, an' a drappie whisky ; an' that's ower little siller.

Curer—Well, I suppose I must give it.

Bowed Shavie—Gie's oor five shillin' then, an we're fixed wi' you an' clear o' a' ither body.

And so, on the payment of these five shillings by way of arles, the bargain is settled, and the men engaged for the next herring-season.

As will be inferred from these details, the fisher-folk, as a body, are not literary or intellectual. They have few books, and many of them never look at a newspaper. It is not surprising, therefore, that only one author has arisen among the fisher-people—Thomas Mathers, fisherman, St. Monance, Fifeshire. We have had many poets from the mechanic class, and even the colliers from the deep caverns of the earth have begun to sing. Mathers' volume is entitled, *Musings in Verse by Sea and Shore*. The following lines will at once explain the author's ambition and exhibit his style :—

> " I crave not the harp o' a Burns sae strong,
>   Nor the lyre o' a sweet Tannahill ;
> For those are the poets unrivalled in song,
> Can melt every heart, and inspire every tongue,
>   Frae the prince to the peasant, at will.

> " To weep wi' the wretched, the hapless to mourn,
>   To glow wi' the guid and the brave ;
> To cheer the lone pilgrim, faint and forlorn,
> Wi' breathin's that kindle and language that burn,
>   Is the wealth and the world I would crave."

The British fisher-people as a class are very sober and industrious, and they are becoming more intelligent, and, it is to be presumed, less superstitious. The children in the fishing villages are being educated; and in time, when they grow to man's and woman's estate, they will no doubt influence the fisheries for the better. Many of the seniors are now teetotal, and while at the herring-fishing prefer tea to whisky. The homes of some of the fisher-folks, on the Berwickshire and Northumberland coasts, are clean and tidy, and the proprietors seem to be in possession of a great abundance of good cheer.

It is, no doubt, considered by some to be an easy way to wealth to prosecute the herring or white fisheries, and secure a harvest grown on a farm where there is no rent payable, the seed of which is sown in bountiful plenty by nature, which requires no manure to force it to maturity, and no wages for its cultivation. But it is not all gold that glitters. There are risks of life and property connected with the fishery which are unknown to the industries that are followed on the land. There are times, as I have just been endeavouring to show, when there is weeping and wailing along the shore. The days are not always suffused in sunshine, nor is the sea always calm. The boats go out in the peaceful afternoon, and the sun, gilding their brown sails, may sink in golden beauty in its western home of rosy-hued clouds; but anon the wind will freshen, and the storm rise apace. The black speck on the distant horizon, unheeded at first, soon grows into a series of fast-flying clouds; and the wind, which a little ago was but a mere capful. soon begins to rage and roar, the waves are tossed into a wilder and wilder velocity, and in a few hours a great storm is agitating the bosom of the wondrous deep. The fishermen become alarmed; hasty preparations are made to return, nets are hauled on board, sails are set and dashed about by the pitiless winds, forcing the boats to seek the nearest haven. Soon the hurricane bursts in relentless fury; the fleet of fishing-boats toss wildly on the maddening waves; gloomy clouds spread like a pall over the scene; while on the coast the waters break with ravening fury, and many a strong-built boat is dashed to atoms on the iron rocks in the sight of those who are powerless to aid, and many a gallant soul spent in death, within a span of the firm-set earth. Morning, so eagerly prayed for by the disconsolate ones who have all the long and miserable night been watching from the land, at length slowly dawns, and reveals a shore covered with fragments of wood and clothes, which too surely indicate the disasters of the night. The *débris* of boats and nets lie scattered on the rocks and boulders, dumb talebearers that bring sorrow and chill penury to many a household. Anxious children and gaunt women—

> " Wives and mithers maist despairin' "—

with questioning eyes, rush wildly about the shore, piercing with their frightened looks the hidden secrets of the subsiding waters; and here and there a manly form, grim and stark and cold, cold in the icy embrace of death, his pale brow bound with wreaths of matted seaweed, gives silent token of the majesty of the storm.

CHAPTER XI.

—◆—

CONCLUDING REMARKS.

Are there more Fish in the Sea than ever came out of it ?—Modern Writers on
the Fisheries—Were Fish ever so abundant as is said ?—Salmon-Poaching
—Value of Salmon—Sea-Fish—Destruction of the Young—Is the demand
for Fish beginning to exceed the Supply ?—Evils of Exaggeration—
Fish quite Local—Incongruity of Protecting one Fish and not another—
Difficulties in the way of a Close-Time—Duties of the Board of White-
Fisheries—Regulation of Salmon Rivers—Justice to Upper Proprietors—
The one Object of the Fishermen—Conclusion.

THE idea of a slowly but surely diminishing supply of
fish is no doubt alarming, for the public have hitherto
believed so devoutly in the frequently-quoted proverb of
"more fish in the sea than ever came out of it," that it has
never, except by a discerning few, been thought possible to
overfish ; and, consequently, while endeavouring to supply
the constantly-increasing demand, it has never sufficiently
been brought home to the public mind that it is possible to
reduce the breeding stock of our best kinds of sea-fish to
such an extent as may render it difficult to re-populate those
exhausted ocean colonies which in years gone by yielded, as
we have been often told, such miraculous draughts. It is
worthy of being noticed that most of our public writers who
venture to treat the subject of the fisheries proceed at once to
argue that the supply of fish is unlimited, and that the sea is
a gigantic fish-preserve into which man requires but to dip his

net to obtain at all times an enormous amount of wholesome
and nutritious food.

This style of writing on the fisheries comes largely into
use whenever there is a project of a joint-stock fishing company placed before the public.   When that is the case
obscure little villages are pointed to as the future seats of
enormous prosperity, just because they happen to be thought
of by some enterprising speculator as the nucleus of a fishing
town ; and we are straightway told that Buckhorn or Kirk-
salt, or some equally obscure place, could be made to rival
those towns in Holland whose wealth and prosperity originated in even smaller beginnings.   We are likewise informed,
on the occasions of giving publicity to such speculations, that
" the sea is a liquid mine of boundless wealth, and that thousands of pounds might be earned by simply stretching forth
our hands and pulling out the fish that have scarcely room
to live in the teeming waters of Great Britain," etc. etc.   I
would be glad to believe in these general statements regarding
our food fisheries, were I not convinced, from personal inquiry,
that they are a mere coinage of the brain.   There are doubtless plenty of fish still in the sea, but the trouble of capturing them increases daily, and the instruments of capture have
to be yearly augmented, indicating but too clearly to all who
have studied the subject that we are beginning to overfish.   We
already know, in the case of the salmon, that the greed of man,
when thoroughly excited, can extirpate, for mere immediate
gain, any animal, however prolific it may be.   Some of the
British game birds have so narrowly escaped destruction that
their existence, in anything like quantity, when set against the
armies of sportsmen who seek their annihilation, is wonderful.

The salmon has just had a very narrow escape from extermination.   It was at one time a comparatively plentiful
fish, that could be obtained for food purposes at an almost
nominal expense, and a period dating eighty years back is

thought to have been a golden age so far as the salmon-fisheries were concerned.   But, in my opinion, it is more than questionable if salmon, or indeed any of our sea or river animals, ever were so magically abundant as has been represented.   At the time, a rather indefinite time, however—ranging from the beginning to the end of last century, and frequently referred to by writers on the salmon question—when farm-servants were compelled to eat of that fish more frequently than seemed good for their stomachs, or when the country laird, visiting London, ordered a steak for himself, with "a bit o' saumon for the laddie," and was thunderstruck at the price of the fish, we must bear in mind, as a strong element of the question, that there were few distant markets available ; it was only on the Tweed, Tay, Severn, and other salmon streams that the salmon was really plentiful.

No such regular commerce as that now prevailing was carried on in fresh salmon at the period indicated.   In fact, properly speaking, there was no commerce beyond an occasional dispatch to London per smack, or the sale of a few fish in country market-towns, and salmon has been known to be sold in these places at so low a rate as a penny or two-pence a pound weight.   Most of these fish, at the time I have indicated, were boiled in pickle, or split up and cured as kippers.   In those days there were neither steamboats nor railways to hurry away the produce of the sea or river to London or Liverpool ; it is not surprising, therefore, that in those good old times salmon could almost be had for the capturing.   Poaching—that is poaching as a trade—was unknown.   As I have already stated, when the people resident on a river were allowed to capture as many fish as they pleased, or when they could purchase all they required at a nominal price, there was no necessity for them to capture the salmon while it was on the beds in order to breed.   Farm-servants on the Tay or Tweed had usually a few poached fish, in the shape of a barrel of pickled salmon, for winter use. At that time, as I have already said in treating of the salmon, men went out on a winter night to " burn the water," but then it was simply by way of having a frolic. In those halcyon days country gentlemen killed their salmon in the same sense as they killed their own mutton—viz. for household eating ; there was no other demand for the fish than that of their own servants or retainers. Farmers kept their smoked or pickled salmon for winter use, in the same way as they did pickled pork or smoked bacon. The fish, comparatively speaking, were allowed to fulfil the instincts of their nature and breed in peace : those owners, too, of either upper or lower waters, who delighted in angling, had abundance of attractive sport ; and, so far as can be gleaned from personal inquiry or reading, there was during the golden age of the salmon a rude plenty of home-prepared food of the fish kind, which, even with the best-regulated fisheries, we can never again, in these times of increasing population, steam-power, and augmented demand, hope to see.

At present the very opposite of all this prevails. Farmers or cottars cannot now make salmon a portion of their winter's store : permission to angle for that fish is a favour not very easily procured, because even the worst upper waters can be let each season at a good figure ; and more than all that, the fish has become individually so valuable as to tempt persons, by way of business, to engage extensively in its capture at times when it is unlawful to take it, and the animal is totally unfit for food. A prime salmon is, on the average, quite as valuable as a Southdown sheep or an obese pig, both of which cost money to rear and fatten ; and at certain periods of the year salmon has been known to bring as much as ten shillings per pound weight in a London fish-shop ! There have been many causes at work to bring about this falling-off in our supplies ; but ignorance of the natural history of the fish, the want of accord between the upper and lower proprietors of salmon rivers, the use of stake and bag nets, poaching during close-times, and the consequent capture of thousands of gravid fish, as well as the immense amount of overfishing by the lessees of fishing stations, are doubtless among the chief reasons.

If these misfortunes occur with an important and indi- vidually valuable fish like the salmon, which is so well hedged round by protective laws, and which is so accessible that we can watch it day by day in our rivers—and that such misfortunes have occurred is quite patent to the world, indeed some of the best streams of England, at one time noted for their salmon, are at this moment nearly destitute of fish—how much more is it likely, then, that similar misfortunes may occur to the unwatched and unprotected fishes of the sea, which spawn in a greater world of water, with thousands of chances against their seed being even so much as fructified, let alone any hope of its ever being developed into fish fit for table purposes?   In the sea the larger fish are constantly preying on the smaller, and the waste of life, as I have elsewhere explained, is enor- mous : the young fish, so soon as they emerge from their fragile shell, are devoured in countless millions, not one in a thousand perhaps escaping the dangers of its youth.   Shoals of haddocks, for instance, find their way to the deposits of herring-spawn just as the eggs are bursting into life, or immediately after they have vivified, so that hundreds of thousands of these infantile fry and quickening ova are anually devoured.   The hungry codfish are eternally devouring the young of other kinds, and their own young as well ; and all throughout the depths of ocean the strong fishes are found to be preying on the weak, and a perpetual war is being waged for daily food, Reliable information, it is true, cannot easily be obtained on these points, it being so difficult to observe the habits of animals in the depths of the ocean; and none of our naturalists can inform us how long it is before our white fish arrive at maturity, and at what age a codfish or a turbot becomes repro-ductive ; nor can our economists do more than guess the per-centage of eggs that ripen into fish, or the number of these that are likely to reach our tables as food.

As has been mentioned in a previous chapter of this volume, the supply of haddocks and other Gadidæ was once so plentiful around the British coasts, that a short line, with perhaps a score of hooks, frequently replenished with bait, would be quite sufficient to capture a few thousand fish. The number of hooks was gradually extended, till now they are counted by the thousand, the fishermen having to multiply the means of capture as the fish become less plentiful. About forty years ago the percentage of fish to each line was very considerable. Eight hundred hooks would take about 750 fish ; but now, with a line studded with 4000 hooks, the fisherman sometimes do not take 100 fish. It was recently stated by a correspondent of the *John o' Groat Journal*, a newspaper published in the fishing town of Wick, that a fish-curer there contracted some years ago with the boats for haddocks at 3s. 6d. per hundred, and that at that low price the fishing yielded the men from £20 to £40 each season ; but that now, although he has offered the fishermen 12s. a hundred, he cannot procure anything like an adequate supply.

As the British sea-fisheries afford remunerative employ-ment to a large body of the population, and offer a favourable investment for capital, it is surely time that we should know authoritatively whether or not there be truth in the falling-off in our supplies of herring and other white fish. At one of the Glasgow fish-merchants' annual soirees, held a year or two ago it was distinctly stated that all kinds of fish were less abundant now than in former years, and that in proportion to the means of capture the result was less. Mr. Methuen reiterated such opinions again and again. "I reckon our fisheries," said this enterprising fish-merchant on one occasion, "if fostered and properly fished, a national source of wealth of more importance and value than the gold-mines of Australia, because the gold mines are exhaustible; but the living, propagating, self-cultivating gift of God is inexhaustible, if rightly fished by man, to whom they are given for food. It is evident anything God gives is ripe and fit for food. 'Have dominion,' not destruction, was the command. Any farmer cutting his ripe clover grass would not only be reckoned mad, but would, in fact, be so, were he to tear up the roots along with the clover, under the idea that he was thus obtaining more food for his cattle, and then wondering why he had no second crop to cut. His cattle would starve, himself and family be beggared, and turned out of their farm as improvident and destructive, who not only beggared themselves, but to the extent of their power impoverished the people by destroying the resources of their country. The farmer who thus destroys the hopes of a rising crop by injudicious farming is not only his own enemy, but the enemy of his country as well." Such evidence could be multiplied to any extent if it were necessary, but I feel that quite enough has been said to prove the point. It is a point I have no doubt upon whatever, and persons who have studied the question are alarmed, and say it is no use blinking the matter any longer—that the demand for fish as an article of food is not only beginning to exceed the supply, but that the supply obtained, combined with waste of spawn and other causes, is beginning to exceed the breeding power of the fish. In the olden time, when people only caught to supply individual wants, fish were plentiful, in the sense that no scarcity was ever experienced, and the shoals of sea-fish, it was thought at one time, would never diminish; but since the traffic became a commercial speculation the question has assumed a totally different aspect, and a sufficient quantity cannot now be obtained. Who ever hears now of monster turbot being taken by the trawlers?

Where are the miraculous hauls of mackerel that used to gladden the eyes of the fishermen? Where are now the waggon-loads of herring to use as manure, as in the golden age of the fisheries? I do not require to pause for the reply—echo would only mock my question by repeating it. Exhausted shoals and inferior fish tell us but too plainly that there *is* reason for alarm, and that we have in all probability broken at last upon our capital stock!

What then, if this be so, will be the future of the British fisheries? I have already, and more than once, in preceding pages, hinted my doubts of the existence of the enormous fish-supplies of former days; in my opinion the supposed plentifulness of all kinds of fish must in a large degree have been a myth, or at least but relative, founded in all probability on the fluctuating demand and the irregular supply. Were there not an active but unseen demolition of the fish-shoals, and were these shoals as gigantic as people imagine them to be, the sea would speedily become like stirabout, so that in time ships would not be able to sail from port to port. Imagine a few billions of herrings, each pair multiplying at the rate of thirty thousand per annum! picture the codfish, with its million ratio of increase; and then add, by way of enhancing the bargain, a million or two of the flat fish family throwing in their annual quota to the total, and figures would be arrived at far too vast for human comprehension. In fact, without some compensating balance, the waters on the globe would not contain a couple of years' increase! If fish have that tendency to multiply which is said, how comes it that in former years, when there was not a tithe of the present demand, when the population was but scant, and the means of inland carriage to the larger seats of population rude and uncertain, the ocean did not overflow and leave its inhabitants on its shores?

It seems perfectly clear that we have hitherto seriously

exaggerated the stock; it could never have been of the extent indicated, because then no draughts could have had any great effect, no matter how enormous they might have been. From various natural causes, some of which I have indicated in a former chapter, the stock has been kept in balance; and it seems now perfectly clear that by a course of fishing so excessive as that carried on at present, coupled with the destruction incidental to unprotected breeding, we must at all events speedily narrow if not exhaust the capital stock. We have done so in the case of the salmon; and the best remedy for that evil which has yet been discovered is cultivation—pisciculture, in fact—which science, or rather art, I have already treated of on its own merits. In ancient days the land yielded sufficient roots and fruits for the wants of its then population without cultivation; but as population increased and larger supplies became necessary, cultivation was tried, and now in all countries the culture of the land is one of the main employments of the people. The sea, too, must be cultivated, and the river also, if we desire to multiply or replenish our stock of fish.

As to the introduction of strange fishes, either sea or river, I for one will be glad to see them, if they are suitable. It would of course be a great misfortune to introduce any fish into our waters that would only become fat by preying on those fishes which are at present plentiful. Some naturalists think that the introduction of *Silurus* is a misfortune; I am not of that opinion, because in the kind of water suitable for the growth of *Silurus glanis* no other fish of any value is to be found, so that no ill could be done. The introduction into our British waters of another fish has been advocated—viz. the *Goorami*. It is a Chinese fish and has been introduced with great success into the Mauritius, and M. Coste is of opinion that it may be acclimatised in France, indeed he is trying the experiment. The Goorami, it seems, is a delicious fish, so far as its flavour is

concerned, and grows to a great size in a short time. I need
not say any more on this part of my subject. If the man is a
benefactor to his country who makes two blades of grass grow
where only one grew before, what shall be said of the man
who introduces to us a new food-fish?

Were we better acquainted with the natural history of fish,
it would be easy to regulate the fisheries. The everlasting
demand for sea-produce has caused the sea-fishing, like the
salmon-fishing, to be prosecuted at improper seasons, and fish
have been, indeed are daily, to a large extent, sold in a state
that renders them quite improper for human food. Another
cause of the constantly-lessening supplies may be also mentioned. Up till a recent period it was thought *all* fish were
migratory, and the reason usually assigned for unsuccessful
fishing was that the fish had removed to some other place!
Thus the fact of a particular colony having been fished up
was in some degree hidden, chiefly from ignorance of the
habits of the animal. This migratory instinct, so far as our
principal sea-fish are concerned, is purely mythical. The re-
discovery of the Rockall cod-bank must tend to dissipate these
old-fashioned suppositions of our naturalists. All fish are
local, from the salmon to the sprat, and each kind has its own
abiding-place. The salmon keeps unfailingly to its own
stream, the oyster to its own bank, the lobster to its particular
rock, and the herring to its own bay. Fishermen are beginning
now to understand this, and can tell the locality to which a
particular fish belongs, from the marks upon it. A Tay salmon
differs from a Tweed one, and Norway lobsters can be readily
distinguished from those brought from Orcadia. Then, again,
the fine haddocks caught in the bay of Dublin differ much
from those taken in the Firth of Forth, whilst Lochfyne herrings
and Caithness herrings have each distinct peculiarities.

In regard to the enormous waste of spawn which I have
chronicled, what more can I say? I have in various pages of

this work shown how fish-roe is wasted, and at the risk of censure for again repeating myself (I have already more than once done so purposely), I must once more ask attention to the millions of cod ova criminally wasted in the French sardine-fishery. I am presuming, in making this allusion, that cod are expressly caught with full roes for the purpose of supplying this bait. The English fishermen can hit on the sprat. shoals without a ground-bait ; surely the French fishermen can do what we do.

The regulation of the herring-fisheries (and the proper protection of the herring) is surrounded with innumerable difficulties, because of our scant knowledge of the natural history of the animal. I have already, and more than once, in the preceding pages of this work, alluded to the striking incongruity of protecting one fish during its spawning time, and yet making the same time in the life of another fish the legal period for its capture. But a close-time for the herring, from the fact of that fish breeding on some part of the coast all the year round, although not impossible, will be difficult to arrange. If, as is pretty certain, there be races of herring that breed in every month of the year, would it be advisable to shut up the fisheries ? and if, as some writers on the natural history of the herring assert, that fish only collects into shoals at the time it is called on to obey its procreative instinct, at what other period of its existence could it be captured, even admitting that at that time of its life it is least fitted to become the food of mankind ? True, we have only gone on fishing for herrings in a routine way at particular seasons of the year, and, were the experiment tried, we might hit on the shoals at a more congenial time. The shoals of particular districts—if, as I assume, the herring is very local—will have each their own spawning time, and there might be a few weeks' close season then—not so much to save the taking of the gravid fish, as to allow them a quiet interval, during which they might deposit their spawn.

The period of the herring's reproduction might, I think, be easily determined by constructing a sea-pond, where a few of these fish could breed, and the growth of the young fish be carefully watched.

In the case of the salmon there is no difficulty about a close-time, because we know the breeding seasons of each river ; but it would be difficult to divide the sea into compartments ; and even if we could, and a close-time were to be instituted, would not the strict logic of the position dictate that the close-time should be for the protection of the fish during their breeding season ?   But again, if it be granted that the breeding season is the only time that we can take the fish, would not such a close-time be practically putting an end to the fishing ?   It is a curious fact, as well as a curious fishing anomaly, that we have had a close-time for herrings on the west coast of Scotland but not on the east coast !   And I can trace no good that the close-time has accomplished ; it is not known that it increases the supply of fish, but it is known that a close-time impedes the prosecution of the other fisheries by depriving the poor men of a supply of bait.   The fishermen often use the herring as a bait for other fishes.

Although Scotland is the main seat of the herring-fishery, I should like to see statistics, similar to those collected in Scotland, taken at a few English ports for a period of years, in order that we might obtain additional data from which to arrive at a right conclusion as to the increase or decrease of the fishery for herring.   So far as the capture and cure of herrings are concerned, we have in Scotland, what ought to be in every country, an excellent fishery police.   The Hon. Mr. Bouverie Primrose, when giving evidence before a fishery commission, described the official duties of the Board of Scottish White-fish Fisheries as being :—" To give clearances to herring-fishery vessels going out to sea, and to receive

notices from curers on shore of their intention to cure ; to see
to the measures for the delivery of fresh herring, as between
buyer and seller ; to the size of the barrel for British white
cured herring, and to the quality of the cure, branding the
first quality, and collecting the fees for the same ; attending
on the exportation ; to inspect the exports in order to see that
they were in proper order ; preventing the use of such nets as
Parliament had declared to be illegal ; protecting the sprat
fishermen in their rights of boundary ; maintaining order on
the fishery grounds, and in connection therewith carrying out
the police regulations for naming and numbering boats and
their sails ; receiving and restoring lost fishing property ;
building fishery piers and harbours ; protecting the spawn of
herring and the herring-fisheries generally, according to Act
of Parliament ; maintaining herring close-time as fixed and
appointed by Parliament ; furnishing returns and statistics of
the herring-fisheries of Scotland and the Isle of Man, and aiding in maintaining the fishery convention with France.   The
functions of the Board extended over the whole coast of Scotland, and in regard to statistics to the Isle of Man, and in
respect to the branding of herring over the northern portion
of the coast of Northumberland."

    Might not the functions of the Board be so extended as to
embrace a statistical inquiry into the capture of haddocks, cod,
and ling (other than those to be cured), turbot, etc., in Scotland?
We all agree heartily enough in Scotland with the Board's
functions of harbour improvement and fishery police, and we
do not grudge, therefore, in any degree, the £15,000 which are
expended for its maintenance.   Scotland gets so small a
portion of the public money in proportion to what it con-
tributes to the revenue that no one would desire to see it
deprived of this small grant.   The only question connected
with it is its proper expenditure.   I object entirely to a
portion of the duties of the Board—i.c. certifying the quality

of the cure. Government might as well step in to certify the manufacture of Dunlop cheese or Glasgow cotton. True, the brand has now to be paid for, and moreover is not at all compulsory, so that curers may trade on their own name if they please, and it is satisfactory to think that they are now doing so in an annually increasing degree.

The salmon-fisheries may be left to their proprietors ; the county gentlemen, and others who own salmon-fisheries, seem now to be thoroughly alive to the great danger of overfishing, which has hitherto been the bane of this valuable animal. The chief requisites for a great salmon river and a series of healthy and productive fisheries are—first, a good spawning ground and a provision for the fish attaining it with the least possible trouble ; second, a long rest during the spawning season ; as also, third, a weekly close-time of many hours. To insure protection to the eggs and to the young fish during the tenderest period of their lives, I would have, as an aid to the natural spawning-beds, artificial breeding-ponds and egg-boxes on every large river ; and it would be well if the proprietors of all our larger salmon streams would agree to work their fisheries, as was long ago proposed, on the plan of a joint-stock company, the shares to be allocated on some equitable plan so that both lower and upper proprietors would share in the produce of the river. It is needless to point out to owners of salmon properties the advantages and saving that would at once accrue from such a mode, and such a plan would especially be the best way of settling the existing differences betwen the upper and lower holders. It was well said by the Commissioners appointed to inquire into the salmon-fisheries of England and Wales, that " it has been found by experience in all the three countries that the surest way to increase the stock is to give the upper proprietors an interest in preserving them. The upper waters are, in fact, the nursery of the fish ; it is there that the breeding operations take place, it is there that the wasteful destruction committed by poachers and depredators, if suffered to have their way, is carried on. It lies with those to whom the rights of fishing, and the lands adjacent to those parts of the streams belong, either to permit the ruinous waste of the breeding fish to go on, or to take measures for protecting them. They cannot take either course without in the one case conferring a benefit, and in the other permitting an injury, to all the parties lower down. But it is almost needless to say that they *will* not make exertions or incur expense to preserve the fish, unless encouraged to do so by being allowed to reap some share of the produce of the waters."

The laws of Scotland as to her salmon rivers are confessedly defective—confessed by the constant efforts to amend them, often ending in only making them worse. This will be eternal if some attempt be not made to act according to the reason of the thing; clearing the ground, and starting on a new and rational principle, instead of tinkering or trying to tinker what is past mending, and never ought to have been. Rivers are subjects entirely different in their nature from lands. A man, having secured a patch of land, may (as is generally understood) do anything he pleases with what he calls "his own" but render it a nuisance. This is wrong; for his obligation to the country, if not to himself, is to use it to the best advantage for the public good. As to rivers, this obligation is more distinct. They are more of the nature of public property, both as regards the public generally and those holding property on their banks and so having private interests in them. No man at the mouth of a river has any moral or legal right to stop the fish from ascending to their breeding-places. This, clear as it may seem, is not generally recognised, and hence the loss to the country, and misery to the useful and valuable animals bred in them, or that might be bred in them, from the ignorant and reckless self-seeking of some, and the negligence or pointed disregard of all interests displayed by others.

I have not in the course of this work intruded many of my own theories as to fish and fishing upon the reader ; but I have not been studying the subject for fifteen years without theorising a little, and when the proper time comes I shall have a great deal more to say about the natural history of our food-fishes than I have said in the present volume. In the meantime I am anxious, as regards the whole of the sea fisheries, to inculcate the duty of obtaining more and better statistics than we have ever yet collected.

Our great farm, the sea, is free to all—too free ; there is no seed or manure to provide, and no rent to pay. Every adventurer able to procure a boat may go and spoliate the shoals; he need have no care for the growth or preservation of animals which he has been taught to think inexhaustible. In one sense it is of no consequence to a fisherman that he catches codlings instead of cod ; whatever size the fish may be, they yield him what he fishes for—money. What if all the herrings he captures be crowded with spawn ? what if they be virgin fish that have never added a quota to the general stock ? That is nothing to the fisherman so long as they bring him money. Our free unregulated fisheries are a thorough mistake. If a fisherman having a capital of £500 in boats, nets, etc., had invested in a breeding-farm, how would he act ? Would he not earn his living and increase his capital by allowing his animals to breed ? and certainly he would never cut down oats or wheat in a green state. But the fish-farmers do all these things, and the Fishery Board stamps them with approval. We must look better into these matters ; and I would crave the expenditure by government of a few thousand pounds definitely to settle, by well-devised experiments, such points in the natural history of the herring and other white fish as clog the prosecution of these particular fisheries. Surely it would not be difficult, as already suggested, to construct a sea-pond, where we could observe fish-spawn from the time of its deposit till the period at which it quickened into life; we could then note the growth of the fish, and so fix beyond cavil the period at which our most important food fishes become reproductive. We want a Fisheries Reform Bill. The time has arrived when the existing laws which govern the British fisheries should be codified and made harmonious; or better still, be repealed in favour of some comprehensive measure that would at once protect the fish, render fish-food more accessible to the public, and guide fishermen into more intelligent methods of working than they at present adopt. What is chiefly needed is a speedy abolition or reconciliation of the many anomalies that en-cumber our knowledge of the industry of the sea, as also a superintending head to administer the laws; overlook the collection and tabulation of statistics; and generally to re-construct, or improve, the economy of our fisheries. In addition to the Scottish Fishery Board we have various fishery inspectors connected with the Board of Works in Ireland—we have inspectors or commissioners of salmon fisheries in England, also of oyster fisheries; but is it not a waste of power to have so many boards? A more con-centrated and responsible authority should preside over an industry so important; and if we are to have the full ad-vantage of the enormous food supply that may be derived from the sea, let us have only one board to watch over and bring into a focus that which we have only the trouble of reaping—which costs us nothing to cultivate, but which is one of the mainstays of the country, namely, the harvest of the sea.

APPENDIX.

—◆—

I. OBSERVATIONS ON FISH-GUANO.

" THE importance of this field of industry has been fully appreciated in France, and a factory has been established at Concarneau, in the department of Finisterre. A full report of a visit to the factory having been made by the distinguished chemist M. Payen, and the well-known agriculturist M. Pommier, to the French Agricultural Society, we purpose presenting our readers with the chief points contained in that report, in the hope that another year may not pass over without some attempt of the like kind being made upon our coasts.

" The experiments which led to the establishment of the factory, of which we are now to speak, were made by a M. de Molon, and have extended over a period of four years. On several occasions he had employed the offal obtained in the preparation of sardines, on the coast of Brittany, to manure his land in Finisterre. The results which he obtained led him to imagine that this offal, and a multitude of marine fish of little commercial value, might furnish an important resource to agriculture. This fact, observed since a long time, especially in countries where deep-sea fishing is a permanent industry, was not new ; but such a manure was by its very nature restricted to the agriculture of the coasts—fish or fish-offal not being capable of being economically transported more than short distances. It is also evident that these materials should be immediately employed—that they are not susceptible of preservation, and that the manure not admitting of being applied to the soil, except at certain seasons, it must at once be evident that the employment of fish-offal, spite of its richness in fecundating elements, could never be generalised, or offer large resources to agriculture.

" M. de Molon, however, conceived that a far vaster and more advantageous agricultural resource might be drawn from this inexhaustible wealth of the ocean, by so treating the offal of the coast fisheries, and the immense quantities of common fish which are of no use to the fishermen, as to ensure their preservation, concentrate their fecundatory properties, and render them as transportable as Peruvian guano—to do, in fine, what we have shown to be practicable in our former article.

" M. de Molon made a number of experiments from this point of view, and finally settled upon this plan : To boil the fish ; to extract as much as possible of the water and oil which they contain ; dry them and reduce them to powder. After he had obtained this powder in a perfectly dry state he had it analysed, first by M. Moride, at Nantes ; then at Rennes, by M. Malaguti ; and finally, by M. Payen, in Paris.

" These analyses, several times repeated, yielded as a mean the following percentage as results :—

Water	1·00
Nitrogenous organic matter	80·10
Soluble salts, consisting principally of chloride of sodium, carbonate of ammonia, and traces of sulphate . .	4·50
Phosphate of lime and magnesia	14·10
Carbonate of lime	0·06
Silica	0·02
Magnesia and loss	0·22
	100·00

" In other words, these repeated analyses indicate that dried fish-powder would contain about—

12 per cent of nitrogen, and
14 ,, of bone earth—

that is to say, it would be nearly as rich as the best Peruvian guano. (According to the results of analyses made on herrings, an average manure made from that fish, and containing 10 per cent of water, would contain about 13½ per cent of nitrogen, and between 11 and 12 per cent of bone earth. The small fish containing but little bone earth accounts for the difference in both cases.) To the scientific analysis M. de Molon wished to add the sanction of practice ; he applied 400 kilogrammes (880·8 lbs.) per hectare (2 acres, 1 rood, and 35 perches), or 3 cwts. 0 qr. 20 lbs. per statute acre, of the fish-powder, half in autumn and half in spring, as a top-dressing to wheat. The results which he obtained were so evident that his doubts were dissipated, his conviction became full and entire, and he resolved to make every effort to discover a means of rendering as economical as possible the manufacture of a manure equally powerful, and which should advantageously compete with Peruvian guano.

"Having made his calculations, his ideas were at once directed to Newfoundland, where the produce of the cod-fishery in a fresh condition amounts to more than 1,400,000 tons annually.

"The cod, previous to being salted and dried, is deprived of its head, its intestines, and the backbone, which together make about one-half of its total weight. This offal, which amounts to at least 700,000 tons, is thrown into the sea, or is lost without utility.

"In 1850 M. de Molon fitted out a vessel, and confided his project to one of his brothers, furnishing him with the utensils necessary to experiment upon and manufacture the fish-powder. The results of this voyage confirmed his anticipations, and M. de Molon junior brought back to France a certain quantity of fish-manure, which was found to be identical in composition with that manufactured in France.

"In 1851 M. de Molon junior again departed for Newfoundland, taking with him all the means of manufacturing, the materials necessary to construct a factory, and houses for one hundred and fifty workmen, whom he also took with him ; finally, all the means necessary to found a permanent establishment. He fixed himself at Kerpon, at the extremity of the island, near the Strait of Belle-isle, on a creek which was visited every year by a great number of fishing vessels, and whose shores abound in fish. At present this establishment is in regular work, and has, we believe, sent within the last two or three months a considerable quantity of fish-manure to France.

"Whilst his younger brother was thus establishing himself in Newfoundland, M. de Molon wished to have in France an establishment of the same kind placed immediately under his own eyes, which would serve to perfect the process of manufacture, and offer to all the practical confirmation of facts, the importance of which hád loñg since been indelibly fixed upon his own mind. It was at this epoch that M. de Molon associated himself with a M. Thurnyssen, who understood the vast field of enterprise which was thus opened up.

"This factory was erected by them at Concarneau, between Lorient and Brest, in the department of Finisterre. This is a mere fishing village, not far from the town of Quimper, containing scarcely two thousand inhabitants, and built upon a rock in the middle of a bay formed by the ocean. The catching and preparation of the sardine, which employs about three hundred to four hundred boats annually, is almost the only industry of the district, if we except a factory for the manufacture of iodine.

"The factory of MM. de Molon and Thurnyssen is placed at the end of the port, and the boats come and discharge their fish under its walls. In its actual condition this factory is capable of manufacturing daily about 4 to 5 tons of fish-manure, in a perfectly dry condition, which represents 16 to 20 tons of fish or of fish-offal in its fresh state. The proprietors receive all the offal of the curing-houses of Concarneau and those of Lorient; and in addition all the coarse fish which were previously thrown into the sea, or which were even abandoned on the very quays of Concarneau, to the great detriment of public health.

"The factory is entirely constructed of deal planks—that is to say, with all the economy possible, and contains the following articles of plant : A steam-engine of ten-horse power, and a boiler of eighteen-horse power; two boiling-pans à la bascule, with steam-jackets for boiling the fish at the temperature of a water bath; twenty-four screw presses to press the material when boiled ; a rasp exactly similar to those employed in beet-sugar factories ; a large stove ; a Chaussenot's coccle-furnace, for heating the stove ; a conical iron mill, similar to a coffee-mill.

"The following is the mode of employing these various utensils : The fish or the offal is introduced by the upper part of the boiling-pans into the interior, one of which is capable of containing about 10 cwts., and the other from 16 cwts. to one ton. The vessel is then hermetically closed, and steam of about 50 to 55 lbs. pressure admitted into the steam-jacket, the steam-room of which is about two inches wide, and into a tube nearly eight inches in diameter, placed vertically in the interior of the pan. The boiling is completed in an hour; then by a simple movement the pan may be made to swing upon its bearings, the steam allowed to escape, and the cover being removed, the boiled fish is allowed to fall into a receptacle. Workmen then convey it in baskets to the presses placed alongside the boilers.

"The great difficulty was to find a means of submitting this fish-magma to the action of the press without losing the fine portions. This was accomplished in this way: Under each of the presses is placed a cylinder of sheet iron open at both ends, about twenty inches high, and twelve inches in diameter. This cylinder is strengthened by four small iron rings or hoops, and is pierced with a number of very fine holes. A loose bottom or wooden plate is fitted into this cylinder, which is then nearly filled with the boiled fish, and upon this is laid another plate of wood similar to the bottom. One or two blocks are then laid upon this cover, and when all the cylinders are filled, a man turns alternately the screw of each press. In proportion as the pressure operates, the water and oil contained in the fish is seen to exude from the perforations of the cylinder. These liquids flow into gutters which conduct them to a common channel by which they flow into barrels placed underneath, and so graduated that when the first is filled, the overflow passes into the second, and so on in succession, without the intervention of any workman. After reposing for some time, the oil floats on the surface, and is collected and stored in barrels in the cellar. The average quantity of fish-oil thus extracted represents very nearly $2\frac{1}{2}$ per cent of the fresh fish.

"When the boiled mass is sufficiently pressed, the presses are loosened, and the cylinders removed and turned upside down, close to the reservoir, to allow any liquid which may have mounted to the surface to flow away; on then tapping the bottom wooden plate, the pressed mass may be taken out of the cylinder in the form of two compact cakes about four inches in thickness. These cakes are immediately conveyed by a workman to the hopper of the rasp, placed close at hand; this rasp, set in motion by the steam-engine, reduces the cakes to a sort of pulp, which is carried by children as fast as formed to the stove.

"The stove, situate on the first floor, is externally 20 metres

long (65 feet 7½ inches), and 5 metres (16 feet 5 inches, nearly)
wide ; it is divided lengthwise into five chambers, 85 centimetres
(2 feet 9½ inches, nearly) wide. Each of these chambers contains
in its length twenty frames or trays, 1 metre (3 feet 3¼ inches) long,
and 85 centimetres (2 feet 9¼ inches, nearly) wide, having a bottom
of coarse linen. These trays rest upon two bars, which run the
whole length of the chamber. Five series of such trays are super-
imposed in each chamber, which makes one hundred in each
chamber, or five hundred in the whole stove. At each end of these
chambers is a number of openings, which can be closed by a door ;
each opening corresponds with a series of trays.

" When the rasped fish-cake is put upon a frame, it is introduced
into the stove through one of the openings just mentioned ; a second
is then introduced, which causes the first to slide along the bars ;
then a third, and so on until twenty have been placed. The second
series of trays is then introduced in the same way by the opening
next above. The operation is proceeded with in this way until the
five series are introduced into each of the five chambers. It takes
about two hours to two hours and a half to fill the stove with the
five hundred trays which it is capable of receiving.

" A current of air heated by the coccle-oven of Chaussenot to a
temperature of from 140° to 158° Fahr., circulates through the five
chambers, according as each is filled with the trays of fish, the
draft being maintained by a chimney.

" As soon as the last tray is introduced into the stove, the first
is fit to be withdrawn. This is effected in the simplest manner ; a
child placed at one extremity of the stove introduces a tray freshly
charged, this pushes without any effort the whole series ranged
upon the bars, and causes the last in the series at the lower end of
the stove to slide out, where it is received by another child ; a fresh
tray is again introduced, and another is pushed out, and so on for
the whole stove. In this way the action of the stove is constant,
being filled as fast as it is emptied, without the workpeople being
exposed to the action of the heat, and without suffering in the least
from it, and being nevertheless able to communicate to one another
the details of the work, the chambers acting as conductors for the
voice.

" This stove constitutes one of the most important features in the system of M. de Molon ; it dries rapidly, regularly, and with comparatively small expenditure of heat, since 100 kilogrammes (220 lbs.) of coal a day are sufficient for heating the coccle ; and the continuity of its action is perfect.

" According as the dried fish is withdrawn from the chambers it is thrown into a heap, on a board close by, from which it is put with a shovel into the mill-hopper by a child.   The mill reduces it to a sufficiently fine and perfectly dry powder, which is at once put in sacks or casks, and sealed in order that there may be no means of adulterating it.

" To any one acquainted with the processes and machinery employed in the manufacture of beet-sugar, it will at once be evident that the organisation of the process just described was the result of an acquaintance with that manufacture.   This is another instance of the benefits conferred upon France by the beet-sugar industry, for to that branch of manufacture it may be truly said to owe the rise of its present manufacturing system.   A branch of industry requiring a combination of chemical and mechanical skill carried on in the midst of a rural population, especially if connected with agriculture, has far more influence upon the permanent prosperity of a people materially and intellectually, than the greatest branch of industry entirely confined to the civic population.

" To carry on all the operations just described, only six men are employed at Concarneau, who receive about 1s. a day, and ten children, who receive from sixpence to sevenpence.   Under those conditions, and without working at night, this factory is capable, as we have already remarked, of producing from four to five tons of dry manure a day, representing about eighteen to twenty tons of fish or offal ; that is, one hundred parts of fresh fish yield about twenty-two parts of fish-powder.   By working at night, which will be done during the ensuing year, when the fishery shall have been better organised, this establishment will be able to produce from eight to ten tons of manure.   M. de Molon estimates the number of days in the year during which the fishermen could fish at from 200 to 250.   In only counting 200 working days, the establishment at Concarneau could thus produce from 1600 to 2000 tons of manure annually, which, at the rate of three cwts. per statute acre, would suffice to manure from 10,000 to 13,000 acres of land, and would represent, at 22 per cent of dried manure, a fishing of 9000 to 10,000 tons. The sardine-fishery and the offal of the curing-houses, formerly lost, would furnish about one-half of that quantity ; but M. de Molon has pointed out a fact from which would appear to result the incontestable facility of obtaining at Concarneau far greater quantities of fish than those mentioned above, by the fishery of the coal-fish, which is sometimes found in immense quantities on the coast, but which the fishermen do not often take, as they could find no sale for them.

"The factory of Concarneau, with the organised fishery which M. de Molon intends to establish (sixty to seventy-eight well-equipped boats), and by doubling its present plant, which is also intended, will quadruple the quantity of dry manure which is now produced in working only ten hours per day.

"In addition to the 180 kilogrammes of coal burned in heating the stove, we may add that 130 more (286½ lbs.) are consumed by the steam-engine, making a total of 230 kilogrammes, or little more than four and a half cwts., or about one cwt. of coal to one ton of manure.

"The fish-manure fetches about 8s. per cwt. in the locality, and is eagerly sought after by the farmers, who expect the most signal results to agriculture from the extension of the manufacture ; while the oil which, as already remarked, constitutes about 2½ per cent of the raw fish, would be worth from 3s. to 3s. 4d. per gallon. These figures show at once that the manufacture must be profitable—a fact which is fully guaranteed by Messrs. Payen and Pommier, who, as a commission sent from the Agricultural Society in order to report upon the project, had the privilege of examining the books of the concern, and of thus satisfying themselves of its com-mercial success.

"The factory of Concarneau, as we have already noticed, was only founded in order to serve as a model, not alone for those which may be established on different points of the French coast, but also in foreign countries. In addition to the factory established under the superintendence of M. de Molon junior, in Newfoundland, and which in its actual condition is capable of furnishing from 8000 to 10,000 tons of manure annually, it is proposed to establish others on the same coast, and also on the coasts of the North Sea, on such a

scale as will furnish sufficient manure to completely replace the
guano now imported from Peru.

" When we recollect what a large amount of offal has hitherto
been wasted upon our coasts, the vast quantity of coarse fish which
have been rejected and thrown again into the sea ; but above all,
when we consider the enormous extent of ocean, teeming with animal life, which has contributed so little to the sustenance of mankind, we cannot help thinking that at Concarneau has been laid the
foundation of a great branch of industry, which is destined to reno-
vate the worn-out soils of the richly-populated countries of Europe."

II. LIST OF AUTHORITIES.

HAVING been frequently asked by correspondents for a list of
the chief authorities on fish, I beg to subjoin the titles of a few
of the works I have had occasion to consult while preparing this
volume :—

A Review of the Domestic Fisheries of Great Britain and Ireland, by
    Robert Fraser, Esq. Edinburgh, 1818.
A Short Narrative of the Proceedings of the Society appointed to manage
    the British White Herring Fishery, etc., by Thos. Cole. London,
    1750.
A Treatise on Food and Diet, by Jonathan Pereira, M.D., etc., 1843.
    London : Longman and Co.
A Treatise on the Management of Fresh-Water Fish, by Gottlieb
    Boccius, 1841. London : Van Voorst.
An Account of the Fish-Pool, etc., by Sir. Richard Steell. London,
    1718.
An Account of Three New Specimens of British Fishes, by Richard
    Parnell, 1837. Royal Society, Edinburgh.
An Essay towards a Natural History of the Herring, by James Solas
    Dodd, Surgeon. London, 1752.
Angler's and Tourist's Guide, by Andrew Young, Invershin, 1857.
    A. and C. Black, Edinburgh.
British Fish and Fisheries. Religious Tract Society.
Ceylon, Notes on, by James Steuart, Esq. of Colpetty. Printed for
    Private Circulation, 1862.
Couch's Fishes of the British Islands, 1865. Groombridge.
Directions for Taking and Curing Herrings ; and for Curing Cod, Ling,

Tusk, and Hake, by Sir Thomas Dick Lauder, Bart. Edinburgh 1846.

Elements de Pisciculture, par M. Isidore L'Amy. Paris, 1855.

Evidence of the Royal Commission on the operation of the Acts relating to Trawling for Herring on the Coasts of Scotland. Presented to both Houses of Parliament by command of Her Majesty. 1863.

Experimental Observations on the Development and Growth of Salmon Fry, etc., by John Shaw, 1840. Edinburgh : A. and C. Black.

Fish and Fishing in the Lone Glens of Scotland, by Dr. Knox, 1854. Routledge and Co.

Fish-Hatching, by Frank T. Buckland, 1863. Tinsley Brothers.

Fisheries, The, considered as a National Resource, etc., 1856. Milliken, Dublin.

Forrester's Fish and Fishing in the United States, 1864. Townsend, New York.

Guide du Pisciculture, par J. Remy, 1854. Paris : Lacroix.

Guide Pratique du Pisciculture, par Pierre Carbonnier, 1864. Paris : Lacroix.

Herring-Fishery, on the Existing State of the, 1854. Herald Office, Aberdeen.

Howitt's Angler's Manual, 1808. Liverpool.

Ichthyonomy, 1857. Swinnerton and Brown, Macclesfield.

Illustrated London Almanac, 1864. London.

Irish Quarterly Review. W. B. Kelly, Dublin.

L'Alienation des Rivages, par M. Coste. Paris, 1863.

La Pêche en Eau Douce et en Eau Salée, par Alphonse Karr, 1860. Paris : Michel Levy Freres.

Letter to a Member of Parliament recommending the Improvement of the Irish Fishery. Dublin, 1729.

Multiplication Artificelle des Poissons, par J. P. J. Koltz. Paris : Lacroix.

Natural History and Habits of the Salmon, etc., by Andrew Young, 1854. Longman and Co.

Natural History of the Salmon, as ascertained at Stormontfield. By William Brown, 1862. Glasgow : Thomas Murray.

Naturalist's Library, by Sir William Jardine, 1843. Edinburgh.

Notice Historique sur L'Etablissement de Pisciculture de Huningue, 1862. Strasbourg : Berger Levrault.

Note sur les Huitrieres Artificelles de Terrains Emergents, par M. Coste. Paris.

Observations on the Fisheries of the West Coast of Ireland, etc., by Thomas Edward Symons, 1856. London : Chapman and Hall.

Oyster, The, where, how, and when to find, breed, cook, and eat it. Trubner and Co.

Pisciculture, Pisciculteurs, et Poissons, par Eugene Voel, 1856. Paris : F. Chamerot.

Pisciculture et la Production des Sangsues, par Auguste Jourdier, 1856. Paris : Hatchette and Co.

Pisciculture et Culture des Eaux, par P. Trigneaux. Paris : Libraire Agricole de la Maison Rustique.

Pisciculture Pratique et sur l'Eleve et la Multiplication des Sangsues, par Quenard, 1855. Paris : De Dusacq.

Propagation of Oysters, by M. Coste and Dr. Kemmerer. Brighton, 1864. Pearce.

Proposals for Printing by Subscription a Complete Natural History of Esculent Fish, etc., by James Solas Dodd.

Report by the Commissioners for the British Fisheries of their Proceedings in the Year ended 31st December 1862, being the Fishing of 1862.

Ditto for the years 1863-64.

Reports of the Commissioners of Crown Lands of Canada, 1863-64-65.

Report of the Royal Commissioners on the operation of the Acts relating to Trawling for Herring on the Coasts of Scotland. Presented to both Houses of Parliament by command of Her Majesty. 1863.

Salmon and other Fish, Propagation of, by Edward and Thomas Ashworth, 1853. E. H. King, Stockport.

Sea-Side and Aquarium, by John Harper, 1858. Nimmo, Edinburgh.

Sea-Side Divinity, by the Rev. Robert W. Fraser, M.A., 1861. J. Hogg and Sons.

Shetland, Description of the Island of, etc., 1753. James, London.

Sketches of the Natural History of Ceylon, by Sir J. Emerson Tennent, 1861. London : Longman and Co.

The Field, the Country Gentleman's Newspaper.

The Herring, its Natural History and National Importance, by John Mitchell, F.R.S., etc. Edinburgh, 1864.

The Interest of Scotland Considered, etc. Edinburgh, 1733.

The Structure and Physiology of Fishes Explained, etc., by Alexander Monro, M.D. Edinburgh, 1785.

The Young Angler's Guide, etc., 1839. J. Cheek, London.

Tweed Fisheries Acts, 1857-59. Eyre and Spottiswoode.

Vacation Tourists, 1862-3. London : Macmillan, 1864.

Voyage d'Exploration sur la Littoral de la France et de L'Italie, par M. Coste. Paris, 1861, Imprimerie Impériale.

Yarrell's British Fishes. London : Van Voorst.

₊ Various numbers of *Macmillan's Magazine*, the *Cornhill Magazine*, etc., have also been consulted, and quoted from, by permission of the publishers.

III. WICK HERRING HARVEST OF 1865.

Date.	Boats out.	Daily Average. Crans.	Daily catch. Crans.	Season's average. Crans.	Season's catch. Crans.	Quality.	Weather.
June 23	19	5	97	0	126	Good	Wet.
,, 24	14	$\frac{1}{2}$	7	0	133	Do.	Cold and blowy.
,, 27	25	2	50	0	183	Do.	Changeable.
,, 28	25	2	50	0	233	Do.	Thick.
,, 30	30	6	180	0	413	Do.	Do.
July 1	34	3	102	$\frac{1}{4}$	515	Do.	Mild and clear.
,, 4	75	0	10	$\frac{1}{4}$	525	Do.	Do.
,, 6	48	0	3	$\frac{1}{4}$	528	Do.	Do.—rains.
,, 11	120	$1\frac{3}{4}$	188	$\frac{3}{4}$	716	Excellent	Do.
,, 12	200	$\frac{1}{2}$	100	$\frac{3}{4}$	816	Do.	Do.
,, 13	50	1	50	$\frac{3}{4}$	866	Do.	Wet.
,, 14	20	1	20	$\frac{3}{4}$	886	Do.	Wet.
,, 15	100	0	10	$\frac{3}{4}$	896	Do.	Fine.
,, 18	20	$\frac{1}{2}$	10	$\frac{3}{4}$	906	Do.	Do.
,, 19	30	0	0	$\frac{3}{4}$	906	...	Do.
,, 20	56	0	0	$\frac{3}{4}$	906	...	Do.
,, 21	120	$\frac{1}{4}$	30	$\frac{3}{4}$	936	Mixed	Do.
,, 22	200	0	20	$\frac{3}{4}$	956	Do.	Mild.
,, 25	500	0	40	1	996	Excellent	Calm and clear.
,, 26	500	0	80	1	1,076	Large	Do.
,, 27	500	0	40	1	1,116	Mixed	Do.
,, 29	60	2	120	$1\frac{1}{3}$	1,236	Excellent	Breezy.
Aug. 1	900	$\frac{3}{4}$	750	2	1,986	Do.	Mild and clear.
,, 2	950	$\frac{1}{2}$	500	$2\frac{1}{2}$	2,486	Do.	Very wet.
,, 3	970	$\frac{3}{4}$	750	3	3,236	Do.	Heavy rain.
,, 4	970	1	970	4	4,206	Do.	Calm.
,, 5	970	1	970	$5\frac{1}{2}$	5,176	Do.	Do.
,, 8	976	$2\frac{1}{2}$	2,440	8	7,616	Do.	Do.
,, 9	970	12	11,640	20	19,256	Do.	Do.
,, 10	976	7	6,832	27	26,088	Do.	Very clear.
,, 11	970	6	5,820	$32\frac{1}{2}$	31,908	$\frac{1}{4}$ spent	Wet and rough.
,, 15	50	1	50	$32\frac{1}{2}$	31,958	Good	Very rough.
,, 16	900	$\frac{1}{4}$	225	33	32,183	Do.	Do.
,, 17	100	1	100	33	32,283	Spent	Do.
,, 18	930	2	1,860	35	34,143	Excellent	Fine.
,, 19	977	$\frac{1}{2}$	487	$35\frac{1}{2}$	34,630	Do.	Do.
,, 22	977	6	5,862	$41\frac{1}{2}$	40,492	Do.	Do.
,, 23	977	6	5,862	$47\frac{1}{2}$	46,354	$\frac{1}{4}$ spent	Breezy.
,, 24	977	12	11,724	$59\frac{1}{2}$	58,978	$\frac{1}{4}$ spent	Mild.
,, 25	977	10	9,770	$69\frac{1}{2}$	67,848	$\frac{1}{4}$ spent	Do.—frost.
,, 26	975	8	7,800	$77\frac{1}{2}$	75,648	$\frac{1}{2}$ spent	Breezy—rain
,, 29	977	0	10	$77\frac{1}{2}$	75,658	Good	Do.
,, 30	30	0	0	$77\frac{1}{2}$	75,658	...	Rough—rain.
,, 31	200	$\frac{1}{4}$	50	$77\frac{1}{2}$	75,708	Do.	Do.
Sept. 1	500	0	0	$77\frac{1}{2}$	75,708	...	Very rough.
,, 5	300	0	0	$77\frac{1}{2}$	75,708	...	Changeable.
,, 12	9	1	9	$77\frac{1}{2}$	75,717	Excellent	Fine.
,, 13	30	1	30	$77\frac{1}{2}$	75,747	Do.	Changeable.
,, 14	50	6	300	78	76,047	Do.	Fine.
,, 15	60	0	3	78	76,050	Do.	Changeable.

IV. TOTAL CATCH of HERRINGS at all the Stations on the North-East Coast during the last Five Years.

Stations.	1861.	1862.	1863.	1864.	1865.
Wick	89,728	90,644	90,099	90,033	76,055
Lybster, etc....	16,828	17,150	24,982	19,120	18,946
Dunbeath	6,720	6,162	6,800	5,248	5,100
Helmsdale......	26,670	26,500	24,982	29,120	13,020
Brora	1,620	1,809	1,554	2,460	1,225
Cromarty	18,060	11,232	13,600	15,000	10,200
Burghhead ...	7,920	9,090	10,320	11,770	10,580
Hopeman	11,614	9,686	10,150	5,824	8,418
Findhorn	1,080	294	...	...	560
Lossiemouth...	10,175	10,881	12,020	5,985	14,742
Portgordon ...	2,783	4,664	4,312	1,160	800
Portsoy	1,974	3,290	2,112	920	1,290
Cullen	2,380	4,200	3,424	1,320	406
Portknockie ...	2,691	3,542	3,092	1,872	2,695
Findochty......	2,660	4,480	3,752	2,040	1,900
Portessie	1,881	2,180	1,350	1,380	1,320
Buckie	5,320	8,600	8,249	3,850	7,700
Whitehills......	2,792	4,753	2,211	1,200	1,624
Macduff.........	4,200	7,884	4,898	2,400	3,962
Gardenstown...	6,642	12,908	6,386	2,948	7,952
Pennan	819	1,215	368	265	520
Rosehearty......	4,620	7,828	6,898	4,602	6,100
Pitullie	1,720	3,768	1,500	720	1,980
Fraserburgh ...	16,581	42,944	24,970	26,793	28,112
Peterhead	32,600	52,461	31,535	32,680	35,741
Boddam.........	5,890	5,445	4,680	3,640	5,358
Total......	285,878	353,610	304,780	272,350	266,211

Estimated Number of Hands Employed—1865.

	Fishermen.	Others.	Total.
Caithness	6,500	3,100	9,600
Sutherland	2,100	1,500	3,600
Cromarty	1,200	1,000	2,200
Moray	1,800	1,200	3,000
Banff..............................	1,800	1,200	3,000
Aberdeen	3,800	2,400	6,200
Total	17,200	10,400	27,600

INDEX.

Printed by R. CLARK, *Edinburgh.*

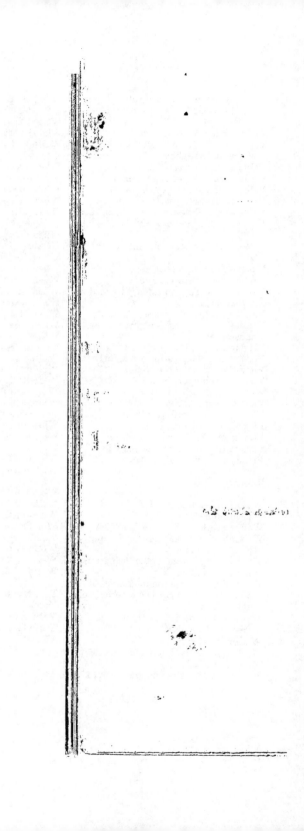

ALBEMARLE STREET, LONDON,
January, 1866.

MR. MURRAY'S

GENERAL LIST OF WORKS.

ALBERT (PRINCE). THE SPEECHES AND ADDRESSES
of H.R.H. THE PRINCE CONSORT, on Public Occasions; with an
Introduction giving some Outlines of his Character. Portrait. 8vo.
10s. 6d.; or Popular Edition. Portrait. Fcap. 8vo, 1s.

ABBOTT'S (REV. J.) Philip Musgrave; or, Memoirs of a Church of
England Missionary in the North American Colonies. Post 8vo. 2s.

ABERCROMBIE'S (JOHN) Enquiries concerning the Intellectual
Powers and the Investigation of Truth. 14th Edition. Fcap. 8vo. 6s. 6d.

———————— Philosophy of the Moral Feelings. 13th Edition.
Fcap. 8vo. 4s.

ACLAND'S (REV. CHARLES) Popular Account of the Manners and
Customs of India. Post 8vo. 2s.

ÆSOP'S FABLES. A New Translation. With Historical
Preface. By Rev. THOMAS JAMES. With 100 Woodcuts, by TENNIEL
and WOLF. 50th Thousand. Post 8vo. 2s. 6d.

AGRICULTURAL (THE) JOURNAL. Of the Royal Agricultural
Society of England. 8vo. Published half-yearly.

AIDS TO FAITH: a Series of Theological Essays. By various
Writers. Edited by WILLIAM THOMSON, D.D., Lord Archbishop of
York. 8vo. 9s.

CONTENTS.

Rev. H. L. MANSEL—*Miracles.*
BISHOP OF KILLALOE—*Christian Evidences.*
Rev. DR. MCCAUL—*Prophecy and the Mosaic Record of Creation.*
Rev. CANON COOK — *Ideology and Subscription.*

Rev. GEORGE RAWLINSON—*The Pentateuch.*
ARCHBISHOP OF YORK—*Doctrine of the Atonement.*
BISHOP OF ELY.—*Inspiration.*
BISHOP OF GLOUCESTER AND BRISTOL.—*Scripture and its Interpretation.*

AMBER-WITCH (THE). The most interesting Trial for Witch-
craft ever known. Translated from the German by LADY DUFF
GORDON. Post 8vo. 2s.

ARMY LIST (THE). *Published Monthly by Authority.* 18mo. 1s. 6d.

ARTHUR'S (LITTLE) History of England. By LADY CALLCOTT.
150th Thousand. Woodcuts. Fcap. 8vo. 2s. 6d.

ATKINSON'S (MRS.) Recollections of Tartar Steppes and their
Inhabitants. Illustrations. Post 8vo. 12s.

AUNT IDA'S Walks and Talks; a Story Book for Children. By
a LADY. Woodcuts. 16mo. 5s.

AUSTIN'S (JOHN) LECTURES ON JURISPRUDENCE; or, the Philosophy
of Positive Law. 3 Vols. 8vo. 39s.

———————— (SARAH) Fragments from German Prose Writers.
With Biographical Notes. Post 8vo. 10s.

B

ADMIRALTY PUBLICATIONS; Issued by direction of the Lords
Commissioners of the Admiralty:—

A MANUAL OF SCIENTIFIC ENQUIRY, for the Use of Travellers.
Edited by Sir JOHN F. HERSCHEL, and Rev. ROBERT MAIN. *Third
Edition.* Woodcuts. Post 8vo. 9s.

AIRY'S ASTRONOMICAL OBSERVATIONS MADE AT GREENWICH.
1836 to 1847. Royal 4to. 50s. each.

———— ASTRONOMICAL RESULTS. 1848 to 1858. 4to. 8s. each.

———— APPENDICES TO THE ASTRONOMICAL OBSERVA-
TIONS.

1836.—I. Bessel's Refraction Tables.
    II. Tables for converting Errors of R.A. and N.P.D. ⎫8s.
        into Errors of Longitude and Ecliptic P.D. ⎭
1837.—I. Logarithms of Sines and Cosines to every Ten ⎫
        Seconds of Time. ⎬8s.
    II. Table for converting Sidereal into Mean Solar Time. ⎭
1842.—Catalogue of 1439 Stars. 8s.
1845.—Longitude of Valentia. 8s.
1847.—Twelve Years' Catalogue of Stars. 14s.
1851.—Maskelyne's Ledger of Stars. 6s.
1852.—I. Description of the Transit Circle. 5s.
    II. Regulations of the Royal Observatory. 2s.
1853.—Bessel's Refraction Tables. 3s.
1854.—I. Description of the Zenith Tube. 3s.
    II. Six Years' Catalogue of Stars. 10s.
1856.—Description of the Galvanic Apparatus at Greenwich Ob-
    servatory. 8s.
1862.—I. Seven Years' Catalogue of Stars. 10s.
    II. Plan of the Building and Ground of the Royal Ob- ⎫
        servatory, Greenwich. ⎬ 3s.
    III. Longitude of Valentia. ⎭

———— MAGNETICAL AND METEOROLOGICAL OBSERVA-
TIONS. 1840 to 1847. Royal 4to. 50s. each.

———— ASTRONOMICAL, MAGNETICAL, AND METEOROLO-
GICAL OBSERVATIONS, 1848 to 1863. Royal 4to. 50s. each.

———— ASTRONOMICAL RESULTS. 1848 to 1863. 4to.

———— MAGNETICAL AND METEOROLOGICAL RESULTS.
1848 to 1863. 4to. 8s. each.

———— REDUCTION OF THE OBSERVATIONS OF PLANETS.
1750 to 1830. Royal 4to. 50s.

———————————————— LUNAR OBSERVATIONS. 1750
to 1830. 2 Vols. Royal 4to. 50s. each.

———————————————— 1831 to 1851. 4to. 20s.

BERNOULLI'S SEXCENTENARY TABLE. *London,* 1779. 4to.

BESSEL'S AUXILIARY TABLES FOR HIS METHOD OF CLEAR-
ING LUNAR DISTANCES. 8vo.

————FUNDAMENTA ASTRONOMIÆ: *Regiomontii,* 1818. Folio. 60s.

BIRD'S METHOD OF CONSTRUCTING MURAL QUADRANTS.
London, 1768. 4to. 2s. 6d.

———— METHOD OF DIVIDING ASTRONOMICAL INSTRU-
MENTS. *London,* 1767. 4to. 2s. 6d.

COOK, KING, AND BAYLY'S ASTRONOMICAL OBSERVATIONS.
London, 1782. 4to. 21s.

ENCKE'S BERLINER JAHRBUCH, for 1830. *Berlin,* 1828. 8vo. 9s.

GROOMBRIDGE'S CATALOGUE OF CIRCUMPOLAR STARS.
4to. 10s.

ADMIRALTY PUBLICATIONS—*continued.*

HANSEN'S TABLES DE LA LUNE. 4to. 20*s.*

HARRISON'S PRINCIPLES OF HIS TIME-KEEPER. PLATES 1797. 4to. 5*s.*.

HUTTON'S TABLES, OF THE PRODUCTS AND POWERS OF NUMBERS. 1781. Folio. 7*s.* 6*d.*

LAX'S TABLES FOR FINDING THE LATITUDE AND LONGI-TUDE. 1821. 8vo. 10*s.*

LUNAR OBSERVATIONS at GREENWICH. 1783 to 1819. Compared with the Tables, 1821. 4to. 7*s.*.6*d.*

MASKELYNE'S ACCOUNT OF THE GOING OF HARRISON'S WATCH. 1767. 4to. 2*s.* 6*d.*

MAYER'S DISTANCES of the MOON'S CENTRE from the PLANETS. 1822, 3*s.*; 1823, 4*s.* 6*d.* 1824 to 1835, 8vo. 4*s.* each.

———— THEORIA LUNÆ JUXTA SYSTEMA NEWTONIANUM. 4to. 2*s.* 6*d.*

———— TABULÆ MOTUUM SOLIS ET LUNÆ.. 1770. 4to. 5*s.*

———— ASTRONOMICAL OBSERVATIONS MADE AT GOT-TINGEN, from 1756 to 1761. 1826. Folio. 7*s.* 6*d.*

NAUTICAL ALMANACS, from 1767 to 1869. 8vo. 2*s.* 6*d.* each.

———— SELECTIONS FROM THE ADDITIONS up to 1812. 8vo. 5*s.* 1834-54. 8vo. 5*s.*

———— SUPPLEMENTS, 1828 to 1833, 1837 and 1838. 8vo. 2*s.* each.

———— TABLE requisite to be used with the N.A. 1781. 8vo. 5*s.*

POND'S ASTRONOMICAL OBSERVATIONS. 1811 to 1835. 4to. 21*s.* each.

RAMSDEN'S ENGINE for DIVIDING MATHEMATICAL INSTRUMENTS. 4to. 5*s.*

———— ENGINE for DIVIDING STRAIGHT LINES. 4to. 5*s.*

SABINE'S PENDULUM EXPERIMENTS to DETERMINE THE FIGURE OF THE EARTH. 1825. 4to. 40*s.*

SHEPHERD'S TABLES for CORRECTING LUNAR DISTANCES. 1772. Royal 4to. 21*s.*

———— TABLES, GENERAL, of the MOON'S DISTANCE from the SUN, and 10 STARS. 1787. Folio. 5*s.* 6*d.*

TAYLOR'S SEXAGESIMAL TABLE. 1780. 4to. 15*s.*

———— TABLES OF LOGARITHMS. 4to. 3*l.*

TIARK'S ASTRONOMICAL OBSERVATIONS for the LONGITUDE of MADEIRA. 1822. 4to. 5*s.*

———— CHRONOMETRICAL OBSERVATIONS for DIFFERENCES of LONGITUDE between DOVER, PORTSMOUTH, and FALMOUTH. 1823. 4to. 5*s.*

VENUS and JUPITER: OBSERVATIONS of, compared with the TABLES. *London*, 1822. 4to. 2*s.*

WALES' AND BAYLY'S ASTRONOMICAL OBSERVATIONS. 1777. 4to. 21*s.*

WALES' REDUCTION OF ASTRONOMICAL OBSERVATIONS MADE IN THE SOUTHERN HEMISPHERE. 1764—1771. 1788. 4to. 10*s.* 6*d.*

BAIKIE'S (W. B.) Narrative of an Exploring Voyage up the Rivers Quorra and Tshadda in 1854. Map. 8vo. 16*s.*

BANKES' (THE HON. GEORGE) STORY OF CORFE CASTLE, with documents relating to the Time of the Civil Wars, &c. Woodcuts. Post 8vo. 10s. 6d.

BARBAULD'S (MRS.) Hymns in Prose for Children. With 112 Original Designs. Small 4to. 5s. Or Fine Paper, 7s. 6d.

BARROW'S (SIR JOHN) Autobiographical Memoir, including Reflections, Observations, and Reminiscences at Home and Abroad. From Early Life to Advanced Age. Portrait. 8vo. 16s.

———— Voyages of Discovery and Research within the Arctic Regions, from 1818 to the present time. 8vo. 15s.

———— Life, Exploits, and Voyages of Sir Francis Drake. With numerous Original Letters. Post 8vo. 2s.

BARRY'S (SIR CHARLES) Life. By his Son, Rev. Alfred Barry, D.D. With Illustrations. 8vo. (In the Press.)

BATES' (H. W.) Records of a Naturalist on the River Amazons during eleven years of Adventure and Travel. Second Edition. Illustrations. Post 8vo. 12s.

BEES AND FLOWERS. Two Essays. By Rev. Thomas James. Reprinted from the "Quarterly Review." Fcap. 8vo. 1s. each.

BERTHA'S Journal during a Visit to her Uncle in England. Containing a Variety of Interesting and Instructive Information. Seventh Edition. Woodcuts. 12mo.

BIRCH'S (SAMUEL) History of Ancient Pottery and Porcelain : Egyptian, Assyrian, Greek, Roman, and Etruscan. With 200 Illustrations. 2 Vols. Medium 8vo. 42s.

BLUNT'S (REV. J. J.) Undesigned Coincidences in the Writings of the Old and New Testament, an Argument of their Veracity : containing the Books of Moses, Historical and Prophetical Scriptures, and the Gospels and Acts. 9th Edition. Post 8vo. 6s.

———— History of the Church in the First Three Centuries. Third Edition. Post 8vo. 7s. 6d.

———— Parish Priest; His Duties, Acquirements and Obligations. Fourth Edition. Post 8vo. 7s. 6d.

———— Lectures on the Right Use of the Early Fathers. Second Edition. 8vo. 15s.

———— Plain Sermons Preached to a Country Congregation. Second Edition. 3 Vols. Post 8vo. 7s. 6d. each.

———— Essays on various subjects. 8vo. 12s.

BISSET'S (ANDREW) History of England during the Interregnum, from the Death of Charles I. to the Battle of Dunbar, 1648–50. Chiefly from the MSS. in the State Paper Office. 8vo. 15s.

BERTRAM'S (JAS. G.) Harvest of the Sea : a Contribution to the Natural and Economic History of British Food Fishes. With 50 Illustrations. 21s.

BLAKISTON'S (CAPT.) Narrative of the Expedition sent to explore the Upper Waters of the Yang-Tsze. Illustrations. 8vo. 18s.

BLOMFIELD'S (BISHOP) Memoir, with Selections from his Correspondence. By his Son. 2nd Edition. Portrait, post 8vo. 12s.

BOOK OF COMMON PRAYER. Illustrated with Coloured
Borders, Initial Letters, and Woodcuts. A new edition. 8vo. 18s.
cloth; 31s. 6d. calf; 36s. morocco.

BORROW'S (GEORGE) Bible in Spain; or the Journeys, Adventures,
and Imprisonments of an Englishman in an Attempt to circulate the
Scriptures in the Peninsula. 3 Vols. Post 8vo. 27s.; or Popular Edition,
16mo, 3s. 6d.

———— Zincali, or the Gipsies of Spain; their Manners,
Customs, Religion, and Language. 2 Vols. Post 8vo. 18s.; or Popular
Edition, 16mo, 3s. 6d.

———— Lavengro; The Scholar—The Gipsy—and the Priest.
Portrait. 3 Vols. Post 8vo. 30s.

———— Romany Rye; a Sequel to Lavengro. Second
Edition. 2 Vols. Post 8vo. 21s.

———— WILD WALES: its People, Language, and Scenery.
Popular Edition. Post 8vo., 6s.

BOSWELL'S (JAMES) Life of Samuel Johnson, LL.D. Including the Tour to the Hebrides. Edited by Mr. CROKER. Portraits. Royal
8vo. 10s.

BRACE'S (C. L.) History of the Races of the Old World. Post
8vo. 9s.

BRAY'S (MRS.) Life of Thomas Stothard, R.A. With Personal
Reminiscences. Illustrated with Portrait and 60 Woodcuts of his
chief works. 4to.

BREWSTER'S (SIR DAVID) Martyrs of Science, or the Lives of
Galileo, Tycho Brahe, and Kepler. Fourth Edition. Fcap. 8vo. 4s. 6d.

———— More Worlds than One. The Creed of the Philosopher and the Hope of the Christian. Eighth Edition. Post 8vo. 6s.

———— Stereoscope: its History, Theory, Construction,
and Application to the Arts and to Education. Woodcuts. 12mo.
5s. 6d.

———— Kaleidoscope: its History, Theory, and Construction,
with its application to the Fine and Useful Arts. Second Edition.
Woodcuts. Post 8vo. 5s. 6d.

BRINE'S (Capt.) Narrative of the Rise and Progress of the Taeping
Rebellion in China. Plans. Post 8vo. 10s. 6d.

BRITISH ASSOCIATION REPORTS. 8vo. York and Oxford,
1831-32, 13s. 6d. Cambridge, 1833, 12s. Edinburgh, 1834, 15s. Dublin,
1835, 13s. 6d. Bristol, 1836, 12s. Liverpool, 1837, 16s. 6d. Newcastle,
1838, 15s. Birmingham, 1839, 13s. 6d. Glasgow, 1840, 15s. Plymouth,
1841, 13s. 6d. Manchester, 1842, 10s. 6d. Cork, 1843, 12s. York, 1844,
20s. Cambridge, 1845, 12s. Southampton, 1846, 15s. Oxford, 1847, 18s.
Swansea, 1848, 9s. Birmingham, 1849, 10s. Edinburgh, 1850, 15s. Ipswich,
1851, 16s. 6d. Belfast, 1852, 15s. Hull, 1853, 10s. 6d. Liverpool, 1854, 18s.
Glasgow, 1855, 15s.; Cheltenham, 1856, 18s.; Dublin, 1857, 15s.; Leeds,
1858, 20s. Aberdeen, 1859, 15s. Oxford, 1860, 25s. Manchester, 1861,
15s. Cambridge, 1862, 20s. Newcastle, 1863, 25s. Bath, 1864, 25s.

BROUGHTON'S (LORD) Journey through Albania and other
Provinces of Turkey in Europe and Asia, to Constantinople, 1809—10.
Third Edition. Illustrations. 2 Vols. 8vo. 30s.

———— Visits to Italy. 3rd Edition. 2 vols. Post 8vo. 18s.

BRITISH CLASSICS. A New Series of Standard English Authors, printed from the most correct text, and edited with notes. 8vo.

Already Published.

I. GOLDSMITH'S WORKS. Edited by PETER CUNNINGHAM, F.S.A. Vignettes. 4 Vols. 30s.

II. GIBBON'S DECLINE AND FALL OF THE ROMAN EMPIRE. Edited by WILLIAM SMITH, LL.D. Portrait and Maps. 8 Vols. 60s.

III. JOHNSON'S LIVES OF THE ENGLISH POETS. Edited by PETER CUNNINGHAM, F.S.A. 3 Vols. 22s. 6d.

IV. BYRON'S POETICAL WORKS. Edited, with Notes. 6 vols. 45s.

In Preparation.

LIFE AND WORKS OF POPE. Edited by REV. WHITWELL ELWIN.

HUME'S HISTORY OF ENGLAND. Edited, with Notes.

LIFE AND WORKS OF SWIFT. Edited by JOHN FORSTER.

BUBBLES FROM THE BRUNNEN OF NASSAU. By an Old MAN. *7th Edition,* with Illustrations. Post 8vo. 7s. 6d.

BUNYAN (JOHN) and Oliver Cromwell. Select Biographies. By ROBERT SOUTHEY. Post 8vo. 2s.

BUONAPARTE'S (NAPOLEON) Confidential Correspondence with his Brother Joseph, sometime King of Spain. *Second Edition.* 2 vols. 8vo. 26s.

BURGON'S (Rev. J. W.) Christian Gentleman ; or, Memoir of Patrick Fraser Tytler. *Second Edition.* Post 8vo. 9s.

———— Letters from Rome, written to Friends at Home. Illustrations. Post 8vo. 12s.

BURN'S (COL.) Dictionary of Naval and Military Technical Terms, English and French, and French and English. *Fourth Edition.* Crown 8vo. 15s.

BURR'S (G. D.) Instructions in Practical Surveying, Topographical Plan Drawing, and on sketching ground without Instruments. *Fourth Edition.* Woodcuts. Post 8vo. 6s.

BUTTMAN'S LEXILOGUS ; a Critical Examination of the Meaning of numerous Greek Words, chiefly in Homer and Hesiod. Translated by Rev. J. R. FISHLAKE. *Fifth Edition.* 8vo. 12s.

———— CATALOGUE OF IRREGULAR GREEK VERBS. With all the Tenses extant—their Formation, Meaning, and Usage, accompanied by an Index. Translated, with Notes, by Rev. J. R. FISHLAKE. *Fifth Edition.* Revised by Rev. E. VENABLES. Post 8vo.

BUXTON'S (SIR FOWELL) Memoirs. With Selections from his Correspondence. By his Son. Portrait. 8vo. 15s. *Abridged Edition,* Portrait. Fcap. 8vo. 2s. 6d.

———— (CHARLES, M.P.) IDEAS OF THE DAY ON POLICY. 8vo.

BYRON'S (LORD) Life, Letters, and Journals. By THOMAS MOORE. Plates. 6 Vols. Fcap. 8vo. 18s.

———— Life, Letters, and Journals. By THOMAS MOORE. Portraits. Royal 8vo. 9s.

———— Poetical Works. Portrait. 6 Vols. 8vo. 45s.

———— Poetical Works. Plates. 10 Vols. Fcap. 8vo. 30s.

———— Poetical Works. 8 Vols. 24mo. 20s.

———— Poetical Works. Plates. Royal 8vo. 9s.

———— Poetical Works. Portrait. Crown 8vo. 6s.

———— Childe Harold. With 80 Engravings. Small 4to. 21s.

———— Childe Harold. With 30 Vignettes. 12mo. 6s.

———— Childe Harold. 16mo. 2s. 6d.

———— Childe Harold. Vignettes. 16mo. 1s.

———— Childe Harold. Portrait. 16mo. 6d.

———— Tales and Poems. 24mo. 2s. 6d.

———— Miscellaneous. 2 Vols. 24mo. 5s.

———— Dramas and Plays. 2 Vols. 24mo. 5s.

———— Don Juan and Beppo. 2 Vols. 24mo. 5s.

———— Beauties. Selected from his Poetry and Prose. Portrait, Fcap. 8vo. 3s. 6d.

CARNARVON'S (LORD) Portugal, Gallicia, and the Basque Provinces. From Notes made during a Journey to those Countries. Third Edition. Post 8vo. 3s. 6d.

———— Recollections of the Druses of Lebanon. With Notes on their Religion. Third Edition. Post 8vo. 5s. 6d.

CAMPBELL'S (LORD) Lives of the Lord Chancellors and Keepers of the Great Seal of England. From the Earliest Times to the Death of Lord Eldon in 1838. Fourth Edition. 10 Vols. Crown 8vo. 6s. each.

———— Lives of the Chief Justices of England. From the Norman Conquest to the Death of Lord Tenterden. Second Edition. 3 Vols. 8vo. 42s.

———— Shakspeare's Legal Acquirements Considered. 8vo. 5s. 6d.

———— Life of Lord Chancellor Bacon. Fcap. 8vo. 2s. 6d.

———— (GEORGE) Modern India. A Sketch of the System of Civil Government. With some Account of the Natives and Native Institutions. Second Edition. 8vo. 16s.

———— India as it may be. An Outline of a proposed Government and Policy. 8vo. 12s.

———— (THOS.) Short Lives of the British Poets. With an Essay on English Poetry. Post 8vo. 3s. 6d.

CALLCOTT'S (LADY) Little Arthur's History of England. 150th Thousand. With Woodcuts. Fcap. 8vo. 2s. 6d.

CASTLEREAGH (THE) DESPATCHES, from the commencement
of the official career of the late Viscount Castlereagh to the close of his
life. Edited by the MARQUIS OF LONDONDERRY. 12 Vols. 8vo. 14s. each.

CATHCART'S (SIR GEORGE) Commentaries on the War in Russia
and Germany, 1812-13. Plans. 8vo. 14s.

CAVALCASELLE AND CROWE'S History of Painting in
Italy, from the Second to the Sixteenth Century, from recent researches, as well as from personal inspection of the Works of Art in
that Country. With 70 Illustrations. Vols. I. and II. 8vo. 42s.

———————————— Notices of the Lives and Works of the
Early Flemish.Painters. Woodcuts. Post 8vo. 12s.

CHARMED ROE (THE); or, The Story of the Little Brother and
Sister. By OTTO SPECKTER. Plates. 16mo. 5s.

CHORLEY'S (H. F.) STUDIES OF THE MUSIC OF MANY
NATIONS; including the Substance of a Course of Lectures delivered
at the Royal Institution. 8vo. (In the Press.)

CHURTON'S (ARCHDEACON) Gongora. An Historical Essay on the
Age of Philip III. and IV. of Spain. With Translations. Portrait.
2 Vols. Small 8vo. 15s.

CICERO: HIS LIFE AND TIMES. With his Character viewed
as a Statesman, Orator, and Friend. With a Selection from his Correspondence and Orations. By WILLIAM FORSYTH, Q'C. With Illustrations, 2 vols. Post 8vo. 18s.

CLAUSEWITZ'S (CARL VON) Campaign of 1812, in Russia.
Translated from the German by LORD ELLESMERE. Map. 8vo. 10s. 6d.

CLIVE'S (LORD) Life. By REV. G. R. GLEIG, M.A. Post 8vo. 3s. 6d.

COLCHESTER (THE) PAPERS. The Diary and Correspondence
of Charles Abbott, Lord Colchester, Speaker of the House of Commons,
1802-1817. Edited by his Son. Portrait. 3 Vols. 8vo. 42s.

COLERIDGE (SAMUEL TAYLOR). Specimens of his Table-Talk.
New Edition. Portrait. Fcap. 8vo. 6s.

COLONIAL LIBRARY. [See Home and Colonial Library.]

COOK'S (Rev. Canon) Sermons Preached at Lincoln's Inn Chapel,
and on Special Occasions. 8vo. 9s.

COOKERY (MODERN DOMESTIC). Founded on Principles of Economy
and Practical Knowledge, and adapted for Private Families. By a
Lady. New Edition. Woodcuts. Fcap. 8vo. 5s.

CORNWALLIS (THE) Papers and Correspondence during the
American War,—Administrations in India,—Union with Ireland, and
Peace of Amiens. Edited by CHARLES ROSS. Second Edition. 3 Vols.
8vo. 63s.

COWPER'S (MARY, COUNTESS) Diary while Lady of the Bedchamber
to Caroline Princess of Wales, 1714—20. Edited by Hon. SPENCER
COWPER. Second Edition. Portrait. 8vo. 10s. 6d.

CRABBE'S (REV. GEORGE) Life, Letters, and Journals. By his SON.
Portrait. Fcap. 8vo. 3s.
———————————— Life and Poetical Works. Plates. 8 Vols. Fcap.
8vo. 24s.
———————————— Life and Poetical Works. Plates. Royal 8vo. 7s.

CROKER'S (J. W.) Progressive Geography for Children. *Fifth Edition.* 18mo. 1s. 6d.

———— Stories for Children, Selected from the History of England. *Fifteenth Edition.* Woodcuts. 16mo. 2s. 6d.

———— Boswell's Life of Johnson. Including the Tour to the Hebrides. Portraits. Royal 8vo. 10s.

———— Essays on the Early Period of the French Revolution. 8vo. 15s.

———— Historical Essay on the Guillotine. Fcap. 8vo. 1s.

CROMWELL (OLIVER) and John Bunyan. By ROBERT SOUTHEY. Post 8vo. 2s.

CROWE'S AND CAVALCASELLE'S Notices of the Early Flemish Painters; their Lives and Works. Woodcuts. Post 8vo. 12s.

———— History of Painting in Italy, from 2nd to 16th Century. Derived from Historical Researches as well as inspection of the Works of Art in that Country. With 70 Illustrations. Vols. I. and II. 8vo. 42s.

CUMMING'S (R. GORDON) Five Years of a Hunter's Life in the Far Interior of South Africa; with Anecdotes of the Chace, and Notices of the Native Tribes. *New Edition.* Woodcuts. Post 8vo. 5s.

CUNNINGHAM'S (ALLAN) Poems and Songs. Now first collected and arranged, with Biographical Notice. 24mo. 2s. 6d.

CURETON (REV. W.) Remains of a very Ancient Recension of the Four Gospels in Syriac, hitherto unknown in Europe. Discovered, Edited, and Translated. 4to. 24s.

CURTIUS' (PROFESSOR) Student's Greek Grammar, for the use of Colleges and the Upper Forms. Translated under the Author's revision. Edited by DR. WM. SMITH. Post 8vo. 7s. 6d.

———— Smaller Greek Grammar for the use of the Middle and Lower Forms, abridged from the above. 12mo. 3s. 6d.

———— First Greek Course; containing Delectus, Exercise Book, and Vocabularies. 12mo. 3s. 6d.

CURZON'S (HON. ROBERT) ARMENIA AND ERZEROUM. A Year on the Frontiers of Russia, Turkey, and Persia. *Third Edition.* Woodcuts. Post 8vo. 7s. 6d.

———— Visits to the Monasteries of the Levant. *Fifth Edition.* Illustrations. Post 8vo. 7s. 6d.

CUST'S (GENERAL) Annals of the Wars of the 18th & 19th Centuries. 9 Vols. Fcap. 8vo. 5s. each.

———— Lives and Characters of the Warriors of the 17th Century who have Commanded Fleets and Armies before the Enemy. 2 Vols. Post 8vo. 16s.

DARWIN'S (CHARLES) Journal of Researches into the Natural History of the Countries visited during a Voyage round the World. Post 8vo. 9s.

———— Origin of Species by Means of Natural Selection; or, the Preservation of Favoured Races in the Struggle for Life. Post 8vo. 14s.

———— Fertilization of Orchids through Insect Agency, and as to the good of Intercrossing. Woodcuts. Post 8vo. 9s.

———— Domesticated Animals and Cultivated Plants; or, the Principles of Variation, Inheritance, Re-version, Crossing, Inter breeding, and Selection under Domestication. With Illustrations. Post 8vo. (*In Preparation.*)

DAVIS'S (NATHAN) Visit to the Ruined Cities of Numidia and
Carthaginia. Illustrations. 8vo. 16s.

———— (SIR J. F.) Chinese Miscellanies : a Collection of Essays
and Notes. Post 8vo. 6s.

DAVY'S (SIR HUMPHRY) Consolations in Travel; or, Last Days
of a Philosopher. *Fifth Edition.* Woodcuts. Fcap. 8vo. 6s.

———— Salmonia; or, Days of Fly Fishing. *Fourth Edition.*
Woodcuts. Fcap. 8vo. 6s.

DELEPIERRE'S (OCTAVE) History of Flemish Literature. From
the Twelfth Century. 8vo. 9s.

DENNIS' (GEORGE) Cities and Cemeteries of Etruria. Plates.
2 Vols. 8vo. 42s.

DERBY'S (EDWARD, EARL OF) Translation of the Iliad of Homer
into English Blank Verse. *Fifth Edition, Revised.* 2 Vols. 8vo. 24s.

DIXON'S (W. HEPWORTH) Story of the Life of Lord Bacon. Portrait.
Fcap. 8vo. 7s. 6d.

DOG-BREAKING ; the Most Expeditious, Certain, and Easy
Method, whether great excellence or only mediocrity be required. With
a Few Hints for those who Love the Dog and the Gun. By LIEUT.-
GEN. HUTCHINSON. *Fourth Edition.* With 40 Woodcuts. Crown 8vo. 15s.

DOMESTIC MODERN COOKERY. Founded on Principles of
Economy and Practical Knowledge, and adapted for Private Families.
New Edition. Woodcuts. Fcap. 8vo. 5s.

DOUGLAS'S (GENERAL SIR HOWARD) Life and Adventures ;
From Notes, Conversations, and Correspondence. By S. W. FULLOM.
Portrait. 8vo. 15s.

———— Theory and Practice of Gunnery. *5th Edition.* Plates.
8vo. 21s.

———— Military Bridges, and the Passage of Rivers in
Military Operations. *Third Edition.* Plates. 8vo. 21s.

———— Naval Warfare with Steam. *Second Edition.* 8vo.
8s. 6d.

———— Modern Systems of Fortification, with special reference to the Naval, Littoral, and Internal Defence of England. Plans.
8vo. 12s.

DRAKE'S (SIR FRANCIS) Life, Voyages, and Exploits, by Sea and
Land. By JOHN BARROW. *Third Edition.* Post 8vo. 2s.

DRINKWATER'S (JOHN) History of the Siege of Gibraltar,
1779-1783. With a Description and Account of that Garrison from the
Earliest Periods. Post 8vo. 2s.

DU CHAILLU'S (PAUL B.) EQUATORIAL AFRICA, with
Accounts of the Gorilla, the Nest-building Ape, Chimpanzee, Croco-
dile, &c. Illustrations. 8vo. 21s.

DUFFERIN'S (LORD) Letters from High Latitudes, being some
Account of a Yacht Voyage to Iceland, &c., in 1856. *Fourth Edition.*
Woodcuts. Post 8vo.

———— Lispings from Low Latitudes, or the Journal of
the Hon. Impulsia Gushington. With 24 Plates. 4to. 21s.

DYER'S (THOMAS H.) History of Modern Europe, from the taking of Constantinople by the Turks to the close of the War in the Crimea. 4 Vols. 8vo. 60s.

EASTLAKE'S (SIR CHARLES) Italian Schools of Painting. From the German of KUGLER. Edited, with Notes. *Third Edition.* Illustrated from the Old Masters. 2 Vols. Post 8vo. 30s.

EASTWICK'S (E. B.) Handbook for Bombay and Madras, with Directions for Travellers, Officers, &c. Map. 2 Vols. Post 8vo. 24s.

EDWARDS' (W. H.) Voyage up the River Amazon, including a Visit to Para. Post 8vo. 2s.

ELDON'S (LORD) Public and Private Life, with Selections from his Correspondence and Diaries. By HORACE TWISS. *Third Edition.* Portrait. 2 Vols. Post 8vo. 21s.

ELLIS (REV. W.) Visits to Madagascar, including a Journey to the Capital, with notices of Natural History, and Present Civilisation of the People. *Fifth Thousand.* Map and Woodcuts. 8vo. 16s.

———— (MRS.) Education of Character, with Hints on Moral Training. Post 8vo. 7s. 6d.

ELLESMERE'S (LORD) Two Sieges of Vienna by the Turks. Translated from the German. Post 8vo. 2s.

———————— Campaign of 1812 in Russia, from the German of General Carl Von Clausewitz. Map. 8vo. 10s. 6d.

———————— Poems. With Illustrations. Crown 4to.

———————— Essays on History, Biography, Geography, and Engineering. 8vo. 12s.

ELPHINSTONE'S (HON. MOUNTSTUART) History of India—the Hindoo and Mahomedan Periods. *Fifth Edition, Revised.* Map. 8vo. 18s.

ENGEL'S (CARL) Music of the Most Ancient Nations; particularly of the Assyrians, Egyptians, and Hebrews; with Special Reference to the Discoveries in Western Asia and in Egypt. With 100 Illustrations. 8vo. 16s.

ENGLAND (HISTORY OF) from the Peace of Utrecht to the Peace of Versailles, 1713—83. By LORD MAHON (Earl Stanhope). *Library Edition,* 7 Vols. 8vo. 93s.; or *Popular Edition,* 7 Vols. Post 8vo. 35s.

———————— From the First Invasion by the Romans, down to the Present Year of Queen Victoria's Reign. By MRS. MARKHAM. *New and Cheaper Edition.* Woodcuts. 12mo. 4s.

———————— (THE STUDENT'S HUME). From the Invasion of Julius Cæsar to the Revolution of 1688. By DAVID HUME. Corrected and continued to 1858. Edited by WM. SMITH, LL.D. Woodcuts. Post 8vo. 7s. 6d.

———————— A Smaller History of England for Young Persons. By DR. WM. SMITH. Woodcuts. 18mo. 3s. 6d.

———————— Little Arthur's History of England. By LADY CALLCOTT. Woodcuts. 18mo. 2s. 6d.

ENGLISHWOMAN IN AMERICA. Post 8vo. 10s. 6d.

ESKIMAUX and English Vocabulary, for Travellers in the Arctic Regions. 16mo. 3s. 6d.

ESSAYS FROM "THE TIMES." Being a Selection from the LITERARY PAPERS which have appeared in that Journal. *Seventh Thousand.* 2 vols. Fcap. 8vo. 8s.

ETHNOLOGICAL SOCIETY OF LONDON, TRANSACTIONS. New Series. Vols. I., II., and III. 8vo.

EXETER'S (BISHOP OF) Letters to the late Charles Butler, on the Theological parts of his Book of the Roman Catholic Church; with Remarks on certain Works of Dr. Milner and Dr. Lingard, and on some parts of the Evidence of Dr. Doyle. *Second Edition.* 8vo. 16s.

FAMILY RECEIPT-BOOK. A Collection of a Thousand Valuable and Useful Receipts. Fcap. 8vo. 5s. 6d.

FARRAR'S (REV. A. S.) Critical History of Free Thought in reference to the Christian Religion. Being the Bampton Lectures, 1862. 8vo. 16s.

———————— **(F. W.)** Origin of Language, based on Modern Researches. Fcap. 8vo. 5s.

FEATHERSTONHAUGH'S (G. W.) Tour through the Slave States of North America, from the River Potomac to Texas and the Frontiers of Mexico. Plates. 2 Vols. 8vo. 26s.

FERGUSSON'S (JAMES) Palaces of Nineveh and Persepolis Restored. Woodcuts. 8vo. 16s.

———————— History of Architecture in all Countries: from the Earliest Times to the Present Day. With 1200 Illustrations. 2 Vols. 8vo. Vol. I. 42s.

———————— History of the Modern Styles of Architecture: forming the Third and Concluding Volume of the above work. With 312 Illustrations. 8vo. 31s. 6d.

———————— Holy Sepulchre and the Temple at Jerusalem; being the Substance of Two Lectures delivered at the Royal Institution, 1862 and '65. Woodcuts. 8vo. 7s. 6d.

FISHER'S (REV. GEORGE) Elements of Geometry, for the Use of Schools. *Fifth Edition.* 18mo. 1s. 6d.

———————— First Principles of Algebra, for the Use of Schools. *Fifth Edition.* 18mo. 1s. 6d.

FLOWER GARDEN (THE). By REV. THOS. JAMES. Fcap. 8vo. 1s.

FONNEREAU'S (T. G.) Diary of a Dutiful Son. Fcap. 8vo. 4s. 6d.

FORBES' (C. S.) Iceland; its Volcanoes, Geysers, and Glaciers. Illustrations. Post 8vo. 14s.

FORSTER'S (JOHN) Arrest of the Five Members by Charles the First. A Chapter of English History re-written. Post 8vo. 12s.

———————— Grand Remonstrance, 1641. With an Essay on English freedom under the Plantagenet and Tudor Sovereigns. *Second Edition.* Post 8vo. 12s.

———————— Sir John Eliot: a Biography, 1590—1632. With Portraits. 2 Vols. Crown 8vo. 30s.

———————— Biographies of Oliver Cromwell, Daniel De Foe, Sir Richard Steele, Charles Churchill, Samuel Foote. *Third Edition.* Post 8vo. 12s.

FORD'S (Richard) Handbook for Spain, Andalusia, Ronda, Valencia, Catalonia, Granada, Gallicia, Arragon, Navarre, &c. *Third Edition.* 2 Vols. Post 8vo. 30s.

———— Gatherings from Spain. Post 8vo. 3s. 6d.

FORSYTH'S (William) Life and Times of Cicero. With Selections from his Correspondence and Orations. Illustrations. 2 Vols. Post 8vo. 18s.

FORTUNE'S (Robert) Narrative of Two Visits to the Tea Countries of China, 1843-52. *Third Edition.* Woodcuts. 2 Vols. Post 8vo. 18s.

———— Third Visit to China. 1853-6. Woodcuts. 8vo. 16s.

———— Yedo and Peking. With Notices of the Agriculture and Trade of China, during a Fourth Visit to that Country. Illustrations. 8vo. 16s.

FOSS' (Edward) Judges of England. With Sketches of their Lives, and Notices of the Courts at Westminster, from the Conquest to the Present Time. 9 Vols. 8vo. 114s.

FRANCE (History of). From the Conquest by the Gauls to Recent Times. By Mrs. Markham. *New and Chaper Edition.* Woodcuts. 12mo. 4s.

———— (The Student's History of). From the Earliest Times to the Establishment of the Second Empire, 1852. By W. H. Pearson. Edited by Wm. Smith, LL.D. Woodcuts. Post 8vo. 7s. 6d.

FRENCH (The) in Algiers; The Soldier of the Foreign Legion— and the Prisoners of Abd-el-Kadir. Translated by Lady Duff Gordon. Post 8vo. 2s.

GALTON'S (Francis) Art of Travel; or, Hints on the Shifts and Contrivances available in Wild Countries. *Third Edition.* Woodcuts. Post 8vo. 7s. 6d.

GEOGRAPHY, ANCIENT (The Student's Manual of). By Rev. W. L. Bevan. Woodcuts. Post 8vo. 7s. 6d.

———— MODERN (The Student's Manual). By Rev. W. L. Bevan. Woodcuts. Post 8vo. *In the Press.*

———— Journal of the Royal Geographical Society of London. 8vo.

GERMANY (History of). From the Invasion by Marius, to Recent times. By Mrs. Markham. *New and Cheaper Edition.* Woodcuts. 12mo. 4s.

GIBBON'S (Edward) History of the Decline and Fall of the Roman Empire. Edited, with Notes, by Dean Milman and M. Guizot. *A New Edition.* Preceded by his Autobiography. And Edited, with Notes, by Dr. Wm. Smith. Maps. 8 Vols. 8vo. 60s.

———— (The Student's Gibbon); Being an Epitome of the above work, incorporating the Researches of Recent Commentators. By Dr. Wm. Smith. Woodcuts. Post 8vo. 7s. 6d.

GIFFARD'S (Edward) Deeds of Naval Daring; or, Anecdotes of the British Navy. New Edition. Fcap. 8vo. 3s. 6d.

GOLDSMITH'S (Oliver) Works. A New Edition. Printed from the last editions revised by the Author. Edited by Peter Cunningham. Vignettes. 4 Vols. 8vo. 30s.

GLADSTONE'S (Right. Hon.W. E.) Financial Statements of 1853,
60, 63, and 64; also his Speeches on Tax-Bills, 1861, and on Charities,
1863. *Second Edition.* 8vo. 12s.

———————— Address on the Place of Ancient Greece in the
Providential Order of the World. *Fourth Edition.* 8vo. 2s. 6d.

———————— Wedgwood :. an Address delivered at Burslem.
Woodcuts. Post 8vo. 2s. *A Cheap Edition,* 1s.

GLEIG'S (Rev. G. R.) Campaigns of the British Army at Washington and New Orleans.. Post 8vo. 2s.

———————— Story of the Battle of Waterloo. Post 8vo. 3s. 6d.

———————— Narrative of Sale's Brigade in Affghanistan. Post 8vo. 2s.

———————— Life of Robert Lord Clive. Post 8vo. 3s. 6d.

———————— Life and Letters of Sir Thomas Munro. Post 8vo 3s. 6d.

GONGORA; An Historical Essay on the Times of Philip III. and
IV. of Spain. With Illustrations. By Archdeacon Churton. Portrait. 2 vols. Post 8vo. 15s.

GORDON'S (Sir Alex. Duff) Sketches of German Life, and Scenes
from the War of Liberation. From the German. Post 8vo. 3s. 6d.

———————— (Lady Duff) Amber-Witch :. A Trial for Witch-.
craft. From the German. Post 8vo. 2s.

———————— French in Algiers. 1. The Soldier of the Foreign
Legion. 2. The Prisoners of Abd-el-Kadir. From the French.
Post 8vo. 2s.

GOUGER'S (Henry) Personal Narrative of Two Years' Imprison-
ment in Burmah. *Second Edition.* Woodcuts. Post 8vo. 12s.

GRAMMARS (Latin and Greek). See Curtius ; Smith ; King
Edward VIth., &c. &c.

GREECE (The Student's History of). From the Earliest
Times to the Roman Conquest. By Wm. Smith, LL.D. Wood-.
cuts. Post 8vo. 7s. 6d.

———————— (A Smaller History of, for Young Persons). By Dr.
Wm. Smith. Woodcuts. 16mo. 3s. 6d.

GRENVILLE (The) PAPERS. Being the Public and Private
Correspondence of George Grenville, including his Private Diary.
Edited by W. J. Smith. 4 Vols. 8vo. 16s. each.

GREY (Earl) on Parliamentary Government and Reform ; with
Suggestions for the Improvement of our Representative System,
and an Examination of the Reform Bills of 1859—61. *Second Edition.*
8vo. 9s.

———————— (Sir George) Polynesian Mythology, and Ancient
Traditional History of the New Zealand Race. Woodcuts. Post
8vo. 10s. 6d.

GRUNER'S (Lewis) Brick and Terra-Cotta Buildings of Lombardy,
Fourteenth and Fifteenth Centuries. From careful Drawings and
Restorations. Engraved and printed in Colours. Illustrations. Small
folio. *Nearly Ready.*

GUIZOT'S (M.) Meditations on the Essence of Christianity, and
on the Religious Questions of the Day. Post 8vo. 9s. 6d.

GROTE'S (George) History of Greece. From the Earliest Times
to the close of the generation contemporary with the death of Alexander
the Great. *Fourth Edition.* Maps. 8 vols. 8vo. 112s.

———— Plato, and the other Companions of Socrates. 3
Vols. 8vo. 45s.

———— (Mrs.) Memoir of Ary Scheffer. Post 8vo. 8s. 6d.

———— Collected Papers. 8vo. 10s. 6d.

HALLAM'S (Henry) Constitutional History of England, from the
Accession of Henry the Seventh to the Death of George the Second.
Seventh Edition. 3 Vols. 8vo. 30s. Or Popular Edition, 3 Vols., Post
8vo, 18s.

———— History of Europe during the Middle Ages.
Tenth Edition. 3 Vols. 8vo. 30s. Or Popular Edition, 3 Vols., Post
8vo, 18s.

———— Literary History of Europe, during the 15th, 16th and
17th Centuries. *Fourth Edition.* 3 Vols. 8vo. 36s. Or Popular Edition,
4 Vols., Post 8vo., 24s.

———— Literary Essays and Characters, Extracted from the
above Work. Fcap. 8vo. 2s.

———— Historical Works. Containing History of England,
—Middle Ages of Europe,—Literary History of Europe. 10 Vols.
Post 8vo. 6s. each.

———— (Arthur) Remains; in Verse and Prose. With Preface, Memoir, and Portrait. Fcap. 8vo. 7s. 6d.

HAMILTON'S (James) Wanderings in North Africa. With Illustrations. Post 8vo. 12s.

HART'S ARMY LIST. (*Quarterly and Annually.*) 8vo. 10s. 6d.
and 21s. each.

HANNAH'S (Rev. Dr.) Bampton Lectures for 1863; the Divine
and Human Elements in Holy Scripture. 8vo. 10s. 6d.

HAY'S (J. H. Drummond) Western Barbary, its wild Tribes and
savage Animals. Post 8vo. 2s.

HEAD'S (Sir Francis) Horse and his Rider. Woodcuts. Post 8vo. 5s.

———— Rapid Journeys across the Pampas. Post 8vo. 2s.

———— Bubbles from the Brunnen of Nassau. With Illustrations. Post 8vo.

———— Emigrant. Fcap. 8vo. 2s. 6d.

———— Stokers and Pokers; or, N.-Western Railway. Post 8vo. 2s.

———— Fortnight in Ireland. Map. 8vo. 12s.

———— (Sir Edmund) Shall and Will; or, Future Auxiliary
Verbs. Fcap. 8vo. 4s.

HEBER'S (Bishop) Journey through the Upper Provinces of India,
from Calcutta to Bombay, with an Account of a Journey to Madras
and the Southern Provinces. *Twelfth Edition.* 2 Vols. Post 8vo. 7s.

———— Poetical Works, including Palestine, Europe, The Red
Sea, Hymns, &c. *Sixth Edition.* Portrait. Fcap. 8vo. 6s.

HERODOTUS. A New English Version. Edited, with Notes
and Essays, historical, ethnographical, and geographical, by Rev. G.
Rawlinson, assisted by Sir Henry Rawlinson and Sir J. G. Wilkinson. *Second Edition.* Maps and Woodcuts. 4 Vols. 8vo. 48s.

HAND-BOOK—TRAVEL-TALK. English, French, German, and Italian. 18mo. 3s. 6d.

———— NORTH GERMANY, HOLLAND, BELGIUM, and the Rhine to Switzerland. Map. Post 8vo. 10s.

———— KNAPSACK GUIDE—BELGIUM AND THE RHINE. Post 8vo. (In the Press.)

———— SOUTH GERMANY, Bavaria, Austria, Styria, Salzberg, the Austrian and Bavarian Alps, the Tyrol, Hungary, and the Danube, from Ulm to the Black Sea. Map. Post 8vo. 10s.

———— KNAPSACK GUIDE—THE TYROL. Post 8vo. (In the Press.)

———— PAINTING. German, Flemish, and Dutch Schools. Edited by DR. WAAGEN. Woodcuts. 2 Vols. Post 8vo. 24s.

———— LIVES OF THE EARLY FLEMISH PAINTERS, with Notices of their Works. By CROWE and CAVALCASELLE. Illustrations. Post 8vo. 12s.

———— SWITZERLAND, Alps of Savoy, and Piedmont. Maps. Post 8vo. 9s.

————KNAPSACK GUIDE — SWITZERLAND. Post 8vo. 5s.

———— FRANCE, Normandy, Brittany, the French Alps, the Rivers Loire, Seine, Rhone, and Garonne, Dauphiné, Provence, and the Pyrenees. Maps. Post 8vo. 10s.

———— KNAPSACK GUIDE — FRANCE. Post 8vo. (In the Press.)

———— PARIS AND ITS ENVIRONS. Map. Post 8vo. 5s.

———— SPAIN, Andalusia, Ronda, Granada, Valencia, Catalonia, Gallicia, Arragon, and Navarre. Maps. 2 Vols. Post 8vo. 30s.

———— PORTUGAL, LISBON, &c. Map. Post 8vo. 9s.

———— NORTH ITALY, Piedmont, Liguria, Venetia, Lombardy, Parma, Modena, and Romagna. Map. Post 8vo. 12s.

———— CENTRAL ITALY, Lucca, Tuscany, Florence, The Marches, Umbria, and the Patrimony of St. Peter's. Map. Post 8vo. 10s.

———— ROME AND ITS ENVIRONS. Map. Post 8vo. 9s.

———— SOUTH ITALY, Two Sicilies, Naples, Pompeii, Herculaneum, and Vesuvius. Map. Post 8vo. 10s.

———— KNAPSACK GUIDE—ITALY. Post 8vo. 6s.

———— SICILY, Palermo, Messina, Catania, Syracuse, Etna, and the Ruins of the Greek Temples. Map. Post 8vo. 12s.

———— PAINTING. The Italian Schools. From the German of KUGLER. Edited by Sir CHARLES EASTLAKE, R.A. Woodcuts. 2 Vols. Post 8vo. 30s.

———— LIVES OF THE EARLY ITALIAN PAINTERS, AND PROGRESS OF PAINTING IN ITALY, from CIMABUE to BASSANO. By Mrs. JAMESON. A New Edition. Woodcuts. Post 8vo. In the Press.

———— NORWAY, Map. Post 8vo. 5s.

———— DENMARK, SWEDEN, and NORWAY. Maps. Post 8vo. 15s.

HAND-BOOK—GREECE, the Ionian Islands, Albania, Thessaly, and Macedonia. Maps. Post 8vo. 15s.

—————— TURKEY, Malta, Asia Minor, Constantinople, Armenia, Mesopotamia, &c. Maps. Post 8vo.

—————— EGYPT, Thebes, the Nile, Alexandria, Cairo, the Pyramids, Mount Sinai, &c. Map. Post 8vo. 15s.

—————— SYRIA AND PALESTINE, Peninsula of Sinai, Eidom, and Syrian Desert. Maps. 2 Vols. Post 8vo. 24s.

—————— BOMBAY AND MADRAS. Map. 2 Vols. Post 8vo. 24s.

—————— RUSSIA, Poland, and Finland. Maps. Post 8vo. 12s.

—————— MODERN LONDON. A Complete Guide to all the Sights and Objects of Interest in the Metropolis. Map. 16mo. 3s. 6d.

—————— WESTMINSTER ABBEY. Woodcuts. 16mo. 1s.

—————— KENT AND SUSSEX, Canterbury, Dover, Ramsgate, Sheerness, Rochester, Chatham, Woolwich, Brighton, Chichester, Worthing, Hastings, Lewes, Arundel, &c. Map. Post 8vo. 10s.

—————— SURREY AND HANTS, Kingston, Croydon, Reigate, Guildford, Winchester, Southampton, Portsmouth, and Isle of Wight. Maps. Post 8vo. 10s.

—————— BERKS, BUCKS, AND OXON, Windsor, Eton, Reading, Aylesbury, Uxbridge, Wycombe, Henley, the City and University of Oxford, and the Descent of the Thames to Maidenhead and Windsor. Map. Post 8vo. 7s. 6d.

—————— WILTS, DORSET, AND SOMERSET, Salisbury, Chippenham, Weymouth, Sherborne, Wells, Bath, Bristol, Taunton, &c. Map. Post 8vo. 7s. 6d.

—————— DEVON AND CORNWALL, Exeter, Ilfracombe, Linton, Sidmouth, Dawlish, Teignmouth, Plymouth, Devonport, Torquay, Launceston, Truro, Penzance, Falmouth, &c. Maps. Post 8vo. 10s.

—————— NORTH AND SOUTH WALES, Bangor, Carnarvon, Beaumaris, Snowdon, Conway, Menai Straits, Carmarthen, Pembroke, Tenby, Swansea, The Wye, &c. Maps. 2 Vols. Post 8vo. 12s.

—————— SOUTHERN CATHEDRALS OF ENGLAND— Winchester, Salisbury, Exeter, Wells, Chichester, Rochester, Canterbury. With 110 Illustrations. 2 Vols. Crown 8vo. 24s.

—————— EASTERN CATHEDRALS OF ENGLAND— Oxford, Peterborough, Norwich, Ely, and Lincoln. With 90 Illustrations. Crown 8vo. 18s.

—————— WESTERN CATHEDRALS OF ENGLAND— Bristol, Gloucester, Hereford, Worcester, and Lichfield. With 50 Illustrations. Crown 8vo. 16s.

—————— FAMILIAR QUOTATIONS. From English Authors. *Third Edition.* Fcap. 8vo. 5s.

HESSEY (Rev. Dr.). Sunday—Its Origin, History, and Present Obligations. Being the Bampton Lectures for 1860. *Second Edition.* 8vo. 16s. Or *Third and Popular Edition.* Post 8vo.

HICKMAN'S (Wm.) Treatise on the Law and Practice of Naval Courts-Martial. 8vo. 10s. 6d.

c

HOME AND COLONIAL LIBRARY. A Series of Works adapted for all circles and classes of Readers, having been selected for their acknowledged interest and ability of the Authors. Post 8vo. Published at 2s. and 3s. 6d. each, and arranged under two distinctive heads as follows :—

CLASS A.
HISTORY, BIOGRAPHY, AND HISTORIC TALES.

1. SIEGE OF GIBRALTAR. By JOHN DRINKWATER. 2s.
2. THE AMBER-WITCH. By LADY DUFF GORDON. 2s.
3. CROMWELL AND BUNYAN. By ROBERT SOUTHEY. 2s.
4. LIFE OF SIR FRANCIS DRAKE. By JOHN BARROW. 2s.
5. CAMPAIGNS AT WASHINGTON. By REV. G. R. GLEIG. 2s.
6. THE FRENCH IN ALGIERS. By LADY DUFF GORDON. 2s.
7. THE FALL OF THE JESUITS. 2s.
8. LIVONIAN TALES. 2s.
9. LIFE OF CONDE. By LORD MAHON. 3s. 6d.
10. SALE'S BRIGADE. By REV. G. R. GLEIG. 2s.
11. THE SIEGES OF VIENNA. By LORD ELLESMERE. 2s.
12. THE WAYSIDE CROSS. By CAPT. MILMAN. 2s.
13. SKETCHES OF GERMAN LIFE. By SIR A. GORDON. 3s. 6d.
14. THE BATTLE OF WATERLOO. By REV. G. R. GLEIG. 3s. 6d.
15. AUTOBIOGRAPHY OF STEFFENS. 2s.
16. THE BRITISH POETS. By THOMAS CAMPBELL. 3s. 6d.
17. HISTORICAL ESSAYS. By LORD MAHON. 3s. 6d.
18. LIFE OF LORD CLIVE. By REV. G. R. GLEIG. 3s. 6d.
19. NORTH - WESTERN RAILWAY. By SIR F. B. HEAD. 2s.
20. LIFE OF MUNRO. By REV. G. R. GLEIG. 3s. 6d.

CLASS B.
VOYAGES, TRAVELS, AND ADVENTURES.

1. BIBLE IN SPAIN. By GEORGE BORROW. 3s. 6d.
2. GIPSIES OF SPAIN. By GEORGE BORROW. 3s. 6d.
3 & 4. JOURNALS IN INDIA. By BISHOP HEBER. 2 Vols. 7s.
5. TRAVELS IN THE HOLY LAND. By IRBY and MANGLES. 2s.
6. MOROCCO AND THE MOORS. By J. DRUMMOND HAY. 2s.
7. LETTERS FROM THE BALTIC. By a LADY. 2s.
8. NEW SOUTH WALES. By MRS. MEREDITH. 2s.
9. THE WEST INDIES. By M. G. LEWIS. 2s.
10. SKETCHES OF PERSIA. By SIR JOHN MALCOLM. 3s. 6d.
11. MEMOIRS OF FATHER RIPA. 2s.
12. 13. TYPEE AND OMOO. By HERMANN MELVILLE. 2 Vols. 7s.
14. MISSIONARY LIFE IN CANADA. By REV. J. ABBOTT. 2s.
15. LETTERS FROM MADRAS. By a LADY. 2s.
16. HIGHLAND · SPORTS. By CHARLES ST. JOHN. 3s. 6d.
17. PAMPAS JOURNEYS. By SIR F. B. HEAD. 2s.
18. GATHERINGS FROM SPAIN. By RICHARD FORD. 3s. 6d.
19. THE RIVER AMAZON. By W. H. EDWARDS. 2s.
20. MANNERS & CUSTOMS OF INDIA. By REV. C. ACLAND. 2s.
21. ADVENTURES IN MEXICO. By G. F. RUXTON. 3s. 6d.
22. PORTUGAL AND GALLICIA. By LORD CARNARVON. 3s. 6d.
23. BUSH LIFE IN AUSTRALIA. By REV. H. W. HAYGARTH. 2s.
24. THE LIBYAN DESERT. By BAYLE ST. JOHN. 2s.
25. SIERRA LEONE. By a LADY. 3s. 6d.

*** Each work may be had separately.

HILLARD'S (G. S.) Six Months in Italy. 2 Vols. Post 8vo. 16s.

HOLLWAY'S (J. G.) Month in Norway. Fcap. 8vo. 2s.

HONEY BEE (The). An Essay. By Rev. Thomas James. Reprinted from the "Quarterly Review." Fcap. 8vo. 1s.

HOOK'S (Dean) Church Dictionary. *Ninth Edition.* 8vo. 16s.

———— (Theodore) Life. By J. G. Lockhart. Reprinted from the "Quarterly Review." Fcap. 8vo. 1s.

HOOKER'S (Dr. J. D.) Himalayan Journals; or, Notes of an Oriental Naturalist in Bengal, the Sikkim and Nepal Himalayas, the Khasia Mountains, &c. *Second Edition.* Woodcuts. 2 Vols. Post 8vo. 18s.

HOPE'S (A. J. Beresford) English Cathedral of the Nineteenth Century. With Illustrations. 8vo. 12s.

HORACE (Works of). Edited by Dean Milman. With 300 Woodcuts. Crown 8vo. 21s.

———— (Life of). By Dean Milman. Woodcuts, and coloured Borders. 8vo. 9s.

HOUGHTON'S (Lord) Poetical Works. Fcap. 8vo. 6s. 6d.

HUME'S (The Student's) History of England, from the Invasion of Julius Cæsar to the Revolution of 1688. Corrected and continued to 1858. Edited by Dr. Wm. Smith. Woodcuts. Post 8vo. 7s. 6d.

HUTCHINSON (Gen.) on the most expeditious, certain, and easy Method of Dog-Breaking. *Fourth Edition.* Enlarged and revised, with 40 Illustrations. Crown 8vo. 15s.

HUTTON'S (H. E.) Principia Græca; an Introduction to the Study of Greek. Comprehending Grammar, Delectus, and Exercise-book, with Vocabularies. *Third Edition.* 12mo. 3s. 6d.

IRBY AND MANGLES' Travels in Egypt, Nubia, Syria, and the Holy Land. Post 8vo. 2s.

JAMES' (Rev. Thomas) Fables of Æsop. A New Translation, with Historical Preface. With 100 Woodcuts by Tenniel and Wolf. *Forty-eighth Thousand.* Post 8vo. 2s. 6d.

JAMESON'S (Mrs.) Lives of the Early Italian Painters, from Cimabue to Bassano, and the Progress of Painting in Italy. *New Edition.* With Woodcuts. Post 8vo.

JESSE'S (Edward) Gleanings in Natural History. *Eighth Edition.* Fcp. 8vo. 6s.

JOHNSON'S (Dr. Samuel) Life. By James Boswell. Including the Tour to the Hebrides. Edited by Mr. Croker. Portraits. Royal 8vo. 10s.

———— Lives of the most eminent English Poets. Edited by Peter Cunningham. 3 vols. 8vo. 22s. 6d.

JOURNAL OF A NATURALIST. Woodcuts. Post 8vo. 9s. 6d.

KEN'S (Bishop) Life. By a Layman, Author of "Life of the Messiah." *Second Edition.* Portrait. 2 Vols. 8vo. 18s.

———— Exposition of the Apostles' Creed. Extracted from his "Practice of Divine Love." Fcap. 1s. 6d.

———— Approach to the Holy Altar. Extracted from his "Manual of Prayer" and "Practice of Divine Love." Fcap. 8vo. 1s. 6d.

KENNEDY'S (GENERAL SIR J. SHAW) Notes on the Battle of
Waterloo. With a Memoir of his Life and Services, and a Plan for
the Defence of Canada. With Map and Plans. 8vo. 7s. 6d.

KING'S (REV. S. W.) Italian Valleys of the Alps; a Tour
through all the Romantic and less-frequented "Vals" of Northern
Piedmont. Illustrations. Crown 8vo. 18s.

———— (REV. C. W.) Antique Gems; their Origin, Use, and
Value, as Interpreters of Ancient History, and as illustrative of Ancient
Art. Illustrations. 8vo. 42s.

KING EDWARD VITH's Latin Grammar; or, an Introduction
to the Latin Tongue, for the Use of Schools. Seventeenth Edition. 12mo.
3s. 6d.

———————————— First Latin Book; or, the Accidence,
Syntax, and Prosody, with an English Translation for the Use of Junior
Classes. Fifth Edition. 12mo. 2s. 6d.

KIRK'S (J. FOSTER) History of Charles the Bold, Duke of Bur-
gundy. Portrait. 2 Vols. 8vo. 30s.

KERR'S (ROBERT) GENTLEMAN'S HOUSE; OR, HOW TO PLAN
ENGLISH RESIDENCES, FROM THE PARSONAGE TO THE PALACE. With
Tables of Accommodation and Cost, and a Series of Selected Views
and Plans. Second Edition. 8vo. 24s.

———— Ancient Lights; a Book for Architects, Surveyors,
Lawyers, and Landlords. 8vo. 5s. 6d.

KING GEORGE THE THIRD'S CORRESPONDENCE WITH
LORD NORTH, 1769-82. Edited, with Notes and Introduction, by
W. BODHAM DONNE. 2 vols. 8vo. Published by permission. From
the Royal Library at Windsor. (In the Press.)

KUGLER'S Italian Schools of Painting. Edited, with Notes, by
SIR CHARLES EASTLAKE. Third Edition. Woodcuts. 2 Vols. Post
8vo. 30s.

———— German, Dutch, and Flemish Schools of Painting.
Edited, with Notes, by DR. WAAGEN. Second Edition. Woodcuts. 2
Vols. Post 8vo. 24s.

LAYARD'S (A. H.) Nineveh and its Remains. Being a Narrative of Researches and Discoveries amidst the Ruins of Assyria.
With an Account of the Chaldean Christians of Kurdistan; the Yezedis,
or Devil-worshippers; and an Enquiry into the Manners and Arts of
the Ancient Assyrians. Sixth Edition. Plates and Woodcuts. 2 Vols.
8vo. 36s.

———————————— Nineveh and Babylon; being the Result
of a Second Expedition to Assyria. Plates 8vo. 21s. On Fine
Paper, 2 Vols. 8vo. 30s.

———— Popular Account of Nineveh and Babylon. A
New Edition. With Woodcuts. Post 8vo. (In the Press.)

LESLIE'S (C. R.) Handbook for Young Painters. With Illustrations. Post 8vo. 10s. 6d.

———————————— Autobiographical Recollections, with Selections
from his Correspondence. Edited by TOM TAYLOR. Portrait. 2 Vols.
Post 8vo. 18s.

———————— Life of Sir Joshua Reynolds. With an Account
of his Works, and a Sketch of his Cotemporaries. By C. R. LESLIE
and TOM TAYLOR. Illustrations. 2 Vols. 8vo. 42s.

LETTERS FROM THE BALTIC. By a Lady. Post 8vo. 2s.
——————— Madras. By a Lady. Post 8vo. 2s.
——————— Sierra Leone. By a Lady. Edited by the Honourable Mrs. Norton. Post 8vo. 3s. 6d.

LEWIS' (Sir G. C.) Essay on the Government of Dependencies. 8vo. 12s.
——————— Glossary of Provincial Words used in Herefordshire and some of the adjoining Counties. 12mo. 4s. 6d.
——————— (M. G.) Journal of a Residence among the Negroes in the West Indies. Post 8vo. 2s.

LIDDELL'S (Dean) History of Rome. From the Earliest Times to the Establishment of the Empire. With the History of Literature and Art. 2 Vols. 8vo. 28s.
——————— Student's History of Rome, abridged from the above Work. With Woodcuts. Post 8vo. 7s. 6d.

LINDSAY'S (Lord) Lives of the Lindsays; or, a Memoir of the Houses of Crawfurd and Balcarres. With Extracts from Official Papers and Personal Narratives. Second Edition. 3 Vols. 8vo. 24s.
——————— Report of the Claim of James, Earl of Crawfurd and Balcarres, to the Original Dukedom of Montrose, created in 1488 Folio. 15s.
——————— Scepticism; a Retrogressive Movement in Theology and Philosophy. 8vo. 9s.

LISPINGS from LOW LATITUDES; or, the Journal of the Hon. Impulsia Gushington. Edited by Lord Dufferin. With 24 Plates, 4to. 21s.

LITTLE ARTHUR'S HISTORY OF ENGLAND. By Lady Callcott. 150th Thousand. With 20 Woodcuts. Fcap. 8vo. 2s. 6d.

LIVINGSTONE'S (Dr.) Popular Account of his Missionary Travels in South Africa. Illustrations. Post 8vo. 6s.
——————— Narrative of an Expedition to the Zambezi and its Tributaries; and of the Discovery of Lakes Shirwa and Nyassa. 1858-64. By David and Charles Livingstone. Map and Illustrations. 8vo. 21s.

LIVONIAN TALES. By the Author of "Letters from the Baltic." Post 8vo. 2s.

LOCKHART'S (J. G.) Ancient Spanish Ballads. Historical and Romantic. Translated, with Notes. New Edition. Illustrations. 4to. 21s. Or Popular Edition, Post 8vo. 2s. 6d.

LONDON'S (Bishop of) Dangers and Safeguards of Modern Theology. Containing Suggestions to the Theological Student under present difficulties. Second Edition. 8vo. 9s.

LOUDON'S (Mrs.) Instructions in Gardening for Ladies. With Directions and Calendar of Operations for Every Month. Eighth Edition. Woodcuts. Fcap. 8vo. 5s.

LUCAS' (Samuel) Secularia; or, Surveys on the Main Stream of History. 8vo. 12s.

LUCKNOW: a Lady's Diary of the Siege. Fcap. 8vo. 4s. 6d.

LYELL'S (Sir Charles) Elements of Geology; or, the Ancient Changes of the Earth and its Inhabitants considered as illustrative of Geology. Sixth Edition. Woodcuts. 8vo. 18s.
——————— Geological Evidences of the Antiquity of Man. Third Edition. Illustrations. 8vo. 14s.

LYTTELTON'S (Lord) Ephemera. Post 8vo. 10s. 6d.

LYTTON'S (Sir Edward Bulwer) Poems. *New Edition.* Post 8vo. 10s. 6d.

MACPHERSON'S (Major S. C.) Memorials of Service in India,. while Political Agent at Gwalior during the Mutiny, and formerly employed in the Suppression of Human Sacrifices in Orissa. Edited by his Brother. With Portrait and Illustrations. 8vo. 12s.

MAHON'S (Lord) History of England, from the Peace of Utrecht to the Peace of Versailles, 1713—83. *Library Edition.* 7 Vols. 8vo. 93s. *Popular Edition,* 7 Vols. Post 8vo. 35s.

———————— " Forty-Five ; " a Narrative of the Rebellion in Scotland. Post 8vo. 3s.

———————— History of British India from its Origin till the Peace of 1783. Post 8vo. 3s. 6d.

———————— Spain under Charles the Second; 1690 to 1700. *Second Edition.* Post 8vo. 6s. 6d.

———————— Historical and Critical Essays. Post 8vo. 3s. 6d.

———————— Story of Joan of Arc. Fcap. 8vo. 1s.

———————— Addresses. Fcap. 8vo. 1s.

———————— Life of William Pitt, with Extracts from his MS. Papers. *Second Edition.* Portraits. 4 Vols. Post 8vo. 42s.

———————— Miscellanies. *Second Edition.* Post 8vo. 5s. 6d.

———————— Condé, surnamed the Great. Post 8vo. 3s. 6d.

———————— Belisarius. *Second Edition.* Post 8vo. 10s. 6d.

MᶜCLINTOCK'S (Capt. Sir F. L.) Narrative of the Discovery of the Fate of Sir John Franklin and his Companions in the Arctic Seas. *Twelfth Thousand.* Illustrations. 8vo. 16s.

MᶜCULLOCH'S (J. R.) Collected Edition of Ricardo's Political Works. With Notes and Memoir. *Second Edition.* 8vo. 16s.

MacDOUGALL (Col.) On Modern Warfare as Influenced by Modern Artillery. With Plans. Post 8vo. 12s.

MAINE (H. Sumner) On Ancient Law: its Connection with the Early History of Society, and its Relation to Modern Ideas. *Third Edition.* 8vo. 12s.

MALCOLM'S (Sir John) Sketches of Persia. Post 8vo. . 3s. 6d.

MANSEL (Rev. H. L.) Limits of Religious Thought Examined. Being the Bampton Lectures for 1858. *Fourth Edition.* Post 8vo. 7s. 6d.

MANSFIELD (Sir William) On the Introduction . of a Gold Currency into India: a Contribution to the Literature of Political Economy. 8vo. 3s. 6d.

MANTELL'S (Gideon A.) Thoughts on Animalcules ; or, the Invisible World, as revealed by the Microscope. *Second Edition.* Plates. 16mo. 6s.

MANUAL OF SCIENTIFIC ENQUIRY, Prepared for the Use of Officers and Travellers. By various Writers. Edited by Sir J. F. Herschel and Rev. R. Main. *Third Edition.* Maps. Post 8vo. 9s. *(Published by order of the Lords of the Admiralty.)*

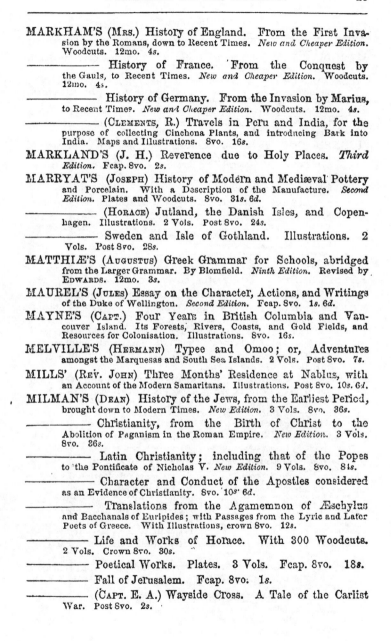

MARKHAM'S (Mrs.) History of England. From the First Invasion by the Romans, down to Recent Times. *New and Cheaper Edition.* Woodcuts. 12mo. 4s.

——————— History of France. 'From the Conquest by the Gauls, to Recent Times. *New and Cheaper Edition.* Woodcuts. 12mo. 4s.

——————— History of Germany. From the Invasion by Marius, to Recent Times. *New and Cheaper Edition.* Woodcuts. 12mo. 4s.

——————— (Clements, R.) Travels in Peru and India, for the purpose of collecting Cinchona Plants, and introducing Bark into India. Maps and Illustrations. 8vo. 16s.

MARKLAND'S (J. H.) Reverence due to Holy Places. *Third Edition.* Fcap. 8vo. 2s.

MARRYAT'S (Joseph) History of Modern and Mediæval Pottery and Porcelain. With a Description of the Manufacture. *Second Edition.* Plates and Woodcuts. 8vo. 31s. 6d.

——————— (Horace) Jutland, the Danish Isles, and Copenhagen. Illustrations. 2 Vols. Post 8vo. 24s.

——————— Sweden and Isle of Gothland. Illustrations. 2 Vols. Post 8vo. 28s.

MATTHIÆ'S (Augustus) Greek Grammar for Schools, abridged from the Larger Grammar. By Blomfield. *Ninth Edition.* Revised by Edwards. 12mo. 3s.

MAUREL'S (Jules) Essay on the Character, Actions, and Writings of the Duke of Wellington. *Second Edition.* Fcap. 8vo. 1s. 6d.

MAYNE'S (Capt.) Four Years in British Columbia and Vancouver Island. Its Forests, Rivers, Coasts, and Gold Fields, and Resources for Colonisation. Illustrations. 8vo. 16s.

MELVILLE'S (Hermann) Typee and Omoo; or, Adventures amongst the Marquesas and South Sea Islands. 2 Vols. Post 8vo. 7s.

MILLS' (Rev. John) Three Months' Residence at Nablus, with an Account of the Modern Samaritans. Illustrations. Post 8vo. 10s. 6d.

MILMAN'S (Dean) History of the Jews, from the Earliest Period, brought down to Modern Times. *New Edition.* 3 Vols. 8vo. 36s.

——————— Christianity, from the Birth of Christ to the Abolition of Paganism in the Roman Empire. *New Edition.* 3 Vols. 8vo. 36s.

——————— Latin Christianity; including that of the Popes to 'the Pontificate of Nicholas V. *New Edition.* 9 Vols. 8vo. 84s.

——————— Character and Conduct of the Apostles considered as an Evidence of Christianity. 8vo. 10s. 6d.

——————— Translations from the Agamemnon of Æschylus and Bacchanals of Euripides; with Passages from the Lyric and Later Poets of Greece. With Illustrations, crown 8vo. 12s.

——————— Life and Works of Horace. With 300 Woodcuts. 2 Vols. Crown 8vo. 30s.

——————— Poetical Works. Plates. 3 Vols. Fcap. 8vo. 18s.

——————— Fall of Jerusalem. Fcap. 8vo. 1s.

——————— (Capt. E. A.) Wayside Cross. A Tale of the Carlist War. Post 8vo. 2s.

MEREDITH'S (Mrs. Charles) Notes and Sketches of New South Wales. Post 8vo. 2s.

MESSIAH (THE): A Narrative of the Life, Travels, Death, Resurrection, and Ascension of our Blessed Lord. By a Layman. Author of the "Life of Bishop Ken." Map. 8vo. 18s.

MICHIE'S (Alexander) Siberian Overland Route from Peking to Petersburg, through the Deserts and Steppes of Mongolia, Tartary, &c. Maps and Illustrations. 8vo. 16s.

MODERN DOMESTIC COOKERY. Founded on Principles of Economy and Practical Knowledge and adapted for Private Families. New Edition. Woodcuts. Fcap. 8vo. 5s.

MOORE'S (Thomas) Life and Letters of Lord Byron. Plates. 6 Vols. Fcap. 8vo. 18s.

——— Life and Letters of Lord Byron. Portraits. Royal 8vo. 9s.

MOTLEY'S (J. L.) History of the United Netherlands: from the Death of William the Silent to the Synod of Dort. Embracing the English-Dutch struggle against Spain; and a detailed Account of the Spanish Armada. Portraits. 2 Vols. 8vo. 30s.

MOUHOT'S (Henri) Siam, Cambojia, and Lao; a Narrative of Travels and Discoveries. Illustrations. 2 vols. 8vo. 32s.

MOZLEY'S (Rev. J. B.) Treatise on Predestination. 8vo. 14s.

——— Primitive Doctrine of Baptismal Regeneration. 8vo. 7s.6d.

MUNDY'S (General) Pen and Pencil Sketches in India. Third Edition. Plates. Post 8vo. 7s. 6d.

——— (Admiral) Account of the Italian Revolution, with Notices of Garibaldi, Francis II., and Victor Emmanuel. Post 8vo. 12s.

MUNRO'S (General Sir Thomas) Life and Letters. By the Rev. G. R. Gleig. Post 8vo. 3s. 6d.

MURCHISON'S (Sir Roderick) Russia in Europe and the Ural Mountains. With Coloured Maps, Plates, Sections, &c. 2 Vols. Royal 4to. 5l. 5s.

——— Siluria; or, a History of the Oldest Rocks containing Organic Remains. Third Edition. Map and Plates. 8vo. 42s.

MURRAY'S RAILWAY READING. Containing :—

Wellington. By Lord Ellesmere. 6d.	Hallam's Literary Essays. 2s.
Nimrod on the Chase. 1s.	Mahon's Joan of Arc. 1s.
Essays from "The Times." 2 Vols. 8s.	Head's Emigrant. 2s. 6d.
Music and Dress. 1s.	Nimrod on the Road. 1s.
Layard's Account of Nineveh. 5s.	Croker on the Guillotine. 1s.
Milman's Fall of Jerusalem. 1s.	Hollway's Norway. 2s.
Mahon's "Forty-Five." 3s.	Maurel's Wellington. 1s. 6d.
Life of Theodore Hook. 1s.	Campbell's Life of Bacon. 2s. 6d.
Deeds of Naval Daring. 3s. 6d.	The Flower Garden. 1s.
The Honey Bee. 1s.	Lockhart's Spanish Ballads. 2s. 6d.
James' Æsop's Fables. 2s. 6d.	Taylor's Notes from Life. 2s.
Nimrod on the Turf. 1s. 6d.	Rejected Addresses. 1s.
Art of Dining. 1s. 6d.	Penn's Hints on Angling. 1s.

MUSIC AND DRESS. By a Lady. Reprinted from the "Quarterly Review." Fcap. 8vo. 1s.

NAPIER'S (Sir Chas.) Life; chiefly derived from his Journals and Letters. By Sir W. Napier. Second Edition. Portraits. 4 Vols. Post 8vo. 48s.

——— (Sir Wm.) Life and Letters. Edited by H. A. Bruce, M.P. Portraits. 2 Vols. Crown 8vo. 28s.

——— English Battles and Sieges of the Peninsular War. Fourth Edition. Portrait. Post 8vo. 9s.

NAUTICAL ALMANACK. Royal 8vo. 2s. 6d. (By Authority.)

NAVY LIST. (Published Quarterly, by Authority.) 16mo. 2s. 6d.

NEW TESTAMENT (The) Illustrated by a Plain Explanatory
Commentary, and authentic Views of Sacred Places, from Sketches
and Photographs. Edited by ARCHDEACON CHURTON and REV. BASIL
JONES. With 110 Illustrations. 2 Vols. Crown 8vo. 30s. cloth ;
52s. 6d. calf; 63s. morocco.

NICHOLLS' (SIR GEORGE) History of the English, Irish and
Scotch Poor Laws. 4 Vols. 8vo.

———— (Rev. H. G.) Historical Account of the Forest of
Dean. Woodcuts, &c. Post 8vo. 10s. 6d.

NICOLAS' (SIR HARRIS) Historic Peerage of England. Exhi-
biting the Origin, Descent, and Present State of every Title of Peerage which has existed in this Country since the Conquest. By
WILLIAM COURTHOPE. 8vo. 30s.

NIMROD On the Chace—The Turf—and The Road. Reprinted
from the "Quarterly Review." Woodcuts. Fcap. 8vo. 3s. 6d.

O'CONNOR'S (R.) Field Sports of France ; or, Hunting, Shooting,
and Fishing on the Continent. Woodcuts. 12mo. 7s. 6d.

OXENHAM'S (REV. W.) English Notes for Latin Elegiacs ; designed
for early Proficients in the Art of Latin Versification, with Prefatory
Rules of Composition in Elegiac Metre. Fourth Edition. 12mo. 3s. 6d.

PARIS' (DR.) Philosophy in Sport made Science in Earnest;
or, the First Principles of Natural Philosophy inculcated by aid of the
Toys and Sports of Youth. Ninth Edition. Woodcuts. Post 8vo. 7s. 6d.

PEEL'S (SIR ROBERT) Memoirs. Edited by EARL STANHOPE
and Right Hon. E. CARDWELL. 2 Vols. Post 8vo. 7s. 6d. each.

PENN'S (RICHARD) Maxims and Hints for an Angler and Chess-
player. New Edition. Woodcuts. Fcap. 8vo. 1s.

PENROSE'S (F. C.) Principles of Athenian Architecture, and the
Optical Refinements exhibited in the Construction of the Ancient
Buildings at Athens, from a Survey. With 40 Plates. Folio. 5l. 5s.

PERCY'S (JOHN, M.D.) Metallurgy of Iron and Steel ; or, the Art
of Extracting Metals from their Ores and adapting them to various purposes of Manufacture. Illustrations. 8vo. 42s.

PHILLIPP (CHARLES SPENCER MARCH) On Jurisprudence. 8vo. 12s.

PHILLIPS' (JOHN) Memoirs of William Smith, the Geologist.
Portrait. 8vo. 7s. 6d.

———— Geology of Yorkshire, The Coast, and Limestone
District. Plates. 4to. Part I., 20s.—Part II., 30s.

———— Rivers, Mountains, and Sea Coast of Yorkshire.
With Essays on the Climate, Scenery, and Ancient Inhabitants.
Second Edition, Plates. 8vo. 15s.

PHILPOTTS' (BISHOP) Letters to the late Charles Butler, on the
Theological parts of his "Book of the Roman Catholic Church;" with
Remarks on certain Works of Dr. Milner and Dr. Lingard, and on some
parts of the Evidence of Dr. Doyle. Second Edition. 8vo. 16s.

POPE'S (ALEXANDER) Life and Works. A New Edition. Containing nearly 500 unpublished Letters. Edited, with a NEW LIFE,
Introductions and Notes, by REV. WHITWELL ELWIN. Portraits.
8vo. (In the Press.)

PORTER'S (Rev. J. L.) Five Years in Damascus. With Travels to Palmyra, Lebanon and other Scripture Sites. Map and Woodcuts. 2 Vols. Post 8vo. 21s.

———— Handbook for Syria and Palestine: including an Account of the Geography, History, Antiquities, and Inhabitants of these Countries, the Peninsula of Sinai, Edom, and the Syrian Desert. Maps. 2 Vols. Post 8vo. 24s.

PRAYER-BOOK (Illustrated), with 1000 Illustrations of Borders, Initials, Vignettes, &c. Edited, with Notes, by Rev. Thos. James. Medium 8vo. 18s. cloth; 13s. 6d. calf; 36s. morocco.

PRECEPTS FOR THE CONDUCT OF LIFE. Extracted from the Scriptures. Second Edition. Fcap. 8vo. 1s.

PUSS IN BOOTS. With 12 Illustrations. By Otto Speckter. 16mo. 1s. 6d. or Coloured, 2s. 6d.

QUARTERLY REVIEW (The). 8vo. 6s.

RAMBLES in the Syrian Deserts among the Turkomans and Bedaweens. Post 8vo. 10s. 6d.

RAWLINSON'S (Rev. George) Herodotus. A New English Version. Edited with Notes and Essays. Assisted by Sir Henry Rawlinson and Sir J. G. Wilkinson. Second Edition. Maps and Woodcut. 4 Vols. 8vo. 48s.

———— Historical Evidences of the truth of the Scripture Records stated anew. Second Edition. 8vo. 14s.

———— Five Great Monarchies of the Ancient World, Chaldæa, Assyria, Media, Babylonia, and Persia. Illustrations. 4 Vols. 8vo. 16s. each.

REJECTED ADDRESSES (The). By James and Horace Smith. Fcap. 8vo. 1s.

RENNIE'S (D. F.) British Arms in Peking, 1860; Kagosima, 1862. Post 8vo. 12s.

———— Peking and the Pekingese: Being a Narrative of the First Year of the British Embassy in China. Illustrations. 2 Vols. Post 8vo. 24s.

———— Story of Bhotan and the Dooar War; including Sketches of a Residence in the Himalayas and Visit to Bhotan in 1865. Map and Woodcut. Post 8vo.

REYNOLDS' (Sir Joshua) Life and Times. Commenced by C. R. Leslie, R.A., continued and concluded by Tom Taylor. Portraits and Illustrations. 2 Vols. 8vo. 42s.

———— Descriptive Catalogue of his Works. With Notices of their present owners and localities. By Tom Taylor and Charles W. Franks. With Illustrations. Fcap. 4to. (In the Press.)

RICARDO'S (David) Political Works. With a Notice of his Life and Writings. By J. R. M'Culloch. New Edition. 8vo. 16s.

RIPA'S (Father) Memoirs during Thirteen Years' Residence at the Court of Peking. From the Italian. Post 8vo. 2s.

ROBERTSON'S (Canon) History of the Christian Church, from the Apostolic Age to the Concordat of Worms, A.D. 1123. Second Edition. 3 Vols. 8vo. 28s.

ROBINSON'S (Rev. Dr.) Later Biblical Researches in the Holy Land. Being a Journal of Travels in 1852. Maps. 8vo. 15s.

———Physical Geography of the Holy Land. Post 8vo. 10s. 6d.

ROME (The Student's History of). From the Earliest Times to the Establishment of the Empire. By Dean Liddell. Woodcuts. Post 8vo. 7s 6d.

——— (A Smaller History of, for Young Persons). By Wm. Smith, LL.D. Woodcuts. 16mo. 3s. 6d.

ROWLAND'S (David) Manual of the English Constitution; Its Rise, Growth, and Present State. Post 8vo. 10s. 6d.

——————— Laws of Nature the Foundation of Morals. Post 8vo. 6s.

RUNDELL'S (Mrs.) Domestic Cookery, adapted for Private Families. New Edition. Woodcuts. Fcap. 8vo. 5s.

RUSSELL'S (J. Rutherfurd) History of the Heroes of Medicine. Portraits. 8vo. 14s.

RUXTON'S (George F.) Travels in Mexico; with Adventures among the Wild Tribes and Animals of the Prairies and Rocky Mountains. Post 8vo. 3s. 6d.

SALE'S (Sir Robert) Brigade in Affghanistan. With an Account of the Defence of Jellalabad. By Rev. G. R. Gleig. Post 8vo. 2s.

SANDWITH'S (Humphry) Siege of Kars. Post 8vo. 3s. 6d.

SCOTT'S (G. Gilbert) Secular and Domestic Architecture, Present and Future. Second Edition. 8vo. 9s.

——— (Rev. Robert, D.D., Master of Baliol) Sermons, preached before the University of Oxford. Post 8vo. 8s. 6d.

SCROPE'S (G. P.) Geology and Extinct Volcanoes of Central France. Second Edition. Illustrations. Medium 8vo. 30s.

SENIOR'S (N. W.) Suggestions on Popular Education. 8vo. 9s.

SHAFTESBURY (Lord Chancellor); Memoirs of his Early Life. With his Letters, &c. By W. D. Christie. Vol. I. Portrait. 8vo. 10s. 6d.

SHAW'S (T. B.) Student's Manual of English Literature. Edited, with Notes and Illustrations, by Dr. Wm. Smith. Post 8vo. 7s. 6d.

——— Specimens of English Literature. Selected from the Chief English Writers. Edited by Wm. Smith, LL.D. Post 8vo. 7s. 6d.

SIERRA LEONE; Described in Letters to Friends at Home. By A Lady. Post 8vo. 3s. 6d.

SIMMONS (Capt. T. F.) on the Constitution and Practice of Courts-Martial; with a Summary of the Law of Evidence as connected therewith, and some Notice of the Criminal Law of England, with reference to the Trial of Civil Offences. 5th Edition. 8vo. 14s.

SOUTH'S (John F.) Household Surgery; or, Hints on Emergencies. Seventeenth Thousand. Woodcuts. Fcp. 8vo. 4s. 6d.

SMILES' (SAMUEL) Lives of British Engineers; from the Earliest
Period to the Death of Robert Stephenson; with an account of their Prin-
cipal Works, and a History of Inland Communication in Britain.
Portraits and Illustrations.   3 Vols. 8vo. 63s.

———— Lives of Boulton and Watt.   Comprising a History
of the Invention and Introduction of the Steam Engine. With Portraits
and 70 Illustrations. 8vo. 21s.

———— Story of George Stephenson's Life, including a Memoir of
Robert Stephenson.   With Portraits and 70 Woodcuts. Post 8vo. 6s.

———— James Brindley and the Early Engineers.   With Portrait
and 50 Woodcuts. Post 8vo. 6s.

———— Self-Help.   With Illustrations of Character and Conduct.
Post 8vo. 6s.

———— Industrial Biography: Iron-Workers and Tool Makers.
A companion volume to "Self-Help." Post 8vo. 6s.

————Workmen's Earnings—Savings—and Strikes. Fcap. 8vo.
1s. 6d.

SOMERVILLE'S (MARY) Physical Geography. *Fifth Edition.*
Portrait. Post 8vo. 9s.

———————— Connexion of the Physical Sciences. *Ninth
Edition.* Woodcuts. Post 8vo. 9s.

STANLEY'S (DEAN) Sinai and Palestine, in Connexion with their
History. Map. 8vo. 16s.

———————— Bible in the Holy Land. Woodcuts. Fcap. 8vo. 2s. 6d.

———————— St. Paul's Epistles to the Corinthians. 8vo. 18s.

———————— History of the Eastern Church. Plans. 8vo. 12s.

———————— Jewish Church. ABRAHAM TO THE CAPTIVITY. 2 Vols.
8vo. 16s. each.

———————— Historical Memorials of Canterbury. Woodcuts.
Post 8vo. 7s. 6d.

———————— Sermons in the East, with Notices of the Places
Visited. 8vo. 9s.

———·———— Sermons on Evangelical and Apostolical Teaching.
Post 8vo. 7s. 6d.

———————— ADDRESSES AND CHARGES OF BISHOP STANLEY. With
Memoir. 8vo. 10s. 6d.

SOUTHEY'S (ROBERT) Book of the Church. *Seventh Edition.*
Post 8vo. 7s. 6d.

———————— Lives of Bunyan and Cromwell. Post 8vo. 2s.

SPECKTER'S (OTTO) Puss in Boots. With 12 Woodcuts. Square
12mo. 1s. 6d. plain, or 2s. 6d. coloured.

———————— Charmed Roe; or, the Story of the Little Brother
and Sister. Illustrated. 16mo.

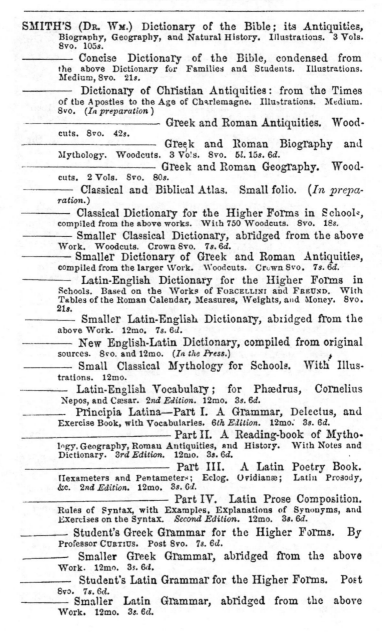

SMITH'S (Dr. Wм.) Dictionary of the Bible; its Antiquities, Biography, Geography, and Natural History. Illustrations. 3 Vols. 8vo. 105s.

———— Concise Dictionary of the Bible, condensed from the above Dictionary for Families and Students. Illustrations. Medium, 8vo. 21s.

———— Dictionary of Christian Antiquities: from the Times of the Apostles to the Age of Charlemagne. Illustrations. Medium. 8vo. (*In preparation*)

———————————— Greek and Roman Antiquities. Woodcuts. 8vo. 42s.

———————————— Greek and Roman Biography and Mythology. Woodcuts. 3 Vols. 8vo. 5l. 15s. 6d.

———————————— Greek and Roman Geography. Woodcuts. 2 Vols. 8vo. 80s.

———— Classical and Biblical Atlas. Small folio. (*In preparation.*)

———— Classical Dictionary for the Higher Forms in Schools, compiled from the above works. With 750 Woodcuts. 8vo. 18s.

———— Smaller Classical Dictionary, abridged from the above Work. Woodcuts. Crown 8vo. 7s. 6d.

———— Smaller Dictionary of Greek and Roman Antiquities, compiled from the larger Work. Woodcuts. Crown 8vo. 7s. 6d.

———— Latin-English Dictionary for the Higher Forms in Schools. Based on the Works of FORCELLINI and FREUND. With Tables of the Roman Calendar, Measures, Weights, and Money. 8vo. 21s.

———— Smaller Latin-English Dictionary, abridged from the above Work. 12mo. 7s. 6d.

———— New English-Latin Dictionary, compiled from original sources. 8vo. and 12mo. (*In the Press.*)

———— Small Classical Mythology for Schools. With Illustrations. 12mo.

———— Latin-English Vocabulary; for Phædrus, Cornelius Nepos, and Cæsar. *2nd Edition.* 12mo. 3s. 6d.

———— Principia Latina—Part I. A Grammar, Delectus, and Exercise Book, with Vocabularies. *6th Edition.* 12mo. 3s. 6d.

———————————— Part II. A Reading-book of Mythology. Geography, Roman Antiquities, and History. With Notes and Dictionary. *3rd Edition.* 12mo. 3s. 6d.

———————————— Part III. A Latin Poetry Book. Hexameters and Pentameters; Eclog. Ovidianæ; Latin Prosody, &c. *2nd Edition.* 12mo. 3s. 6d.

———————————— Part IV. Latin Prose Composition. Rules of Syntax, with Examples, Explanations of Synonyms, and Exercises on the Syntax. *Second Edition.* 12mo. 3s. 6d.

———— Student's Greek Grammar for the Higher Forms. By Professor CURTIUS. Post 8vo. 7s. 6d.

———— Smaller Greek Grammar, abridged from the above Work. 12mo. 3s. 6d.

———— Student's Latin Grammar for the Higher Forms. Post 8vo. 7s. 6d.

———— Smaller Latin Grammar, abridged from the above Work. 12mo. 3s. 6d.

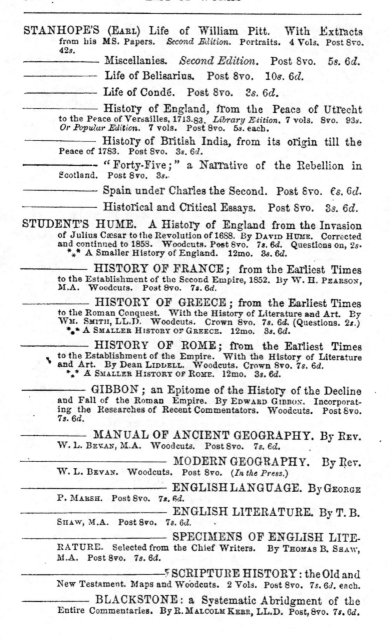

STANHOPE'S (EARL) Life of William Pitt. With Extracts from his MS. Papers. *Second Edition.* Portraits. 4 Vols. Post 8vo. 42s.

——— Miscellanies. *Second Edition.* Post 8vo. 5s. 6d.

——— Life of Belisarius. Post 8vo. 10s. 6d.

——— Life of Condé. Post 8vo. 2s. 6d.

——— History of England, from the Peace of Utrecht to the Peace of Versailles, 1713.83. *Library Edition.* 7 vols. 8vo. 93s. Or *Popular Edition.* 7 vols. Post 8vo. 5s. each.

——— History of British India, from its origin till the Peace of 1783. Post 8vo. 3s. 6d.

——— "Forty-Five;" a Narrative of the Rebellion in Scotland. Post 8vo. 3s.

——— Spain under Charles the Second. Post 8vo. 6s. 6d.

——— Historical and Critical Essays. Post 8vo. 3s. 6d.

STUDENT'S HUME. A History of England from the Invasion of Julius Cæsar to the Revolution of 1688. By DAVID HUME. Corrected and continued to 1858. Woodcuts. Post 8vo. 7s. 6d. Questions on, 2s.
 *** A Smaller History of England. 12mo. 3s. 6d.

——— HISTORY OF FRANCE; from the Earliest Times to the Establishment of the Second Empire, 1852. By W. H. PEARSON, M.A. Woodcuts. Post 8vo. 7s. 6d.

——— HISTORY OF GREECE; from the Earliest Times to the Roman Conquest. With the History of Literature and Art. By WM. SMITH, LL.D. Woodcuts. Crown 8vo. 7s. 6d. (Questions. 2s.)
 *** A SMALLER HISTORY OF GREECE. 12mo. 3s. 6d.

——— HISTORY OF ROME; from the Earliest Times to the Establishment of the Empire. With the History of Literature and Art. By Dean LIDDELL. Woodcuts. Crown 8vo. 7s. 6d.
 *** A SMALLER HISTORY OF ROME. 12mo. 3s. 6d.

——— GIBBON; an Epitome of the History of the Decline and Fall of the Roman Empire. By EDWARD GIBBON. Incorporating the Researches of Recent Commentators. Woodcuts. Post 8vo. 7s. 6d.

——— MANUAL OF ANCIENT GEOGRAPHY. By REV. W. L. BEVAN, M.A. Woodcuts. Post 8vo. 7s. 6d.

——— MODERN GEOGRAPHY. By Rev. W. L. BEVAN. Woodcuts. Post 8vo. (*In the Press.*)

——— ENGLISH LANGUAGE. By GEORGE P. MARSH. Post 8vo. 7s. 6d.

——— ENGLISH LITERATURE. By T. B. SHAW, M.A. Post 8vo. 7s. 6d.

——— SPECIMENS OF ENGLISH LITE-RATURE. Selected from the Chief Writers. By THOMAS B. SHAW, M.A. Post 8vo. 7s. 6d.

——— SCRIPTURE HISTORY: the Old and New Testament. Maps and Woodcuts. 2 Vols. Post 8vo. 7s. 6d. each.

——— BLACKSTONE: a Systematic Abridgment of the Entire Commentaries. By R. MALCOLM KERR, LL.D. Post, 8vo. 7s. 6d.

ST. JOHN'S (Charles) Wild Sports and Natural History of the
Highlands. Post 8vo. 3s. 6d.

———————— (Bayle) Adventures in the Libyan Desert and the
Oasis of Jupiter Ammon. Woodcuts. Post 8vo. 2s.

STEPHENSON (George and Robert). The Story of their
Lives. By Samuel Smiles. With Portraits and 70 Illustrations.
Medium. 8vo. 21s. Or Popular Edition, Post 8vo. 6s.

STOTHARD'S (Thos.) Life. With Personal Reminiscences.
By Mrs. Bray. With Portrait and 60 Woodcuts. 4to. 21s.

STREET'S (G. E.) Gothic Architecture in Spain. From Personal
Observations during several journeys through that country. Illustrations. Medium 8vo. 50s.

———————— Brick and Marble Architecture of Italy in the
Middle Ages. Plates. 8vo. 21s.

SWIFT'S (Jonathan) Life, Letters, Journals, and Works. By
John Forster. 8vo. (In Preparation.)

SYME'S (Professor) Principles of Surgery. 5th Edition. 8vo. 12s.

TAIT'S (Bishop) Dangers and Safeguards of Modern Theology,
containing Suggestions to the Theological Student under Present Difficulties. 8vo. 9s.

TAYLOR'S (Henry) Notes from Life, in Six Essays on Money,
Humility and Independence, Wisdom, Choice in Marriage, Children,
and Life Poetic. Fcap. 8vo. 2s.

THOMSON'S (Archbishop) Sermons, Preached in the Chapel of
Lincoln's Inn. 8vo. 10s. 6d.

THREE-LEAVED MANUAL OF FAMILY PRAYER; arranged
so as to save the trouble of turning the Pages backwards and forwards.
Royal 8vo. 2s.

TREMENHEERE'S (H. S.) The Franchise a Privilege and not a
Right, proved by the Political Experience of the Ancients. Fcap. 8vo.
2s. 6d.

TRISTRAM'S (H. B.) Great Sahara. Wanderings South of the
Atlas Mountains. Map and Illustrations. Post 8vo. 15s.

TWISS' (Horace) Public and Private Life of Lord Chancellor Eldon,
with Selections from his Correspondence. Portrait. Third Edition.
2 Vols. Post 8vo. 21s.

TYLOR'S (E. B.) Researches into the Early History of Mankind,
and the Development of Civilization. Illustrations. 8vo. 12s.

TYNDALL'S (John) Glaciers of the Alps. With an account of
Three Years' Observations and Experiments on their General Phenomena. Woodcuts. Post 8vo. 14s.

TYTLER'S (Patrick Fraser) Memoirs. By Rev. J. W. Burgon,
M.A. 8vo. 9s.

VAUGHAN'S (Rev. Dr.) Sermons preached in Harrow School.
8vo. 10s. 6d.

VENABLES' (Rev. R. L.) Domestic Scenes in Russia. Post 8vo. 5s.

WAAGEN'S (Dr.) Treasures of Art in Great Britain. Being an Account of the Chief Collections of Paintings, Sculpture, Manuscripts, Miniatures, &c. &c., in this Country. Obtained from Personal Inspec-. tion during Visits to England. 4 Vols. 8vo.

WALSH'S (Sir John) Practical Results of the Reform Bill of 1832. 8vo. 5s. 6d.

VAMBERY'S (Arminius) Travels in Central Asia, from Teheran across the Turkoman Desert, on the Eastern Shore of the Caspian to Khiva, Bokhara, and Samarcand in 1863. Map and Illustrations. 8vo. 21s.

WELLINGTON'S (The Duke of) Despatches during his various Campaigns. Compiled from Official and other Authentic Documents. By Col. Gurwood, C.B. 8 Vols. 8vo. 21s. each.

———————— Supplementary Despatches, and other Papers. Edited by his Son. Vols. I. to XII. 8vo. 20s. each.

———————— Selections from his Despatches and General Orders. By Colonel Gurwood. 8vo. 18s.

———————— Speeches in Parliament. 2 Vols. 8vo. 42s.

WILKINSON'S (Sir J. G.) Popular Account of the Private Life, Manners, and Customs of the Ancient Egyptians. *New Edition.* Revised and Condensed. With 500 Woodcuts. 2 Vols. Post 8vo. 12s.

———————— Handbook for Egypt.—Thebes, the Nile, Alexandria, Cairo, the Pyramids, Mount Sinai, &c. Map. Post 8vo. 15s.

———————— (G. B.) Working Man's Handbook to South Australia; with Advice to the Farmer, and Detailed Information for the several Classes of Labourers and Artisans. Map. 18mo. 1s. 6d.

WILSON'S (Bishop Daniel) Life, with Extracts from his Letters and Journals. By Rev. Josiah Bateman. *Second Edition.* Illustrations. Post 8vo. 9s.

———————— (Genl. Sir Robert) Secret History of the French Invasion of Russia, and Retreat of the French Army, 1812. *Second Edition.* 8vo. 15s.

———————— Private Diary of Travels, Personal Services, and Public Events, during Missions and Employments in Spain, Sicily, Turkey, Russia, Poland, Germany, &c. 1812-14. 2 Vols. 8vo. 26s.

———————— Autobiographical Memoirs. Containing an Account of his Early Life down to the Peace of Tilsit. Portrait. 2 Vols. 8vo. 26s.

WORDSWORTH'S (Canon) Journal of a Tour in Athens and Attica. *Third Edition.* Plates. Post 8vo. 8s. 6d.

———————— Pictorial, Descriptive, and Historical Account of Greece, with a History of Greek Art, by G. Scharf, F.S.A. *New Edition.* With 600 Woodcuts. Royal 8vo. 28s.

BRADBURY, EVANS, AND CO., PRINTERS, WHITEFRIARS.

CPSIA information can be obtained
at www.ICGtesting.com
Printed in the USA
BVHW08*1349210918
528174BV00010B/167/P